Wall Street

WALL STREET

—

WALTER WERNER
AND
STEVEN T. SMITH

Columbia University Press   New York

Library of Congress Cataloging-in-Publication Data
Werner, Walter, 1915–
Wall Street / Walter Werner and Steven T. Smith.
p.   cm.
Includes bibliographical references and index.
ISBN 0-231-07302-X
1. New York Stock Exchange—History—19th century.
2. Securities—United States—History—19th century.
3. Finance—United States—History—19th century.
4. United States—Economic conditions—To 1865.
I. Smith, Steven T., 1961–   . II. Title.
HG4572.W44 1991   90-39369
332.64'273—dc20   CIP

Columbia University Press
New York   Oxford
Copyright © 1991 Columbia University Press
All rights reserved

Casebound editions of Columbia University Press books
are Smyth-sewn and printed on permanent
and durable acid-free paper

Printed in the United States of America
c 10 9 8 7 6 5 4 3 2 1

Contents

Part II.
Participants in New York Securities Markets,
1790–1840

Part III.
Corporate Governance, Law, and the Public Corporation,
1790–1840

Part IV.
The Road to Today

Appendixes

Foreword

ONE WARM summer afternoon in the early 1980s, Walter Werner went to the country post office near our home and reluctantly painfully mailed what he announced was absolutely the final version of "Corporation Law in Search of its Future," an article for the *Columbia Law Review* on a subject which was the focus of his professional career. He had worked on the article for months, chosen each word with the greatest of care to say precisely what he meant, added what seemed to me a mountain of footnotes, and after many drafts, changes, and frantic phone calls from the young *Review* editor, released the product of his mind to a larger world.

That was the beginning of this book.

The suitably absent-minded law professor did not then contemplate that the concept he continued to write about through the next years would emerge between hard covers. Walter taught corporation law. Like many of his colleagues, his concern was to illuminate the law, present and future, for his students and the community. The focus of his nonstop study of this vast, critical subject was on the past.

These were years of mounting turmoil on Wall Street. Control was out of hand, takeovers were the order of the day. There was a rush for stricter regulations; authorities assembled to draft new laws. In 1986, Ivan Boesky's inside trading was a scandal, amazing the nation; a year later the stock market crash stunned the world. Everywhere people talked and worried.

Meanwhile, Walter somewhat smugly said he was not at all surprised at the turn of events, it being part of the continuous growth of Wall Street that he was discovering. He spent his free time peacefully at work in the library at the law school or at the New York Historical Society, where he was often the lone reader, fascinated by what the past was telling him about the present. He feasted on stacks of letters exchanged in those pre-telephone days, read newspapers two centuries old. He saw patterns visible only in a long perspective, and discovered some firmly rooted answers to the present Wall Street dilemma.

At first he did not say he was finding answers. He would come home with tales of the legendary king of Wall Street, Nathan Prime, an unknown lad who came to New York in the early 1800s to make his fortune and did, building the just-born securities market in the process. Or of Jacob Little, a notorious pioneer speculator who made and lost many fortunes and finally went bankrupt for $10 million (nevertheless, Walter was to conclude that "speculation," as a memo scrawled on a yellow pad a week before he died says, "is the essential native genius of Wall Street.")

Fascinating stories described the building of railroads, the early bank scandals and inside thefts, what really happened under the buttonwood tree, the nineteenth century panic caused by the failure of Jay Cooke & Co. which lost many fortunes and closed the stock market for days—the 3x5 card files burgeoned. The true history of Wall Street was becoming clear, and startling.

Walter's conceptual views deepened. He identified some basic, hitherto unchallenged, misconceptions which had been taken as gospel through the years. Now they appeared to be leading to dangerous conclusions and needed definition, a less than popular undertaking. He showed that even the renowned Adolf Berle's thesis was not based on fact and devoted seven footnotes to proof of its flaws.

The harvest of years of research took on a life of its own, insisting on seeing the light of publication as a consistent whole. As the book took shape, Walter spent more and more of his time, when not teaching, in writing. He was completely engrossed in this work when he was appointed to be the first occupant of a new Chair at Columbia Law School, named for none other than Adolf Berle. Delighted and unphased, Walter happily described the event as "the peak of my career." A few days later, he discovered that he had a fatal illness.

He worked harder than ever during the next months. His determination to add to the understanding of American business with his book was fundamental to him, and I am certain, prolonged his life. He could not quite finish, and never had the satisfaction of holding this volume in his hands, although I believe that he somehow knew it would find its way into minds concerned with a bright future.

With great good fortune, Walter found in Steven Smith a careful concerned person in whom he had complete confidence. First as a law student, then as a full-fledged lawyer, Steve helped with research for the book, later, he spent many hours discussing its completion with Walter, by then in a hospital bed. The brilliant and absorbing task which Steven Smith performed to bring this book into being has earned deep and abiding gratitude, surely from Walter in absentia, and from all here and now who will benefit from the result, one way or another.

ANNE W. WERNER

March 1990

Acknowledgments

T HE HISTORY of early American securities markets was one of
Walter Werner's passions. Anyone fortunate enough to have heard
him speak on the subject was inspired by the way he could make the events
and people of the period come alive. Had he been able to, he would have
finished this book himself. His devotion to the project kept him at it until he could do no more. I was honored to complete the task, and have
done my best to keep the book consistent with what he would have written.

Thanks for Walter to his fellow faculty members and students at
Columbia Law School. Their informed interest encouraged this project
from its start. And thanks to close friends who gave caring time and at-
tention to see this book safely to publication after Walter's death: Dorothy
Olding, literary agent, Charles Lieb, legal counsel, and Walter's Literary
Trustees—his wife, Anne W. Werner, John Oakes, and Professor Albert
Rosenthal.

The historians and archivists who helped to collect the vital primary
source material deserve immense credit, particularly those at the New York
Historical Society, the New York Stock Exchange Archives, and the
Columbia University Libraries. Indispensable contributions were made by
other researchers, including many research assistants over the years.
Columbia Law School provided important support during the period that
the manuscript was being written. The comments of those who reviewed
the manuscript, particularly Professor Stuart Bruchey, are also greatly appreciated. Finally, the support and real contributions made by my wife
Karen were invaluable when at times the work seemed as though it would
never be done.

S.S.

Introduction

I N NOVEMBER 1986, Ivan Boesky admitted to insider trading. Although the scale of Boesky's transgression was astonishing, his crime was nothing new. The pantheon of market manipulators and traders on inside information stretches back hundreds of years. The scandal, however, became a national crisis, and spawning a national debate and providing the focus for an examination of major developments in the world of high finance. As never before, the importance of securities markets to corporations was scrutinized. The hostile takeovers and leveraged buyouts that remodel institutions as huge as Gulf Oil, TWA, and Phillips Petroleum, were closely analyzed. Greenmail, junk bonds, white knights, crown jewels, and poison pills were condemned afresh as symptoms of a desperately ill or wildly perverse corporate system gone beserk.

Less than one year later, the stock market crash of October 1987 stunned the world; hundreds of billions of dollars vanished in one day of panic. Losses hit across the entire spectrum of securities holders. Mergers and takeovers stopped dead in their tracks. Market mechanisms were stretched to the limit when trading on the New York Stock Exchange soared over 600 million shares two days in a row. Around the globe, all financial markets were in turmoil. The NYSE responded to the crunch with limits on computerized program trading and with reduced trading hours. Eventually, the spectacular tumble reached bottom, but for weeks trading volume remained high and prices were unstable. Caution and uneasiness pervaded the financial scene.

Confused investors, issuers, traders, and analysts sorted through the rubble. What caused this crash? Why did it happen in October 1987? Was it a signal of more profound economic malaise? Was government management of the economy to blame? Would so great a loss lead to hard times? Had the stock market simply gotten out of control? Desperate for answers, the public devoured miles of newsprint, listened to untold hours of discussion. Explanations were cheap, solutions scarce.[1]

By 1989, investors seemed to have forgotten the 1987 crash. While the Dow Jones Industrial Average reached new heights, corporate battles also reached a new pinnacle with the $25 billion takeover of RJR Nabisco. The Boesky episode was eclipsed as Drexel, Burnham, Lambert, Inc., agreed to settle charges with the SEC for an unprecedented $650 million. Drexel itself foundered, fell victim to a crisis of confidence, and collapsed. Soon thereafter Drexel's star, Michael Milken, apologized with tears in his eyes when he pled guilty to six counts of securities fraud as part of a settlement requiring him to pay $600 million in fines.

Wall Street,[2] the legendary symbol of high finance, has provided the arena for these corporate struggles, the opportunity for corporate looting, the setting for the market collapse. The media, paying tribute to Wall Street's awesome power, have swept such stories off the financial pages and into every American home, an exposure that has dramatized the influence wielded by modern financial markets.

Alongside its flashy displays, Wall Street's might has been harnessed to perform for the corporate world the more vital, albeit more humdrum, task of attracting and distributing capital.[3] By bringing customers and issuers together, securities markets enable public corporations to tap the funds of many savers and set those funds working toward society's economic objectives. Securities markets are instrumental in the most important decisions made in our economy;[4] they determine what new enterprises deserve capital, and they help existing corporations decide how to make the best use of the capital at their disposal.[5] Such commonplace market tasks are rarely front page news.

Many contemporary discussions of both the dramatic and the run-of-the-mill aspects of securities markets begin from the premise that an unpredictable 1980s stock market dominates the corporate world as never before. But securities markets have not taken up this mantle only recently. Today's elaborate financial instruments, flamboyant manipulators and insider traders, hostile takeovers and market crashes may be understood as the flowering of seeds planted in the United States more than 200 years ago. As this book documents, these modern manifestations are merely another stage in the steady, joint evolution of public corporations and securities markets.[6]

Transplanted to American soil, the English roots of public corporations and securities markets flourished in the climate of an eager, risk-taking, and growth-seeking people. Before independence was won, the first American business corporation had already been formed. In the early 1790s, the infant country boasted a thriving securities market. A major stock market crash in 1792 followed the ratification of the Constitution by only four years.

In the wake of the 1792 collapse, a group of securities professionals signed the famous Buttonwood Agreement, pledging to give each other a preference in their trading. This agreement was not, as has been repeatedly claimed, the result of competition between brokers and auctioneers. It merely formalized preferential relationships among a specific group of securities traders. The Buttonwood Agreement soon lapsed, as did the trading frenzy of the early 1790s, but its principles were later to serve as the foundation of the New York Stock & Exchange Board, the forerunner of today's New York Stock Exchange.

Developments in trading methods and forums kept pace with increasing numbers of marketable securities and expanding trading volume. By 1808, fifteen different stocks and bonds were traded in New York. Daily trading volume rose to 3,500 shares in 1824, 14,000 in 1835. Securities trading activity concentrated in New York City from the start, boosting New York's growth as a financial center.

The important purchasers in American securities markets between 1790 and 1840 can be divided into investors and speculators. As investors cautiously seeking security of principal and regular dividends, governments, financial institutions, and foreign and domestic individuals purchased shares of seasoned institutions like the two Banks of the United States, or put their money into federal government bonds. Trading of these conservative investment issues in the New York market was often slow, compared with trading in the get-rich-quick securities. In contrast, speculators hustled in early markets. Their trading, based on predicting changes in securities prices, was the heart of early Wall Street. Traders could capitalize on their ability to forecast price changes by entering into time bargains, often without paying any cash up front. Time bargains constituted the bulk of securities business during the first 1790–1792 boom and bust, and for the next fifty years, speculative trading regularly made up a major portion of market activity.

Trading activity both encouraged, and was encouraged by, the growing class of professional securities dealers who practiced in New York. Securities specialists emerged among men of finance, and, by the 1820s, some devoted their entire time and resources to securities operations. Like the brokers and investment bankers of today, they facilitated the trades that kept the market functioning. They brought buyers and sellers together, made markets, contracted loans, and occasionally even engaged in large transactions for their own accounts. The growing volume of their business led to specialization: one branch of the industry concentrated on contracting for government debt issues, another consisted of brokers and dealers in the trading markets.

While customers and securities professionals nurtured the growing trading market, corporations and governments issued securities to raise funds. Before the 1830s, securities markets were utilized to raise capital only for those corporations that could entice investors by promising some form of return. The stock market had little or no significance for other corporations unable to spark investors' interest. Financial corporations, notably profitable banks and insurance companies, were among the first able to raise money through issuance of shares. Later, profitable nonfinancial corporations and railroads copied from their example.

This trading market was of vital importance to public corporations, working its magic in several ways. Healthy trading of stocks in a particular type of venture stimulated promoters to organize new but similar ventures. The trading market allowed new businesses to raise capital even before they proved that they would be profitable. Speculators bought and held securities during the trial period, selling at a profit if the venture succeeded, and walking away with little loss if it failed. Once an issue had been sold, the securities market allowed publicly owned corporations to continue operations without impairment of capital, even as the suppliers of that capital regularly changed. Securities markets also offered guidance on the cost of capital to business management, which in turn helped determine appropriate levels of investment. In addition, distribution in the share market directly influenced corporate financial policies, because most shareholders looked for dividends, and some laws required all profits to be paid as dividends.

All early corporations, including those capable of raising capital in the public securities markets, received government assistance in some form. State governments were active in promoting corporations as engines of economic development. Regulation did not impose restrictions to shield shareholders from corporate abuse. Their control over the corporations they owned was not protected; nor were other shareholder rights generally available. Similarly, trading in the securities market was virtually unregulated, except for a few futile efforts to restrict speculation. Any who chose to put money into securities were taking risks known well to all.

They took those risks because securities were attractive investments. By standing ready to convert securities to cash, the trading market conferred important benefits upon the owners of corporate shares. Marketability, always useful, was particularly desirable when few forms of wealth had it, and marketable shares became more attractive and valuable than those not regularly traded. In addition, the trading market furnished prices and quotations, thereby giving shareholders a constantly updated measure of their investment's value.

From the start, customers of securities markets treated the shares they purchased as financial assets. Voting in corporate elections was a "side-issue"; beyond exiting from the corporation when departure seemed in their interest, shareholders had little desire to intervene in corporate decision making.[7] Further, securities markets created large, dispersed groups of shareholders who found acting in concert cumbersome. Thus, it was often the manager, not the shareholders, who controlled public corporations. Managers orchestrated shareholder votes and engineered directors' elections to keep themselves in power. This separation of ownership from control was a product of the stock market: investors surrendered claims to affect corporate decision making in exchange for the marketability of their shares.

Though nonvoting, investors in public corporations were not ignored or abused; if dissatisfied with management, they could sell their shares. As a result, corporate officers had sufficient incentives to pursue the interests of shareholders in order to sustain share prices. Thus, the securities markets, extensions of the corporations whose shares they traded, operated much as they do today—as the external adjunct of the public corporations' internal government structures. Securities trading even created a market for control of the first public corporations. Just as they are now, occasional battles to topple managements were waged in early nineteenth century stock markets. Shrewd operators could also exploit the market for control with such "modern" corporate raiding tactics as greenmail.

A long view of United States corporate history demonstrates that the line of development from the corporate system[8] of 1790 to today is direct and continuous. In their growth, public corporations and securities markets have been pushed through various stages. Each successive era set the stage for the next, and all have built on the foundations laid during the period from 1790–1840, called here the Bank Age. Joseph Davis' statement that "Before 1801 a . . . basis had been laid on which the 19th Century could build,"[9] can be applied to each period in its turn.

Too many corporate historians have misread the significance of early securities markets in the maturation of the corporation. Some have focused on corporations and treated early securities markets as institutions that have affected them, but not greatly.[10] Others have denigrated early securities markets because of their large speculative components.[11] Additional corporate scholars, attempting to place early securities markets into a larger picture, have been hampered by the lack of complete studies and accurate facts. For example, an early historian of the Exchange pointed to March 16, 1830, when 31 shares traded hands, as the dullest day in stock market history.[12] This "fact" has been often repeated as an indication that the market had little significance at this time. However, there were other duller days, and many when no shares traded hands. More importantly, there were years in the 1820s and 1830s when the regular sustained trading volume was many thousands of shares. Clearly, only a relatively sophisticated market could handle such activity.[13]

Another factor distorting American corporate history has been overgeneralization.[14] Historians have examined the roots of today's big corporations by examining the development of all corporations without differentiation, but all enterprises organized as corporations are not the same and never were. Although all corporations have had similar legal organizations, in economic reality they fall into two groups: one with publicly quoted and traded shares, valuable property interests held by a relatively large number of shareholders; the other, without such direct relationships with securities markets. Today, these corporations are termed "public" and "private," respectively. They have developed quite differently, due largely to the market which quoted and traded their shares.

Consequently, those corporate historians who have focused on the numerous enterprises not utilizing the securities markets during the earliest years have downplayed the importance of those other corporations with publicly issued and traded shares. To account for the later preeminence of the public corporation, many historians explain that the corporate system was fundamentally transformed sometime in the nineteenth century to become like the corporate system we know today, an institution founded in the securities market.[15]

We offer a different perspective, concentrating on public corporations and the influence of securities markets in the 1790–1840 period, with a briefer discussion of how the roots put down during these first fifty years matured during the next fifty years.[16] We believe that, for a thorough understanding of their earliest years in America and all that has since ensued, the interdependence of public corporations and securities markets dictates that they be examined together. Rather than the corporate revolution that others have seen, we view the history of the corporate system as a process of continuous maturation, in which securities markets and public corporations have always been of vital importance to each other.[17]

PART ONE

Origins and Attributes
of New York Securities
Markets, 1790–1840

CHAPTER ONE

The Roots of American Securities Markets

EARLY SECURITIES MARKETS IN ENGLAND

"EXCHANGE ALLEY" in London boasted a thriving securities market at the beginning of the eighteenth century. By 1720, England had all the essentials of securities markets as they exist today. First, there was a group of actively traded securities, representing both the government and private companies. Second, in accessible places like the coffee houses, there was continuous trading with publicity of prices and quotes. Third, there were professional brokers and dealers specializing in trading securities. Fourth, and perhaps most importantly, there was an investing public eager to buy and sell.[1] Specialized securities traders, "stock jobbers" in common parlance, were the cornerstones of this market, each day buying and selling government bonds, shares in profitable business corporations such as the East India Company, and shares in joint-stock companies formed by enterprising groups of English businessmen.[2]

In 1711, to help finance extended intervention in the War of Spanish Succession, an issue of government debt was floated in this London securities market.[3] Because there was little faith in the government's ability to repay its obligations, the bonds were sold at a heavy discount from par, their nominal issue price. To bolster unenthusiastic sales, a new financing package provided that these bonds could be exchanged for shares in the South Sea Company, formed with a monopoly on the potentially lucrative trade with India. Investors bought the depreciated government bonds, and were able to convert them at par, often twice their acquisition price, for issues of South Sea stock. Sales boomed, and as they did, the speculative "bubble" grew. The South Sea Company took on a mountain of debt while promising investors extraordinary dividends and profits. Investors became caught up in what appeared to be a way to make easy and certain money.

South Sea shares were traded heavily in Exchange Alley. The public's enthusiasm, buoyed by rising prices, soon spilled over to securities generally. Londoners, and then people from all parts of England, became obsessed with stock trading. Hysteria set in. Securities of every description were traded constantly and recklessly.[4] Demand for stocks and the money to buy them became fierce. Interest rates on some notes rose to 100 percent.

Shares were issued by myriad new joint stock companies, many no more than schemes to bilk frenzied securities purchasers. Schemers created companies to make salt water fresh, to make boards from sawdust, to build a perpetual motion machine. The craving for investment grew so intense that "A Company for Carrying On an Undertaking of Great Advantage, but Nobody to Know What It Is" raised over £2,000 in one day. On the next day, the shrewd promotor left London, never to be seen again.[5] Over one hundred such schemes soon earned the name of "bubbles:"

> Set on foot and promoted by crafty knaves, then pursued by multitudes of covetous fools, which at last appeared to be, in effect, what their vulgar appellation denoted them to be—bubbles and mere cheats.[6]

This rage for securities, dubbed the South Sea Bubble, was perhaps the most spectacular speculative episode of the eighteenth century. The heights reached by the trading fever only made the inevitable crash more devastating. After inquiries were launched into the affairs of various bubble companies, including the South Sea Company, South Sea directors flooded the market with their large holdings of shares, and a panic followed. Share prices fell catastrophically to their intrinsic value, which often was nothing. The disaster was widespread, many were bankrupted, and the credit of the English government was nearly ruined.[7]

EARLY SECURITIES MARKETS IN AMERICA

THE FURIOUS securities trading of the South Sea Bubble did not spread to the English colonies in America, primarily because the colonies had no significant securities trading market.[8] Joint-stock companies were rare in colonial America.[9] The few corporations were predominantly chartered towns, churches, and schools—entities with shares that were not attractive as financial assets. There were some indigenous securities available for trading in the colonies,[10] and European securities occasionally circulated in the large commercial centers of New York, Philadelphia, and Boston,[11] but there is no record of any substantial or public securities trading before the Revolutionary War.

The main activity in early United States financial circles was centered instead on the various currencies overprinted by the states. One effect of the prevalence of paper money was a strengthening of the gambling spirit stimulated by the instability of its value.[12] "The revolutionary 'shin-plasters' as the irreverent already styled them, were spread over the land in such plenty that there were a hundred dollars to each inhabitant. Something was to be made therefore from the fluctuations to which they were unhappily liable."[13]

America's first sustained and regular securities trading market arose in the bonds issued by the states and the Continental Congress to finance the Revolutionary War.[14] Each of these obligations, issued in innumerable forms, had some speculative or real value,[15] and they were traded regularly as early as the closing years of the conflict.[16]

Securities dealings increased as the postwar economy recovered and as the Constitution made the rounds of the ratifying conventions.[17] Trading expanded further when funds began to flow from Europe for investment in American securities.[18] A political controversy brewed, as debt certificates were accumulated by American and European men of wealth.[19] Some decried the opportunism involved in buying securities at bargain prices from veterans and widows desperate for cash; others felt that the purchasers of the public debt "show at least as much confidence in the public faith as those who sell them."[20]

On August 4, 1790, this widely dispersed securities trading gained additional coherence and legitimacy. Congress, as part of Hamilton's program to establish the fiscal integrity and federal supremacy of the infant United States government, authorized three new bond issues to redeem the debts of the national and state governments.[21] Trading of government bonds stabilized and concentrated in these standard refunding issues, and securities markets in New York City and other Atlantic seaboard communities blossomed. Prices in the refunding issues rose steadily as the prospects for their repayment brightened.[22] Respectable merchants, brokers, and auctioneers of goods and land added securities trading to their other activities.

This first sustained American securities trading was not directly associated with the earliest United States corporations. Unlike their English prototypes, whose shares were attractive financial assets, most United States business corporations were not destined to be money makers. Their shares were not desirable as financial assets, and no regular trading market developed for them. Only financial assets with some promise of return could survive in this market. The competition for funds was brisk; for investors, loans on local real estate or a share in a ship offered the most profitable and secure investment,[23] while large speculators were heavily involved in land schemes and small ones were deep into innumerable lotteries.[24] Nonetheless, in 1791, a stock market was born in New York as an adjunct to the existing bond market when shares in two important corporations were issued: the Bank of the United States, chartered in February by Congress to serve as the federal government's bank, yet largely owned by the public,[25] and the Bank of New York, organized as a joint-stock company in 1784 but not chartered by New York state until August 1791.[26] Both banks were virtually guaranteed profits by their monopoly holds on important functions such as issuing currency, and their stock issues were quickly oversubscribed. It took only five minutes to fill subscriptions for the Bank of New York, and a lively trading market sprang up immediately.[27] For a time, shares of the Society for Useful Manufactures, the first American manufacturing company to go public, were also actively traded in New York.[28] In this manner, the separate evolution of early corporations and securities markets in America first came together, marking the start of a long and fruitful alliance.

Securities markets in New York took on a high profile. All five major securities—the three different federal debt issues and shares in two important banks—were traded continuously, with increasingly brisk volume. Public auctions of securities were held daily in New York, and then twice daily from August 1791 to April 1792.[29] Newspapers published securities quotation and prices of consummated transactions at these auctions alongside reports of the newly inaugurated Washington administration.

Many of these securities were purchased as income-producing long-term investments. Investors held them steadfastly, collected dividends, and watched the value of their holdings increase.

Speculators, however, seeking profit by forecasting securities price fluctuations, were primarily responsible for the substantial trading activity. Elaborate financing techniques allowed speculative campaigns to be waged by persons of moderate means. Borrowing stocks and dealing on credit became a normal course of business.[30] The logic behind borrowing stock allowed a trader to operate for a fall in prices. If borrowed stock were sold at a high price, and then replacement stock to return to the rightful owner were repurchased at a lower price, the one who borrowed the stock would profit from the fall in prices. Another similar and common financing technique was using stocks as collateral for loans. Time bargains, also known as wager contracts, were also executed. In time bargains, stocks could be bought and sold in the future without the outlay of cash at the present. Time bargains allowed the parties to settle contracts at a stipulated future date by paying or receiving the difference between contract price and cash price on that date. These contracts differed from other credit dealings insofar as they did not require the handling of a security certificate.[31] Aided by all of these contrivances, speculation in stocks flourished.[32]

Contemporary stories of how "all sorts and conditions of men and women became devotees of the stock market" are commonplace; the opportunity for quick riches attracted throngs of speculators.[33] Rufus King describes "mechanicks deserting their shops" to join shopkeepers and merchants in the spirited trading while "neglecting the regular & profitable commerce of the city."[34] James Sullivan wrote of:

> The rage in the present day for acquiring property by accident. Some men are supposed to have made large fortunes by speculations in the stocks and banks: And they who have not been thus fortunate, can discover no reason why their neighbors should be thus favorably distinguished from them. And too many are ready to lay aside their ordinary business, to pursue Chance as the only goddess worthy of human adoration.[35]

Not even the lotteries, so much in favor at the time, could match securities markets' capacity to cater to the risk-oriented.

With this great influx of traders and high turnover of securities, prices fluctuated wildly. Scrip, temporary certificates that could later be converted into shares in the Bank of the United States, issued in July 1791 at $25, hit a peak price of $280 in August, dropped to $110 the next month, and then rose again.[36]

Understandably, the obsession with securities speculation was criticized. In August 1791, one observer wrote: "The scriptomania is at its full height," another: "A frenzy runs through all the nation."[37] Madison wrote to Jefferson about New York: "stock jobbing drowns every other subject. The coffee house is an eternal buzz with the gamblers."[38] Newspapers in other cities took particular delight in deriding the antics of New York speculators.[39]

America's own bubbles were launched. In January, 1792, a joint-stock company was created for The Million Bank of the State of New York with a capital of one million dollars in $500 shares.[40] In less than one day, it was oversubscribed tenfold, and the next day subscriptions opened for another joint stock company, the Tammany Bank, whose 4000 shares at $500 each were also oversubscribed instantly. Shares in these projects were traded, as were shares in another less speculative joint-stock company, theTammanial Tontine Association.[41] The thirty thousand New Yorkers now had no fewer than nine securities to choose from.

Securities trading spelled the difference between money made or lost to most market-minded men. To Hamilton, the architect of the nation's first financial plan, the market's significance was more profound. As he made clear in his famous Report on Manufactures, the United States had to make up for its "deficiency of pecuniary capital," and therefore had to excite "the confidence of cautious sagacious capitalists, both citizens and foreigners."[42] The securities market was particularly useful for achieving these objectives. By encouraging the transformation of capital sunk in specific projects into marketable securities, it helped to cure the deficiency of pecuniary capital, and by setting prices that reflected the judgment of buyers and sellers of the new securities, it excited the confidence of sagacious capitalists, domestic and foreign. The speculation ingrained in the American spirit was also vital; capital flows induced by hopes of speculative gain could be converted into useful inland navigation projects and manufactures.[43]

In addition, bond prices measured confidence in the ability of the new government to survive and prosper, while determining the interest rate for government borrowings. Hamilton, therefore, did not sit idly by and let the market determine prices unassisted. His financial scheme strengthened demand for federal bonds by allowing them to be used for the purchase of shares in the new Bank of the United States.[44] When bond prices threatened to fall below par, Hamilton supported those prices by ordering strategic market purchases. The federal government bought bonds in New York as early as 1790 and whenever something occurred to make the market low, thereby stabilizing prices and strengthening the trading market.[45] Securities holders and traders were quick to realize that Treasury would protect its new debt instruments.

Hamilton was not alone in his efforts to influence market prices. William Duer, who had been Hamilton's assistant at Treasury, masterminded an elaborate securities trading program.[46] He profited openly from his association with Hamilton and his access to government information.[47] Spread thin in numerous ventures, Duer nevertheless found time to participate in promoting the Society for Useful Manufactures and the Scioto Land

Company, both highly speculative ventures that failed sensationally.[48] Duer's most famous and catastrophic speculation occurred in securities markets.

Early in 1792, Duer was riding high. An experienced securities trader, he had speculated with great success in the bull market of 1791. On December 29, 1791, he and Alexander Macomb, a wealthy New York businessman, agreed to join forces in their securities trading.[49] Duer, who had the larger financial stake in the venture, provided the market knowledge, while transactions were executed in Macomb's name.[50] Supported by associates who followed their lead, Duer and Macomb then speculated heavily. Duer was constantly cash poor, and he borrowed from every available source to finance these operations. He sold his father-in-law's country home at auction and "borrowed" funds which had been entrusted by the Society for Useful Manufactures.[51] He paid interest rates of three to four percent a month to: "persons of all descriptions . . . merchants, tradesmen, draymen, widows, orphans, oystermen, market women, churches,"[52] all of whom were attracted by the high yield and by Duer's social standing.

The nature of Duer's strategy is unclear. He might have attempted to corner the floating supply of one or more issues, to obtain sufficient Bank of New York shares to participate in control, or to engineer a takeover of the Bank of New York by the Bank of the United States.[53] It is more plausible, however, that Duer and his cohorts were operating on the bigger fool theory: no matter how much a buyer pays for a security in a rising market, he will be able to sell to a bigger fool who will pay even more.

Duer's fortunes clearly rested on a bull market. Rising prices would enable him to cash in on time bargains and then make new contracts to push prices up even further. The Duer-Macomb partnership's trading stimulated the extraordinarily heavy speculation of January and February, 1792.[54] In early March, Duer made large purchases in two weeks time, betting on continued price increases. Unfortunately for him, prices fell, and his losses prevented him from making payment on his promissory notes.[55] Overnight, Duer's credibility vanished, and creditors clamored for their money.[56] As though these misfortunes were not enough, the coup de grace came when Duer was named defendant in a suit by the federal government to recover funds that he was alleged to have accounted for improperly while employed by the Treasury.[57] The bottom fell out from under Duer's paper empire, and by March 23, 1792, he was in debtor's prison.

Duer's troubles quickly became the troubles of the entire city. Many of Duer's associates had endorsed his notes, and they, too, were unable to meet their obligations. The wave of insolvencies had a domino-like effect. Each failure affected creditors of the defaulting party, and many not directly associated with Duer were forced into insolvency. Private and public confidence were shaken to the core.[58] The bubble in the securities market burst. Inflated securities prices collapsed.[59] The speculative New York joint-stock companies failed.

Only two years after the birth of regularized trading, the New York market had suffered its first crash.[60] The city was in shock. Seth Johnson, a knowledgeable observer of the New York scene, wrote to a friend on April 1: "The present Month is dreaded, as would be some general Calamity."[61]

Effects were felt throughout the country. Standish Forde of Philadelphia wrote to Peter Anspach of New York: "The whole of our misfortunes we may certainly charge to the New York failures, for no person would have stopped here if it had not been for their indorsements on the notes of New Yorkers. Their own losses on stocks they could have borne."[62]

Hamilton intervened again with Treasury purchases, and a steady securities market returned by June,[63] but purchasers were chilled from speculative transactions. The New York legislature then made public auctions of stocks illegal.[64] For a time, New York securities markets moved out of the spotlight.

NATURALIZATION OF THE BUSINESS ETHIC

THE EVENTS of 1790–1792 were, in one dimension, astounding. The United States has experienced many speculative securities market booms and busts over the years, but this first one took place almost two centuries ago in a new nation, an agrarian economy that was chopping a place for itself out of a vast wilderness.

The explanation for the presence of sophisticated financial institutions and practices that could lead to a securities market boom and crash in a simple economy is that none of these elements was new. From the start, the young United States contained the seeds of capitalism and a market economy based on bargain and sale, money and credit. Its law embraced notions of private property and freedom of contract. Its most influential citizens were merchants and the lawyers who served them. The uses and abuses of paper money were well known. Businessmen handled bills of exchange, promissory notes, warehouse receipts, and other intangibles.

Government's goal was to raise the standard of living by increasing the net output of goods and services. These financial arrangements and institutions, although primitive by today's standards, were highly sophisticated on the broad canvas of world economic development. The United States thus began with a legacy of commercial and financial institutions that had been evolving for centuries across the Atlantic.

The legacy was not universally admired. Many who distrusted these institutions sensed a clash between the values of farmer and artisan and those of moneylender and securities speculator. Proponents of the simple life resisted expansion of the world of finance. The outcome, however, may well have been sealed in 1607, when the first settlers landed at Plymouth Rock. By the time of Independence, business attitudes and institutions were too ingrained in American society to be excised or even contained. Hamilton did little more than describe the inevitable when he wrote in 1791 that the nation's need was to foster the "spirit of enterprise."[65]

These business-oriented attitudes found their highest expression in the naturalization of securities markets and publicly owned business corporations. Both securities markets and public corporations took on characteristics of their predecessors in England and adapted them to the pioneer spirit. Speculative capitalists and risk-taking entrepreneurs were united in these two institutions that were to play vital roles as they carried the United States' economy into the Bank Age.

CHAPTER TWO

The Buttonwood Agreement

THE TRADITIONAL STORY

O N A spring day in 1792, twenty-four men signed the compact generally viewed as marking the birth of organized stock trading in New York. The Buttonwood Agreement, which takes its name from legendary Wall Street trading beneath a buttonwood tree, asserts the fundamental principles that later shaped the New York Stock Exchange and other securities markets in the United States.

> We the Subscribers, Brokers for the Purchase and Sale of Public Stock, do hereby solemnly promise and pledge ourselves to each other, that we will not buy or sell from this day for any person whatsoever, any kind of Public Stock at a less rate than one quarter per cent Commission on the Specie value, and that we will give a preference to each other in our Negotiations. In Testimony whereof we have set our hands this 17th day of May at New York, 1792.[1]

In 1931, Margaret Myers restated the orthodox version of the Buttonwood myth:

> The first trading in securities was carried on by merchants and by auctioneers as a part of their regular business in other commodities. By 1792 the activity in Wall Street was sufficient to produce a group of specialists in stock trading. When five of the auctioneers, seeing a part of their business about to be taken from their hands, proposed to establish a daily regular auction of stocks, the brokers were forced into a compact for self-defense, and drew up the first informal agreement for a Stock Exchange. They mutually promised not to patronize the auctioneers, not to charge a commission of less than one-fourth of one

percent, and to give each other preference in sales. This effectually nipped the scheme of the auctioneers, and since the one-way type of market was less satisfactory than the two-way market provided by brokers, the market was practically left to the brokers.[2]

In essence, auctioneers and brokers had competing business interests: auctioneers acted to protect their interests by proposing regular daily auctions, and brokers countered by signing the Buttonwood Agreement. These propositions provoke troubling questions.

WERE BROKERS AND AUCTIONEERS ADVERSARIES? — A CLOSER LOOK

REGULAR DAILY securities auctions in New York were first reported on July 1, 1791. Pintard and Bleecker advertised "Sale of Public Securities at Auction, This evening at the Coffee House Long Room at VII O'Clock."[3] A few days later they announced a schedule of fees for the auctions, which then took place three times a week at 1 P.M. and three times at 7 P.M.[4] Soon there were two auctions daily, two-way auctions in which both buyers and sellers entered quotations. Brokers and dealers participated in the auctions, then used auction prices as the starting point for trading between themselves in the coffee houses and on the street.[5] The auctioneers' market and dealers' market complemented each other, and both thrived.[6]

Auctioneers could have acted against the interests of other securities professionals by allowing the public to participate in their auctions without the aid of brokers, or by attracting customers to auctions and then dealing with them privately. Either practice would have deprived brokers of commissions, furnishing the basis for legitimate broker grievances. Auctioneers, however, had more to gain by cooperating with other securities professionals. The nature of a securities transaction was far more complex than the sale of a commodity, and it required considerable follow-up. In a cash deal, the trade was settled with the exchange of cash for an appropriate certificate and a recording of the transfer with the securities issuer. For a time bargain, the principals had to execute a formal contract. It was easier for an auctioneer to complete trades by working together with securities professionals than by dealing directly with members of the public.

It appears that a cooperative arrangement between auctioneers and securities professionals was established in 1791. A printed broadside reports
an agreement by the "dealers in the public funds," on September 21, to
be bound by fourteen rules governing public auction sales of securities.[7]
The rules are comprehensive, covering methods of submitting bids, settlement of trades, execution of time bargains, and sanctions to be imposed on defaulting parties. A principal objective seems to be protecting
the brokers' interests. The first rule asserts that securities professionals will
do business only with auctioneers who agree to employ a broker in any
dealings for their own account.[8] Another rule provides that each lot put
up for sale will be "subject to the usual Commission on Sales."

We do not know the extent to which these rules became effective or
how well they were enforced. At least one rule, that calling for only one
auction daily, was abrogated or revised when the dealers began attending
two auctions daily.[9] There is no known press comment on the 1791
agreement, and it is not mentioned by historians of the early market who
might be expected to have known of its existence.[10] Nevertheless, the
printing of the broadside is strong evidence that the dealers did adopt the
fourteen rules. In addition, numerous references to "sworn brokers" in
contemporary security professionals' advertisements[11] could be references
to those who agreed to comply with rule 1 of this agreement.[12] These
references to sworn brokers appear both before and after the Buttonwood
Agreement, which suggests that the earlier 1791 agreement could have
continued in force after the Buttonwood Agreement was signed.[13] If this
earlier agreement endured, it is possible that the Buttonwood Agreement
was primarily a modification required by the end of public auctions in
1792. Even if the broadside reports an agreement that was never implemented, it demonstrates that brokers and auctioneers attempted to accommodate each other's interests in securities trading in the fall of 1791.[14]
Brokers' continued participation in auction sales after the adoption of the
fourteen rules confirms that whatever differences may have existed among
securities professionals were not obstacles to a working relationship.

In early 1792, after auctions had been proceeding on a regular basis for
more than seven months, the auctioneers published this notice in the
February 15 *New York Daily Advertiser*:

Stock Exchange Office

This day will be opened, at No. 22 Wall Street, a large convenient
room for the accommodation of the dealers in stock, and in which pub-

lic sales will be daily held at noon, as usual, in rotation, by the public's much obliged humble servants.

> A. L. Bleecker and Sons
> John Pintard,
> M'Evers and Barclay,
> Cortland and Ferrers,
> Jay and Sutton[15]

Feb. 6

"As usual." The announcement confirmed continuance of the auctions, now to be held in more spacious quarters to accommodate securities dealers. The new arrangement was apparently expected to be permanent enough, and the relationship between auctioneers and securities dealers firm enough, to warrant its characterization as the "Stock Exchange Office."

Nothing in this action suggests, as the myth would have it, that the auctioneers saw part of their business about to be taken away or that the brokers, viewing the auctioneers' action as hostile, were forced into a compact for self-defense. Brokers had no reason to fear the auctions. By generating publicity, auctions actively fed securities speculation. Daily publication of auction prices on a trade-by-trade basis invigorated the bull market in the same way a rising ticker tape was to stimulate demand in a later day. Brokers and auctioneers were not in any way adversaries; they were simply responsible for different segments of one integrated process.

THE REAL STORY OF THE BUTTONWOOD AGREEMENT

AS WE have seen, the New York securities market was on the verge of a short but devastating panic in 1792. The fall of William Duer and the market collapse in March merely confirmed earlier fears, widely expressed, that securities speculation was a particularly virulent kind of gambling and should be banned.[16] On August 13, 1791 the *New York Daily Advertiser* published a typical blurb from another paper, *Claypool's Daily Advertiser:* "A frenzy runs through all the nation/For soon or late, so truth advises/Things must assume their proper sizes—/And since as death all mortals trips/Thousands will rue the name of SCRIPS." The collapse of New York's speculative market was widely ridiculed elsewhere as well.[17] All brokers and auctioneers were tarred for running the market which had made the cataclysm possible, and some, unable to meet their obligations, were forced into insolvency, earning the ignoble title: "lame ducks."[18]

If, as the traditional story goes, the brokers had wished to oust the auctioneers from the business, the collapse of the market and the con-demnation of auctions in the press created the perfect opportunity. Yet the brokers did not immediately boycott the auctions, a somewhat sur-prising failure. Auctions may have fueled the speculation that got out of hand, but they were good publicity for the securities business. Instead, on March 21, the "Merchants and Dealers in Stocks in the city of New York" met at Corre's Hotel and resolved:

> That after the 21st of April next, they will not attend any sale of stocks at public auction; and

> That a committee be formed to porvide a proper room for them to assemble in after April 21, and to report such regulations relative to the mode of transacting their business, as in their opinion may be proper.[19]

Thus the brokers and auctioneers, who clearly had some form of organi-zation, merely contemplated moving their market from the street to a "proper room." On March 25, public auctions were reduced from two to one daily, but they were not ended.[20] Finally, on March 31, presumably on account of the growing seriousness of the situation, the dealers re-solved to attend no more auction sales of stock,[21] and without public no-tice or fanfare, the last public auction was held on April 2.[22]

On April 10, after the auctions had already stopped, the New York legislature made them illegal through a statute that outlawed sale "at public vendue or outcry" of securities created by the federal government or any state.[23] The law also voided time bargains and wagers on the prices of government and corporate issues. The legislature's action underscored public concern over the factors that had apparently brought on the panic.

Under pressure, but still alive, securities trading continued in New York.[24] Securities dealers must have gathered at their accustomed haunts and transacted some business as before. Traders who weathered the crisis settled maturing time bargains, perhaps made new ones. The market, however, had changed in an important respect. Where trading had pre-viously been widely publicized, it was now curtailed in silence. After a single incomplete price report on April 10, the press did not carry daily summaries of prices or quotations.[25] Nothing more from the dealers was heard for weeks, nor was there any notice of the committee report due on April 21. This secrecy in New York is the more striking because the press in other cities continued to print daily summaries of securities trading. The blackout of information suggests some kind of understanding among the securities dealers that, in light of the Duer debacle, it would be prudent for them to lie low and for the market to operate without publicity of any kind.

Securities professionals now appreciated the dimensions of the disaster that their market had brought to the entire city. They recognized that public auctions and the publicity given their prices encouraged speculation. For the first time, government had intervened in their market to make those auctions unlawful, and had added its weight to the popular clamor that stigmatized securities dealing. The challenge for the brokers and dealers was to find an alternative to auctions that could preserve their market while eliminating, or at least minimizing, the conditions that had brought on the panic.[26]

The Buttonwood Agreement resulted. Professionals banded together in an arrangement that would establish a structured securities market without auctions. The signatories include a number of the auctioneers whose advertisement on February 15, according to the orthodox version, were antagonistic to the interests of the brokers.[27] Obviously the product of meticulous draftsmanship, the agreement states its principles clearly and concisely.[28] Signers would charge nonsigners the same fixed minimum commission rate, and each signer would give preference to the others in their dealings.[29] Signers thereby obtained an economic edge over nonsigners, who included other securities dealers as well as retail customers.[30] By its very nature, the agreement separated signers from nonsigner securities professionals. This noncompetitive aspect is the Buttonwood Agreement's greatest claim to fame. The real conflict in the securities industry was not between auctioneers and brokers, but was created by the compact itself, because it was signed by only some of the people in the securities business.

The extent to which the Buttonwood Agreement affected securities trading is difficult to gauge. A flurry of advertisements by signing securities brokers and dealers appeared about the time of its birth, testifying to a securities trading market in New York.[31] Certainly the agreement had some useful life; two brokers did not sign up until November, 1792. They were, however, the last to join a group that should have regularly taken in new members as long as it was functional.

Furthermore, if the Buttonwood Agreement were to be effective, its principles needed the teeth that could only be found in a more formal association of securities dealers, such as a stock exchange. One would at least expect the signers to meet daily to conduct their own private auction and set prices that would become the basis for interdealer trading.[32] There is, however, no evidence of a broker's organization at this level before the creation of the New York Stock & Exchange Board in 1817, which leads us to conclude that the Buttonwood Agreement never lived up to its potential.

The Buttonwood Agreement's primary claim to fame is its presumed place as the first formal broker's agreement in New York. It is widely recognized as the ancestor of the New York Stock & Exchange Board. Yet the brokers' meetings of February and March 1792 seem to have an equally valid claim to that place in history.[33] The earlier broadside of September 1791 could be a contender as well.

CHAPTER THREE

The New York
Stock and Exchange Board

THE FOUNDING

I N A typical public notice, Bernard Hart advertised the 1792 opening of his stockbroker's office at "No. 196 Water Street, near the Coffee House": "The subscriber intending to devote himself entirely to purchase and sale of STOCK on commission, begs leave to offer his services to his friends and the public, and hopes by assuidity and attention, to merit their favors."[1] Although Hart was competing with other brokers for the public's patronage, his business—like that of other securities professionals—ultimately depended on his rivals. Not only did he have to check securities prices and availability with other brokers, but when he found a favorable deal, he would generally execute it with another broker. Recognizing their mutual need, brokers came together during the active trading of 1791 and 1792 to adopt formal rules, including the Buttonwood Agreement. But once the trading market tapered off in the wake of the 1792 crash, incentives to further formalize arrangements among brokers dwindled.

Over the next twenty-five years, securities trading in New York gradually increased, but few traces of collective action by securities professionals can be found. What evidence exists indicates that trading likely took place in an over-the-counter market, one without any enduring exchange structure.[2] As Medbery tells us: "The little league of New York brokers gradually increased in numbers and in a sense of their own importance. They met during stormy or wintry days in a chamber of the old Tontine Coffee House, high up under the eaves. On pleasant afternoons they consulted in a solemn manner on the open pavement of Wall Street."[3]

Yet the *New York Commercial Advertiser* listed "Prices of stocks this day at One O'Clock" from January 1804 to January 1807, implying that there may then have been some broker's organization. Interestingly enough, some historians suggest that an organization of brokers functioned throughout this period,[4] while others simply disregard the question. We have found no first-hand evidence to confirm that there was any formal brokers organization between the time of the Buttonwood Agreement and the NYS&EB. Although it is probable that New York brokers made some cooperative arrangements, it is doubtful that these were long-lasting or formal, and equally doubtful that the 1792 Buttonwood Agreement principles governed the brokers' dealings.[5]

With the rapid expansion of securities trading in New York during the War of 1812, pressures mounted for a routine meeting place for buyers and sellers. According to legend, the brokers of Philadelphia had organized into an exchange before the New Yorkers,[6] who did not hesitate to copy their example.[7] On February 25, 1817, twenty-four New York brokers met for an organizational meeting at the office of Samuel Beebee. The records listing gentlemen present and absent at this February meeting suggest that the group had been formed earlier.[8] The committee resolved:

> That it is desirable to constitute a Board or Association of Brokers in this city for the transaction of their business at their Board, and
>
> That a committee of three be appointed to draw up a report, at another meeting articles of association.

At this meeting, Nathan Prime was designated president and John Benson, secretary.[9] With the reporting and passing of the rules on March 8, 1817, the New York Stock & Exchange Board was born.[10]

Immediately, the new trading center began regular operations. Its first few years, however, can best be characterized as a trial period. But after it passed the critical test of being useful for its members, the NYS&EB attracted more and more business. In 1820, a newly increased membership and a new constitution reinforced the organization, now thirty-nine brokers strong. In fact, one contemporary argued that 1820 marked the true birth of the Exchange, as only subsequently did it become the vehicle for major stock transactions of the most active investors and brokers.[11]

On each business day, members would gather in the Exchange's board room, and, when the President called securities, state their bids and offers. Unlike the public auctions of 1791–1792, this bidding was restricted to Exchange members, who participated either as brokers or as principals for their own accounts. Not even a handshake was required to complete a transaction, duly recorded by the secretary in his call book.

Disputes were kept to a minimum because the NYS&EB promulgated comprehensive rules on trading practices, offers and acceptances, fictitious trades, methods and times of payment, and interest rates on credit deals. Unless a question was raised within a limited time, the parties to a trade were considered bound. Upon the raising of a question, the Exchange settled the dispute by arbitration and proceedings before the Board. In the 1820s, minutes of the NYS&EB are packed with reports of disputed sales between members and with resolutions suspending and readmitting members according to their financial integrity. Without resorting to the courts, members of the Board would sit in committee and pass judgment on their fellows. [12] Punishment for violations took the form of sanctions ranging from fines to expulsion from Exchange membership. There was no appeal from the Board's final determination. [13]

Once this organizational base was in place, securities markets functioned more efficiently than they had under less formal trading arrangements, benefiting both members of the Exchange and their customers. It must, however, be noted that the chief aim of the NYS&EB was not some high-minded notion of serving public utility with an efficient trading forum. Brokers formed the NYS&EB solely to maximize their income—the pursuit of gain brought them together and molded America's securities markets. [14]

In this pursuit of gain, and to insure the profitability of members' business, two interrelated devices were established. One device was an agreed-upon minimum commission rate—carefully set at a level to assure profit—that each member would charge for his services. As a result, members could operate with the confidence that they would lose no business to other members willing to charge a lower commission. Additionally, member brokers gave each other preferential treatment by charging nonmembers higher commission rates. An October 11, 1817, resolution expressly required members to collect the stipulated commission on trades executed for any nonmember. [15]

The second device made NYS&EB brokers' privileges exclusive. Only members could trade at the Board and be privy to the transactions and prices set there. Not only did keeping membership exclusive maintain the price-fixing cartel, it also sustained the practice of charging outsiders higher commission rates. In addition, the exclusivity allowed members to use the information obtained at the Board for their own advantage in trades with nonmembers. [16]

Although there was no express ceiling on the number of NYS&EB brokers, admission to the Board was a difficult process. New members had to meet Board criteria for trustworthiness and creditworthiness. More-over, an 1817 rule required that applicants first serve a two-year appren-ticeship to a member of the Board. Next, the applicant would be pro-posed by a member, and all would vote; "three black balls shall exclude." New members were added regularly, especially in peak trading years, but it was equally common for applications of brokers possessing the highest character and business qualifications to be summarily rejected.[17] Cus-tomers and those brokers who were not members could trade in the NYS&EB market only through a member, and only by paying the non-members' commission rates. By that stroke, the NYS&EB divided the New York securities traders into two groups, members and nonmembers, much as the Buttonwood Agreement would have.[18] Whereas nonmember se-curities professionals had formerly done business on an equal footing, they now were relegated to an over-the-counter market on the streets and in the coffee houses, competing against rivals who enjoyed an edge.[19]

In the 1830s, these pressures led excluded brokers to establish a rival exchange, a "New Board," which attracted business by slashing commis-sion rates. For a time, the New Board thrived, particularly in the specu-lative boom of 1835 and 1836, when its trading volume occasionally sur-passed that of the NYS&EB, or "Old Board."[20] Of course, the NYS&EB could not tolerate a rival within its own market area, because its chief attraction was offering to the public the best market with the most orders executed. Accordingly, the Old Board fought back, taking business away from nonmembers by prohibiting its own members from trading stocks with nonmembers on the street.[21] As it happened, the contest was re-solved in the crash of 1837, when more than two-thirds of the New Board brokers failed. That organization never fully recovered, and was discon-tinued later in the decade, with many of the surviving brokers absorbed into the NYS&EB.[22]

THE EFFECTS OF THE NYS&EB
ON SECURITIES TRADING

FROM THE start, the NYS&EB was no paper tiger. With members of the stature of Nathan Prime, Leonard Bleeckie, William Godet Bucknor, and Samuel Ward, all important in New York's business and social life, the Board enjoyed a nucleus of business which in turn at-tracted the patronage of others. Like a snowball, increased business im-proved the market at the NYS&EB, narrowing the differential between bid and asked quotations and guaranteeing the best executions, which further increased business.[23] Soon, the Exchange attracted much of the supply and demand for securities it traded, clearly becoming New York's foremost securities trading center.[24]

After some preliminary hesitation, the NYS&EB made sure that its prices became widely known. In truth, the initial reluctance stemmed chiefly from the prized secrecy of the Exchange's boardroom sessions: price information was valuable property, for members only. Slowly, however, some members began to see that publishing securities prices was the best possible advertisement for member business, certain to attract public orders.

As a compromise, members voted to publicize, but with limits: only the secretary was authorized to release price information, and only on a weekly basis.[25] Later, price information was released daily, and by 1828 volume information was also reported to the press.[26] Both nonmember securities professionals and members, who did much of their trading away from the Exchange, relied on those prices as a starting point for their trading throughout the day.[27] This price-setting function was vital, as the securities traded by the NYS&EB made up virtually the entire roster of securities traded in New York.[28]

Many of the trades entered into at the NYS&EB were speculative, large numbers taking the form of time bargains. Traders anticipating a price rise would contract to purchase shares at a stipulated price, within a stipulated period that might be as long as six months. As part of the procedure, traders paid a small deposit as collateral security for their obligation to take the stock should the price decline. Time bargains rarely consisted of a direct exchange of cash for stock; the parties were more likely to settle by paying the difference between contract and market prices. Hence, each party was forced to rely on the integrity and credit of the other.[29]

Time bargains came to be such an integral part of NYS&EB activity that elaborate rules were adopted to govern them.[30] By requiring a broker executing a time bargain to vouch for his customer's ability to perform and to assume the customer's obligation, in the event of nonpayment, the Exchange minimized the risk of default. Breach of the member's duty subjected him to the ultimate sanction: expulsion from the Exchange.

As a consequence, securities traders soon found that the Exchange was uniquely qualified to insure that the "losing" party discharged his contractual obligation. Since time bargains were unenforceable at law,[31] this consideration was crucial. Such ability to act outside state law, to act under a different set of rules, gave the brokers on the Exchange a powerful advantage, and it is easy to understand why public customers preferred this protection that only the Exchange offered.[32] Speculators whose risk decreased were not the only ones to benefit; brokers also profited from commissions generated by rapid-fire traders engaged in repeated time bargains.

Time bargains, though the core of innumerable rash speculative schemes, appear tame compared to other bold operations that occurred behind the NYS&EB's doors in its early days. Those attributes that made the Exchange a good marketplace—concentration of supply and demand to set widely publicized prices—also made it a ripe target for manipulation. "Operators" could control trading at the Exchange to a degree not feasible in the over-the-counter market. A scant five days after the NYS&EB's founding, a fictitious sale of fifty shares of Manufacturing Bank was engineered in order to establish a false price. From that day forward, the Board forbade fictitious sales on pain of expulsion, but, in a move foreshadowing later Exchange responses to manipulation, the perpetrators were not punished. The sale was merely expunged from the Exchange's record.

Later, choosing the guise of bull or bear, kings of the street did battle on the Exchange floor, driving prices up or squeezing them down.[33] The most visible of such contests occurred when operators cornered the market in outstanding shares of a company. By so doing, operators forced others—obligated to deliver now unobtainable shares—to pay outrageous sums in settlement.

Twice in the 1830s, when corners were completed upon operators insufficiently wary, the NYS&EB stepped in and gave the losing brokers some relief.[34] On January 9, 1835, the NYS&EB suspended sales of Morris Canal & Banking Company stock, due to the sudden sharp fluctuations, and thereupon established a committee to investigate. In consequence, the stock was struck from the trading list on January 17, not to be restored until May 11.[35] Ultimately, the Exchange invalidated short sales and thereby relieved the cornered bears from the obligation of repurchase at artificially inflated prices.[36]

Such action was not enough to protect the Exchange from criticism for being the vehicle of the great corners, particularly when those corners affected share prices of such established institutions as the Bank of the United States.[37] As *The Journal of Commerce* editorialized:

> that most reprehensible practice, gambling in stocks upon fictitious contracts . . . is a practice alike opposed to the laws of the land, the laws of God, and the peace of society. We trust that now every gentleman of the Board (and there are many of the most estimable character)

will sign the pledge, or at least firmly resolve, never again to have any part in such transactions. . . . If the Board were determined in honesty, to put an end to this wicked business, it would be ended instanter. After this fearful exhibition [the Morris Canal corner] of the gulph to which such gambling leads, we have no doubt that we speak the language of public sentiment in saying that any Broker who continues it ought to be branded as a gambler, and classed with black-legs; and if it is not suppressed at the Board, the Board ought itself to be suppressed by the overwhelming voice of public opinion.[38]

Reaching an early peak in the 1830s, tumultuous securities speculation, also attracted the attention of the New York legislature,[39] resulting in the 1836 proposal of a bill to outlaw sales at private stock exchanges under penalties of fine and imprisonment. With its life at stake, the NYS&EB fielded a remarkable petition.[40] In this "Memorial," the Exchange first praised itself by describing its valuable social function.[41] Then, the memorialists warned the legislature that too much regulation would scare important business away to rival Philadelphia. In a noteworthy passage, the NYS&EB's role in fostering men's speculative spirits was downplayed:

The love of gain, and the desire of vastly too many to live without labor, begets a spirit for speculation which in all times of abundance of money, as was the case last season, is more easily indulged in. At such a period it pervades a larger space in the community. If the individual who is actuated by it happens to prefer stock instead of merchandise, cotton, lands or manufactures, to play hazard with, stocks would be selected as the proper means for indulgence. It may well be questioned whether any legislation, however, moral or wise, can change man's nature in this respect, or limit his desire to acquire money, or to live in some way other than "by the sweat of his brow."[42]

The memorialists further declared that an unjust prejudice had been created against the brokers as a body through ignorance of the way they transacted business. For a conclusion, they boldly suggested legislative reforms favorable to themselves, in particular making time bargains legal and enforceable.[43] Whatever the effect of this petition on the legislature, the proposed law to outlaw private exchanges was never enacted.

Though the Exchange could successfully resist the passage of unfavorable legislation, its unsavory public image was another matter. As early as 1818, only one year after the NYS&EB's formation, the *National Advocate* printed a letter complaining about the "unchartered and dangerous body."

It is a confederacy to loan money at certain prices—to affix a wanton and fictitious value to stock and bank notes—to play into each others hands—to shut the doors of banks and compel persons to bring them their notes for discount. . . . Some restrictions must be legally imposed on this fraternity or the evil will increase until a remedy can no longer be applied. [44]

The Exchange was quick to respond with a spirited defense:

Be assured, sir, there is no confederacy in this Board to affix a uniform or fictitious value for stock. . . . In the purchase and sale of stock, there is always a fair competition and any member is liable for expulsion for making a false sale. [45]

From that day forward, however, the Exchange was on the defensive on two fronts: against those who did not understand its functions, and against those losing speculators who understood them too well.

For example, it was claimed that: "the organization had grown to be a power but a power for evil rather than good since it stimulated in the community a thirst for speculation."[46] Nonetheless, while promoting this "evil," the NYS&EB grew rapidly in size and importance. Though it attracted tremendous speculation, it attracted tremendous investment. Though it provided a forum for manipulators, it provided a forum for companies and governments seeking to raise capital. While many individual fortunes were made and lost through the NYS&EB's spasms, overall trading volume established it as the nation's premier securities market. These positive roles paralleled the steadily growing importance of securities markets and public corporations in the burgeoning American economy.

CHAPTER FOUR

An Overview of New York Securities Markets: 1792–1840

THE CONSOLIDATION: 1792–1816

THE DISASTROUS 1792 crash engendered a long-term contraction of New York securities markets. Statistical evidence, presented in appendix A, reflects slow trading in New York throughout the 1790s. So thoroughly had securities markets been deflated that press coverage did not return to its 1792 level until the War of 1812.[1] Wary of securities, speculators found their outlet in lotteries or land schemes, while investors used their money to fund American shipping.[2]

Although transactions in federal bonds were the heart of the 1790s securities market, new federal bond issues were not fully subscribed.[3] In 1796, subscription books were opened for a $5 million government loan, but only a paltry $80,000 was subscribed.[4] In 1800, the federal government could borrow only $5 million of the $8 million sought, even at generous 8 percent.[5] Moreover, the new-issue market for corporate shares was emasculated. It took a long six years after the 1792 crash for the publicly quoted trading lists to add the shares of a new corporation, the New York Insurance Company.[6]

Around the turn of the century, securities trading quickened when numerous business corporations obtained charters from the New York legislature. Regular chartering of financial institutions was particularly important to securities traders: banks were virtually guaranteed a profit by their state-granted privileges, and insurance companies were careful to instill confidence by stocking their boards of directors with the most respectable men. As a result, initial offerings of shares in these companies were usually oversubscribed. After the first gust of transfers, trading activity in any one issue would subside as corporate shares were stashed away by investors, yet each additional issue served to augment the public stock market as whole. From 1798 to 1803, securities quoted and traded lists doubled—from six issues to twelve—and continued to expand. The amount of capital invested in shares of publicly owned corporations increased apace.

During the years after the turn of the century, the number and variety of issues in the stock market continued to swell, seemingly impervious to the large swings in economic fortune in the United States. For example, a broad recession reportedly occurred in 1801–1802.[7] A boom followed until 1808, at which point European belligerents greatly interrupted American trading by seizing American vessels. The ultimate result was 1808–1809 embargo, which in turn, encouraged a spurt of American manufactures.[8] Foreign trade and finance were, however, substantially harmed, and the trading deadlock ultimately contributed to the War of 1812. Nevertheless, in both good times and bad, the prewar securities market managed to grow.

Naturally, the War of 1812 itself caused disarray in financial markets, yet it also stimulated securities trading.[9] Because the federal government needed money to finance the war, it floated new bond issues. The Treasury issued $16 milion in short-term notes as well as $109 million in long-term bonds.[10] New York City also contributed to securities market growth by flotating a loan in 1812.[11]

In addition, four new banks were incorporated in New York during 1812: the Phoenix Bank, the Franklin Bank, City Bank, and Bank of America. Against a sense of financial insecurity, this glut of new issues was more than the securities market could easily digest.[12] The Bank of America had difficulty attracting subscriptions for its shares, resulting in depressed bank stock prices.[13] The significance of this sluggish market is not the slow absorption of new issues, but that the floating of so many public issues of corporate shares could be attempted. Even in a bad year, the market was by now more vibrant than it had been in the quiet years before 1800.

Speculation in federal debt issues and in currency caused wartime securities trading to surge. United States 6 percent bonds of 1814 were sold for a time at $50 in specie, $70 in New York currency.[14] This speculation did not spread to shares in sound financial institutions, manifest evidence of the rift between bond and stock components of early securities markets.[15]

When the war drew to a close, the economy was exhausted, with 1815 and 1816 described as depression years.[16] The stock market was weak; speculation was dampened. This lack of trading, and the decreased value of bank and insurance shares, occasioned a June 1816 *New York Courier* report that bank stocks, once one of the best properties in the United States, were now among the worst.[17] Fortunately, peace was around the corner. Share prices rebounded later in the year when the economy improved.

The steady growth of public securities markets despite the turbulent 1792-1816 years suggests that the short-term fate of those markets was not contingent on the economy, nor was economic success contingent on the markets. Although securities markets at this time were a mere appendage to markets in other goods—lacking the strength to function as an independent economic force—securities trading was nevertheless important.[18] Although markets were quiet, there were already performing many of the same functions they do today. They allowed investments to be liquid, a vital step toward mobilizing the capital sorely needed for economic development. The markets also began to wield their influence on the corporate and government issuers whose securities were traded. The lessons taught by experience to customers, issuers, and securities professionals alike were crucial in preparing the market for its later greater roles, roles already clearly evident by 1816.

THE EMERGENCE: 1816-1840

NEW BANKS and insurance companies had been formed in the commercial revival following the War of 1812. As the economy recovered, speculation in bonds subsided. By 1817, the 6 percent war loans were selling for $109\frac{1}{4}$.[19] Currency values also stabilized; new securities issues proliferated.[20]

In 1816 alone, seven securities were added to the publicly quoted trading lists, among them the tremendous issue of $28 million worth of shares in the Second Bank of the United States. The Second Bank of the United States' capital was set at $35 million and, like the First Bank of the United States, the federal government subscribed to one-fifth of the outstanding capital. The public's shares received a mixed reception; the $28 million was not subscribed within the twenty-day initial offering period, despite subscription books opened in twenty cities.[21] The shares were eventually absorbed, partially due to the ability to purchase them with federal bonds.[22]

In addition to the Second Bank stock, the first of the popular Erie Canal bonds, the New York "sixes," or 6 percents, were also floated in New York in 1817. Over the next eight years, $7 million of New York canal securities were floated in New York securities markets.[23]

Both of these stock offerings were in successful, highly profitable ventures, and prices of their securities steadily increased. Regular trading in these, and the growing variety of other less prominent issues, added a new dimension and a new vitality to New York securities markets. In recognition of this spirit, the brokers of the time were encouraged to launch the New York Stock & Exchange Board (or, the NYS&EB).[24]

An examination of a crude indicator of this securities market's size— the number of publicly-quoted issues—indicates astonishing growth of New York trading during this period. The number of issues publicly quoted in New York doubled between 1816 and 1822. It doubled again by 1827, by which time more than 100 different securities were regularly traded in New York. Nonfinancial enterprises, such as the Delaware and Hudson Canal Company and the New York Gas and Light Company, began to appear on the trading lists.[25] Issues from outside New York were added as well, beginning with the Louisiana Bank in 1828.[26]

Fortunately, during portions of this period, we can examine public securities markets through an indicator more accurate than the number of publicly quoted issues. Beginning in 1818, regular records of share trading volume, records kept by the NYS&EB and reported in the press, are available. Not suprisingly, volume was more sensitive to the fortunes of the economy than was the number of issues quoted. For example, the brief but painful panic of 1819 coincided with significantly reduced securities trading volume. An overextension of bank credit and the formation of new banks were the probable cause of the panic. When the federal bonds used to purchase Louisiana from France had to be repaid in Europe with specie, the Second Bank of the United States tightened credit, and specie became scarce.[27] As a result, securities trading was lethargic from then until 1821.

By contrast, in periods of speculative fever, such as 1824 and 1825, trading volume and share prices both rose sharply, with little regard to underlying economic circumstances.[28] Speculation inflated trading volume on the NYS&EB from a daily average of 175 shares in 1818 to 1,309 shares in 1824. The rush to invest in stocks was on. Medbery captured the spirit of that euphoric time:

> The Water Works Company was authorized to hold two millions of capital, and ten millions were subscribed. The Morris Canal and Banking Company, whose capital was fixed at $1,000,000, had twenty millions of subscriptions! In Philadelphia the Bank of Southwark opened its books on a certain day to the public, and the rush of capitalist sub-

scribers was like a mob. Noses were smashed, hats jammed in, and the police court was at work over the wounded for weeks after.[29]

This speculative peak also inspired the launching of new companies, some derisively dubbed "bubbles" by a number of commentators. Companies have "dissolved into air—thin air . . . bubbles, set afloat with deliberate intent to 'make money,' honestly if they might—but rascally, if they must." Niles, in his influential newsletter, refers in particular to the fraudulent New Hope Delaware Bridge Company and Bank which issued notes by the carload, notes as intricate and beautifully printed as they were worthless.[30]

Some members of the public were apparently willing to purchase shares of any kind. A common advertisement in the press blared:[31] TO CAPITALISTS—AN INTEREST IN A VALUABLE CHARTER FOR SALE. The offering describes in detail the organization of the company, the price of shares, and the methods to pay for them. Investors are enticed with promises that the lucrative investment will "in all probability produce an income from 8 to 10 percent and probably 10 to $12\frac{1}{2}$ percent per annum." There is a guarantee that: "The whole capital invested can no doubt be returned in about three years." The offering, however, nowhere mentions the project that the company will undertake, because "an entire public explanation, further than the above, is not deemed necessary." Without compunction, such fraud was routinely practiced by the unscrupulous on those unacquainted with corporate mechanisms.

Perhaps not too surprisingly, the 1825 speculative fling was not prevented by lessons learned from prior crashes. At the time of wild speculation in cotton and "various gambling projects of the stock jobbers," Niles pointed out that earlier calamities "are now forgotten.[32] Many soon relearned the hard way that a crash would likely follow a speculative peak. Late in 1825, the securities market bubble burst. Expansive buying and selling shifted to cautious liquidation and retrenchment. According to Gouge, a violent reaction set in about July or August, and lasted through 1826.[33] The Franklin Bank, the Marble Manufacturing Company, and other New York firms failed.[34] Annual trading at the NYS&EB, which had reached a peak of 380,000 shares by 1824, sagged to a mere 15 percent of that number by 1829, remaining low through 1831.[35]

This collapse triggered healthy trading in bonds, as securities purchasers gravitated to less risky investments. In value, the bond trading surge accounted for more than half the trading on the NYS&EB in 1828. Once the economy began pulling out of this conservative slump in the early 1830s, speculators returned to corporate securities. Bond trading then reverted to its accustomed minor portion of NYS&EB activity.

In 1831, securities prices and trading volume again rose noticeably, particularly in the newly-introduced railroad stocks.[36] Once again, securities markets were on the ascent, lurching toward their largest boom yet. Although unsettling, neither Andrew Jackson's veto of the Bank Bill in 1832 nor the withdrawal of federal deposits from the Second Bank of the United States in 1833 checked the securities market climb. Even the short recession of 1834 did not manifest itself in slower trading on the NYS&EB.[37] This spirit of optimism was boosted by easy money late in 1834, and financial markets heated up. Prices advanced sharply. Trading volume soared.[38]

During this period, newspapers focused increasing attention on Wall Street.[39] Market reporting improved in frequency and sophistication. For example, the reporting of issues quoted became better organized. Different types of companies were reported together, in different segments of the trading lists.[40]

While speculative fever set in, intrepid operators continued to manipulate trading with outrageous schemes. Shares in one railroad and then another became a fad, or fancy, and it was not uncommon for a railroad's entire outstanding shares to be traded in a month. In a notable example, in July and August 1835, 64,000 shares of Harlem Railroad stock were sold for future delivery, despite the fact that only 15,000 shares had been issued. In such an atmosphere, prices of railroad stocks fluctuated rampantly. More seasoned stocks were also rocked, although their prices fluctuated less than those of the new railroad fancies.[41]

Incidental to this immense activity were corresponding "irregularities;" bank cashiers defaulted, operators disappeared with funds and members of the New York state legislature were deeply involved in the fraud and gambling. The infamous Senator Kemble, for example, made a speech opposing the capital enlargement of the Harlem Railroad. When the news hit Wall Street, the price of Harlem inevitably rose, and at the top of the market Kemble's broker sold short. Kemble then pushed a bill through the legislature enlarging Harlem's capital. The price plummeted. Kemble was caught red-handed, and what little money he reportedly made was no compensation for expulsion from the senate.[42]

Speculation, gambling, and manipulation of so wild an ilk made the securities market of the late 1830s no place for the cautious. In the context of other "commercial" activity of the time, however, this securities speculation was not so outrageous as it may now seem. The 1830s, at least before 1837, was a time of speculation in all things. Speculative land booms, in particular, corresponded with the cycles of speculation in securities markets.[43] Both often depended on easy money; and, because land was largely bought on credit, land policy became entangled with banking and monetary issues.[44] Astounding examples of land speculation are evident alongside the stock market boom of 1790–1792, and they continued during speculative periods throughout the early nineteenth century.[45]

Playing the stock market, even a rigged market, was simply another form of speculation, one that made it easy for the "little man" to participate in the action and to do so with a small stake.[46] During a boom in the stock market cycle, Josiah Quincy told how "that enormous increase in wealth without labor which has come to fortunate speculators . . . seems to make the invocation of chance legitimate business."[47] Chevalier commented near the speculative peak of 1835: "Everybody is speculating, and everything has become an object of speculation."[48]

In December 1835, the greatest fire that New York has ever seen swept through the city and destroyed, among other things, the Merchant's Exchange, where the NYS&EB brokers had been holding their meetings. A chest full of trading records, containing irreplaceable information concerning various speculative movements underway, was heroically rescued.[49] Trading was suspended for a week while new quarters were found, yet the brokers' speculative fever was hardly affected. Speculation also flourished in land and in commodities, but the growth of securities markets had made speculation in stocks comparatively easier and more attractive. Volume and prices in the market soared.

As before, this heady rise to the speculative peak of 1837 was followed by the inevitable fall. In a panic, securities trading volume and prices dropped precipitously. In January 1837, the average number of shares traded per day was 7,393. By June, the average had fallen to 1,534.[50] The crisis was spread far beyond the stock market, as many banks failed or suspended specie payments.[51] Renewed prosperity in 1838 was short-lived.[52] The depression that then set in has been described as "one of the greatest panics in the history of the country" and "one of the most disastrous crises the nation has ever experienced,"[53] although a more recent examination suggests that the economic downturn of the late 1830s was "indeed dramatic, but its effects were not disastrous."[54]

After 1837, securities were traded less frequently. Nonetheless, intrepid new issues continued to appear, causing expansion of the public trading list both in 1839 and 1840.[55] In addition, an infusion of investment from abroad, combined with a marked rise in state government expenditures, bolstered sagging securities markets.[56] Unfortunately, state governments were poorly disciplined. They borrowed money excessively, printed bonds wildly, and incorporated innumerable banks. When much of the state paper was repudiated, the crisis in securities markets only worsened. In 1841 and 1842, nine states, finding themselves unable to pay the interest due on their bonds, defaulted.[57] As a result, hard-hit European investors lost confidence in America. When their foreign capital dried up, many state projects went under.[58]

The securities market contraction resulting from all of these forces lasted well into the 1840s, with volume sluggish, investors wary, and new securities offered only by the most solid issuers.[59] Brokers, dealers, and bankers in New York failed en masse; only twelve of the ninety-one NYS&EB members trading in 1840 had escaped failure in the previous five years.[60]

This securities market collapse of the late 1830s was a world apart from that of the 1790s. Whereas the earlier securities speculation was primarily generated by securities traders, the 1830s speculation was less self-contained. By the 1830s, the New York securities markets had become an integral part of the financial system. Their fortunes rose and fell with the fluctuations of other financial institutions and of the economy. Their influence had grown as the number of publicly traded securities burgeoned. Moreover, daily trading had long outgrown a handful of independent brokers and dealers. It now depended on the smooth functioning of the NYS&EB, an Exchange strong enough to survive the crises of the 1830s. It was a financial marketplace transformed.

During the half-century that witnessed this transformation, New York securities markets first revealed patterns repeated down to today: tremendous booms and busts, trustworthy issuers in need of capital and charlatans in search of lambs to shear, shareholders without power in corporate governance and managers with control, periods of government acquiescence and others of government meddling, market leaders and market makers, winners and losers. These same statements could describe New York securities markets over the next 150 years.

One crucial and recurring characteristic of these early New York securities markets was that while customers of all stripes and predispositions bought and sold securities, the trading market was dominated by speculators. The markets might have evolved differently if the NYS&EB had fallen under the control of older, conservative members who discouraged time bargains, or if the New York legislature had insisted on "reform," but by 1840 there was no turning back. At that point, the New York securities market had realized its ultimate native genius: its capacity for unrestrained speculation.[61]

EARLY UNITED STATES SECURITIES MARKETS COMPARED

D URING THE New York securities markets' formative years, significant markets also existed in Philadelphia, Boston, and to a lesser extent elsewhere.[62] As early as the 1790–1792 boom and bust, securities prices varied among cities, and dealers surmounted significant transportation barriers in order to arbitrage.[63] Already, however, it was New York that set the pace and the prices for the other markets to follow. The large volume of trades executed by speculators made New York the nation's leading securities trading market.[64]

After the 1792 crash, the smaller Philadelphia market grew slowly and gradually, projecting from the start a more cautious character.[65] Rather than a forum for speculation, all indications point to a Philadelphia market geared to the investor. The distinction was obvious from the vantage point of a Philadelphian. The *Financial Register* noted that:

> Our readers can scarcely have failed to observe the great difference in amount between the transactions in the stock market of New York and those of Philadelphia. This difference, we presume, is more an evidence of a speculative temperament, than a proof of an actual transference of capital from one species of investment to another. . . . Perhaps it would be found that in reference to a large proportion of the sales at New York, the only capital employed or required was the simple amount of the difference between the buying price and the possible selling price at the expiration of a week or a month. . . . If the buyer was in good credit the transaction might be conducted by a note, so as to require no capital at all. A very large portion of stock sales are nothing but wagers on the price of stocks.[66]

New York securities markets grew in the beneficial climate of a thriving commercial center, but it is not altogether clear why New York became the most important speculative securities market. One hypothesis centers on the characters of the peoples of the different cities and the manner in which their capital was put to work. Boston had its heritage of frugal Puritans, likely to put their money into shipping and later into manufactures. Philadelphia had both Quakers, who eschewed gambling, and aristocrats, who lavished money on their palaces. New York, on the other hand, as the port of embarkation of new immigrants, had a population more willing to take risks. Hammond, sounding this theme, characterizes Philadelphia as a city of wealth, while New York was a city of enterprise where a "newer and more aggressive spirit, in both politics and business, flourished."[67]

Although New York was the primary securities trading market, Philadelphia, Boston, and other cities also had pools of capital to tap, and it is generally accepted that early in the nineteenth century, New York was not the country's leading market for raising investment capital. When local funding proved insufficient to finance large southern railroads in the 1830s and early 1840s, they appear to have turned to Philadelphia for their financing,[68] and when midwest railroad promoters sought capital in the 1840s, they went first to Boston.[69] Both Philadelphia and Boston capitalists were eager to promote railroads in order to counter New York's advantages stemming from the Erie Canal, while many New Yorkers were cool to the idea of aiding those competing with their source of livelihood.[70] Although local railroads managed to raise capital during this period by opening subscription books in New York, and nonrailroad issuers successfully obtained New York financing,[71] it was not until perhaps 1850 that New York came into its is own as the nation's chief source of railroad funds.[72]

In the meantime, New York aided capital-hungry railroads in its own fashion. The New York secondary trading market quickly absorbed the stock of railroad companies, at first those with a terminus in New York, but soon roads chartered and operating in other states as well. The new railroad stocks were financial assets that lent themselves admirably to the speculative capabilities of New Yorkers: they were the issues of a glamorous new industry, made up of many entrants, some destined for success and profitability, others to failure and liquidation. Share prices and trading volume in New York were high. Speculation kept New York securities markets liquid. Buyers and sellers could execute their trades at short notice, often without substantial changes in price from the previous quote. Because trading volume gravitates to the market that assures best execution, Wall Street became the primary center for trading railroad shares.

While Boston and Philadelphia securities markets kept their focus on local customers, New York's orientation became increasingly national.[73] New York eventually became the place where issues could be sold to many investors, the place where the funds of the multitudes with modest savings could be tapped. Both Philadelphia and Boston had their turn as wholesale markets, but they never developed significant retail markets where shares could be bought and sold. When the deep pockets in Boston and Philadelphia were emptied, all that was left were the savings of millions of smaller investors from across the country which were tied to Wall Street. At that point, New York became the center for issuers to raise funds as well as the premier trading market.

To finance the voluminous New York stock trading, a market developed for "call loans." Banks lent money repayable on demand, with securities as collateral. Demand for call money arose "almost wholly out of speculative transactions in securities."[74] Banks found call loans attractive because they were highly liquid, yet also interest-bearing. The call loan market became secondary in liquidity only to specie, and was preferable for banks because the loans were interest-bearing.[75] Call loans were also attractive to purchasers, because speculation could be financed with a small downpayment. Call loans became so popular, and amounted to such a large market, that commercial borrowers complained of neglect in favor of them.[76]

Since extensive high-interest call loans helped New York banks to pay rates generally higher than those of other cities, funds flowed to the city. The source of these funds was twofold: 1) correspondent banks in rural areas, and 2) New York merchants who prospered from trade with the West.[77] Speculation in the stock market and call loans fed upon each other: the stock market provided banks with borrowing customers holding liquid collateral and willing to pay high interest rates, while the banks encouraged those customers to keep speculating by providing them with funds. Ultimately, a close relationship was forged between New York's chartered banks and the stock market. The growth of speculative activity in securities then directly affected the increasing importance of New York's banks.

Call loans and securities markets alone did not ensure New York's financial primacy; geographic, economic, political, and personal elements also contributed. New York's pre-1800 importance as a harbor and center of foreign trade expanded during the nineteenth century.[78] In addition, New York became a center for domestic commerce, especially after the Erie Canal cornered the market on western trade.[79] Furthermore, the demise of the Second Bank of the United States ended Philadelphia's ability to compete with Wall Street for financial primacy.[80] In addition, New York had the largest urban population in the United States after 1810.[81]

Nevertheless, securities markets were crucial to New York's growth. Because they were the center of speculation, New York securities markets overwhelmed all rivals to become the primary market, first in the United States, and later worldwide. In turn, the vitality of Wall Street helped fuel New York's rise to become the financial capital of the United States.

PART TWO
Participants in
New York Securities
Markets, 1790–1840

CHAPTER FIVE

Securities Professionals:
The Market's Nucleus

THE FIRST AMERICAN SECURITIES
PROFESSIONALS

B Y ACCEPTING Revolutionary War securities for payments in lieu of cash, merchants became the first securities professionals in America.[1] The steady flow of state and federal debt certificates, including obligations to unpaid American soldiers, spawned a regular trading market. By 1784, brokers, like Joshua Eaton of Boston, began to specialize in securities and advertised their intentions: "Public Securities of every denomination Negotiated: Business on Commission, transacted with attention and punctuality, and every favor gratefully acknowledged."[2] Similar evidence reveals securities brokers doing business in New York by 1786.[3]

During the 1790–1792 boom, the infant American securities market grew large and complex enough that specializations divided the securities profession into traditional segments. There were dealers who purchased securities for others and for their own account. There were also stock-jobbers who dealt in securities for themselves and held those securities for speculative reasons.[4] Brokers, on the other hand, bought and sold only for others on commission, and were expected not to operate on their own account lest they make a deal favorable to themselves at the expense of their clients.[5] In fact, regulations in London, copied by some American cities, required brokers to be sworn before the mayor and to abstain from trading on their own account.[6] In New York it was the auctioneers, responsible for the public sales, who were required to be licensed by the mayor.[7]

Distinctions among these various specializations were not rigid. Some professionals were, for example, both auctioneers and brokers.[8] More generally, each type of securities activity was accomplished by men with other business interests. Perhaps, for a time, a handful of New Yorkers devoted their energies exclusively to their securities business, but, after the 1792 market collapse, most of them returned to related occupations handling foreign exchange, circulating bank notes, discounting commercial paper, trading commodities, managing lotteries, or speculating in land.[9]

NATHAN PRIME

I N 1795, a remarkable young man arrived in New York City with an ambition that outweighed his modest capital. Nathan Prime had been born in Rowley, Massachussets, in 1768.[10] Little is known of his early personal life until he became a coachman to William Gray, a Boston merchant and early director of the First Bank of the United States, who reportedly exposed Prime to the world of finance and loaned him the money to enter it.[11]

Prime's choice to make his mark in New York securities markets in 1795 was bold. Public securities auctions had been banned in 1792, and many dealers active during the speculative bubble were gone. Customers were scarce; they spent their money and energy on less risky endeavors. Few new issues were floated, and securities trading markets were generally slack. Occasionally, newspapers reported stock prices or ran a broker's advertisement, but press coverage did not nearly approach the 1790–1792 level. There was precious little to suggest that a livelihood might be earned in the securities business. Nevertheless, Prime plunged in, starting his career as a broker—an appropriate occupation for a young man relying primarily on his business acumen and aggressiveness.[12]

Prime did not confine his brokerage to stocks and bonds. He became deeply involved in note shaving, that is, buying and selling at discount the notes of incorporated banks, notes redeemable only at the place of issue. This form of brokerage became important with the increase in number of incorporated banks after 1800, particularly in the years between the First and Second Banks of the United States. The newspapers of the time regularly listed various banks and the discounts that their notes were commanding in New York.

Prime is said to have "bravely got ahead" in currency trading as a note shaver.[14] He also undoubtedly brokered mortgage loans, insurance, and other kinds of business dealings.[15] His early success at these endeavors was marked by his entrance into New York society when he married Cornelia Sands, the daughter of a wealthy merchant.[16]

Within five years, Prime's brokerage profits allowed him to expand his activities to operate not only as a broker for others, but also as dealer, buying and selling securities for his own account.[17] His name appears frequently in the stock register of The Manhattan Company, New York City's second incorporated bank. He bought and sold Manhattan Company shares regularly, making a profit from price markups. This "dealer's turn" more than compensated him for the risk he assumed in maintaining an inventory of stocks with constantly fluctuating values.

Prime's activity was so extensive that he was undoubtedly "making a market" for Manhattan Company shares, helping other brokers to find the matching sides of their customers' orders. Without auctions or a stock exchange to bring buyers and sellers together, Prime was the focal point for Manhattan Company trading. He maintained an inventory of securities and held himself out to other brokers and dealers as prepared to buy or sell those issues on demand. He priced both sides of the market, the "bid" or "offer" representing the price he would pay sellers, and the "asked" representing the amount he would charge.

Securities professionals likely made markets as early as 1790, but Prime's operation in Manhattan appears to be the earliest documented instance of this type of securities activity.[18] By 1802, Prime published the prices of ten securities on a weekly basis, and it is likely that he was making a market in them all.[19] Whenever trading activity in an issue was great enough to warrant assumption of the dealer's risk, Prime seems to have made markets, thereby providing a service to all other brokers and dealers.[20] Similar patterns appear repeatedly in the development of New York's securities markets; when a need was felt strongly enough and the prospects for profit were enticing enough, some enterprising financier like Nathan Prime would step in.

Prime's securities operations proved to be a springboard for activities in allied fields. In 1805, identifying himself as "Stock and Exchange Broker," Prime announced that he would pay a premium for dollars.[21] The letters of one of his customers, David Parish, reveal that Prime dealt extensively in currency and bills of exchange, domestic and foreign.[22] These activities paved the way for Prime to function as a private banker. He held customer's funds on deposit and loaned them money. Deposits grew as customers (like Parish) left funds with Prime after completion of securities sales or as Prime collected dividends paid to his customers by corporate issuers.[23] Although he did not issue large volumes of notes that circulated as currency, as did other private bankers, such as Jacob Barker of New York and Stephen Girard of Philadelphia, Prime's bills of exchange, when traded, usually commanded a premium price.[24] Just as market-making was vital to securities markets, particularly in the absence of a functional stock exchange, this type of private banking was an important component of the early New York financial system as an alternate to additional incorporated banks.

Prime was not only a pioneer private commercial banker, he was also directly involved in the fledgling field of investment banking. Before the War of 1812, there were no American investment bankers to speak of, because new issues were commonly distributed without intermediaries. Issuers announced the opening of subscription books at various centers throughout the country, and prospective purchasers signed these books, committing themselves to pay for the stocks or bonds. In 1813, however, Secretary of the Treasury Albert Gallatin found it impossible to sell a large bond issue in this manner to a nation deeply divided over the merits of the war with England. Instead, the government accepted sealed bids and sold a substantial quantity of bonds to a small syndicate who purchased the bonds with the intention of resale. American loan contracting was born.[25] Prime was given the opportunity by his friend Parish to participate in the syndicate's purchase of the 1813 bonds, but declined the offer because off his opposition to the war.[26]

Loan contracting was a natural outgrowth of Prime's complementary activities. Brokerage provided him with a roster of domestic purchasers, and exchange dealings with foreign bankers opened the door to foreign investors. Private banking provided him with the capital needed to pay for new issues. Market-making sharpened Prime's ability to appraise securities values, and familiarity with securities markets enabled him to advise issuers on how best to structure and sell their offerings.[27] These experiences added up to an extraordinary ability to compete in purchasing new securities issues for distribution to others.

Although Prime's first efforts at loan contracting appear to have failed,[28] he persevered, and in 1824, he won the bid for an Erie Canal loan.[29] Thereafter, Prime and the firms he founded became leading American loan contractors. Acting alone, or occasionally in association with firms such as Thomas Biddle of Philadelphia, Prime purchased sizable bond issues backed by New York, Ohio, Louisiana, and Mississippi.[30] Prime's success as a loan contractor led to the expansion of his market-making when his customers later looked to him to provide liquidity for the new issues he had distributed.

Many of the bonds Prime purchased in bulk were sold retail to foreign investors through correspondent relationships with eminent London banking houses such as Baring Brothers and the Rothschilds. Ultimately, Prime's firm became the most important ally and correspondent of Baring Brothers, enjoying a better credit line than Baring extended to other American loan contractors.[31] Connections with the sources of foreign capital that were essential to the young American economy and its securities markets further enhanced Prime's prestige and financing ability.

These international connections also contributed to Prime's extensive endeavors in foreign exchange markets. The dealings of Prime's firm in foreign exchange were at times second only to those of the Bank of the United States.[32]

Prime had begun his career as an individual operator, but in order to accommodate his constantly growing roster of customers and services, he built progressively larger partnerships. He chose partners as skillfully as he developed his business. They were leaders in New York and well known in other large financial centers. In 1808, his firm became Prime & Ward, in 1816 Prime, Ward & Sands, and in 1826 Prime, Ward & King.[33]

By this time, there were many other private bankers and loan contractors operating in New York City who had entered the lucrative securities industry from various related fields. Merchants who invested their capital in inventories of bonds became loan contractors.[34] European financial firms sent representatives to the United States, some of whom entered business for their own accounts.[35] Lottery agents became involved in note shaving, and from there moved into securities distribution.[36] Incorporated banks, particularly the Second Bank of the United States, also served as loan contractors.[37] This tremendous competition notwithstanding, it was Prime, Ward & King which became Wall Street's most highly regarded securities and private banking house.

Prime not only built a firm among firms, he also played important roles in other financial institutions, predating the time when investment bankers such as J. P. Morgan would command the financial world by holding interlocking directorships in banks and insurance companies. Prime has indeed aptly been termed the Morgan of his day.[38] He was commonly known as a "king" of Wall Street. He was instrumental in the organization of the New York Stock & Exchange Board,[39] he became a director of various insurance companies, and he was nearly elected a director of the Second Bank of the United States.[40] Prime's influence was demonstrated by his belief that his outspoken demands for interest-on-demand deposits might actually cause the Bank of the United States to follow the lead of English banks and change their long-standing no-interest policy.[41] His firm's unique and powerful position in the market was further manifested by its being chosen to quietly sell securities for the Bank of the United States.[42]

Prime, Ward & King was a highly profitable enterprise.[43] Prime himself was reputed to be the third wealthiest man in New York in 1830.[44] He speculated heavily in stocks and bonds, accumulated considerable real estate, and dabbled in bankrolling shippers and merchants.[45] His children were intermarried with the Hoffmans, Jays, Costers, Rays, and other prominent New York families.[46]

The estate listed in Prime's will showed how well he had prospered in the securities profession that he had helped to build. He owned six residences and over twenty parcels of land, including a country house in Westchester and a veritable palace at the corner of Broadway and the Battery.[47] Tragically, Prime's material success did not bring happiness; his death was reportedly a suicide.[48]

Prime retired in 1832, but the firm which was his most significant progeny lived on. It proved its stature in 1838, leading the way in encouraging New York banks to resume operations after suspension of specie payments.[49] Without Prime's cohesive force, however, the firm soon dissolved. Samuel Ward was distracted by his later endeavors as president and successful molder of the Bank of Commerce,[50] and James Gore King withdrew to establish his own firm, which soon became a prominent investment house in its own right.[51] Extensive losses on foreign exchange dealings ultimately led to the failure of Prime & Ward in 1847.[52]

More important than these direct descendants of his firm, however, is Nathan Prime's example. He demonstrated that the securities industry, in brokering, note-shaving, market-making, private banking, loan contracting, and international financing could and would be a successful and integral component of the growing American economy.

THE OTHER BRANCH OF THE SECURITIES INDUSTRY

B Y THE end of Nathan Prime's career, securities business in New York had grown from a handful of part-time brokers and dealers to a full-fledged industry. The New York Stock & Exchange Board was now the nation's chief securities market, handling orders from all parts of the country. The trading list numbered over 100 stocks and bonds, many from outside New York. The securities industry was made up of various firms, stretching from tiny one-man enterprises to large and prestigious private banking houses. Although they all had securities in common, a division ran through these firms, separating those in the distribution market from those in the trading market.

Relatively few solidly financed firms like Prime, Ward & King were pioneers in investment banking. As private bankers and loan contractors, they dealt primarily in trustworthy securities, usually debt instruments. Their patrons were investors who bought these securities for steady dividend income and safety of principal. These firms handled their customers' stock trading, but probably avoided time bargains and other speculative operations. They were cautious and conservative businessmen, the embodiment of the rational, bourgeois strain of the capitalist spirit.

The other group of securities professionals, smaller in size and capital but more numerous by far, handled business in the trading market. It was as easy to enter this side of the business as it was to become a merchant. Men became brokers simply by hanging out a shingle. They might profess to be doing only a commission business, but nothing prevented them from trading for their own accounts. They represented the adventurous, risk-taking side of the securities industry, and attracted as customers the risk-oriented members of the public—some, astute risk-takers; many, rash gamblers. By the late 1830s, Wall Street brokers of this ilk were notorious for their speculative abilities.[53]

Jacob Little exemplified these brokers. He began as a clerk to Jacob Barker, himself a maverick private banker. Little prospered, and in 1822 opened his own office.[54] In 1825, Little joined the NYS&EB in order to nurture his brokerage business.[55]

By the 1830s, Little had become a well-known operator, not only trading for his own account, but doing so visibly and spectacularly.[56] He was perpetually engaged in speculation, devoting his mornings to cotton and other staples, his afternoons to securities.[57] The only thing remarkable about this gentleman, an observer of the time stated, was his extraordinary appetite, "for he has been known to gorge and digest more stock in one day than the weight of the bulk of his whole body in certificates."[58] Little made an enormous killing by investing in early railroads, and he soon owned so much stock that he was called by some the "Napoleon of Wall Street."[59] Because he regularly operated on the short side of the market, profiting from price declines, he would also be pointed out to visitors as "the Great Bear."[60]

Little was the first operator to make stock corners a commonplace occurence. He is said to have been responsible for one of the early coups in market manipulation, the corner in 1835 of Morris Canal & Banking Company shares.[61] Armstrong describes another Little operation to raise the price of Norwich and Worcester Railroad stock. Little joined a clique with Boston operators, and bound himself under a penalty of $25,000 that he would not sell the stock below 90, and would do all in his power to advance the price. Foreseeing that the operation was destined to fail, he quietly sold all of his stock to his colleagues, who were forced to buy it to keep the price up. They lost enormously when the crash came, and he simply sent them the $25,000, "Their rage was unbounded, and they asserted in a very emphatic manner that if Mr. Little ever visited Boston he would inevitably part company with his ears."[62] In a similar notorious episode, Little escaped from a corner in Erie Railroad stock. The Erie Gang controlled all the Erie Railroad stock in the New York market and Little was obligated to deliver shares to them in the future. Trapped in a vise, Little sent to England and obtained convertible Erie Railroads bonds in time to cover his contracts. This action so infuriated the Erie Gang that they pushed through a NYS&EB rule on time limits for options contracts to prevent others from following this example of obtaining overseas relief.[63]

Little's accomplishments attracted speculative customers looking for tips, or points as they were known in those days.[64] Like all agents, securities brokers owe their principals the fiduciary obligations of care and loyalty, but, due to the nature of their product and customers, securities brokers enjoy many opportunities to neglect fiduciary obligations. Manipulating customers was easy for brokers like Little, and he could rationalize that if he did not shear the money from these lambs in a bear trap, some bullish broker would take it from them instead. Little would use these small-time buyers and sellers as pawns in the game, providing them with the proper tips to aid him in accomplishing his larger designs. In addition, the trading he prescribed for them, often in the form of time bargains, generated substantial commissions.[65]

During his lifetime, Little made and lost a number of fortunes.[66] He repeatedly came out solvent, but he was finally brought down in the crash of 1857. He had sold 100,000 Erie Railroad shares short, "expecting" the crash, but a last "bulge" before the collapse found him overextended and unable to maintain his position, and he failed for $10 million.[67]

The extent of Little's operations was a forerunner of trading later in the century; he was the pioneer of that class of speculators of which Daniel Drew, Commodore Vanderbilt, and Jay Gould were soon to become conspicuous examples. The fact that he, alone, for a time could so dominate securities trading reveals the intimate character and size of the market in his day. The market had seen speculators before, but it had grown enough by the 1830s to have a full-time one. Soon, the market could and would accommodate many more.

Because of operators like Little, the brokerage segment of New York's securities industry established an unsavory image. American securities brokers had been accepted genially at first, but by 1841, "Mr. Broker" in New York was described as a practitioner of the "black art," who sacrificed customers to his own interests, and whose roguery, when discovered, "established his character for shrewdness."[68] Conservative New York securities professionals may well have been unhappy over the negative effect of speculative trading on the industry's image, but they were powerless against the wave of speculation and the brokers who rode its crest, especially after the NYS&EB became the center of speculation in the 1830s.

Nathan Prime and Jacob Little, loan contractor and broker, epitomize the extremes of the securities industry during this formative period. Not all loan contractors met the standard of Prime, Ward & King, nor were all brokers notorious operators like Jacob Little. Many securities professionals of both varieties earned reputations as cautious, prudent advisors.[69] They were the less colorful rank and file of the profession, who, day by day, did their part and ultimately contributed as much as Nathan Prime or Jacob Little to the building of American securities markets.

CHAPTER SIX

The Supply of Capital: Purchasers of Securities

M OST SECURITIES market customers can be conveniently divided into two groups—investors or speculators. Investors use securities markets as the rough equivalent of a savings bank. They maintain the purchasing power of their wealth and the income it produces with low-risk securities that promise safety of principal and steady dividend payments. Investors pay cash and store their certificates in strong boxes, expecting to hold them for long periods of time.[1] Speculators, on the other hand, assume risks willingly and use the market to obtain new wealth. They predict securities price changes, and often borrow funds to trade accordingly.[2] When they believe a price will rise, they purchase securities for resale. When they expect a fall, they sell short, planning to cover their sales by later purchases at a lower price. Their time horizon is brief; they are in and out of the market quickly.

There are those who fit in neither category. Additional customers, relatively few in number, are interested in shares because of the voting rights they carry, ultimately perhaps leading to control of a corporation.[3] Some others contribute capital to support socially desirable projects, even though the securities they purchase will never become valuable financial assets.[4] Still another group buys securities to obtain influence in enterprises on which their related businesses depend.[5] In the early American securities trading market, these atypical customers were neither as important nor as numerous as the two dominant groups: investors and speculators.[6]

EARLY AMERICAN INVESTORS

T HE NEW York stock market's dramatic first speculative episode from 1790–1792 was not soon repeated; investors were the primary customers during the next quarter century.[7] Even during the first boom, many bonds and stocks were purchased by investors who held on to them. Many of the original shareholders of the Bank of New York, for example, were not involved in trading during 1791 and 1792.[8]

Investors picked securities from a small, select, but growing list of publicly traded issues that were likely to provide safety of principal and stability of income: federal bonds, shares in banks and insurance companies, and, later, state bonds. Before the turn of the century, federal bonds yielded 6 percent or more, and until the government paid off its debt in the 1830s, yielded at least 5 percent. In contrast, state bonds, Erie Canal bonds in particular, resulted in relatively lower returns during the 1820s and early 1830s, although after the wholesale repudiation of state bonds in the late 1830s, state issues had to offer higher yields to attract wary investors.[9]

Early stocks were generally less secure investments than bonds. The guarantee of repayment from a group of entrepreneurs was never as solid as that from a government. Consequently, bank shares provided a somewhat higher return than bonds. Purchasers of shares in The Manhattan Company and the First Bank of the United States obtained annual yields of between 5 percent and 6 percent on their investments. Insurance company shares, apparently considered riskier, provided even higher returns. Various investors held portfolios of these stocks and government bonds, collected their dividends, and watched the value of their holdings gradually increase.

Institutions, particularly banks, were a significant group of early American investors.[10] They bought securities both for retention as investments and for resale at a profit or commission.[11] Federal and state bonds were nearly as valuable and liquid as specie, and many chartered banks held them as reserves against the currency they issued.[12] Banks also functioned as intermediaries in the capital mobilization process. They gathered the funds of many savers and funnelled them into securities. For a prominent example, The New York Savings Bank was chartered expressly to collect funds from small savers in order to invest the money in larger projects. It subsequently became an important purchaser of Erie Canal bonds.[13] The so-called improvement banks, such as the notorious Morris Canal & Banking Company, were similar. They were chartered to invest in the securities of canals and other social capital endeavors.[14]

Fire and marine insurance companies were also significant corporate investors. In the nature of their business, they collected premiums that would sit idle until required to pay off claims. Consequently, they required investments that would earn money on that capital, yet could be quickly converted to cash. For these reasons, they invested heavily in securities, concentrating on seasoned issues that could be easily sold at a favorable price.[15]

The securities purchases of another important class of investors, state and local governments, can be divided into two categories: some promoted economic development by supporting corporations that could not otherwise raise sufficient funds;[16] others raised money without resort to taxes.[17] New York state, for example, owned bank shares and United States bonds amounting to nearly $2 million in 1795,[18] investments it held onto for many years.[19] New York steadily built its portfolio of income-producing securities, and by 1836, owned stock in seventy-seven state banks. Dividends from these investments provided the state with a significant amount of non-tax earnings.[20] Similarly, New Jersey built a large portfolio of investment-grade stocks, aided by the legislature's practice of reserving for the state shares in the enterprises it chartered. These exactions from the promoters of chartered corporations became a major source of New Jersey's revenue.[21] Similar investments in securities were held by Pennsylvania,[22] Massachusetts, Maryland, Virginia, and Connecticut.[23]

Another significant force in the early American investment market were European securities purchasers.[24] They were warmly received in the United States from the time of Hamilton's famous Report on Manufactures, which encouraged the importation of foreign capital. Before 1840, surplus savings earned relatively low interest from Old World banks. As a result, foreign investors, who were willing to take slightly larger risks for a larger return, looked to the rapidly developing New World. By and large, they bought investment-grade securities; they avoided the risks that bold American speculators were accustomed to.[25] Foreign investors were first attracted to the bond market, where at the turn of the century they purchased United States bonds to get a 6 percent return, well above the 4 percent generally available in London.[26] By 1824, foreigners were estimated to own over a quarter of the federal bonds then outstanding[27] English investors with extensive experience in canals also jumped on the Erie Canal bandwagon, eventually holding more Erie Canal bonds than Americans.[28] The confidence in American securities that this tremendous foreign investment represented was further bolstered by payment of the federal debt in 1832; never before had a country extinguished its debt.[29] By the late 1830s, foreign investment in United States securities amounted to over $200 million, a tremendous sum in those days. [30]

Such foreign investment, in the form of pounds and guilders, usually found its way to the United States through correspondent relationships with New York securities professionals. London or Amsterdam firms would buy securities in New York with the aid of New York brokers and loan contractors, like Nathan Prime, and then sell the securities on their local retail market. [31] American enterprises would undertake more direct attempts to tap foreign capital in periods of high demand by sending securities salesmen to bargain directly with European purchasers. For example, in 1829 and 1830, the representative of the cities of Washington, Alexandria, and Georgetown, a Mr. Rush, with the collaboration of the important London banking house of Rothschild, solicited subscriptions to a loan of $3 million at 6 percent. "Nearly five times as much was subscribed, in Holland, on opening the books, as was needed, and the stock instantly rose about ten percent." [32]

For domestic enterprises, the results of heavy foreign investment were mixed. The influx of capital was obviously helpful, even crucial, for numerous projects. Also, because foreign shareholders were often precluded from voting on corporate matters, many local investors gained power and voting rights disproportionate to the number of shares they held. [33] Others, however, feared the results of foreigners owning too much stock, even if they had no vote. Pennsylvania in 1825 passed a statute prohibiting transfer of stock in the important Bank of North America to noncitizens, except citizens of Holland, unless the foreigner had declared the intention of becoming a citizen of the United States. [34] Foreign investments in the Banks of the United States were so extensive that they became a national political issue. In 1809, foreign investors owned three-fourths of the shares of the First United States Bank, [35] and a similarly large foreign involvement in the Second Bank of the United States was one of the reasons cited by President Jackson when he announced his intention to veto its charter in 1832. [36]

Despite the wealth and stature of institutional, governmental, and foreign investors, the majority of investment-grade securities in early America were purchased by domestic individuals. From the scarce and widely dispersed information available, it is difficult to make many generalizations about this group, particularly since all indications are that they were a group equally diverse as the great mass of individual investors today.

As might be expected, issuer records indicate that the individuals purchasing investment-grade securities made both large and small investments. For example, numerous individual original subscribers to the important New York banks invested anywhere from a few hundred dollars to many thousands. Original subscribers to the $500 par value Bank of New York shares included some who signed for 34 shares and many who signed for a half or one share.[37] Of the 1,372 subscribers to The Manhattan Company, 497 subscribed to two shares only.[38] Similar patterns were repeated for both United States Banks.[39]

Government bonds were also typically sold both to a few large investors and to many more of moderate means. When New York state floated its first public loan in 1815, sixteen subscribers signed for $10,000 or more, thirty-eight between $3,000 and $10,000, and eighty-five for $3,000 or less.[40]

Wealthy investors, such as J. J. Astor, were known to make sizable securities investments. Astor was typical of the business and professional men of his time who invested in securities. A majority of these men were from New York City, and among them, many were merchants who had accumulated capital in the ever-growing trade with the West.[41] In a speech before the Senate and Assembly in 1812, Governor Tompkins of New York echoed the widespread belief that: "Bank stock is generally owned by the speculating, wealthy, and aspiring part of society."[42] Shares in some enterprises, customarily manufacturing and textile companies, discouraged any but the wealthy from participating by issuing securities with par values as high as $1,000.[43]

Although influential individual investors such as J. J. Astor are long remembered, the mainstays of the early American securities market were the more numerous men of moderate means: tradespeople, merchants, and farmers.[44] They bought securities cautiously, a few at a time, when they had extra cash on hand sitting idle. Some enterprises had shares with par values as low as $25, allowing for widespread participation by the small saver and the small investor. Many other small savers who did not put their money directly into securities contributed indirectly to securities markets by putting their funds into banks, which in turn used them to purchase securities.

This pattern of dispersed holdings of investment-grade securities held true in regard to regions, as well as economic classes. Individual investors were not exclusively located in New York City where the most important securities trading market thrived, and many did not live in cities at all. In 1827, half of The Manhattan Company's shares were held by 384 shareholders who lived outside of New York, and nearly half of the Bank of New York shares as well, were held outside of New York. One out-oftowner owned 5,000 Manhattan Company shares, one-eighth of the bank's stock.[45] Likewise, the shares of the Second Bank of the United States in 1831 were distributed throughout the country, with large holdings in Pennsylvania, South Carolina, and Maryland.[46] Federal bonds were also held by investors from nearly every state.

The dispersion of shareholders and potential shareholders among classes and across the country created a challenge to issuers wishing to sell shares. The first hurdle was to identify possible purchasers, so that a sales pitch could be made. That accomplished, early enterprises seeking money from individual investors faced the same difficult task that similar enterprises face today. Investors, large or small, have always been slow to be convinced; they do not part with their money before they have an assurance that they have something to gain and some confidence that they have little to lose. This cautiousness was especially evident in large landholders who "short of capital and frequently in debt . . . maintained a conservative outlook where ventures involving the risk of precious capital were to be considered."[47]

For an example, consider the history of investment in the Erie Canal: "smart money" did not subscribe to the first Erie Canal loans until the success of the enterprise was established, preferring instead stock in the Second Bank of the United States.[48] It was not until 1821, four years after the first Erie Canal bonds were sold, that many wealthy individuals became interested in the canal and invested along with banks and other institutions.[49] Ultimately, when the Erie Canal success became glaringly obvious, wealthy investors and prominent brokers clamored to obtain the bonds, and their sale was considerably simplified.[50]

This Erie Canal episode also illustrates that investors had at least as much difficulty in the early days as they do today in identifying safe investments, or financial advisers who could lead them to such investments. The great need was for accurate market and corporate information. Accordingly, we find John Rathbone, an investor, writing from Zanesville, Ohio, in 1829 to his nephew and broker, James Bleecker, in New York. Rathbone explains that he has $2,000 "which I wish to put out on interest, or invest in stocks: will you have the goodness to advise me by the Bearer what Pct. interest can be obtained for in New York on good security or what kind of stock you would recommend to purchase."[51]

In a regular correspondence, Rathbone informed Bleecker of the economic situation in Ohio, particularly the "renegade unincorporated banks,"[52] while requesting information from Bleecker concerning securities prices in New York.[53] Theirs was a symbiotic relationship. When

Rathbone received good advice, he returned the favor by referring new customers to his broker.[54] Yet it was Rathbone who was out of touch with the market and who was forced to rely on his broker. After ordering that fifty shares of Manhattan Company be purchased at an advantageous price, Rathbone wrote: "I have seen no price current of stocks lately. . . . I rely very much on your good judgment in this business."[55] Such correspondence is characteristic of Rathbone's communications to Bleecker throughout a period of some fifteen years, correspondence which reads like a customer's correspondence with a broker today.

Accordingly, information about securities: yields, issuers, interest rates, and the like, grew in importance as the American securities market grew in complexity. When the number of publicly quoted stock issues increased, investors were forced to become more discriminating in selecting securities for their portfolios. Eventually, even the pillars of the securities markets, bank issues that had at one time been treated as solid investment-grade securities in almost every case, became suspect. As early as 1804, we find Matthew Clarkson, a New York merchant and broker, advising a client to purchase government bonds "because I am of the opinion that banks are getting to be too numerous." This advice was given at a time when the Merchants Bank was struggling to be chartered as New York City's third bank.[56] The proliferation of banks during the War of 1812 and the emergence of so-called "wildcat" banks, produced many banks that were managed ineptly, some fraudulently.[57] Investors were then faced, as they are now, with the knotty problem of sorting the good investments from the bad.

For a customer carefully calculating his or her eventual return, the task of choosing the proper investment was made all the more difficult as a different type of customer became increasingly common in the securities markets and his trading influenced market prices. Rather than viewing securities investments simply as good, liquid, financial assets, this type of customer was willing to take great risks, and often simply gamble with securities, in the hope of spectacular gain.

EARLY AMERICAN SPECULATORS

WHILE INVESTMENT dominated the New York market before 1817, the hectic years from 1790—1792 were a notable exception. The large trading volumes, tremendous price volatility, predominance of time transactions, and the boom-bust syndrome are all symptoms of a period when speculation flourished. Given the right conditions, early Americans securities purchasers were clearly capable of expressing a spirit of speculation.

Although not so widespread or notorious, the trading of speculators continued in the years following the 1792 collapse. Any opening of subscription books for new issues provided an opportunity for speculators who paid the first installment of the purchase price, sometimes as little as 5 percent. If heavy demand materialized, they would capitalize on it by selling promptly at an advance in price. If the price did not rise, the speculator could abandon the security and lose only his original down payment. The pattern of spirited trading immediately following the initial public offering of shares in The Manhattan Company in 1799 and the Eagle Insurance Company in 1806 illustrates this type of speculative activity.[58] Even some Bank of New York shares, later to be infrequently traded as investors held on to them, were traded heavily when first issued during the 1791 boom.[59]

The War of 1812 also brought typical wartime speculation, much of which centered on the price volatility of Treasury notes and bonds sold to finance the war. Large amounts of this speculative bond trading were centered in New York City, which by this time had clearly become the nation's foremost arena for securities speculators. The end of the war took the wind from the sails of bond speculation,[60] and securities speculators turned their attention more fully to corporate stocks. By 1817, speculative stock trading became the dominant activity in New York securities markets.

For persons of a gambling turn, speculating became a career, and in those days, just as now, that career was hazardous. In 1818, the troubles and dealings of an overextended speculator, Bernard Hart, were summed up in one long document.[61] On September 28, 1818 Hart was unable to repay $6,300 he owed to Henry Coster. Coster refinanced the loan, extending its duration and increasing its amount to $10,000, on the following consideration: First, any profits arising from a number of Hart's time bargains would go to Coster, including an overdue contract to deliver 250 Bank of the United States shares, a contract to deliver 100 Bank of the United States shares on February 1, another contract to deliver 100 Bank of the United States shares on February 15, and a contract to deliver 50 Franklin Bank shares on April 1; second, if the National Insurance Company stock Hart had pledged as collateral on three other outstanding loans was sold to cover those loans, Coster would get any profits that otherwise would have been returned to Hart;[62] and third, Hart pledged additional stocks to Coster as collateral.[63] Not only does this agreement show the diversity of holdings and transactions of a speculator of this period, it also demonstrates the growing practice of lending money with stocks or stock transactions as security.

JOHN MICHAEL O'CONNOR

THE CORRESPONDENCE and trading records of another securities trader in New York in the 1820's provides a clear picture of the goals and trading methods used by contemporary speculators.[64] We know more about John Michael O'Connor's securities transactions than almost any other facet of his short life. Born in Pennsylvania in 1790, O'Connor joined the army and rose to the rank of major during the War of 1812.[65] His interest in the securities market began while he was still in uniform, when he invested in conservative stocks and bonds.[66] His appetite for securities trading was apparently whetted by these investments, for from the time O'Connor was decommissioned in 1821 until his death in 1826, he used New York as his base for extensive securities dealings.

O'Connor often traveled to other parts of the country. Fortunately, his absences from New York were occasions for an extended correspondence with his brokers, and many of these letters still exist. Together with O'Connor's detailed notes of some transactions, they provide a unique picture of an early speculator's trading habits. They also provide a basis for believing that O'Connor, who does not appear to have originated his trading methods, was trading in the same way as other speculators of the day, and that market considerations important to O'Connor and his brokers were also relevant to others.

O'Connor relied largely on information provided by his agent, Thomas Hutchinson, while he actually placed most of his orders with two brokers, Clarkson & Co., and Ralph Wells, neither of whom appear to have been members of the NYS&EB.[67] O'Connor concentrated much of his activity in bank and insurance stocks, which twenty or thirty years before would have been exclusively bought and sold by investors. Among these stocks, Bank of America, Ocean Insurance Company, and Hope Insurance Company were his favorites.

Although most of O'Connor's trades were speculative, it appears that he did keep inventories of stocks such as the Hope Insurance Company, presumably as long-term investments. As a speculator, he generally operated on the long side of the market, looking for price rises. On occasion, however, he would also sell short when he expected a price decline.[68]

O'Connor knew the advantage of speculating with borrowed money; he could obtain larger blocks of shares with the hope of great gain, and the risk of total loss.[69] His purchases were primarily financed with loans using the stocks he acquired as collateral, and his borrowing arrangements were remarkably fluid. At times, he was both lender and borrower, with brokers, insurance companies, banks, other traders, or acquaintances as counterparties to his transactions.

Although market and individual securities information was crucial to O'Connor, information he could use was difficult to obtain. Wells, O'Connor's broker, wrote in 1825, that "I can do little more than give you the quotations of the day. The information which can be obtained by any stockholder in any of our monied incorporations is very imperfect, and even the correctness of that little cannot be relied on."[70] Such a state of affairs did not prevent O'Connor from seeking whatever information might affect securities prices. Some was news concerning individual companies, such as casualty losses suffered by insurance companies. More often, it was information likely to influence the movement of stock prices as a whole. Frequently, Hutchinson wrote to O'Connor of changes in the money supply, with their subsequent effect on interest rates. On May 2, 1822, Hutchinson wrote to O'Connor that money demand was such that interest rates were at 1 percent per month. Five months later, on October 7, 1822, he reported that money was plentiful once again.[71] O'Connor also received letters regarding changes in the economic and political environment, as in Hutchinson's report of March 9, 1825, that "the election of Mr. Adams seems to have been received here with considerable coolness."[72] In addition, Hutchinson informed O'Connor of changes in economic conditions abroad, particularly in England.[73] O'Connor used the two or three letters a week to stay ahead of other traders, who could only rely on the sporadic financial press of the time.

As might be expected, O'Connor's securities trading activity was extensive. His notes and receipts for the first seven months of 1824 show more than thirty illustrative transactions: purchases and sales of securities, and loans to and from his brokers.[74] Moreover, it is plausible that the surviving records provide a mere glimpse of the totality of O'Connor's transactions. He could have been dealing with other brokers whose records are not available; he could have executed trades for cash; or he could even have executed some of his trades himself; and, for these less complicated trades, O'Connor had no need to keep the same detailed records required by the complicated dealings described below.

Some of O'Connor's trading during this period was relatively straight-forward. On May 15, 1824, he purchased 200 Bank of the United States shares, pledging the shares as collateral for a loan that paid for them. When the market price of these shares rose quickly, O'Connor sold them on June 15 and repaid the loan. This trade showed a small profit in a deal that never required O'Connor to put up his own money.

In contrast, other transactions were quite complex. For example, on January 30, 1824, O'Connor added 300 shares to his holdings of Hope Insurance Company stock. Wells, O'Connor's broker, in effect loaned him the funds to finance the purchase, charging a fee equivalent to interest and retaining possession of the shares.[75] A month later, O'Connor repaid most of this loan with the proceeds from a sale of 43 Bank of America shares. He pledged 100 Hope Insurance Company shares as collateral on the remainder of the initial loan, a loan which he did not fully repay until April.[76]

From March through April 1824, O'Connor built his position in Ocean Insurance Company stock in a rising market. The heavy trading volume in Ocean Insurance on the NYS&EB during this period suggests it was a "fancy" of its time.[77] O'Connor purchased Ocean Insurance shares and pledged them as collateral for loans with individuals and insurance companies. Then, as the price continued to rise, the proceeds of O'Connor's loans on the collateral of the Ocean Insurance stock were used to purchase additional shares. In July, the price of Ocean began to turn down, and O'Connor unwound his complicated transactions in order to free up the stock and sell it.[78] When the price stabilized in August, O'Connor repledged his still unsold Ocean Insurance Company shares as collateral for another loan at a favorable interest rate.[79]

This intricate series of transactions, typical of O'Connor's deals, suggests a number of patterns and repeated interests. One important point is that many of O'Connor's securities purchases were financed on credit, by what was the equivalent of trading on margin. In the accepted view of securities transactions on credit, time bargains prevailed in Wall Street until 1840, and were gradually replaced by margin trading by 1860.[80] Analysis of O'Connor's trading, however, demonstrates that securities he purchased in the 1820s frequently served as collateral for loans which then financed that, or other, purchases. The shares involved often did not even pass through O'Connor's hands. Instead, they went directly from the broker to the financer. Where one was involved, the institutional lender was generally an insurance company, not a bank. The possibility arises that insurance companies pioneered loans to finance margin trading, so that when Wall Street banks created the call loan market, they were building on an already established practice.[82]

In addition, O'Connor's records reveal that his relationships with brokers were wide-ranging and flexible. At times, Wells would act like a banker, as O'Connor borrowed money from him. On the other hand, Clarkson suggested that O'Connor withdraw his funds on deposit at the Bank of New York, presumably earning no interest, and lend them to Clarkson, who not only would pay interest but also would pledge stocks as collateral.[83] This arrangement appears to be an early version of modern-day customers' credit balances in brokerage accounts. Throughout these transactions, it is also clear that a solid customer like O'Connor was able to purchase shares on credit and then pledge those shares as collateral for a loan. Without immediately advancing any of his own money, he could thereby speculate and lock in a transaction at a favorable price.

When O'Connor's health faded in 1825 and 1826, he was forced to spend considerable amounts of time in climates milder than New York. This did not deter him from speculating from afar. Even as his death approached, he retained a keen interest in the market. Yet his speculations had not made him a rich man. His will was modest, leaving a gold watch and his library to his friend and agent Hutchinson, and an estate not even sure to raise the $500 annual sum he provided for his sister.

SPECULATIVE METHODS IN EARLY AMERICAN SECURITIES MARKETS

T HE NEW York Stock & Exchange Board, organized in 1817, left behind a pool of regular data on share volume and market prices. While for some years the data are lacking, a fairly accurate picture can be drawn of the market as it swung in and out of cycles of speculation. All evidence indicates that, after 1817, market activity was largely conducted by speculators, with volume and prices surging in alternating cycles of intense activity and of calm.[84] Throughout these swings, stock transactions fell into two classes: those requiring immediate transfer of securities for cash, and those involving some type of credit.[85] From the first active stock trading in 1791–1792 onward, large volumes of purchases were leveraged—financed with borrowed money. For such purchases, time bargains, option contracts, and puts and calls were frequently utilized.

Time bargains, an institution borrowed from English tradition where they had been practiced since at least 1730, were the most popular credit transactions in early American securities markets. Essentially futures contracts, they were agreements based on a future transfer of securities at a price agreed upon at the present. They were cheap, and they were simple. They required little cash when entered into, and they were frequently settled on the day they expired by payment of the difference between market and contract prices.[86] Essentially, time bargains were wagers on the future prices of stocks. Although not illegal, they were unenforceable at law, which forced the parties executing them to rely on each others' personal honor and credit.[87]

Time bargain trading was a cornerstone of the early New York securities market. According to Hedges, during the first quarter of the nineteenth century, "the majority of sales were time transactions of some description, probably involving up to six months or even longer."[88] Yet speculative trading was so extensive in early American securities markets that time bargains alone could not satisfy speculators.

Option contracts were also common. Like time bargains, options allowed betting on the future price of securities without putting down the full purchase price. The most favored were buyer's or seller's options. A price would set, and the buyer had the right to require delivery (buyer's option) or the seller had the right to make delivery (seller's option), on any day within the option period. Neither party was required to put up cash until the option was exercised. If the option were not exercised, the customary practice at the time required performance on the final day of the option period.[89]

"Puts" and "calls" also came into vogue. A "put" is the privilege of the seller to deliver stocks at an agreed price at any time within a given period; a "call" is the privilege of the buyer to demand delivery. The purchaser of a put expects a fall in price; the purchaser of a call expects a rise. Puts and calls differed from options contract in that, if they were not exercised by the end of the period, they lapsed and no obligations were incurred.[90]

Together, these various types of speculative trading, time bargains, buyers' and sellers' options, and puts and calls, overshadowed investors' cash purchases at the NYS&EB, both in volume and in effect on securities prices.

SPECULATIVE EXCESSES

T HE SPECULATOR, according to theory, assumes the risk of price fluctuations. He wins if he forecasts changes accurately; loses, if the market moves against him. Taking a cue from early speculators in Amsterdam and London, some New York speculators discovered that they could eliminate the risk of market fluctuations if they controlled prices. Sporadic instances of manipulation before 1830 grew into institutionalized practices.[91] By 1833, the terms "bull" and "bear" were being applied to members of warring cliques of traders who sought to drive prices up or down. "Neither party is satisfied to await the influence of natural events, but makes every effort to bring about such a result as each desires" (in other words, they do what they can to fix prices).[92] Today, deliberate control of prices is prohibited under federal securities laws,[93] but during the NYS&EB's early days, and for virtually a century thereafter, manipulation violated no statute.

Even Nicholas Biddle, the venerable president of the Second Bank of the United States, was known to operate in Bank of the United States stock. In 1833, Wall street was heavily short in the Bank of the United States, and it had been sold down to 102. As the settlement date approached, "there were frantic efforts to break the market," but they all failed, and the price lifted to 111. Speculators on Wall Street lost heavily.[94]

Bold manipulators boasted of their exploits and were widely admired for their enterprise and daring. They played the game according to the rules and were simply more aggressive and imaginative than their fellows. The game took the form of a battle. Prominent speculators served as unofficial generals of rival armies, mounting campaigns of bulls and bears to control prices. Their arsenal, in addition to the financial resources of each clique, ring, or pool, included false tips, wash sales, or any other artifice that might do the job.

The king operators, men like Jacob Little, Jacob Barker, and Samuel Beebee "knew everything."[95] They could control bull pools or conduct bear raids and had countless other arrangements for driving stock prices up or down. The editor of the *New York American* explained: "By artful management, assiduous puffing, manifest predictions, and supplies of stock skillfully curtailed as the demand increases . . . stocks may be blown up to an absurd rate—and spared, as a favor, to the public."[96] Fowler himself a veteran of these forays describes one as follows:

Various methods are adopted to entice operators to sell short the stock which a pool have under their manipulation. Sometimes the price is made to simulate a weakness which deceives the street by producing the false impression that the price will soon be lower. This is the partridge trick. That game bird, it will be remembered, flutters as if wounded, in order to draw the hunter away from her young. As soon as the price of a stock looks "weak," it becomes the mark for short sales. The bears rush in and sell it under the expectation of a further decline. After a sufficient number of the contracts of these gentlemen have been taken by the pool, the price is lifted again, and the short sellers find themselves in the trap. This in the slang of the street is known as the "scoop game."[95]

Two-bit speculators, then as always yearning for sudden, easy riches, rushed into the market when beckoned by the operators. Whoever emerged as winners in the large battles on Wall Street, the masses of small investors generally lost their savings, while the brokerage community profited handsomely.

The most flamboyant manipulations were attempts by the bulls to corner markets, to obtain control over all available shares and prevent the bears from covering their short positions. A corner is a result arrived at when one combination, secretly holding the whole or greater part of any stock or species of property, induces another combination to agree to deliver a large further quantity at some future time. When the time arrives, the second combination, if the corner succeeds, suddenly finds itself unable to buy the amount of the stock or property necessary to enable it to fulfill its contracts, and the first combination fixes, at its own will, the price at which differences must be settled. The corner fails or is broken when those who have agreed to deliver succeed in procuring the stock or property, and fulfill their contracts.[98]

A corner enabled the person or syndicate in control of the stock to set the price at which they would settle with those who had agreed to deliver items that could not be obtained. Profits of 200 percent were common on successful corners and often resulted in bankruptcy for the unfortunates caught in them.[99]

In the 1830s, market corners became the order of the day at the NYS&EB. The Canton Company corner of 1834 and 1835 was remarkable in driving the price of shares from 60, their par value, to 300.[100] In January 1835, the famous Morris Canal & Banking Company corner culminated, and the price of its shares jumped from almost nothing to 185.[101]

Shares of stocks that were involved in a corner or were otherwise "in play" were traded at a spectacular pace. Turnover numbers for some of these stocks are sobering; it was not uncommon for an entire issue of shares to be traded more than ten times in a year. All of the outstanding shares of some corporations were traded twenty or even thirty times over in the course of only twelve months. These stocks were clearly passed around like hot potatoes—"footballs," to use the jargon of the time. To make this trading practicable, stock certificates were generally not passed around this rapidly. Many transactions were time bargains where the stocks never changed hands, only the difference in the contract price and the market price at the time of settlement was transferred. When discussing the Canton Company corner, Niles mused: "In all this mighty amount of business done, it is most probable that not a single share of stock had been delivered."[102]

Other stocks were also traded briskly during speculative peaks. Some, the "fancies," were traded solely as vehicles of speculation, not because the companies had any prospect of earning a profit. As Armstrong described them:

> [Fancies] are, generally speaking, of no particular or known value, and represent worthless or embarrassed corporations, which have failed in the undertakings for which capital was contributed, and most generally have never paid a dividend, and are never expected to. Their real worth, or rather worthlessness, is so little known, that it seldom interferes with an unlimited expansion or contraction in prices, as according to the wealth or talent employed on either side may preponderate. Harlem Rail Road Stock, for instance, has sold for both seven and nearly two hundred per cent, within the same year.[103]

Many of the purchases and sales of these fancy stocks were financed by call loans. Thus, the purchaser had the choice of either entering into a time bargain—where he could avoid transferring the stock, or financing his purchase through a call loan—where he could avoid the outlay of his money.[104]

THE IMPORTANCE OF SPECULATION

S UCH SPECULATIVE excesses as corners, market fixing, and fancy stocks, which stand in stark contrast with the more "legitimate in-

vestment" practices in securities markets, have often caused all speculative practices to be condemned. Yet speculation and speculators make their
own vital contributions to the functioning of securities markets.

The sale of new issues to investors who place their funds at the disposal of corporations is the cornerstone of the securities markets' contribution to the mobilization and allocation of capital. If investors merely
hold on to their stock, neither needing to liquidate their investment nor
wishing to switch their capital to a different enterprise, they have little
additional use for securities trading markets—although, typically, they
regularly check quotations to put a value on their investment.[105] There
are, and always have been, many investors who operate this way.

It matters little to the issuer of securities in the new issue market whether
the purchaser is an investor or a speculator: both place new money at the
disposal of the enterprise. True, the speculator may purchase with the
express intention of reselling the next day at a higher price, but, when
that resale is consummated, the speculator is simply replaced by a new
securities holder and his capital, while the issuer's capital is unaffected.[106]
The impact on capital formation is the same whether the original purchaser is an investor purchasing to hold the security or a speculator purchasing with speculative designs. Both speculators and investors purchase
shares, both can and do contribute funds to corporate enterprises, and
both make it easier for corporations to raise money in the stock market.

Speculators have always been particularly important for launching risky
projects. First, innovators propose new ventures; then speculators provide the financing. Together, they sponsor enterprises, both good and
bad, that might not otherwise get off the ground. Speculation in the early
securities market made it the institution, as much as any, that anti-
cipated and implemented the "feverish ardor" with which, in de
Tocqueville's words, "Americans pursued their prosperity."[107]

By subscribing to the capital stock and paying a small downpayment,
speculators gave new unproven corporations their first chance in early
America. If the project succeeded, speculators would continue to contribute when the board of directors called for funds. Otherwise, speculators would sell their stakes in successful ventures at a profit. If an enterprise failed, speculators would simply abandon it. In this manner,
speculators gave both the Society for the Establishment of Useful
Manufactures and the Bank of the United States their chance in 1791.
When the success of the S.U.M. appeared unlikely, shareholders stopped
paying on their subscriptions;[108] but when prospects for success of the Bank

of the United States were certain, speculators sold their scrip at a profit or held it and paid the required contributions. In broad terms, speculators in the 1790s, like speculators today, provided the risk capital which helped to develop the economy. [109] By forecasting the future and then trying to put their money there, speculators have always made important contributions to economic growth and development. [110]

Traditionally, securities speculators are more active in the secondary trading market than in the new issue market. Transactions in the trading market, whether executed by investors or speculators, affect issuers only indirectly. They merely change the identity of the securities holder. The issuer's ability to raise additional capital can, however, be affected by the trading market. For example, when potential purchasers know that the shares they contemplate purchasing have an active trading market, typically fueled by speculation, and that shares can thereby easily be converted to cash, new issues can be floated more easily. [111] Thus, speculators, responsible for keeping trading activity high, help securities markets absorb new issues.

Speculators' trading in the secondary market impacts issuers and customers alike when it affects prices. Because the price a security commands is an indication of investors' enthusiasm, and thus a reflection of the enterprise's economic health, managers have strong incentives to keep their share prices up. Speculators, however, can and do distort the prices of shares away from their intrinsic value, [112] sending improper signals to managers while also harming customers who cannot buy or sell their shares for what they should be worth. Such distortions are, fortunately, short-run phenomena. If an enterprise is successful and pays dividends, its share prices will eventually stabilize. If an enterprise fails, its share prices will eventually collapse.

Moreover, intelligent speculation will contribute to the process of bringing prices into line with underlying values. If shares are over-or under-valued, speculators who recognize the distortion will predict the return to proper prices. When they trade on these predictions, speculators bring prices and values together. In 1865, Hamon explained this process colorfully:

> Both classes of operators are useful, and even essential. But for the bulls, no enterprise would ever be carried into effect; and when rogues try to gull the public with fraudulent schemes, and to foist worthless stock on unsuspecting investors, the bear looms up as the protector of

his species, and, by selling the trash *short*, develops its want of value, and warns the dupes of their danger. When values are too low, the bull reinstates them; when they are too high, the bear interposes and checks the enthusiasm of the sanguine.[113]

Speculators' trading also increases overall trading volume, in turn allowing prices to change more smoothly, less erratically. Constantly traded shares have more orderly markets and fewer sharp price fluctuations, while thin trading markets display sharp price rises and falls disastrous for both investor and speculator. The customer of an actively traded stock is likely to buy or sell at a price close to the previous transaction. Speculative traders not only increase volume, they also fill in trading gaps by assuming risks that others do not wish to carry. In addition, by providing a more continuous market, speculative trading can lessen the spreads between bid and asked prices.[114]

Speculators not only add important elements to the new issue market and make contributions to orderly trading in secondary markets, they have also been a driving force behind securities market growth. Thanks to its large volume of speculative trades, New York City became the place where a customer could find the best execution for a securities contract in the first years of American securities trading. In a self-fulfilling cycle, this fact made New York City the best securities market. Speculation in securities also encouraged the growth of call loans, collateralized by securities and payable on demand, again strengthening New York's banks. The role of speculation in New York's rise to the financial capital of the United States can hardly be overstated.[115]

In turn, New York securities market growth played a vital role in mobilizing the capital society so desperately needed, by funneling speculative enthusiasm into worthwhile projects. Speculative boom periods have always been times of feverish economic activity, capital accumulation, and optimism. As Chevalier wrote in 1835:

> In the midst of all this speculation, while some enrich and some ruin themselves, banks spring up and diffuse credit; railroads and canals extend themselves over the country; steamboats are launched into the rivers, the lakes, and the sea; the career of speculators is ever enlarging, the field for railroads, canals, steamers and banks goes on expanding. Some individuals lose, but the country is a gainer; the country is peopled, cleared, cultivated; its resources are unfolded, its wealth increased. Go Ahead![116]

Only a few years after Chevalier's enthusiastic note, securities markets crashed along with the economy and many fortunes were crushed.[117] However, too many who examine this boom and bust, or the boom-bust syndrome in general, see only the bust and ignore the boom. Typically, following a cyclical upswing and crash, securities markets are left in a stronger position than before the upswing. They take two steps forward, one step backward. As Stedman observed in 1905: "Each succeeding era of speculative enthusiasm will leave after its recession the values of honest securities higher than they lay where the preceding wave had flowed and ebbed."[118]

Overall, speculation in securities plays an important role in the mobilization of capital. Every project funded represents risks taken: the more risks taken, the more projects funded. Not only is speculation as important as investment in the new issue market, it also allows innovators to raise capital. It keeps the volume of trading high, which encourages investors who know that their investments can be converted to cash. High volume also tends to dampen the suddenness of market price swings. While speculation may distort trading prices in the short run, it also corrects them in the long run.

It seems reasonable to conclude that investors in new issues have not been the only legitimate players in the securities markets. The indirect, less easily discernable roles played by speculators have been equally important to the market's success as an instrument for raising and allocating capital.

The vital and positive contributions made by speculation and speculators are often overlooked, in particular by those who consider speculation a destructive practice at odds with beneficial "investment." The opinion—long-held by earlier generations of historians and market analysts—that the securities markets' true function is only as an investment market has led many to view in isolation the role played by investors purchasing new issues. Other elements of securities markets have been discounted or ignored. Securities speculation in particular has been considered gambling, morally suspect at the least, and socially undesirable. Consequently, its significance has long been overlooked.[119] Because speculation frequently constituted the bulk of securities market activity in the earliest years, the picture of the early American securities market has been skewed.[120]

Contemporary analyses show that the sharp line that once separated investment from speculation has largely been erased.[121] Taking chances in securities markets is no longer shameful, it is generally acceptable behavior.[122] Market participants continue to have the same goals that motivated the classic investor and speculator. Now, however, no opprobrium beclouds the activities of those who seek stocks that will show the greatest price increase over the shortest time period, precisely that for which the old-time speculators were condemned.[123] Speculation has come of age; it can sit quite comfortably side by side with investment; and it is as legitimate and necessary as the securities markets themselves.

CHAPTER SEVEN

The Demand for Capital: Issuers of Securities

THE FIRST AMERICAN PUBLIC CORPORATIONS

THE FIRST publicly owned business corporations were created when the British government, lacking the resources to develop and exploit India and the New World, offered inducements to merchant adventurers in order to attract the capital that was required. Business corporations such as the East India Company and the Hudson's Bay Company were launched, combining attributes of earlier corporations chartered by the crown to provide public services—such as schools and churches—with attributes of joint-stock companies organized for profit by businessmen.[2] To encourage these important enterprises, the government granted them privileges ranging from monopolies to shareholder insulation from enterprise debts. Eager investors purchased shares in these projects, and many realized phenomenal returns on their investments. The Crown also benefited from this alliance of government and private enterprise when important objectives, such as the colonization of America, were achieved.[3]

After the American Revolution, the newly independent governments in the United States, eager to promote economic growth, sought the roads, bridges, and canals that would enhance local commerce. Because taxation to finance such projects was no more popular in the 1790s than it is today, legislatures turned to the familiar device of chartered business corporations as instruments for attracting private capital. Within two decades of Independence, the new states had chartered more than 300 business corporations,[4] far more than had been created in England up to that time.[5]

Securities markets capable of absorbing the shares issued by these corporations were in place in America by the 1790s. Enterprises with attractive risk-reward relationships could sell stock to the public, not because securities purchasers wanted to promote some project or service that was needed for the social good, but because individual securities purchasers were convinced that they would obtain liquid and income-producing financial assets. Generally, corporate stocks were marketable as long as their institutions were sound and profitable.

Banks were the first American public corporations, the first capable of raising capital by issuing shares, the first whose shares were traded regularly in the public market.[6] Although the Constitution prohibited states from coining money, it allowed state-chartered banks to issue notes that functioned as currency[7] and the earliest banks, such as the Bank of North America, the Bank of New York, the Bank of Massachusetts, and the First Bank of the United States, had a virtual monopoly on printing money. Consequently, they were highly profitable.[8] They had no difficulty filling initial share subscriptions, and demand for their shares in the trading market was generally strong. Sound banks were sound investments, and a broad array of investors could be convinced to part with their money for stakes in enterprises that promised generous returns at low risks.[9] Even the wholesale issuance of bank charters after the demise of the First Bank of the United States in 1811 did not dim the attractiveness of stock in banks that were conservatively managed.

Bank profitability and the resulting attractiveness of bank stock encouraged the development of numerous publicly owned banks. Bank promoters knew that eager investors could be found. Fueling this cycle, stock prices quoted at a premium advertised the success of early banking corporations and stimulated the promotion of others, usually over the fierce resistance of the first.[10]

While the constellation of publicly owned banks expanded steadily, many banks became more or less indistinguishable. Nevertheless, the two Banks of the United States, the largest and most powerful corporations of their times, stood apart from state-chartered banking corporations in their size, their ability to perform some rudimentary central banking functions, and their level of federal government involvement.[11] These distinctions, however, had only a negligible effect on their operation as corporate bodies. In issuing shares, the election of directors, or the declaration of dividends, they were similar to any other public corporations. The actively traded shares of the Banks of the United States were stock market volume leaders, and were benchmarks by which other securities' prices were measured.[12] Investments in the First Bank of the United States by a wide spectrum of shareholders, combined with the publicity given to the Bank's affairs, were crucial to the development of public corporations in America because they served to familiarize the public with public corporation and securities markets.

Bank shares were not the only corporate issues in the trading markets; insurance company stocks were also in demand. When operated conservatively, insurance companies realized stable earnings and paid handsome dividends, occasionally as high as 20 percent.[13] They appealed to potential policyholders, and implicitly to investors as well, by boldly proclaiming their responsibility in newspaper advertisements that listed their directors, all pillars of the local community.[14] In 1828, Boston insurance company stock was described in these glowing terms:

> for solidity and safety, is not surpassed by any stock . . . in the United States; their capitals are generally entire and in many cases will command a premium; the mode of investment is restricted by the legislature and the amount which they are authorized to take on any one risk is limited to 10% on each respective capital.[15]

Thus, insurance shares were seen as attractive financial assets and were actively quoted and traded.

Shares in both banks and insurance companies were investment-grade corporate securities. Their retention of value and steady dividends, combined with their easy convertability into cash, attracted conservative investors. Many of those investors profited handsomely, and continued to support the financial institutions whose shares they held. In the 1880s, many shares of the Bank of New York were still held by the heirs of the original founders "as a permanent investment."[16] The shareholders benefitted because the profitability of the shares was maintained for many years, while the bank in turn had the advantage of a stable and supportive group of shareholders. This relationship typifies the development of successful public corporations utilizing securities markets. Relationships of this variety are commonplace today, but in the earliest years of the American economy, that situation was new. By issuing desirable shares, banks and insurance companies were the first American enterprises to prove the public corporation's unique ability to mobilize investors' capital through the securities market and put that capital to work in important projects.

UNTRADED CORPORATIONS

I N THE earliest years of the Republic, hundreds of nonfinancial corporations, ranging from textiles to turnpikes, could not raise sufficient capital from the public, and shares in these corporations were not publicly traded. Over three hundred business corporations were chartered by the new states before 1801, yet at that time fewer than ten had securities that were regularly quoted and traded.[17]

Scarcity of capital is one reason often given for the stock market's failure to mobilize the funds needed by many of the young nation's enterprises around the turn of the century.[18] Evidence suggests, however, that the failure of corporations, "the ordinary agency of private enterprise," to mobilize capital for inland transportation projects "was not due to any lack of adequate supplies of capital."[19] In a trial-blazing essay, Guy Callender blames instead the cautiousness of those who controlled the available capital. Before 1830, Callender claims, there were few "speculative investors," very numerous by the end of the nineteenth century, "who devote a part of their savings to investments involving a great risk and requiring a long period of time to yield a return."[20]

The facts are otherwise. Rather than there being few "speculative investors," risk-takers were plentiful. Joseph Davis, foremost historian of the pre-1800 corporation, was on the mark when he stated that:

> Not only was capital readily forthcoming for every undertaking likely to pay and *seen* to be likely, but it came forth for innumerable undertakings in which the risk was very great and the chances of success were remote. . . . [Liquid capital] was really abundant, eagerly seeking investment, and ready to take in other lines risks as high as those of the sea.[21]

Investors put money into attractive securities and speculators played the market regularly, at times furiously. Few, however, were prepared to buy shares in a venture that was unlikely to succeed and provide a fair opportunity to make a profit.[22] The reasons that the public corporation as an institution did not mobilize capital for the projects society needed were not a lack of capital or a lack of entrepreneurial risk-takers; they were, instead, the natures of the enterprises seeking money from investors. Simply put, securities markets were no place for fundraising by corporations whose shares were not desired as financial assets.

Inland transportation corporations, glaring examples of enterprises unable to raise capital from the public, were seen by potential investors as probable financial failures. There were many such corporations. Two-thirds of the corporations granted charters between the revolution and 1801 were for transportation enterprises: warfs, canals, turnpikes, and bridges.[23] Roads, canals, and bridges tended to be fraught with engineering, management, and labor problems, yet their charters often restricted the tolls they could charge. The reward potential they offered to investors was strictly limited. Before the attention of the young nation turned westward, convincing investors that they would enjoy a financial return from an investment in a massive canal project that might take five years or more to build was especially difficult.[24] Many transportation enterprises were not even organized for profit. They were established, instead, to serve the public interest.[25] Some shareholders participated in them as a matter of patriotism.[26] Others might have hoped that their investments would show profits and pay dividends, but also invested to obtain the services such corporations would render or to enhance the value of nearby real property they owned.[27] Few, however, invested in such projects with great expectations of making money from their shares.

Understandably, issuers that did not promise to be money makers could not raise sufficient funds from the public, and there was little demand for their shares in the trading market.[28] Investors looked to secure financial assets, and speculators sought better opportunities for a return on their capital. Making money seemed more likely by entering into a time bargain than investing in a bridge project that was as likely as not to fail. Unattractive corporations had to look elsewhere for their financing, usually to government aid.[29]

Rudimentary corporate finance techniques compounded the difficulties for enterprises unable to stimulate investors' enthusiasm. Issuers announced that they would open subscription books on certain days in certain places. At the time of subscription, purchasers were generally required to pay only a small fraction of the purchase price, 5 or 10 percent of the par value, obligating themselves to pay the balance in installments. Each time a payment was called for by the board of directors, subscribers had a chance to reassess their investment, and, if the venture's prospects appeared dim, they defaulted.[30] The issuer was then left with burdensome, and often unsuccessful, actions at law against defaulting shareholders.[31] Many early public corporations failed when they had a bad year, as young enterprises are apt to do, and could no longer collect money from their shareholders.

Early United States corporations' capital-raising capabilities were also restricted by a reliance on common stock, to the exclusion of senior securities that might have attracted additional investment by offering lower risks to securities purchasers.[32] Some corporate promoters appear to have been familiar with senior securities, and there are a few examples of their use in the 1820s, but these were isolated instances. The earliest preferred stock we have found in the Unted States was issued in 1822.[33] Before 1840, however, senior securities were rare; they were not regularly traded, and their full potential to raise funds from cautious investors was untapped.

One reason for corporations attempting to raise capital from the public to ignore senior securities in the earliest years of America's securities markets was the clear example of financial corporations, which raised all the capital they required by sale of common stock. The absence from the corporate new-issue market of securities professionals, who might have understood senior securities more readily than did entrepreneurs, also retarded their use. If securities professionals had gotten involved with corporate stocks, rather than dealing primarily in contracting for bond issues, they could have merchandised either preferred or common stocks more aggressively than corporate promoters did, which in turn could have improved corporate financing capabilities. Once demand was already assured, professionals operated in the corporate common stock trading market but they rarely promoted new corporate issues by aggressively selling them to customers.[34]

Alongside corporations that unsuccessfully attempted to tap public supplies of capital but failed, due to the unattractiveness of the enterprise to investors, or inadequate corporate finance techniques, or both, there were many close corporations, most conspicuously manufacturing enterprises, that, for the most part, did not try their luck with public issues.[35] Although incorporated, early close corporations, like those of today, resembled partnerships. They relied on the same small group of people to furnish capital, operate the business, and divide profits and losses.[36] With personal, not standardized, management, success often depended on the abilities of the firm's founder.

While some manufacturing companies flourished, many failed. For an investor, it was difficult to distinguish the good investments from the bad. Because shares in most manufacturing enterprises were considered risky investments, particularly before the War of 1812, purchasers in public securities markets were wary of them.[37] One famous manufacturing corporation, the Society for the Establishment of Useful Manufacturers, had tapped public capital during the bull market of 1790–1792, when demand for any and all securities was extremely high.[38] The market collapse of 1792, however, deeply wounded the company.[39] The ensuing conspicuous failure of this public corporation undoubtedly chilled prospects for subsequent manufacturing ventures, ventures that might have considered selling shares to the public. Because of the riskiness of manufacturing enterprises, compounded by the hefty amounts required to purchase expensive manufacturing corporation stock (typically $1000 a share), no significant trading market developed.[40] This lack in turn damaged the new-issue market for subsequent manufacturing enterprises. Shares could not be sold easily to inverstors who plainly did not believe it would be simple to resell them.

Generally, the nature of both the enterprises and of corporate finance explain why sufficient public capital could not be raised by many nonfinancial corporations before 1820. Issuers could successfully appeal to the public for money only if they offered to investors participation in a venture that would be viable, earn a profit, and pay dividends. As banks and insurance companies were such issuers, they could attract public supplies of capital. For these profitable enterprises, there was no failure of the securities market. Other issuers would have been able to raise capital had they been organized to promise profit and minimize risk. "Let any project be started which will insure an interest of seven or eight per cent. (and that was though to be quite a moderate profit six or seven years ago), and millions of dollars are ready to meet and support it," wrote Niles in 1821.[41]

That was indeed the problem: securities markets were unable to raise capital for most early corporations primarily because attractive issuers were scarce. As a result, when enterprises could not raise sufficient capital from the public directly, through securities markets, states competing for the opening of the West had little choice but to invest capital themselves.[42]

BONDS AND THE ERIE CANAL

GOVERNMENTS—FEDERAL, state, and local—were perhaps the most important issuers in the earliest American securities markets, particularly before 1800. Bonds were attractive from an investor's perspective because they were liquid, income-producing, and guaranteed return of the invested capital.[43] After Hamilton made certain that the federal government would vigorously support its obligations, United States bonds became stable and secure financial assets, and, with the exception of the speculative 1812 war issues, investors were drawn to them. Following in the wake of successful federal bonds, came state bonds and city bonds.[44] By 1829, twenty different government bonds were traded in the New York market.

The financing of the Erie Canal demonstrates the importance of a government guarantee that an investment is secure. The need for a waterway to connect the eastern seaboard with the West had been felt before 1800.

In 1792, the New York legislature chartered two corporations to connect the Hudson River with the Great Lakes. Despite state aid with stock purchases and loans, one corporation collapsed almost immediately, and the other, the Western Inland Lock Navigation Company, puttered along aimlessly for years. Both projects suffered from wholly inadequate planning, financing, management, and timing.[45] As might be expected, wary investors avoided shares in these corporations that showed no promise of success.

These and other canal-building failures by enterprises financed through corporate stock were coupled with a growing need to reach the nation's interior. An intense regional rivalry developed, as each state wanted the benefits of trade with the West for its own citizens. On both national and state levels, the appropriate method for financing canals was debated, a debate that ended in New York with the legislature's determination that a canal between the Hudson River and Lake Erie should be financed by sale of bonds secured by the state's credit.

Although the legislature selected this course with considerable trepidation,[46] the issue was an overwhelming success, and Erie Canal bonds were sold in forty-two separate flotations between 1817 and 1825.[47] In constructing an inland waterway, New York state succeeded brilliantly where public corporations had failed miserably. Clearly, among its advantages, the state-built canal reflected careful planning, engineering, and management lacking in the prior corporate ventures. In addition, the state's project was begun a full quarter-century later, when public pressure to build the facility was far greater. Nevertheless, the state's accomplishment is largely attributable to its ability to tap private savings, an ability that the earlier attempts had lacked. Whereas the earlier corporate shares had not been, the Erie Canal bonds were marketable primarily because they carried a low risk. New York obligated itself to honor the bonds even if the canal proved to be a failure. The state guarantee was the crucial factor giving investors an adequate assurance against major risk in putting their money to work in a canal.

Also aiding the state's fundraising success was the vibrant New York securities market, now capable of comfortably handling such a financing. Not only was the New York Stock & Exchange Board in place, but securities professionals had learned how to contract for bond issues and resell them to others. The public had also become familiar with arrangements for the purchase and sale of securities.[48] Purchasers could rely on regular press reports of quotations to provide a composite judgment on the relative risks of various investments.

The New York success in selling bonds stimulated other states to finance projects in a similar manner, and resulting state debt issues were traded actively at the NYS&EB.[49] While regular trading improved the liquidity and attractiveness of the various state bonds, it also strengthened and broadened the New York securities market. In addition, the successful absorption of state bonds into the securities trading markets paved the way for nonfinancial corporations to raise capital from the public by issuing marketable securities. The example of the Delaware and Hudson Canal Company graphically demonstrates the next stage in this evolution.

THE DELAWARE AND HUDSON CANAL COMPANY

WHILE CAMPING in northeastern Pennsylvania, the Wurts brothers had found rich deposits of anthracite possessing remarkable qualities as a fuel.[50] It was relatively easy to transport the bulky product from the mines to Philadelphia, but by the 1820s when the brothers decided to mine and sell the coal, other entrepreneurs were already delivering coal to Philadelphia via the Schuylkill Canal. The brothers sought an alternate market in New York City, their major obstacle being a stretch of countryside that at some points reached a height of 900 feet above sea level. It was essential to carry the exceedingly heavy coal over these points at a cost allowing it to be sold profitably in New York.

The Wurts brothers proceeded to meet the challenge. First, they obtained control of the coal deposits. Next, they surveyed the terrain to determine whether a waterway would be feasible, retaining for that purpose Benjamin Wright, who already enjoyed a national reputation as chief engineer for the Erie Canal. Recognizing that the nation was in the grip of a canal-building mania, the brothers determined that the climate was favorable for floating an issue of stock, and they orchestrated a program aimed at tapping public funds for their enterprise. In 1823, they organized two corporations, one chartered in Pennsylvania to mine the coal and to canalize the Lackawaxen River, the other, the Delaware and Hudson Canal Company, chartered in New York to establish water communication between the Delaware and Hudson Rivers, purchase lands, transport the anthracite, and raise an authorized common stock of $1.5 million.[51]

The brothers next embarked upon a stock-merchandising campaign in New York City. Late in 1824, they shipped some Lackawaxen coal to New York via sloop and prevailed upon the Tontine Coffee House to install a grate so that they might demonstrate the qualities of the new fuel. A press dispatch commented that New York's "citizens will have an opportunity of examining and testing the quality of this coal; the rich mines of which it is intended to open to the New York market by means of a canal."[52] An offering circular extolling the advantages of the proposed canal and the coal it would carry to the city gave notice that shares could be subscribed on January 7, 1825.[53] Support was enlisted from such solid citizens as former Governor De Witt Clinton and Philip Hone, soon to be mayor of New York.

Despite rival companies which mounted a vigorous last-minute dirty-trick press campaign,[54] the issue of Delaware and Hudson Canal Company stock was largely oversubscribed.[55] Within a few months, shareholders chose a board of managers consisting of people well-known in New York's civic life as well as one member of the Wurts family. Philip Hone became the company's first president, serving for a short time before his election as mayor. By mid-1825, the first contracts for construction of the canal were let. A year later, 2,500 men were building its various stages.

In 1827, with a large portion of the canal completed, the company appears to have run out of money, as it applied to the New York legislature for assistance. The company was granted a loan of $500,000 in state bonds, secured by a mortgage on the company's properties, that was increased two years later to $800,000.[56] By October 1829, about three years after the start of construction, canal operations began. The 108 miles of canal held four feet of water between banks thirty-six feet apart at the waterline, twenty feet across at the bottom. If evaluations of the company's official biographers are accepted, the Delaware and Hudson Canal was one of the engineering marvels of its time. Although only one-third the length of the Erie Canal, it contained more locks and crossed higher terrain.

Between the time of the ill-fated corporate effort in the 1790s to build a canal from the Hudson River to the Great Lakes and the Wurts brothers' successful effort to build a similar waterway in the 1820s, engineering, planning, and management had advanced considerably. These developments alone, however, could not have been fully utilized if enterprises like the Delaware and Hudson Canal Company had not been able to raise enough money. Fortunately for the Wurts brothers and a good many like them, the securities markets had also developed sufficiently to enable a large nonfinancial business to obtain the bulk of its financing by selling stock.[57]

Following on the heels of successes like the Delaware and Hudson Canal Company, the public corporation came into its own as a powerful device to raise funds for nonfinancial corporations. Railroad promoters in the 1830s studied and copied this example, and soon exploited the intrinsic advantages of the public corporation and securities markets that had always existed.

EFFECTS OF THE TRADING MARKET ON PUBLIC CORPORATIONS

BEFORE THE Civil War, the new-issue market, where corporations sold securities to the public, and the trading or secondary market, where those shares were transferred, were considerably more distinct then they are today. Funds were initially raised by a corporation through subscription rather than by a sale of securities in the open market. Issuers were most concerned with the success of their issues at subscription, less concerned with the secondary trading of their shares.[58] Issuers could not, however, ignore this secondary trading.

Corporations looked to the secondary trading market for shares in other, similar enterprises before offering shares to the public. If insurance company shares were all commanding premium prices, it was probably a good time to launch a new insurance company. The trading market was important for an initial distribution. It encouraged investors to buy shares; the ability to convert shares to cash quickly and easily made them more desirable as financial assets.[59] The trading market was also vital for the initial share distributions for new untested enterprises. Speculators would buy shares and give a corporation enough capital to begin and prove itself. If the venture failed, the speculators lost: if it succeeded, speculators resold their shares to investors at a profit.

Once an issue was sold, the trading market allowed issuers to continue operations and maintain their capital while the suppliers of that capital constantly changed. The market created a large and diversified group of shareholders interested in the enterprise and offering their funds and other support. Disbursed holdings of shares resulting from effective trading markets also gave managers more power vis-a-vis scattered shareholders, who found it difficult to act in concert. At the same time, share marketability left shareholders less disturbed about this separation of their ownership from the powers of managers to control the corporation. If shareholders in a publicly traded corporation felt aggrieved by managers' actions, their remedy was simple; they sold their shares.[60]

Buying and selling in the secondary market sent an important signal to managers. Solid demand reflected in steady share prices indicated investors' perceptions of the enterprise's economic health. Comparing share prices of rival companies was similarly instructive. These considerations were important for a corporation as it considered issuing additional stock or borrowing money from a bank. If investors were enthusiastic, additional funds could be raised more easily. Managers thus had strong incentives to keep their share prices up.[61] The securities markets also provided guidance on the cost of capital to management, which in turn helped them to determine the appropriate levels of investment. In addition, corporate officers typically owned large blocks of shares in their enterprises, the value of which they had an interest in keeping as high as possible. The first directors of The Manhattan Company, for example, signed for 12,000 of that company's 40,000 shares.[62] For these reasons, managements of public corporations were concerned with the prices their shares commanded in the secondary trading market.

The Delaware and Hudson Canal Company illustrates the relevance of the early trading market to an issuer immediately after the successful distribution of its stock. Completion of the canal did not assure financial success or a return on shareholders' investment. Even before completion, the stock market was monitoring the company's progress and reacting to its problems. The first quotation of Delaware and Hudson Canal Company stock at the NYS&EB took place on January 26, 1825 at an opening price of $101.75, slightly up from the original purchase price of $100.[63] The price then rose throughout the spring to a high of $112 by May. Yet by 1828, with the canal unfinished and prospects uncertain, the stock had dropped to $71.[64] Thereafter, the market reflected changes in the company's prospects. For example, once the canal was complete, a railroad had to be built to carry the coal the ten miles from the mine face to Honesdale, New York. When it appeared that this railroad was not functioning properly, the share price dropped precipitously.[65] The price dropped again when complaints were publicly voiced, apparently with some justification, concerning the coal's price and quality.

The stock market's evaluation was a cause of deep concern to the company's managers. In January, 1831, when Delaware and Hudson Canal Company shares were selling for $70, the managers knew that shares in the rival Schuylkill Navigation Company were commanding a price of

$176.[66] Management attributed the low market price of its shares in the early 1830s to maneuvers by its rivals to depress the price and chill the company's favor with stockholders and the public.[67] The stock market was, of course, equally accessible to a company's enemies as it was to supporters.

Although the low share price was probably due both to manipulation on the part of rivals and the company's poor performance, the managers responded by concentrating on improving performance. They sought to appease shareholders with a pamphlet summarizing the virtues of the company and its product, and forecasting a share price of over $200 within two years. The promised increase did not occur, but the company did put its house in order. John Wurts, the newly elected president, embarked upon a program of financial austerity, sale of nonessential properties, private borrowings,[68] and an expansion of merchandising efforts to sell coal for manufacturing and steamboat use. By the end of 1831, the Delaware and Hudson Canal Company had turned the corner. It was selling an acceptable product at a price substantially less than the competition, and showed a modest profit of $34,000 for the year's operation.[69] A year later, it declared a semiannual dividend of $3\frac{1}{2}$ percent.

This success in operations did not immediately stabilize the price of Delaware and Hudson shares in the stock market. For a time, while the profitability of the enterprise was increasing, the share price did not respond. Delaware and Hudson Canal Company stock became a captive favorite of speculators on the Exchange, accounting for over 20 percent of total trading volume at the NYS&EB each year in the late 1830s. Its prices fluctuated wildly, from $75 to $125.[70] Speculators traded shares of Delaware and Hudson Canal Company with such abandon that the company's entire outstanding capital stock was turned over three times in 1832 and 1833, and more than twenty times in 1836!

Speculators were not concerned with the devastating impact this kind of trading could have on a company. The Morris Canal and Banking Company and the Harlem Railroad both functioned only for a short time after their shares became "footballs" on the Exchange. By 1848, as Armstrong described it, most of the favorite stocks of the speculators were "dogs," or "miserable abortions."[71] Whether the stocks became worthless because of the trading of speculators, or whether the speculators traded them heavily because they became worthless, is difficult to determine. Regardless, managers of corporations were not happy to see their stocks heavily traded. Wild speculation in a company's stock wreaked havoc with corporate control and with additional financing. Henry Varnum Poor was later to warn railroad managers that every means must be used to prevent the securities of their roads from becoming speculators' footballs. It was fatal to the "character" of the stock for it to become involved in such operations; "in the end too often it becomes fatal to the value of the property it represents."[72] The same stock market that had helped the Delaware and Hudson Canal Company to raise funds operated at times against the company's interests as well.

Fortunately for the Delaware and Hudson Canal Company, wild speculation, though alarming to managers, was not necessarily fatal to an enterprise. Early speculation in shares of the Bank of New York or the Second Bank of the United States did not prevent them from later becoming profitable institutions, nor did it prevent their shares from becoming investment grade. If an institution were sound, its shares would ultimately weather the storm. In the short run, the market and speculators may distort values, but, in the long run, the market will reflect corporate earnings.[73] When earnings were high, even though the share price was low, the Delaware and Hudson Canal Company could be considered successful.[74] Everyone knew that if earnings were maintained, the stock would increase in value. Thus, the company was able to sell small issues of stock to investors in the 1830s at or near par, even while prices in the trading market were fluctuating violently.[75] The speculators' time bargains on the Exchange did not eliminate the cash market for shares.[76]

Nor did the heavy speculative trading volume in Delaware and Hudson Canal Company shares destroy the company. The Wurts family and other investors continued to hold on to their shares, and we are told that by 1840, the company had survived this early stage of rampant speculation in its shares, and that the stock "came to be recognized, for the first time, as a security suitable for permanent investment."[77] Trading records, however, indicate that the company's shares were still traded with unnerving velocity at that time. The entire outstanding issue was traded twelve times over in 1840, and the price was generally in the low seventies in 1839 and 1840—even while dividends were increasing.[78] Finally, in the 1840s, with the Delaware and Hudson Canal Company's advancing prosperity, its stock did become investment grade, paying high dividends and commanding a steady share price.[79] Many successful years followed. The peak of the canal's traffic was not reached until after the Civil War.

As the Delaware and Hudson Canal Company example makes clear, early public corporations were deeply affected by the stock market. It was a place to raise funds, both at the project's inception and at other critical junctures of need. Share trading in the secondary market was also important to issuers, affecting their ability to raise money and influencing other decisions made by management. The two institutions, public corporations and securities markets, were closely entwined, and both the links with, and responses to, securities markets greatly distinguished public corporations from those whose shares were not traded.

PART THREE

Corporate Governance, Law, and the Public Corporation: 1790–1840

CHAPTER EIGHT

Government and the Corporate System

GOVERNMENT AND SECURITIES MARKETS

I N THE late sixteenth century, when Holland was a thriving center of world trade and an important source of capital, a Viennese botany professor innocently imported a consignment of tulip bulbs to Amsterdam. Soon, they became the rage of fashion.[1] Originally a wealthy man's amusement, by 1634 tulipmania had filtered down to the middle classes, by then keen traders. Tulips commanded high prices, particularly exotic strains. The more expensive bulbs became, the more people viewed them as smart investments.[2] All the familiar vehicles of speculation—options, futures, and short sales—were called into play as stupendous fortunes were made in days. Regulations were drawn up for the guidance of dealers in tulips, and special tulip-notaries were created to record the transactions.[3] Stories are told of tulip bulbs worth many times more than the ships that transported them.[4]

Clearly, the market was bloated beyond the intrinsic value of tulips, and, in due course, Holland suffered the inevitable collapse. When the crunch came in 1638, the panic rapidly snowballed to the point where credit was impossible to obtain, and a depression gripped the country.[5]

Government attempts to shore up prices and bolster confidence were unsuccessful. A compromise wherein contracts made during the height of the mania were declared null and void, and those made after could be settled for 10 percent of the purchase price, gave satisfaction to none.[6] Judges refused to enforce payment of any debts arising from tulip trading, on the grounds that debts contracted in gambling were not recognized at law.[7] Here the matter rested, with tulip traders' enthusiasm thoroughly dampened. The Dutch government did not outlaw similar action in the future. They relied on the example of all those who had lost money to chill the prospects for renewed speculation.

Eighty years later, England became the site of another spectacular speculative episode, the South Sea Bubble, when the public became obsessed with stock gambling of the most audacious kind.[8] In 1720, Parliament responded with the "Bubble Act," forbidding the issuance of transferable stock certificates by unincorporated joint-stock companies,[9] but the trading fever was hardly affected. Even after the Lords in Council declared over one hundred of the bubble companies issuing the heavily traded stock to be illegal, the frantic activity continued.[10] When the bubble finally burst, it was due to the general realization that stock values were extremely overinflated, not to the restraining influence of the Bubble Act. Yet the Bubble Act remained after the crisis was past, supposedly to prevent any repetition of the disaster.

The Bubble Act's enduring influence stretched far beyond the evils it was intended to remedy. Corporations were not outlawed, but corporate charters were sparingly granted in England for decades, and entrepreneurs were reluctant to propose schemes involving transferable shares.[11] Business ventures attempting to pool the savings of many investors were thus severely shackled by the law. Ingenious ways were found to avoid the Bubble Act,[12] and for some years later in the eighteenth century it was apparently not enforced,[13] but it was always there, discouraging any enterprise with transferable shares.[14] After a renewed spate of early nineteenth century prosecutions, the Bubble Act was finally repealed in 1825 and replaced with more modern statutory regulations.[15]

Although the Bubble Act's prohibitions on joint stock companies were sweeping, they did not prevent uncontrolled securities speculation from reappearing in London fewer than fifteen years later. During the reign of George II, stock speculation became so prevalent and assumed so many different forms of gambling that the whole business community again became infected.[16]

Stock brokers, those lawfully entitled to buy or sell shares for others on commission, did a booming business. In London, regulations originating as early as 1285 required brokers in all goods as well as securities to be sworn before the mayor on an oath of good behavior.[17] These regulations did nothing, however, to restrict the brokers' activities or their contributions to the speculative ferment. Although illegal, other buying or selling of securities by those not officially brokers was continuous. Stock-jobbing, dealing in securities for oneself and holding those securities for purely speculative reasons, likewise flourished. Time bargains, the dominant form of speculative trading, proliferated even as they were roundly condemned.

In 1734, Parliament attempted to curb this time bargain trading with "An Act to Prevent the Infamous Practice of Stock-Jobbing," otherwise known as "Sir John Barnard's Act."[18] The act was apparently aimed at quashing what the drafters viewed as wagering in securities markets. One hears echos of the old dichotomy between healthy "investment" and unhealthy "speculation" in the preamble laying out the act's legislative aims: "Whereas, great inconveniences have arisen, and do daily arise, by the wicked, pernicious and destructive practice of stock jobbing, whereby many of his Majesty's good subjects have been and are diverted from pursuing and exercising their lawful trades and vocations . . . to the utter ruin of themselves and families, to the great discouragement of industry, and to the manifest detriment of trade and commerce." Although the act intended to end time bargains by making them unenforceable and void, adding a penalty of 500 pounds,[19] it never succeeded in stopping time bargains. It only made them riskier for brokers entering into them for their clients, and brokers simply charged higher commissions to compensate.[20] The act was simply misguided; it placed blame on "the infamous practice of stock-jobbing," while the schemes of unscrupulous promoters, the greed and gullibility of the public, and the corruption of politicians were really the responsible parties.[21] As such, the law was aimed at the manifestations of a problem rather than at its causes. Eighteenth century legislators did not fully understand the functioning of securities markets, and to them, outlawing time bargains was a simple method of restricting what they viewed as immoral gambling. Later legislators more familiar with securities markets realized at last that efficiency was best achieved when dealings were left to the discretion of businessmen, even at the cost of allowing speculation.[22] Eventually, Sir John Barnard's Act was repealed.[23]

Comparing the responses of the Dutch after tulipmania and the English after the South Sea Bubble, it appears that the Dutch approach—relying on the recollection of previous losses to prevent future speculative activity—avoided the risks of unforeseen results from undue government interference. An approach like the English one, blaming the problem on its symptoms, resulted in companies, brokers, and investors scrambling to get around laws that interfered with their ability to do business and to trade securities as they wished. Many businessmen ignored these laws as a result, which had the perverse effect of increasing their scorn and disregard for the legal system.

Repercussions from English securities regulations sounded across the

Atlantic in the American colonies. The Bubble Act's initial impact was slight, especially after the Massachusetts attorney general took the position that it did not apply to America.[24] Parliament responded by expressly extending the Bubble Act to the colonies in 1741,[25] and, from then to the Revolutionary War, it may have placed a slight damper on the capitalization of American enterprises.[26] With independence, however, whatever influence the Bubble Act had on American business was swept away.

Whether Sir John Barnard's Act restricted securities trading in the American colonies in the years before the Revolutionary War is uncertain.[27] There is no documented American time bargain trading before the 1790s, and it is impossible to discern whether the presumed lack of such trading was due to Sir John Barnard's Act or due to more fundamental causes such as the scarcity of securities appropriate for time bargains and the lack of speculators interested in securities.[28] Nonetheless, soon after independence, the trading practices that Sir John Barnard's Act had attempted to stamp out in England surfaced in the United States, particularly in New York, and played a commanding role in the great speculative bubble and burst of 1792. Following the English example of a regulatory response, the New York legislature passed "An Act to Prevent the Pernicious Practice of Stock-Jobbing, and for Regulating Sales at Public Auction."[29]

Article III of this law, copied from Sir John Barnard's Act, nullified time bargains and option trading of any kind "unless the party so contracting to sell be in possession of the certificate at the time of making such contract." Article II also outlawed sales of public securities or stock at "public vendue or outcry" under penalty of 100 pounds.[30] By its timing, it is clear that this law was a response to the disorder in New York in the wake of the 1792 crisis, but since time bargains and wagers had been unenforceable under the common law, the new statute did not create a new sanction against them. Furthermore, because public auctions of securities had already stopped, the statute simply recognized that auctions were not the best methods for trading securities, something securities professionals had already determined.[31] Ultimately, the New York statute was not nearly as effective at discouraging time bargains as were the burned fingers of the market traders. In the years after the 1792 crash, the lack of investor confidence made securities markets conservative in a manner that a law never could. The legislature's action was important, nonetheless, in underscoring the public's disapproval of the stockbrokers and their market. Both were blamed for bringing on the panic.

The effect of New York's nullification of time bargains matched England's action. The law was acknowledged, but time bargains were not stopped. Brokers continued them on a private basis. The act simply required further agreements among brokers to secure the extralegal enforcement of these speculative contracts.[32] That this act made NYS&EB time bargains illegal was well known at the Exchange, but time bargains continued there regardless. In fact, the ability to engage in time bargains without risk of default was one of the pillars of the early NYS&EB. Generally, in the face of this law, New York brokers continued to engage in time bargains and, like their London cousins, they passed the costs of increased risks on to their clients in the form of higher commissions.

The American movement to regulate securities trading was not limited to New York state. The Pennsylvania legislature considered, and then tabled, a bill to forbid futures contracts.[33] The fact that Philadelphia brokers had the advantage of transacting business without any constraints from such a law was later cited by members of the New York Stock & Exchange Board as one of the reasons why securities trading in the rival city flourished.[34]

The New York prohibition of public securities auctions and the nullification of time bargains were items continually before the legislature. It repeatedly revived and restated this law, sometimes under confusing titles. The linkage between securities market restrictions and the regulation of auctions—the more commercially significant sections of the statute—kept this securities regulation in force.

Throughout its tenure, this New York securities law did not greatly discourage the gambling and speculation at which it was aimed, nor did it eliminate time bargains. It was the response of an irritated but not well-informed legislature which had attempted to outlaw a desire which could not be outlawed—the propensity of speculators to take risks while seeking riches. Time bargains and speculation flourished in New York, while the law languished. Finally, after a long but not very useful life, these restrictions were repealed by the New York legislature in 1858.[35]

The only other New York legislative actions that dealt with securities markets at this time were attempts to regulate the New York Stock & Exchange Board in response to the wild speculation of the 1830s. In 1834, a Committee Report suggested that brokers at the NYS&EB "mislead and deceive their employers to a fearful and dangerous degree" and recommended a bill to criminalize stockjobbing,[36] and, in 1836, "An Act to Regulate the Sale of Stocks and Bills of Exchange" was proposed.[37] Neither bill was passed.

Additional state government involvement with securities markets in the days before the blue-sky laws of the early twentieth century[38] centered on providing a forum for the common law actions of misrepresentation, deceit, or rescission of contract.[39] Litigation concerning share transfer also produced a number of decisions, including rulings that a transfer may be valid between the parties even though not recorded in the corporation's books as prescribed by the charter,[40] and that a corporation is liable to a purchaser of shares for refusing to enter a share transfer on its books.[41] These causes of action and rulings did not affect securities markets to any significant extent.

Federal regulation did not greatly affect securities markets either. There were no comprehensive attempts to regulate securities issue or transfer before the securities acts of the 1930s. Federal policy was hands-off securities markets as it was hands-off generally. The age of regulation had not yet arrived. Throughout the nineteenth century, the most important federal action in respect of securities markets was the repeated use of securities as the vehicle to finance the national debt, thereby stimulating securities markets' growth.

The overall effect of securities market regulation during the first years of the United States was typical of regulations attempting to forbid speculative trading. It failed to prevent speculation and its perceived evils. As Dos Passos reminded his readers in 1882:

> In almost every instance in which statutes attempting to curb speculation have been adopted, after lingering for years on the books, scorned and violated by the "unbridled and defiant spirit of speculation" despite the earnest efforts of the courts to enforce them, they have finally been repealed. It is perhaps better to allow the evil to correct itself, as it surely does, than to bring the administration of justice into contempt by filling the books with useless laws, which are at times openly violated and laughed at, and which seem hardly more effective to prevent the practices at which they are aimed, then legislation directed against the laws of nature.[42]

Early attempts to restrict American securities trading fit this vivid description. They were generally futile efforts to restrain the avarice of a growing population in an expanding economy. Not only were they ineffective and counterproductive, but they also revealed a paucity of understanding of the mechanisms of the markets and their links to corporations. While with one hand, governments encouraged business corporations through generous charter grants, general incorporation laws, and the like, with the other, they attempted to restrict the securities markets that were the public corporation's lifeblood of capital. On balance, effects of the promotion of public corporations greatly outweighed effects of the feeble restrictions on securities markets.

GOVERNMENT AND PUBLIC CORPORATIONS

E ARLY AMERICAN business corporations were formed, and operated, without excessive government controls. This free market was not, however, based on an absolute hands-off approach. Where necessary, pragmatic government action fostered the business corporations required for growth and prosperity.[43] As the policies of Alexander Hamilton amply illustrate, if Congress had to create a bank in order to stabilize money and energize capital, it did.[44] In innumerable ways, state government also promoted business corporations of all kinds. When private capital could not be raised, states sponsored and helped to finance the internal improvement corporations that met the young economy's urgent needs for roads, canals, and other infrastructure, while for those businesses that held out prospects of profit, such as banks and insurance companies, state governments eagerly chartered the business corporations that would be publicly owned.

A corporate charter typically offered two valuable attributes to a business enterprize: limited shareholder liability, which only a state could grant, and unrestricted share transferability, which could also be achieved by private contract. Some ventures, notably insurance companies, required limited shareholder liability in order to attract investors who were wary of being held liable for the losses their company might suffer. Because insurance was an indispensable service to merchants and businessmen, vital to trade and commerce, legislatures regularly limited the liability of insurance company shareholders.[45] Consequently, insurance companies that promised to make a profit were able to attract the funds they required from public investors.

Many enterprises that could prosper without limited shareholder liability were formed as individual proprietorships, partnerships, and, when they became large, as unincorporated joint stock companies.[46] Like the chartered corporations of their day, these organizations could provide for centralized direction of large pools of assets amassed by sale of freely transferable securities. To entrepreneurs seeking a form of organization for their businesses, and to state governments encouraging businesses of all kinds, unincorporated entities provided viable alternatives to chartered corporations.

Although not necessary to give practical or legal form to a business venture, charters were actively sought by corporate promoters as vehicles for larger packages of benefits. The rights to make corporate contracts and affix seals thereto were not vital. What most charter-seeking entrepreneurs were truly after were bounties: monopolies, land grants, tax exemptions, rights to conduct lotteries or state aid in financing the enterprise. Many ventures that did not promise to return a profit to investors could not get off the ground without such state aid. Enterprises that legislatures found most desirable and investors found least attractive—such as long expensive canals in remote regions—were granted numerous privileges in order to encourage investors.[47] Intense haggling over these items was typical.[48] As a result, similar enterprises were often granted quite different charters.

In the earliest years, such business corporations with their state-granted privileges were considered to be agents of the state pursuing public purposes. Little legislative distinction was made between forming a corporation for a church, a school, or a municipality on the one hand, or a business enterprise like a bank, an insurance company, or a manufacturing company on the other. Business corporations, however, which "the American people had shown remarkable facility in forming," were quickly found to pursue both public service and private gain.[49] But when the private gain from a project outweighed the potential public benefit, states were often miserly in the privileges they granted,[50] and many American business corporations had to seek their funds elsewhere. Though legislatures continued to support these publicly owned companies and chartered them regularly, the states were unwilling to provide bonuses if ample support was available from individual investors.

Some business corporations were inherently profitable, particularly such monied corporations as insurance companies and banks. Outside of the charters themselves, states were never required to provide many benefits for them. Numerous banks did not even deem a charter necessary; private banking was a big industry in early New York. For example, the Bank of New York operated without a charter from 1784 to 1791.[51] Unchartered banks, however, competed against those banks with charters that wished to maintain their market shares, and, in 1804, the New York legislature responded to the pleas of the six existing chartered banks by prohibiting unchartered banks.[52] Although these restrictions may have been clothed as the best method of serving the public interest by protecting people from unscrupulous bankers operating without charters, their effect was to grant a windfall to the operators of existing chartered banks.[53] With a growing market for their services and a legal restriction on competitors, regular profits were practically guaranteed.

Legislators, acknowledging the inherent profitability of banking, used their power to grant banking privileges to support other less profitable business ventures. In order to attract public investors to corporations that did not promise quick and sure profits, legislatures granted them banking privileges instead of direct financial support. Many successful businesses, including the Delaware and Hudson Canal Company, were aided in this manner during their earliest years.[54]

The most famous of such combinations, the Morris Canal and Banking Company, was given banking powers to help finance a canal that would have competed with the Delaware and Hudson Canal. Niles, the editor of the influential Niles Weekly Register, was strongly antibanking, yet he approved at first: "Canal-making and bank-making have no natural union between them. We shall however, be glad to find by the result, that the two different projects worked well together—and for the good of a new canal will be willing to bear with the evil of a new bank."[55] Launched at the height of mid-1820s speculation, $20 million were said to have been subscribed for the $1 million authorized Morris Canal and Banking Company stock.[56] Unfortunately, this legislative attempt to aid the canal project backfired. The banking powers proved "fatal to the success of the company" when management became exclusively interested in financial aspects of the business, ignored the canal, and soon became engaged in irregular and criminal schemes.[57]

Most chartered banks were more successful. In recognition of the fact that a bank charter was a profitable prize,[58] potential bank organizers often competed to make concessions to the legislature rather than the other way around. Bank charters were frequently granted only on the condition that the state retain an option to purchase shares, or after the promoters agreed to pay a bonus to the state. Maryland banks paid an annual fee for their charters.[59] New Jersey at first reserved the right to subscribe to bank stock, which it would sell at a profit. Later, banks paid bonuses to the New Jersey legislature.[60] Similarly, the Second Bank of the United States paid a $1.5 million bonus to Congress for its charter.[61]

With bank charters so valuable, entrepreneurs seeking permission to establish a new bank freely dispensed favors to legislators. Gouge reports that in 1826 General Root, then speaker of the Senate, made a speech in which he claimed that proprietors of the New York State Bank had

offered him shares in return for support for their charter. Other such stories are common. "A member of the legislature merely intimated his
will to have a certain number of shares and his wish was gratified." In
Pennsylvania, the practice of "log-rolling" (a task that many had to join
together to do) was common. Legislators had to support bank charters
and other private bills sponsored by their peers if they wanted return support for their public bills.[62] When the scandals associated with the Bank
of New York charter in 1812 reached a fever pitch, Governor Tompkins
suspended the legislature from sitting for two months.[63]

The 1821 amendment to the New York Constitution requiring a two-
thirds vote of both houses to pass an act of incorporation for a bank was
meant to end some of this graft, but with more legislators to convince,
the corruption involved in the consideration of bank charters simply increased.[64] Upon investigating the passage of the Chemical Bank charter
in 1824, a legislative committee found that "the evidence . . . afforded
a most disgusting picture of the depravity of the members of the legislature."[65] Characterized as the most important event in American banking
history before 1936,[66] New York's 1838 general incorporation statute for
banking attempted to eradicate this corruption by making it easier to establish banks. Although the "Free Banking Act" did not end the corruption accompanying the granting of bank charters, it did remove some obstacles to the formation of banks.[67]

The Free Banking Act was a latecomer in a steady series of general
incorporation statutes. Consistent with its tradition of aiding business
corporations that were building the economy, the New York legislature
had attempted in various ways to aid domestic manufacturing during the
troubled period of Jefferson's embargo and Madison's war. Among the most
important legislative actions was the 1811 general-incorporation statute
for manufacturing enterprises.[68] Enacted essentially as an emergency
measure to encourage investments in enterprises that would produce thread
for household weaving while the European textile supply was cut off, it
remained the law of New York long after the crisis passed.

This 1811 statute, the first effective general incorporation law for business corporations, furthered the evolution toward standardization of charters
and the process for their approval. It had been foreshadowed by other
commonplace general incorporation acts for schools, churches, municipalities, and the like, corporations which could be given similar attributes and similar state assistance or regulation.[69] Moreover, the statute
built on the practice after 1800 of using provisions from existing charters
as models for new ones.[70] Other state legislatures, copying the prototype

New York law, enacted general incorporation laws for specific types of enterprises.[71] Regardless of the forms of the statutes or the types of enterprise they targeted, general incorporation laws were at first not widely used. Until late in the nineteenth century, the special charter process, existing alongside general incorporation laws, continued to be the primary vehicle for corporations that sought benefits beyond those offered by general incorporation schemes.[72]

Using both special charters and general incorporation laws, states promoted large numbers of business corporations. Although charter policy varied state by state,[73] and within each state by industrial classification,[74] the pattern was that business charters were generously granted, rarely denied. "Not many charters were sought in vain," writes Joseph Davis, "and these because of local objection to the project."[75] After 1800, charters abounded for enterprises operating unabashedly for the self-interest of their promoters and shareholders.[76] By the 1830s, the corporate privilege appears to have been granted in virtually every instance in which it was actively pursued. Massachusetts alone, which Professor Dodd characterizes as "very ready to respond to the desires of entrepreneurs," had issued more than 800 business charters by 1830.[77] Chancellor Kent, writing at that time, reported that legislatures were dispensing corporate privileges "lavishly."[78]

Some important corporate historians, however, including Justice Louis D. Brandeis, have looked at the popular rhetoric of the time and drawn a different conclusion. Corporations were attacked in the early American press as artificial creatures lacking moral responsibility or feeling, and as legal shields for individual malefactors. Dubbed "heartless money-machines," business corporations were accused of undermining the republic's character.[79] Brandeis built up from this criticism as if the words signified policy in action.

According to Brandeis, states regulated early business corporations by limiting their number.

> Incorporation for business was commonly denied long after it had been freely granted for religious, educational and charitable purposes. It was denied because of fear. Fear of encroachment upon the liberties and opportunities of the individual. Fear of the subjection of labor to capital. Fear of monopoly. Fear that the absorption of capital by corporations, and their perpetual life, might bring evils similar to those which attended mortmain. There was a sense of some insidious menace inherent in large aggregations of capital, particularly when held by corporations. So, at first, the corporate privilege was granted sparingly;

and only when the grant seemed necessary in order to procure for the community some specific benefit otherwise unattainable.[80]

These fears were indeed felt. Anticharter sentiment dates back to the controversy in 1785 over the Bank of North America, the nation's first business corporation.[81] It is also true that the earliest charters were granted for canals, banks, or other public service activities. Yet neither the existence of popular fears nor the early corporate performance of public and quasi-public functions supports the conclusion that business charters were commonly denied or sparingly granted. Opposition to corporations as such was generally no more than the storming of a vocal minority.[82] Accordingly, while the press raged against business corporations, governments nurtured them and businessmen promoted them. Banks were the only business corporations that faced significant obstacles to obtaining a charter, but these obstacles were rooted in the greed of legislators and the resistence of established bankers, not in a fear of corporations or a public policy against them. The push by the states, regardless of rhetoric, was for economic growth. They did everything they could to make it happen, particularly the promotion of numerous business corporations.

GOVERNMENT AND SHAREHOLDERS

A LTHOUGH GENERAL incorporation statutes were not at first widely used, they were important for the development of business corporations because of their recognition of the principle of limited shareholder liability for corporate debts.[83] The 1811 New York general incorporation statute for manufacturing companies provided:

> for all debts which shall be due and owing by the company at the time of its dissolution, the persons then composing such company shall be individually responsible to the extent of their respective shares of stock in the said company and no further.[84]

The operation of this statute restricted shareholder liability,[85] which in turn promoted the advancement of more risky business ventures. Corporations that could limit investors' potential losses could attract their funds more readily than partnerships that could not. Building on general incorporation statutes, the principle of shareholders' limited liability for corporate debts become generally accepted by the 1830s.[86] The rule of limited liability, combined with other encouragements of business corporations, fostered the growth and later dominance of the corporate form of organization.[87]

Adolph Berle, an eminent corporate historian, offers a different perspective on general incorporation statutes.[88] According to Berle, before the advent of general incorporation statutes, states restricted corporate managements in order to protect shareholders by controlling the contents of the charter:

> Substantially every contract was separately legislated into the law of the state by a separate act. . . . To be valid . . . the powers granted to the corporate management had to be thoroughly thrashed over with the state authorities.[89]

Shareholders were protected by the "rule of a single defined enterprise," which insured that the shareholder knew "the type of business in which his capital was to be embarked."[90] Shareholders could restrict management from excursions off the clear path laid out by the legislature, through suits claiming management actions were "ultra vires," or beyond the corporations's granted power.[91] In addition, Berle suggests that legislatures protected shareholders before the age of general incorporation by rigidly supervising capital contributions. States permitted a corporation to start business only after a certain amount of its shares had been paid up, a practice that provided protection against dilution of the shareholder's interest.[92] Similarly, legislatures protected shareholders by insisting on "a rigid capital structure. . . . Shares even in those early days could be classified."[93]

All of these protections, Berle writes, vanished by 1900 due to the general incorporation laws that eliminated the legislative scrutiny accompanying the enactment of special charters. General incorporation statutes, eventually construed as permission for a corporation to engage in as many different businesses as the organizers chose, effectively ended the "rule of a single defined enterprise." Promoters utilized these laws to write charters giving maximum discretion to managers, minimum protection to shareholders.[94] State governments no longer protected shareholders from management as they had in the past.

A reexamination of these assertions suggests that, before the advent of general incorporation, states regulated corporations in order to protect shareholders from corporate management far less than Berle understood. In the years of thorough legislative scrutiny which preceded general incorporation acts, legislatures were not concerned with safeguarding shareholders. They were concerned with promoting business ventures. If they looked to protect anyone, they protected consumers and corporate creditors, not shareholders.[95] Because the notion of the corporation as distinct from its shareholders developed slowly and awkwardly in the law,[96] protecting shareholders from managers was at first as conceptually difficult as protecting someone from himself. Furthermore, legislators saw little reason to intervene on behalf of shareholders who, after all, voluntarily associated themselves with an enterprise. If an investor chose to buy shares in a corporation, he took the risks involved, risks known well to all.

The rites of legislative passage were not aimed at producing regulation for the benefit of shareholders. On the contrary, the charter process generally involved bargaining for favors, not limiting managements' powers. It is true that legislatures did not write blank charters, but there is no evidence that single-purpose charters, however carefully limited, were either conceived or operated as a safeguard for shareholders. With few exceptions, applicants did not seek charters for more than one business activity. Furthermore, although applicants had to describe the activity to be chartered, this description was frequently very general,[97] and the shareholder remedy of claiming that a corporation's actions were ultra vires was not often used to restrict corporations from entering new areas of business.[98]

Nor did states rigidly supervise capital contributions. Early practice called for a public corporation to begin business when a threshold portion of its shares had been subscribed to, not paid up. Subscribers paid a small fraction of the par value of their shares, generally not more than ten percent, obligating themselves to pay the balance in installments called by the board of directors.[99] The volume of legal actions to enforce such obligations demonstrates the difficulty involved in converting a stated promise to actual cash, after early prospects for the corporation's success had faded. Capital contributions for some corporations, particularly banks and insurance companies, were supervised more rigorously than for bridges or manufacturing enterprises, but these measures were designed to protect depositors, noteholders, policy holders, and other creditors, not shareholders, and commonly these statutory controls were unenforced. Many bank shareholders actually paid for bank "scrip" by borrowing from the bank.[100] Some banks were able to use this method to begin operations without any infusion of capital, in the usual sense of that word, from investors. The New York Daily Advertiser, May 21, 1819, provides a typical complaint when reporting on an Illinois bank with capital of $4 million that is to go into operation when $15,000 is paid in—"almost a two hundred and sixty sixth part of its capital paid in!"[101]

Finally, during the United States' first half-century capitalization consisted almost entirely of a single class of common stock. Legislatures made no effort to control capital structures until well into the 1840s, and, even then, there was no indication of solicitude for the common shareholder.[102]

Thus, the comprehensive shareholder protections that Berle argues were lost upon entering the era of general incorporation really did not exist before then. Other safeguards in the law that were useful to shareholders did not empower them much further. The right to inspect the corporation's share transfer books was important,[103] but shareholders often had to go to court for an order allowing them to inspect books of account, books which even then they would have little reason to expect were accurate.[104] Other regulations detailed in charters on such matters as the size and power of boards of directors did not protect those shareholders who did not concern themselves with voting or whose few votes could not change policy anyway.[105] The basic model of the corporation may have appeared to be strictly defined, and that appearance is what Berle saw, but, in fact, corporations and corporate managements were not greatly restrained by legal sanction.[106]

Of course the absence of legal constraints to protect shareholders does not mean there were no constraints. Shareholders of the Bank of New York expected and got an administration of the corporation for their benefit, without regard to legal niceties created by fiduciary duties of care or loyalty. Most small shareholders, however, never had any meaningful legal rights in the control of the corporations they invested in. Shareholders were at the mercy of management, and, if they felt aggrieved, their remedy was to sell their shares rather than to rely on the law for protection.[107]

Earlier in this century, both Brandeis and Berle examined the history of corporate law and found a process of decay. Brandeis saw limits on the numbers of corporations evaporate, as legislatures became less concerned with protecting the public from them. Berle saw restrictions that were written into each charter in order to protect shareholders fade, as legislators ended their one-by-one chartering approach. Each of these scholars in his own way saw state regulation of corporations giving way to more a more permissive era. Both men, however, began their analyses from shaky premises. Early corporate regulation was not as extensive as they envisioned. Charter policy was designed to promote, not to restrict, the activities and growth of business corporations. Early corporate law did not restrain corporate managements in order to protect shareholders from their corporations to any significant extent. Nor did early regulations restrict securities markets. Instead, as the development of limited shareholder liability for corporate debts illustrates, public policy and law were forces on the side of the integrated system of securities markets and public corporations, in their individual pursuits of gain and their aggregate contributions to economic development.

CHAPTER NINE

The Separation of Ownership and Control

THE MECHANISM OF CORPORATE OWNERSHIP AND CONTROL

T HOUGH SHAREHOLDERS own corporations, they typically control them only indirectly. Shareholders elect boards of directors, who in turn delegate the day-to-day decision making to officers responsible for managing the enterprise. This three-tiered pyramid with shareholders at the bottom, directors in the middle, and management at the top has always been the model corporate structure. [1]

This model poorly reflects where the power to control corporations truly resides. It does not flow smoothly from shareholders to directors to managers. Shareholders only have significant input into corporate government if they can choose directors, [2] and in public corporations, the shareholders' "choice" is often mere ratification after the decision has been made by top officers. Managers propose candidates for election to the board, usually including officers of the corporation among those candidates, and then collect proxies from shareholders in order to elect the managers' slate. Because the power to affect directors' decisions follows from the power to appoint them, these directors, who should be the representatives of shareholders and watchdogs over management, instead typically ratify management's decisions.

Managers, as agents of the owners, should look after shareholders' interests, and often they do. Sometimes, however, the interests of managers and shareholders diverge. Managers may have incentives to pursue corporate growth in order to increase their power or justify their salaries, even if that growth is not the most efficient path for the corporation to take, and will not result in maximum enhancement of shareholders' wealth. Shareholders, on the other hand, may not be as concerned with the long-term plans of the corporation as they are with short-term gains that will quickly, if only temporarily, raise the price of their shares. In the most dramatic example of conflicting interests, shareholders can be happy with a corporate raider who will pay a premium to buy shares and then proceed to oust current managers.

When there are conflicting interests, management usually controls. Management manipulates the proxy process and packs the board of directors. As a recent commentator describes it:

> The truth of the matter is that the public corporation has generally been a benevolent autocracy. Managers have run the show. Shareholder meetings have been elaborate ceremonies. Proxy votes have been foreordained rituals. People who have served as directors on boards have usually been friends of the boss.[3]

This separation of ownership and control occurs in a public corporation unless one shareholder holds all the voting stock. Such complete control exists primarily in untraded close corporations, incorporated partnerships, or one-person corporations. Usually, those who own all of the shares of an enterprise either direct and manage it themselves or closely supervise those they appoint.[4]

In cases of majority share ownership—common in small corporations but rare among giants—the majority shareholder has nearly the same powers as a complete owner. The majority's power, however, may be curbed if the minority shareholders are well organized, particularly in important corporate matters that require votes of two-thirds of the shareholders.[5] Otherwise, minority shareholders are effectively disenfranchised. They can vote, but the majority will prevail. For minority shareholders in this situation, the divorce of ownership and control is practically complete.[6]

Some control can be exercised by minority shareholders in corporations where shares are widely dispersed and there is no clear majority.[7] "Working control" can be achieved without a majority of the shares, if opposing interests are splintered or control even fewer shares. Minorities, particularly if allied with management, may be able to attract enough other proxies to support their position and thwart any effective challenge.[8] Those shareholders not a part of this empowered minority, however, have little or no control over corporate decisions.

In cases of complete control, majority control, or effective minority control, some shareholders' votes have significance. In other "managerial corporations," the ordinary shareholder's vote is generally an empty ritual. If the owner does not combine with other ordinary shareholders, that vote is simply a drop in the bucket. Only in the case of a proxy battle, where those vying for control court the ordinary shareholder, does the individual right to vote have any real meaning.[9]

Typical small shareholders are not overly concerned about this lack of voting power. They frequently purchase shares for the very reason that they admire current management and expect it to continue in office.[10] So long as their confidence is maintained, they give their proxy to management or vote with it, if they vote at all. If management's performance fails to meet their standards, their remedy is likely to be a sale of shares.

This ability to sell is the second important right shareholders possess. Shares have a dual nature; not only do they represent part ownership of an enterprise entitling the owner to some portion of corporate governance, they are also financial assets. By virtue of securities markets, a shareholder can at any time sell shares for the best price they will command. The small invester's ability to cash the investment lessens his or her dependence on the management of the corporation and blunts any inclination to exercise voting rights in directors' elections.

It is this ability to sell securities quickly and easily through the public stock market that has undermined the possibility of unifying ownership and control in the small stockholder.[11] Clearly, separation of ownership from the responsibilities of control is necessary for the unrestrained trading of shares: property which demands personal intervention from its owner has limited liquidity. Given the choice, most shareholders prefer liquidity over power to influence corporate affairs. They purchase shares for the return they expect to realize, not for the chance to participate in corporate decision-making. As a result, small shareholders exchange control for marketability through securities markets.[12]

THE EROSION DOCTRINE

ADOLPH BERLE and Gardiner Means, in *The Modern Corporation and Private Property*,[13] set forth the traditional view of early corporations and their unity of ownership and control. Early corporations were small affairs where shareholders exercised the rights they were intended to possess. "The number of shareholders was few; they could and did attend meetings; they were business-men; and their vote meant something."[14] Certain powers were delegated to managers, Berle concedes, but shareholders were protected by fixed rules allowing managers little latitude.

The management of the corporation was indeed thought of as a set of agents running a business for a set of owners; and while they could and did have wider powers than most agents, they were strictly accountable and were in a position to be governed in all matters of general policy by their owners. They occupied, in fact, a position analogous to that of the captain and officers of a ship at sea; in navigation their authority might be supreme; but the direction of the voyage, the alteration of the vessel, the character of the cargo, and the distribution of the profits and losses were settled ahead of time and altered only by the persons having the underlying property interest.[15]

According to this view, corporations once behaved as they were supposed to. The shareholders who owned corporations controlled them. Although they elected a board of directors to whom they delegated management powers, shareholders retained effective residual control. These early corporations where ownership and control were united were unaffected by the stock market because corporate shares were not publicly traded and owners were locked into an enterprise described today as a close corporation or incorporated partnership.[16] It was only after the advent of the railroads that the quasi-public corporation began to come into its own. Railroads used the securities markets to obtain capital and to consolidate smaller lines into larger systems. After the war, the quasi-public corporation gradually came to dominate practically every sector of the economy, with mining and manufacturing leading the way. Acting within this model, the first corporations, run by their proprietors and constrained by law, exercised state-granted privileges to further the public interest.

After Berle describes his view of early corporations, he explains how he believes the states curtailed regulation, shareholders abdicated control, and this Eden came to an end. "The stockholders' position, once a controlling factor in the running of the enterprise . . . declined from extreme strength to practical impotence."[17] Shareholder control over direction of the enterprise, manifested chiefly by the right to vote, disappeared. Shareholders lost the right to block "striking change" in the nature of the enterprise[18] and the right to remove directors at will.[19] The emergence of proxy voting further diluted shareholders' power, as management used proxies to strip shareholders of the control they were supposed to exercise.[20]

In addition, corporations grew larger and their shares came to be traded in the public market. That market fragmented ownership among thousands, even hundreds of thousands, of shareholders. The ordinary shareholder, owning a relatively small part of the company's shares, had little incentive to initiate a proxy contest to displace inadequate management or to institute legal action to protect his rights. The incentives for shareholders to participate were further reduced by the ease with which they could convert their shares to cash. Shareholders were no longer locked into the corporation. They had in effect exchanged control over the corporation for liquidity of their investment.

As the shareholders abdicated their original control position, managers filled the vacuum, becoming the new princes of industry.[21] Managers no longer implemented corporate policy articulated by a board of directors that represented the interests of shareholders. On the contrary, they set corporate policy and designated the slate of directors for shareholders to elect at an annual meeting, which became a meaningless ritual.

Out of these changes, according to Berle, emerged a wholly new kind of corporation, the "modern" or managerial corporation, in which ownership and control were divorced. The modern corporation was owned by shareholders who did not control it, controlled by managers who did not own it. The atom of ownership and control had been split, and the traditional logic of profits had been destroyed. The conflict between owners and managers raised the specter of great concentrations of economic power operated by men who do not own them.[22] Shareholders no longer had any basis for believing that their corporation would be run for their benefit. Society would also suffer because the conflict of interest might impair the efficiency of big corporations, now vital to the capitalist economy, but run by managers who were accountable only to themselves, managers who could blink at obligations to shareholders and to society.

THE INHERENCE THESIS

T HE HISTORICAL facts of early corporations and their relationships with shareholders bring into question the erosion doctrine as articulated by Berle and described above. It appears that shareholders have always had rights similar to those they have in today's modern corporations, and shareholders have always exercised those rights in the same manner. As we have shown, early state regulations did not protect shareholders or restrict corporations in the way either Berle or Brandeis describes.[23] Nor did the distribution of power within the corporation protect shareholders from managers, either. From the time of the first public corporations, shareholders were owners who did not directly exercise control over their property. There never was an admired era in which shareholders possessed and exercised more rights in public corporations than they do today, and there has never been an erosion from such an era.[24]

To begin with, Berle's analysis was based on some misconceptions. Early shareholders did not have the critical voting powers Berle attributes to them. A dissenting shareholder faced with a "striking change" in the nature of an enterprise could not veto that change, but was only entitled to the fair value of his shares.[25] There is also no evidence that shareholders in business corporations ever had the power to remove directors at will.[26] Furthermore, the right to vote by proxy did not emerge in the early nineteenth century as a device to limit shareholder power; it was an important and basic right from the beginning. Proxy voting clauses were virtually boilerplate in the charters of the first corporations, not only in the United States, but in England.[27] The earliest American business corporation—the Bank of North America, the Bank of New York, and the First Bank of the United States—all provided for voting by proxy. Proxies were also freely transferred just as they are today. Blank proxy forms were available in New York as early as the 1790s.[28] Moreover, from the beginning, managers used the proxy machinery to control corporations and entrench themselves.[29]

While early shareholders may not have had the voting rights Berle attributed to them, they did have a stock market which Berle overlooked. By starting from the private corporation, whose shares were not traded in public securities markets, in order to examine development of the "quasi-public" corporation, whose shares were regularly traded, the erosion doctrine ignores the impact of the early securities markets on early public corporations. Since law had not distinguished between the first public and close corporations, the erosion doctrine did not either. Thriving securities markets, however, grew in tandem with the public corporations they served. These markets fostered the separation of ownership and control, which has existed as long as stock markets have existed, and which is inherent in corporations with publicly traded shares.[30]

The securities market separated ownership and control by reducing the owners' incentives to exercise control, while increasing their propensity to passively allow managers to make decisions. Even where they had the right to vote, shareholders in the first public corporations did not exercise it. Those who held shares as investments attended shareholder meetings as rarely as they do now. At the 1841 annual meeting of the Massachusetts First National Bank of Boston, there were eight shareholders present and 227 votes represented out of 3,200 shares.[31] Shareholders generally voted, if at all, by proxy.[32] They made the trade-off of control for marketability. They regarded themselves, not as citizens of a corporate state, but as investors seeking a financial return. Speculators looking for quick gains from share price fluctuations were even less concerned than investors with the voting rights attached to their shares. Thus, even when shareholders had latent power, they did not exercise control. Berle, in missing this fact, paid more attention to the black letter of the law and corporate charters than to the way that people behaved under them.

Securities markets also separated ownership and control by attracting investors with small stakes. Few public corporations were dominated by shareholders with large enough holdings to be controlled outright. Most public corporations had a few large, but not dominant, shareholders and many small ones. Of the 400 initial shareholders of the Merchant's National Bank, only two had more than 400 shares.[33] The largest eleven subscribers to the Baltimore & Ohio Railroad held less than 20 percent of the shares.[34] There were 900 shareholders of the Mechanics Bank in 1833, most owning five to ten shares.[35] It was reported in 1831 that of the 4,145 domestic shareholders of the Second Bank of United States, 1,449 owned ten shares or less, 900 were women, 329 were executors and trustees, and 126 were corporations and charitable societies.[36]

Securities markets, which spread shares far and wide, also separated ownership and control by making it difficult for shareholders to act in concert even had they desired to have an impact on managers' policies, and by making it easier for managers to maintain control over their corporations.[37] In addition, securities markets created, as an adjunct to the corporate structure, brokers and dealers whose activities further distributed shares, thereby further increasing the separation of ownership and control.[38]

THE ROLES OF DIRECTORS AND MANAGERS

OFFICERS OF corporations have always spent more time and energy conducting their enterprises than responding to shareholders. Managers of early banks, insurance companies, canals, and other corporations were kept busy making difficult operating decisions similar in kind to those made by managers today. It was essential to define tasks and relationships even within a single-unit enterprise run by few employees. It was also necessary to devise accounting principles and methods to measure earnings, distinguish the interests of the enterprise from those of the shareholders, separate income and capital, and ensure that dividends were properly paid.[39]

Although management was far less of a challenge in banking than in canal building and other early corporate activities, there was, nonetheless, a need for effective administration.[40] The pressure in early banks was for consistent dividends. At first, directors of some banks involved themselves in these corporate affairs. They met once a week, passed on loan applications, conducted routine business, and chose a member to serve for a week as "sitting director" or chief executive officer.[41] In this respect, corporate governance for some early banks resembled Berle's model of director supervision more closely than it does today.

Directors, however, quickly tired of this direct participation. Their most immediate concerns were their own livelihoods, not the economic health of the enterprise, and they entrusted increasing power to committees and to the cashier of the bank, the senior employee.[42] By 1815, directors commonly delegated large amounts of authority to the president, relying on his judgment and ratifying his actions.[43]

As different at the Second Bank of the United States was from state banks in other respects, the dominant position played by Nicholas Biddle was typical of chief executive officers in big city banks of that era.[44] Biddle ran the Bank of the United States as his own province, asking others for advice, but making most important decisions himself.[45] He enjoyed the advantage, as bank president, of being the only director who could be reelected and serve continuously.[46] Biddle's leadership position was hardly challenged, and under him shareholders had virtually no control over the bank.[47]

Tendencies to centralize management in full-time administrators and to diminish participation of outside directors were among the essential elements that made banks in this period similar to big corporations today.[48] Management of public corporations engaged in insurance, canal, toll bridge, and other activities were centralized as well.[49] These managers controlled corporations they did not own, often for the benefit of management and shareholders both.

In the familiar case of the Delaware and Hudson Canal Company, the Wurts family controlled the company,[50] although it appears that they did not own a majority of the shares. The Wurts brothers installed as directors and officers people such as Philip Hone, soon to be mayor of New York, who were not decision makers but merely window dressing to attract investment. While they centralized control, the Wurts brothers did not act malevolently. They operated the Delaware and Hudson Canal Company for the benefit of shareholders as well as themselves.

However, managers and directors of some other corporations exercised control in their own self-interest. It was common for fringe benefits to include jobs for family and friends. Business could be done with the corporation on favorable terms; lower insurance rates or better credit lines were available. Some corporations, particularly banks, seemed to be run for the benefit of directors only. Shareholders and the general public alike were regarded as outsiders.[51] Directors often cemented this type of influence by reserving large blocks of shares in the corporation for themselves.[52]

In the earliest corporations, such power was typically not abused at the expense of bank earnings and dividends. Management did not pilfer from ordinary shareholders. There is no evidence of the abuse of control by dominant shareholders in the Bank of New York and other early conservative New York banks. No conflict between owners and managers surfaced because of the self-restraint, community position, conservatism, or sense of morality of those who held sway over the enterprises. The potential for mistreatment of ordinary shareholders was always present, however, and as banks and other corporations proliferated, so did abuse.

The motivation of those in control was sometimes pernicious. Directors and managers exploited their offices to engage in self-dealing that flouted even embryonic fiduciary standards. They resold shares to the corporation at a profit just before it folded, or disseminated false financial information and then traded shares on the true inside information.[53] They collected high salaries, made improper loans to themselves, or purchased the bank's notes at a discount in order to put them into circulation in distant places at much higher prices. They operated in violation of their charters and refused to disclose their books even to legislative committees.

The Farmers Bank of Virginia paid small dividends because of high officers' salaries.[54] Bank of Hudson officers borrowed nearly one half more than the capital of the entire bank.[55] The State Bank of Tennessee cashier refused to surrender books to a legislative committee, and would not disclose the names of the friends he had allowed to overdraw to the amount of $250,000.[56] The cashier of the Planters Bank in Maryland absconded with that bank's funds.[57] The wreck of the City Bank of Baltimore was due to the large overdrawing permitted by the former cashier.[58] Through such devices, regularly reported in the press, avaricious officers plundered what would otherwise have been sound institutions,[59] such as the Morris Canal and Banking Company, ruined in large part because the management was more concerned with stock speculation than with running the business.[60]

Shareholders who were left holding the bag when these institutions folded were not the only ones who suffered. The public who had to rely on the notes issued by banks for currency were often jilted as well. One young operator took control of a Rhode Island country bank in 1809 and converted it into a personal money machine. He kept the cashier up late every night signing $800,000 worth of small-denomination notes that the bank manufactured on a capital that at one point amounted to only $45.[61] The notes, needless to say, were worthless. Many banks had as capital nothing more than the promissory notes of their directors and principal officers. The New Jersey Lombard and Protection Bank "was no more than a swindling mill." Its notes were forced into circulation immediately before its collapse. The capital of the bank contained $4,000 in specie and a $100,000 note from the president, while the outstanding obligations were $170,000.[62] When the vaults of one bank were examined by a legislative committee, the bank borrowed for that one day $50,000 in specie from another bank, and the committee certified that the bank was sound.[63] Other similar deceptions were practiced on legislatures and the public alike, so that even banks generally considered to be sound were often found to lack a sufficient capital base.[64] As the *New York American* explained in 1819:

> Country banks are perverted to the exclusive accommodation of the directors and some of their influential friends—while the public for whose advantage they were contemplated, are left to struggle with difficulties, created in a great measure by these very institutions.[65]

Shareholders did not restrain these managers. They rarely joined together to vote dishonest managers out of office, nor were many managers kept in check by the potential that shareholders might throw them out. Corrupt managers regularly received proxies from those they were robbing. As the *New York Daily Advertiser* admonished in 1819: "The temptations to misconduct are strong, and the opportunities to defraud, are great in Banks. Stockholders necessarily trust much to their agents—it seems they sometimes discover, when it is too late, that they may trust too much."[68] The same year, a stockholder warned his fellows in a letter published in the *New York Daily Advertiser* that: "The custom of stockholders giving their proxies to officers of banks, to be used at their discretion, to keep in, put in, or turn out who they please is fatal to their interests."[67]

Perhaps the most notorious example of such abuse was practiced by the first directors and management of the Second Bank of the United States, before the glory years of Nicholas Biddle. Initially issued in 1818, much of the stock was grabbed by speculators who inflated its price in the hopes of unloading it on European investors. Their aim, like that of most speculators, was to "sell out as soon as the balloon is sufficiently inflated by puffing, and before the pressure of too much gas causes it to burst."[68] With rising prices, small shareholders were encouraged to give up their shares and the stock accumulated in relatively few hands. The price rose quickly to $155–$160 for $100 paid.[69] Four individuals were rumored to hold $6 million worth of the stock, and half the shares were owned by fewer than fifty people, many of the largest shareholders being directors.[70]

The directors were deeply involved in this speculation. They kept the share price high either by purchasing shares as they came into the market or by making loans to others, who would purchase shares and then use them as collateral on additional loans. Other lending policies were equally questionable. Lending was concentrated in the Baltimore region, the home of an influential group of shareholders, and many loans were made to directors or to their business associates.[71]

Directors maintained this abusive system and kept themselves in office by voting their own shares and by manipulating the proxy process.[72] The bank's charter provided that no shareholder, no matter how many shares he owned, could cast more than thirty votes, but the directors and the large shareholders circumvented this restriction by dividing up large holdings of shares and claiming they were being voted in the names of people who, in reality, neither owned nor had any interest in them.

Once these abuses came to light, an inquiry was brought in Congress, where it was confirmed that directors and officers were deeply involved in speculation in the stock. They were charged with keeping share prices up in their own interest, a charge they could not defend. The Congressional report found that:

> The root and source of all these instances of misconduct was the illegal and reprehensible division of stock. By the first fundamental article of the charter, no person, copartnership, or body politic shall be entitled to more than 30 votes; and yet in violation of this provision, it will appear that it was common and general practice, well known to the judges of the election and to the directors, to divide shares into small parcels, varying from one to twenty shares, held in the names of persons who had no interest in them, and to vote upon the shares thus held, as attorneys for the pretended proprietors. . . . So long as the

large stockholders can control the choice of directors, so long as they can hold and acquire immense amounts of stock, by the proceeds of notes discounted on their shares, and so long as they can obtain such discounts, they can control the election of directors. The system places the property of the other stockholders, of the government, the credit of the bank, and of individuals, and in a measure, that of the nation, at the mercy of a few large stockholders, who, without really having contributed to the wealth or value of the institution, have control of its concerns. [73]

After this report, the price of United States Bank stock plummetted, and William Jones resigned the office of president. A committee of shareholders sought limitations on the powers of management and on their ability to trade in bank stock. [74] Yet even in response to such clear abuses by management, there was not enough concern for the small shareholders to prompt Congress to add additional restrictions on management to the bank's charter. [75] It would have been possible for an equally unscrupulous management to run the bank similarly in the future, as long as they obtained the required proxies through legal means. [76] Fortunately, the subsequent administrations were more responsible than the first.

Another shareholder attempt to rectify management abuse of its controlling power appears in an open letter to the shareholders of the Hope Insurance Company from our old friend John Michael O'Connor, who, it should be recalled, invested heavily in Hope Insurance Company stock. [77] In a lengthy diatribe, O'Connor asserts the rights of shareholders who are unhappy with the management of their companies. He writes:

> To The Stockholders of the Hope Insurance Company:
>
> A fellow sufferer by this Institution, who supposes your patience, like his own, to have been long since exhausted, ventures to address you on the scandalous mismanagement of the President and Board of Directors, and to propose the only remedy left to save the miserable wrecks of your property from utter destruction—a fate from which nothing can now save you but a total change of the Direction and Officers of the Institution at the approaching election.

O'Connor's specific complaints begin with the drop in share value and the lack of dividends. He invokes the suffering of widows and orphans who have been hurt as a result. He blames the incumbent management—who do business on ruinous terms, who pay extreme salaries to themselves, who insure their own ships at low rates, and who are allegedly involved in trading shares on inside information. He asserts that his feelings of annoyance are "aggravated by the refusal of the President and Directors to make a statement of the situation of the company and by the most impertinent denials of information as to the state of his property; as if they were the proprietors and not the stewards of the company."[78]

Clearly, O'Connor felt mistreated by managers who were not the owners of the company, but were in control. His remedy for the situation involved replacing those in control with men of "high standing in society" who would pay back the capital to the stockholders if they could not do a good business. He also called for regulations to protect shareholders which would require incorporated companies to regularly disclose the state of their affairs, and he threatened a lawsuit to compel the managers to provide an accounting.[79] Additionally, he suggested that the shareholders rather than managers should set the dividends. Finally, he proposed that no director be allowed to purchase insurance from the company.

This plea for shareholders to act in concert and use their dormant power to control managers is a dramatic illustration that such shareholder power was not commonly used at this time. Managers of public corporations controlled them, often to the detriment of shareholders or the public. We do not know if, in response to this call by O'Connor, the management of the Hope Insurance Company was unseated at the next election. We do know, however, that O'Connor's calls to comprehensively limit the powers of management were ahead of their time. Effective restraints against self-dealing on the part of management did not evolve until the twentieth century.

BATTLES FOR CORPORATE CONTROL

N OT ONLY was ownership separated from control in the first public corporations, but there also existed a marketplace for that control, much like the one that exists today. Shares were bought on credit primarily to obtain their voting rights, and proxies were solicited in order to collect votes for various resolutions or slates of managers. Managements were affected or even changed by outsiders who managed to obtain enough votes and, consequently, enough influence.

Short of taking over the corporation or waging a proxy battle, large shareholders could gain some control over corporate policies without actually acquiring enough shares to vote out management. They could do business on advantageous terms. For example, in 1815, the *New York Courier* advertised: "For Sale Twenty Shares of York & Jersey Steam Boat

Ferry Co., which will entitle the holder to free passage."[80] At banks, shareholders received good credit lines and could readily discount their notes, and at insurance companies, they could get their ventures protected, sometimes at favorable rates. A large group of shareholders in early Massachusetts textile firms were merchants who "attempted to cement their sources of supply by investment in textile production."[81] Nathan Appleton, the moving force in a large Massachusetts manufacturing enterprise, bought shares in railroads primarily because they were good for his other businesses.[82] Ownership of large blocks of stock could even pave the way to election on a board of directors, which in turn could lead to better business deals and open the door to affecting the manner in which the corporation did business with rivals.[83]

Influence over corporate policies was not enough for some ambitious shareholders who sought complete control. Shares were purchased, proxies were solicited, and battles were waged. Many corporations had limitations on voting large blocks of stock. Shareholders in the Bank of New York, for example, were allowed one vote for each share not exceeding four, five votes for six shares, six votes for eight shares, seven votes for ten shares, and one vote for every five shares above ten.[84] As a result, shareholders with large holdings placed shares with friends and family in order to avoid these restraints and enjoy maximum voting power.[85]

Although directors were generally elected and reelected without opposition,[86] proxy battles did occasionally occur when rival factions vied for control. Some early proxy contests reached the courts.[87] At times of heated proxy contests, the voting rights of the small shareholders were crucial to the control-minded.

Those attempting to change management by obtaining enough shares and enough votes found the securities trading market to be a double-edged sword. While the securities market allowed controlling shares to be purchased by challengers, it also aided managers in their efforts to keep themselves in power. By dispersing shareholdings, the market facilitated reelection of the incumbents; it made the challenger's task of collecting shares or votes more difficult.

Corporate raiders in early control contests confronted managers whose maneuvering showed the same ingenuity that characterizes such contests today. Incumbent managers altered bylaws to suit their needs and improperly called shareholder meetings. Managers used their mastery of the proxy machinery to vote the shares of inert shareholders, and bolstered their position by voting treasury shares, voting proxies without authorization, and denying the opposition the right to vote. Yet, even in the face of blatant management abuses designed to maintain their position of control, outsiders were on occasion able to accumulate the shares or votes they needed to outmaneuver and unseat the incumbents.

By 1825, successful hostile takeovers were being completed with sufficient regularity to elicit editorial comment. The *New York American,* in 1825, reported that the members of one syndicate had purchased target company shares for $105 per share, using $5 of their own funds and borrowing the balance by pledging the shares. With this small stake,

> They are thence enabled to be operating in the stock of many companies at once, till, having acquired control in the several concerns, they turn out all the old administrators, put in their own men, and then go to work with renewed energy, and means increased by the whole amount of the capitals they have thus acquired the control of.[88]

The *New York Inquirer* in 1826 reported that a "confederacy" worth $100,000 had seized control of companies with a nominal capital of $4 million. Still another "gang of stock jobbers" had employed similar tactics to obtain control of thirty-four companies.[89] Some of these escapades ended in litigation.[90]

One takeover involved the ancestor of today's Citibank.[91] During the early 1820s, the bank's earnings had declined, largely due to extensive loans to directors, and the stock fell below par. In an effort to boost the stock's price, the bank bought back 20 percent of its shares on the open market. That did not prevent Charles Lawton from acquiring a majority of the shares. In July 1825, Lawton used his power to oust the existing board of directors and replace it with one more suitable to him. Then, in what appears to have been an early instance of greenmail, Lawton sold his controlling interest to the new directors at a profit.[92] The directors bought the shares in order to prevent him from selling his control of the bank to interests "fatal to the character and credit of the institution." Lawton subsequently resigned as director.[93] Corporate representatives like these directors who could pay greenmail were able to act in the interest of their own survival without much concern for the interests of shareholders.

Then, as today, attempts by shareholders to gain control were exceptions to the rule that ownership and control of public corporations are typically separated. Control battles were rare in comparison with the number of times an election simply followed the plan set forth by management, when ordinary shareholder's votes were practically meaningless. The existence of early battles for corporate control through the stock market, however, demonstrates that, on occasion, entrepreneurs bought shares in order to effect changes in control.[94] The share-trading market thus worked as a check on managers who improperly ran public corporations. Management could be unseated if their mismanagement allowed the share price to fall low enough for someone to purchase control and replace them.

THE SIGNIFICANCE OF THE INHERENCE THESIS

T HIS SEPARATION of ownership and control is not a phenomenon that developed as corporations were corrupted from an ideal state. The first publicly traded corporations had shareholders protected at law less than they are protected now, shareholders who were generally as disinterested in corporate management and as supine in corporate governance as the shareholders of today. The securities trading market allowed investors to treat their shares as financial assets rather than as vehicles for participation in corporate affairs. Managers of corporations controlled them, and battled for this control in the securities markets. These foundations of the corporate system existed in the first public corporations. There has been no erosion from an earlier, more pristine era to the distortions of today. There has been, however, significant fallout from the erosion doctrine.

The erosion doctrine sprang from the need to find some explanation for the depression of the 1930s. Traditional thinking could not explain the breakdown of the economy, nor could the orthodox prescription, a laissez-faire posture for government, cure it. According to Berle and Means, the essence of the change in the economy was the "new" separation of ownership and control in the modern corporation. They understood that nonowner controllers could lack the owner-entrepreneur's incentive to maximize profits, the bedrock of classic theory. They also demonstrated that controllers motivated by desire for personal monetary gain could use their power position against the interests of shareholders.[95]

In response to what they viewed as new developments, Berle and Means considered two possible regulatory reactions for the protection of the economy and shareholder rights. One alternative focused on utilizing the shareholders' right to sell their shares in the securities market. To be effective, the securities markets had to be free, open, and honest, providing shareholders with accurate corporate information and with remedies for fraud and manipulation.[96] Berle and Means' prescriptions for market regulation along these lines were largely carried out.[97]

The second alternative, which Berle and Means considered and then rejected, involved empowering shareholders with an effective voice in corporate governance. Berle and Means dismissed the notion that shareholders could run the modern companies they owned.

With the fair and effective securities market the key to shareholder protection, there was little need to deplore the separation of ownership and control. Although shareholders surrendered claims to participate in corporate governance in exchange for share marketability, their interests were not ignored because of this lack of direct control. Shareholders could still vote with their feet, and sell shares when they were dissatisfied. A rash of sales would depress the share price and alert management to investor dissatisfaction.

Managers were concerned with keeping their shares desirable and keeping their share prices up because the existence, or even prospect, of a good share market expedited purchase of newly issued shares. It was a symptom of the corporation's economic health taken into account by creditors making lending decisions. In order to have access to additional capital when necessary, managers had to act in the interests of existing shareholders. Managers had added incentives to keep share prices up, ranging from the value of their own share holdings to fending off hostile takeovers.

Shareholder satisfaction, as measured by prices in the trading market, thus disciplined management. It replaced the nexus between shareholder and corporation that the dispersion of ownership and control was supposed to create. So what if shareholders could not mandate their corporation to maximize earnings on their behalf through voting their shares? So what if the corporate franchise is meaningless in the great majority of cases? Whether a shareholder voted his ten shares for or against the Bank of New York's slate of directors was irrelevant. But if the Bank of New York lost ground to The Manhattan Company or the Merchants Bank, and if it did not do something about it, the stock price was going to fall and management was going to be changed. The earliest American stock market was an extension of the corporations whose shares it traded. It operated then—much as it does today—as the external adjunct of the public corporation's internal government structure.

PART FOUR
The Road to Today

CHAPTER TEN

The Railroad Age: 1840–1890

T HE FIRST fifty years of American securities markets and public corporations, particularly the experience of banks and other financial corporations, established the foundations for all that followed. The following examination of the next fifty years, called here the Railroad Age, explores some of the continuities built upon the characteristics of the Bank Age.

The United States took its first giant steps toward today's trillion-dollar economy during the Railroad Age. Whether measured by GNP or income per capita or tangible wealth or financial assets, growth was explosive. Historians debate the details, but nearly all give railroads the chief credit for bringing the United States from its agricultural heritage to the brink of the industrial era.[1]

Launching the railroads was a tremendous undertaking for a young economy. Costs for each enterprise were astronomical, risks were great, and rewards were usually a long time coming. Railroad promoters were innovators, speculators, people willing to take big chances. Disdaining the path of reasonable profit on carefully invested capital, railroadmen were out to make personal fortunes.[2] The American people, eager to see the country grow and looking for huge returns on their investments, were willing to take the necessary risks. By 1830, the stage was set, the country was ready for railroads, and the twin institutions of public corporations and securities markets were equal to the task.

The business corporation, the organizational form used successfully by banks and insurance companies for decades, had proven workable for nonfinancial enterprises like the Delaware and Hudson Canal Company. Railroads copied from these examples and adapted business corporations to their purposes. It is likely that railroads would have been built without public corporations and securities markets, but it is difficult to imagine just how. Without limited shareholder liability and unlimited corporate duration, railroads would have faced tremendous obstacles to growing as large as they did. Raising the vast sums railroads required would have been nearly impossible without the public corporation's ability to tap broad-based supplies of capital. True, money might have been accumulated through retained earnings, but growth along this route alone was bound to be slower than if the enterprise could also attract the savings of others. The securities market was the necessary mechanism; the enthusiasm of the general public was channeled into material aid for the railroads by sales of railroad stock.

For the railroads, securities markets and public corporations formed an integrated system for business activity. As was stated at the time:

> The colossal achievements in railroad development would not have been possible but for the New York Stock Exchange, which affords a market for the disposal of the stocks and bonds of the various companies, and has been an unerring guide to the public of the values thereof. The corporation is the vehicle for industrial activity, including the building and operating of railroads, and the securities markets are the vehicle for financing those operations.[3]

Other corporations were created during this period—thousands of them. Manufacturing corporations were numerous and important, particularly toward the end of the Railroad Age. It was the exciting new technology of the railroads, however, that was able to stir the interests of investors and mobilize large amounts of capital. As a result, it was the railroads that realized the full potential of securities markets and public corporations that had been developing in America for fifty years. It was also the railroads, forced to meet new challenges accompanying large public corporations, which produced the innovations in corporate finance, organization, and management to set the pace for all corporations that followed.

American railroads were started in the 1820s, and they caught on quickly.[4] When shares of the Mohawk & Hudson Railroad were first traded at the NYS&EB in 1830, a new generation of corporations relying on securities markets was born.[5] As the railroads grew, everyone wanted to participate in this national project, everyone wanted to go along for the ride. Merchants, manufacturers, professional men, practically anybody who had capital to invest purchased shares in the new steel highways. By 1834, the shares of nine railroads were already actively traded on the NYS&EB,

and trading of railroad stock soon outstripped all other NYS&EB activity. Railroads overran the securities markets just as they conquered the plains and the imaginations of the American people. By 1832, no fewer than twenty-five railroads presented applications for charters to the New York legislature.[6]

Some railroad shares were bought for investment,[7] but more were bought for speculation. Railroad stocks lent themselves admirably to the speculative capabilities demonstrated by New York securities traders. They were the issues of a glamorous new industry, made up of many entrants, some destined for success and profitability, others to failure and liquidation. A risk-taking spirit was rife in nineteenth-century America, notably in real estate, commodities, and lotteries,[8] but in many ways speculation in stocks was more attractive. Stocks could be bought and sold quickly and easily, and stock investments did not require the sizable sums often necessary to purchase land or tangible commodities.

Margin trading, an innovation indigenous to the United States, made speculation in stocks simpler still. Margin trading allows a purchaser to put down only a small amount of the purchase price, with the broker financing the rest. The broker holds the shares for the customer, and the customer can order them sold at a gain if the price of the security rises. If the price of the security falls, the customer must either put up more money on margin, or the broker will sell the security and recover the money advanced to finance the original purchase. The broker is protected against default by holding the security. Margin trading thereby had an advantage over time bargains, in which there was little protection against default beyond the word of another broker. Time bargains also technically violated the law as wagering contracts; margin trading did not. As a result, time bargains seem to have come to an end sometime between 1840 and 1860.[9]

With margin trading, $5 sent to a broker could buy $50 of stocks.[10] Trading pools were created wherein each individual would put up $200 and would sometimes find brokers to handle their account on 2 percent margin, buying or selling short in the morning and reversing course in the afternoon.[11] To use the jargon of the street, every farmer and shopkeeper seemed engaged in "carrying" some favorite security "on a margin." This leveraging of investors could lead to great gains,[12] but, in the end, many of these small-time investors or speculators lost their shirts to the big operators, or they paid out their profits in commissions to brokers who always made a killing in a trading frenzy.

In many railroad stocks, trading volume was high, with sharply fluctuating prices leading to periodic cyclical booms and panics.[13] In broad terms, the 1840s were consolidation years after the economic downturn of the late 1830s.[14] The success in the War with Mexico and the gold rush in California brought new life and optimism to the American economy late in the decade, resulting in a speculative spurt early in the 1850s.[15] A stock market boom was sustained until the failure of the Ohio Life and Trust Company triggered the collapse of August 1857. On October 13, 1857 eighteen New York City banks suspended specie payments, followed by many banks throughout the country. Securities sold for bargain prices, and bank presidents stood at their doors urging the public to be calm and not to hastily withdraw their deposits.[16] By 1859, the heights of the stock market showed how quickly the wounds of this panic were healed. With the discovery of oil in Pennsylvania, a small oil rush was on.[17] The stock markets' glow then faded as the Civil War approached and gloom settled over the nation and the economy.[18]

The war itself brought to the North new corporations and strong incentives to industrialize. Profusely printed paper money caused prices to swell. The spirit of speculation flourished in securities markets, optimism rising and falling with the tides of Union victories and defeats.[19] After the issuance of greenbacks in 1862, even holding onto currency was a speculative venture; its value changed from one day to the next. As Henry Adams explained:

> The Civil War in America, with its enormous issues of depreciating currency, and its reckless waste of money and credit by the government, created a speculative mania such as the United States, with all its experience in this respect, had never before known. Not only in Broad Street, the centre of New York speculation, but far and wide throughout the Northern States, almost every man who had money at all employed a part of his capital in the purchase of stocks or of gold, of copper, of petroleum, or of domestic produce, in the hope of a raise in prices, or staked money on the expectation of a fall.[20]

Under such an influx of demand, the NYS&EB, continuing a steady course of twice-daily calls of stocks, was unable to handle drastically increased securities trading. To deal with the glut, an annex developed in an adjoining room where quotations could be heard and repeated. Those brokers not admitted to the NYS&EB paid up to $100 a day for the privilege of listening at a keyhole.[21] In addition, an alternate market grew in the street to accommodate the overflowing business. Specialized exchanges appeared: a mining board traded shares in mining companies, many of which were little more than bubbles and fraudulent enterprises,[22] and a petroleum board was also established and soon merged with the mining board.[23] A Gold Exchange was formed after the issuance of federal paper money.[24] In addition to these niche exchanges, a second large exchange, the Open Board of Brokers, was formed in 1864, holding calls at 1:00 and 3:30 P.M. to alternate with the 10:30 A.M. and 2:30 P.M. calls at the NYS&EB.[25] During the Civil War, there was even an evening exchange to cater to speculators who traded day and night.[26]

These rival exchanges, the offspring of speculative booms, were at the mercy of the market and were doomed in downturns. Most collapsed of their own weight with scandals and fraud.[27] Trading in the evening and mining exchanges dried up after the NYS&EB, the Open Board, and the Gold Exchange gave these unwanted half-brothers the final push by forbidding their own members from trading in them on pain of expulsion.[28]

The two major legitimate stock exchanges, the New York Stock & Exchange Board, renamed the New York Stock Exchange in 1863,[29] and the Open Board of Brokers, competed directly for business. In 1865, continuous trading was established in a "Long Room" opened to the public in the basement of the New York Stock Exchange building. By 1866, the Open Board and the Long Room grew in importance while the significance of the calls at the New York Stock Exchange (the NYSE) decreased. The NYSE "looked with great disfavor on its young rival (the Open Board); a bitter contest arose, in which, the former had the advantage in wealth and established position, the latter in fire, energy, and numbers."[30]

While these exchanges contended for trading, securities activity steadily increased. Lee's surrender buoyed trading in stocks and gold to over $20 million each day.[31] The effects of easy money were long-lasting, and speculation prospered. Speculation had become so well established that it no longer required the fluctuating values of national credit, or the extravagant spirit of army contractors grown suddenly rich, to insure its continuance. Stock market operators raged, railway empires were built and destroyed, fortunes were made and lost in weeks—or days—or hours. The late 1860s was truly a "gilded age," a riotous period in society reflected in the Crédit Mobilier in corporate finance, the Tweed Ring in government, the Erie Gang, and the gold conspiracy. 1860s speculation passed through two dominant phases: first, the struggle of a few strong men for railroad supremacy; second, manipulation of the gold market.[32]

Among the most celebrated speculative chapters in the history of New York stock markets are contests waged over railroads. Operators used the markets to amass fortunes, break their rivals, and, in famous battles, to obtain control of enterprises they coveted. Such maneuverings became regular features of the corporate scene.[33] Commodore Vanderbilt of the New York Central in this manner amassed a railroad empire second to none. When he matched up against Daniel Drew and the Erie Gang, however, the fierceness of their clash on Wall Street was unprecedented.

During 1867, Vanderbilt attempted to gain control over the Erie Railroad, as he had already obtained possession of the New York Central, by purchasing a majority of the outstanding stock.[34] Daniel Drew and the Erie directors sold Vanderbilt all the stock he could take, and then at the last moment, and in direct violation of a court injunction Vanderbilt had obtained, issued new stock by the carload, as much more stock as was required to defeat the acquisition.

The ensuing struggle was violent, with the Erie directors held in contempt of court and hiding out in New Jersey behind a wall of armed men. The legal battle was waged with armies of lawyers and allegedly bribed judges who overruled and contradicted each other. The issue was brought before the New York legislature where money to influence the decision flowed freely, and, finally, the issuance of Erie shares was ratified. Ultimately, Drew triumphed. Vanderbilt abandoned the contest to obtain control. The Erie corporation paid Vanderbilt a large sum to reimburse his alleged losses, and Drew was released in full from responsibility for any wrongdoing with which he might be charged. The exhausted Erie Railroad was left under the control of Jay Gould and James Fisk, Jr., whose reign began in July 1868.[35]

This contest, perhaps the most famous attempt during this period to obtain control of a corporation through the stock market, was but one of similar campaigns waged regularly and ruthlessly. In the attempt by the Erie Gang to wrest control of the Albany and Susquehanna Railroad from its original president and guiding spirit, Joseph Ramsey, the struggle was so vicious that it approached armed combat. At one point, a locomotive filled with Ramsey supporters crashed into an Erie locomotive and set off a pitched battle. The militia went on alert to assure the peace; the contest moved to the courts. Ultimately, the Erie Gang was kept from the road, and Ramsey sold out to the powerful Delaware and Hudson Canal Company.[36]

Also common at this time were securities market operations aimed not at control but merely at excessive profits. Vanderbilt and other kings of Wall Street were involved in stock market corners on a regular basis. In one notorious corner, Vanderbilt nearly bankrupted the New York city

council, which had tried to ruin him with excessive regulations concerning the Harlem Railroad.[37] In another, Vanderbilt almost sent the entire
speculation-crazy state legislature to the poorhouse.[38] These notorious
corners pale, however, in comparison with the attempt made in 1869 by
Jay Gould and Jim Fisk, Jr.

Gould and Fisk operated heavily in the Gold Exchange,[39] an arena of
large-scale speculation with far-reaching effects. Speculation in gold affected the entire economy, insofar as it changed the value of currency.
The conspirators saw in the awesome importance of the gold market an
opportunity for sizable profit.

In September 1869, at a time when the available supplies of gold in
the United States amounted to less than $25 million, Gould and Fisk
made contracts to purchase $50 million or more, raising the price of gold
tremendously.[40] Because they controlled all the available gold and many
brokers had commitments to deliver gold to them in the near future, Gould
and Fisk were in a position to demand either delivery of gold no one could
obtain or settlements at outrageous prices. Their attempt to corner the
market was working, and on Black Friday, September 24, 1869, they put
the squeeze on and raised the price. With each advance, more and more
investors and speculators in gold were bankrupted. Each alternative spelled
disaster: selling gold that could not be acquired and delivered was madness, while buying it at an inflated price only to hand it over to Gould
and Fisk to honor earlier, lower-priced contracts meant certain ruin.

All financial markets were in chaos. As gold lost its value, the stability
of the financial system was jeopardized. Because of the lack of federal action in the face of this turmoil, the Grant administration was suspected
of complicity in the scheme. When the Treasury stepped in with an offer
to sell a large amount of gold, making it clear that the government would
protect the economy and keep the price from going too high, it came as
a surprise. This action broke the rise, and by the end of Black Friday the
gold price fall was as precipitous as its earlier gain.

Gould and Fisk hid themselves in their offices protected by hired thugs
while pandemonium filled the streets.[41] No one knew where he stood.
Many contracts had been made, but none were sure of being kept because
of the hundreds of firms and brokers who failed. Some committed suicide. The crisis rippled through financial circles and the economy. Gold
markets remained closed through September 30 while attempts were made
to settle outstanding contracts. Somehow Gould and Fisk emerged practically unscathed.[42]

The government proposal to sell gold prevented the Black Friday crisis

from wreaking more havoc than it already had. Direct intervention quieted the market as no regulation could. Earlier attempts to curb speculation in gold trading through regulation had failed miserably,[43] the most
notable among them a drastic federal statute that had made it a crime for
gold to be sold for future delivery.[44] This statute was intended to bring
the price of gold down, but instead destroyed confidence in the market.
When gold prices rose rapidly and speculation flourished,[45] Congress,
alarmed at the effect of its own folly, repealed the prohibition within a
month, and gold again receded.[46]

Meanwhile, the NYSE could not shake off the competition from the
Open Board, and, in order to retain the advantages of being the central
market, agreed to a merger of the two organizations in 1869.[47] This consolidation made even more powerful and efficient the trading forum which
made the marketplace. A near monopoly on trading was assured, and
brokers attempting to steal business by cutting commission were no longer
a serious threat. Continuous trading hours ran from 10 A.M. to 4 P.M.,
with the calls in stock decreasing in importance.[48]

Other improvements in efficiency resulted from the technology of the
stock ticker, telegraph, and, later, telephone. Trading orders were wired
in from all over America and Europe. The specialist trading system took
root, and soon each security came to be traded at a particular location on
the exchange floor.[49] Seats on the exchange became salable; what was
once a privilege became a valuable property right. With each of these
improvements the power of the NYSE was enhanced, and Fowler could
write in 1871, "The Board of Brokers is a wheel within a wheel, an im-
perium in imperio—a government in itself. It makes laws and regulations
which bear upon its members as strongly as the laws of the land."[50]

These developments in the marketplace were accompanied by profound changes for the burgeoning securities industry. In increasing numbers, professionals in the trading market dedicated themselves to brokerage alone.[51] Others served as brokers' brokers, handling commission
business for their fellows. Brokers' specialties developed, and soon experts
dealt only in bonds or a particular variety of stock. Business boomed; the
three largest brokerage firms in 1865 bought and sold more than $150
million worth of stocks and gold, each trading fifteen times more securities than the entire NYS&EB market only thirty years before.[52] Other
smaller firms came and went regularly.[53]

Alongside the trading market, the distribution or new issue market also
developed rapidly.[54] When railroads sold their massive securities issues
they relied on middlemen from Philadelphia, Boston, and New York to

market the issues.[55] From this platform, investment banking as we know it developed.[56]

By 1860, investment bankers were vital to railroads. They were the most important link in the chain supplying funds,[57] and they developed increasingly cozy ties with the issuers whose securities they sold. Investment bankers' securities marketing function often opened the way to other relationships with their clients, such as serving as corporate fiscal agent responsible for transfers of securities and payments of interest and dividends. Thus, clusters of interrelated services began to cement the continuing association between corporations and investment banks.

Investment bankers also nurtured relationships with securities purchasers, particularly foreign capitalists.[58] Investors began to rely on investment bankers' advice, which in turn required the better and larger houses to establish research and statistics departments that could evaluate railroads and their securities. Some houses began to issue letters to acquaint customers with developments in financial markets.

Jay Cooke's distributions of bonds for the federal government during the Civil War built on these advances in merchandising securities.[59] Cooke sold hundreds of millions of small denomination "baby bonds" to small investors through high pressure sales campaigns that supplemented the basic appeal to patriotism. He also organized other bankers into syndicates that were pioneers in managing the market by supporting prices systematically during a securities distribution.[60]

After Cooke's successes, investment banking flowered. Responsibilities extending beyond the limits of Wall Street and into corporate boardrooms demonstrated that investment bankers had become crucial to public corporations and to the economy. They formed a powerful part of the financial community.[61] By the 1880s, J. P. Morgan and his firm were establishing themselves at the top of the heap. They became the leading specialists in railroad finance.[62] In a nation pressed for funds to meet the needs of an expanding economy, these men who controlled the supply of security capital became leaders of a new business elite.[63] By the end of the Railroad Age, they were not only distributing railroad securities, but were also reorganizing railroads and consolidating them into systems, systems which they themselves often either controlled or strongly influenced.[64]

Powerful investment bankers acquired much of their influence over corporations by introducing new financing methods which proved to be the most significant developments on the corporate scene in this period. Public corporations of the Bank Age had depended on a combination of capital contributed by both shareholders and various kinds of state assistance. The capital-hungry railroads received even more public help, from state government charters, to federal land grants, to subsidies from local municipalities. Although it would be difficult to overemphasize the importance of this public assistance in promoting the railroads that presented the greatest risks and required the largest amounts of capital,[65] for large railroads government help was merely the beginning.

In essence, railroads could be built only by tapping private capital, the target of other allurements. Promoters of new railroads obtained their initial capital through opening subscription books and selling common shares to the public. In the case of some early Massachusetts railroads, common stock provided all the necessary funds.[66] Later promoters had to reach a broader market, and, with the advice of investment bankers, they developed a variety of techniques for this purpose.

A typical strategy began with aggressive marketing of common stocks. Promoters sought funds throughout the territory to be served by the railroad, and subscription books were opened at offices set up in towns along the proposed right of way, as well as at the company's main office. Public meetings, parades, petitions, and door-to-door canvassing were organized to remind the community of the benefits of a rail link to the outer world and of the dangers of eclipse by neighboring communities.[67] Subscribers were encouraged to pay for shares with labor or goods instead of cash. Financing arrangements were developed to allow subscribers to borrow the purchase price of the shares on collateral of their farm or property.[68]

The shining dividend performance of the early railroads helped subsequent promoters to raise capital.[69] Small investors by the thousands bought railroad stocks with expectations of regular dividends. The heavy trading of railroad stocks in New York helped tremendously as well. The existence of this active trading market where investors could convert their shares to cash when necessary, strengthened sales in the new issue market. Soon, there were many investors eager to purchase common shares in railroads, and issues were often oversubscribed. Regular press reports of oversubscribed railroads appeared as early as 1831.[70]

It was clear, however, that even the combination of public assistance and contributions of common shareholders was insufficient to finance railroad projects limited in size only by the imaginations of their promoters. Therefore, railroad men and investment bankers devised new financial instruments to draw needed funds not attracted by common shares.[71] Corporate values were sliced up into equity, which was divided between common and various classes of preferred stock,[72] and debt, which was divided into a variety of bonds. [73] The concept met with success: securities tailored to different risk preferences attracted wider sources of funds, and the capital formation potential of the corporate system was greatly enlarged. [74]

The use of senior securities had profound consequences for public corporations. Senior securities leveraged corporations [75] and made common shares more attractive to risk takers. [76] Preferred stock also facilitated government aid to railroads by allowing unconvinced legislatures to take on reduced risks. In addition, corporate managers were forced to disclose additional financial information to satisfy senior securities holders who had greater stakes in the soundness of the enterprises.

Senior securities also enhanced promoters' ability to raise capital without giving votes to major contributers of money. Ironically, many senior securities holders who provided large amounts of capital could not vote for directors. [77] Common shareholders' votes now elected boards of directors to manage larger pools of assets. [78] Securities markets helped to build corporations so large that majority control was impossible for even the wealthiest of individuals, [79] and the great army of small shareholders was so widely dispersed that each individual was nearly powerless. For common shareholders, the franchise was worth exercising only in a proxy contest.

Thus, managers had the upper hand, as shareholders were disenfranchised or divided. The principles of control by management or by minority shareholders were understood by publicly traded corporations of the Bank Age before the Railroad Age began and before securities markets were well developed, but the expansion of securities markets refined these principles. Corporate officers devised capital structures that assured control of enterprises built with other people's money. In the 1850s, $2 million of stock, mostly not paid for, controlled the Pittsburgh, Fort Wayne, & Chicago Railroad financed with $16 million of borrowing. [80] In the very large Pennsylvania Railroad, J. Edgar Thompson and other professional managers exercised the same power as share-based controllers without even obtaining control over the limited pool of common stock. [81] Because these promoters and managers handpicked the directors, who were dummies or "ciphers," stockholders had little direct input on corporate affairs.

Other managers, such as Gould and Fisk of the Erie Railroad, enlisted the aid of the legislature to entrench their control. During the winter of 1869, Gould marshalled through the New York Assembly a bill to abolish the former system of annual elections for the entire board of Erie directors. As a result, Gould and Fisk could remain directors of the Erie Railroad for five years, notwithstanding any attempt by the stockholders to remove them.[82]

With their power over immense corporations, many managers of the Railroad Age made great strides toward efficient management. They built on developments pioneered by early banks and other public corporations, reorganizing firm structures, refining accounting methods, transforming the theory of business enterprise.[83] Because railroads were the largest and most complicated business enterprises of their time, railroad management faced challenges and developed modern managerial structures earlier than did nonrailroad industries. These managers of public corporations used their power to move industrial America forward.

Some managers, however, used their power for ill-gotten gains. Here, the best-known illustration is the control of the Erie Railroad by the Erie Gang, who discovered that clever manipulation of the securities market could produce more for them than could sound operation of the corporation. Using this tool, the Erie Gang was able to use its control over the corporation to mold corporate behavior and publicity in ways to suit their own securities market machinations. Consequently, these promoters could manipulate prices upward when they wanted to unload their own securities at artificially inflated prices, or they could drive down prices when they wanted to squeeze out other securities holders.

Another strategem was to water stock. Watered stock—the issuance of additional shares to raise capital, without purchasing new assets or creating new value—was popularized by the Erie's Daniel Drew. When he was a cattle drover, Drew had fed his animals salt so they would drink excess water just prior to sale. He explained the application of that principle to the issue of new securities in this way:

> If a fellow can make money selling a critter just after she has drunk up fifty pounds of water, what can't he make by issuing a lot of new shares of a railroad or steamboat company and then selling this just as though it was the original shares.[84]

In the short period of four years, the Erie Railroad was recapitalized by raising the outstanding common stock from $17 million to $78 million.[85] During the Railroad Age, overcapitalization of this sort became a common device to defraud shareholders.[86]

Minority shareholders in corporations run by corrupt managements were swept along by policies that provided no special place for their rights. Purchasers of common shares who were taken by crooked railroad barons went in with their eyes wide open. Abuses by corporate officers were well known. The shareholders' main line of defense was to protect themselves by not purchasing common stock in highly leveraged, risky railroad ventures. Investors who were truly "investors" could seek out responsible advice from honest, competent bankers and brokers. Those who did business with speculation-minded securities businessmen, or who traded on margin on the exchanges, were considered gamblers and received little sympathy from legislators, the press, or the general public.

The notion of government action to protect investors as a class appears to have been foreign to the thinking of the time. The early, but not very effective, stirrings of laws to protect shareholder's interests can be found in preemptive rights giving existing shareholders first crack at purchasing any new shares issued by the corporation, in requirements that all shareholders were liable to pay their subscriptions to shares, and in developments toward making corporate officers liable for wrongs against the corporation.[87] Although other state regulations did set limits on a corporation's area of activity and its equity capital, these restrictions were aimed more to protect creditors than to protect shareholders.[88]

Another victory for investors was access to the additional corporate information reaching the marketplace on the urgings of investment bankers, exchanges, and some state regulations requiring financial reports. The quality of such information improved, as accounting practices became more standardized. The NYS&EB deserves considerable credit in the movement toward corporate disclosure. Its requirements for listing securities involved releasing increasing amounts of information to the public. In 1847, the NYS&EB required that a transfer office for all listed securities be maintained in New York.[89] In 1853, applications for listings had to be approved by members and had to include financial disclosures.[90] A standing committee on securities, formed in 1861, attempted to obtain information concerning all securities on the trading list.[91]

In a test of strength during the exciting days of the various Erie Railroad battles, both the NYS&EB and the Open Board sought to force the registration of securities to prevent overissuance. The exchanges wanted notice to the public before issuance of new stock. When the Erie Railroad did not comply, its stock was stricken from the trading list for a time. After the failure of a rival Erie Trading Board set up by Jim Fisk, the Erie Railroad succumbed to the requirements of the NYS&EB and was relisted.[92]

In related corporate regulation, state governments were permissive. They set ever more lax ground rules for corporate organization, rules that did not inhibit corporate growth. Charter provisions restricting limited shareholder liability and corporate duration were phased out. By the 1880s, states were chartering corporations to engage in any legitimate business activity. Corporate enterprise came to serve the community in the broad sense that the pursuit of private gain in a free market served the public interest.

The federal government also assisted corporate expansion at this time, actively encouraging postwar growth in the North, reconstruction in the South. The Union Pacific and other railroads were chartered with land grants and federal loans. High tariff walls were created to protect young American industries. The floodgates of immigration were opened, providing large pools of labor. The banking system was buttressed with the National Bank Act.[93] In addition, corporations gained significant rights in federal courts. They earned valuable guarantees against undue interference by state legislatures,[94] and they were granted unrestricted access to the federal judicial system.[95] The Supreme Court repeatedly played the role of overall corporate protector, defending corporations from harm at the hands of leveling influences jealous or afraid of corporate accumulations of wealth and power.[96]

While these legal developments were unfolding, securities markets maintained their cyclical swings. A sharp panic in 1873 was triggered by the failure of the powerful Jay Cooke & Co.[97] The NYSE closed for ten days, many fortunes were lost, and economic confidence vanished.[98] Following the depression of 1873, railroad building was stopped for almost five years. In the late 1870s and early 1880s, economic activity heated again, fostering the final great burst of railroad building.[99] Securities markets also recovered in the 1880s. Annual trading volume on the NYSE rose from less than 40 million shares in 1876 to over 114 million in 1881.[100] The failure in 1884 of Ulysses Grant's firm, Grant and Ward, set off a small panic, but a bull market returned by 1885.[101] In December 1886, a million-share trading day was reached at the NYSE.[102]

By this time, the Railroad Age was drawing to a close. The concern of legislators and securities markets broadened from a fascination with railroads to expanded interests in industrial corporations, trusts, and monopolies.[103] Speculation had moved beyond the railroads, too. The wave of speculation that began after the panic of 1890, which led to the larger panic of 1893, was conducted largely in the shares of the new industrial combinations.[104] The days of railroad primacy on the NYSE and in the economy had given way to an era in which the industrial corporations were becoming increasingly important.

The system of securities markets and public corporations had carried the railroads and the American economy to this point. At the beginning of the Railroad Age, this system was in its infancy, but all of its characteristics were present. The Railroad Age was the adolescence, in which the unique genius of the American system of securities markets and public corporations was fully appreciated and utilized.

By the end of the Railroad Age, the financial side of the corporation dominated. Capital was the prerequisite for success, and corporate promoters had to know how and where to get it. Once capital was obtained, the rest could follow. Closer ties with investment advisors were one consequence, as were new types of managements. Corporate officers looked to securities markets in formulating their financial plans, in creating new kinds of securities and financing arrangements, in setting dividend policies, and in releasing financial and operating data. Thus, while growing tremendously in size and efficiency, securities markets continued to influence the corporations they served so well. [105] Securities markets and public corporations nourished each other's development, and together they made vital contributions to the Railroad Age and the prosperity it brought. Thereafter, securities markets and public corporations acting together launched the second—and even more profound—century of progress.

CHAPTER ELEVEN
Conclusions

CONTINUITIES IN THE HISTORY OF AMERICAN SECURITIES MARKETS AND PUBLIC CORPORATIONS

BETWEEN 1790 and 1840, banks were the largest, best-known, and most controversial public corporations, the ones with the most shareholders and the most active trading market. These and other publicly traded corporations contained the essential elements of big corporations today: a tripartite internal government structure, a share market that dispersed shareholdings and separated ownership from control, and tendencies to centralize management in full-time administrators. While securities markets were important to bank shareholders as a means to make their investments liquid, they were crucial for banks as a source of funds, as an aid in appealing to investors who preferred liquid assets, and as a measure of performance.

Railroads built upon this foundation and took advantage of the banks' experience with public corporations. Utilizing an exciting new technology, railroads offered tempting profit possibilities. As a result, their shares were frequently oversubscribed. They quickly became the nation's second glamour industry. From the start, railroads were public corporations, with national share trading markets and thousands of shareholders. Securities markets were indispensable to the railroad builders. The markets tapped savings, inspired new types of securities issues, made consolidations easier, and facilitated government aid.[1]

By 1900, the railroad's glow had faded. Industrials replaced them as the nation's glamour securities. Securities markets were crucial to the industrials, too. Without a ready market for industrial issues, the spread of stock ownership would have been delayed, the emergence of professional managers would have been postponed, and the creation of the big industrial mergers would have been incalculably more difficult.[2] Raising capi-

tal was an important as producing marketable products, and managers relied upon their financiers and securities markets as never before. The
speculative component of the New York trading market was also crucial
to the young industrials. With heavy demand and robust trading, notice
was given through the securities markets that the public was eager to invest its money in industrial combinations.

In the twentieth century, shareholders and securities markets were
greatly affected by federal securities legislation, designed to protect investors from fraud and breaches of fiduciary duty.[3] Federal legislation legi-
timized securities markets with the implicit seal of approval that they are
the best mechanism for allocating capital. Shareholders later in the
twentieth century, offered a vast and smoothly functioning securities trading
market, became increasingly interested in "performance": the rapid appreciation in share price. An efficient stock market, able to react quickly
to corporate prospects, forced corporate managers to keep share prices high.

Current corporate managers, responding to the ever-present threat of
takeovers, are making their enterprises perform and are keeping up the
price of their shares. Corporate raiders and targets, their eyes glued to
securities markets, look for vulnerabilities or shore up defenses.[4] The per-
vasiveness of takeovers has made corporate ownership and control more
fluid than ever; management is now more likely to end up in the hands
of those able to use it most effectively. Securities markets have improved
corporate discipline and efficiency, while also allowing corporations the
flexibility and the financing to continue their tremendous growth.

This history shows that expanding securities markets and public corporations have kept pace with a dynamic American economy for two
hundred years, moving from the wings to center stage and becoming today's most important social institutions. Throughout this tremendous
growth, the solid roots of the corporate system put down in the first years
of the republic have remained essentially intact. Commercial and financial enterprises and practices that developed in New York during the 1790s
closely resemble those we know today. Each of the components of the
1790s securities markets finds descendants bearing a close resemblance
today.

New and larger stock exchanges, for instance, have responded to increased trading volume and improved technology, but the great trading
forums of today still perform the same functions their forebears did: they
provide for the most traders the quickest execution at the best price. They
furnish a meeting place for buyers and sellers and enhance share marketability with lower commission costs and steady, knowable quotations.

Purchasers have patronized and built up the exchanges best able to meet these needs, and trading has gravitated to whichever city and exchange has offered the best market. Just as trading in railroad shares concentrated in New York in the 1830s, trading in futures and options has centered in Chicago in the 1980s.

As specialized, regional, and rival exchanges have come and gone in response to fluctuating trading pressures, the New York Stock Exchange and its ancestors have kept their position as the most important stock markets in the United States. By law, the NYSE is no longer a restricted club, although the high price of NYSE seats retains its exclusivity. The NYSE also no longer has a fixed commission structure to prevent price-cutting competition, but its dominant position in the market is so secure that stock trading gravitates there, regardless.

Keeping pace with the markets, the securities industry has grown in size, complexity, and specialization. Securities professionals have evolved in each age, responding to the needs of issuers and investors, but their fundamental function of lubricating investors' and issuers' access to the markets has not been altered. Merrill Lynch's brokerage business today is similar to Leonard Bleecker's in 1790. Goldman, Sachs and Company makes markets just as Nathan Prime did in 1800. Other investment bankers, in stabilizing or pegging markets for new issues, are simply building on the example of Alexander Hamilton's strategy to support the market for United States bonds.

From the beginning, securities professionals have been an integral part of the corporate system, and cannot be viewed as outsiders simply because they may not own shares or hold offices within the corporate framework. They have profoundly influenced trading in securities markets, which in turn has helped to mold corporations.[5] Securities professionals have guided shareholders in need of advice when confronted with proxy contests or offers to purchase their shares. They have also often been the driving force pushing the market onward toward new securities or bringing new financing strategies to corporate management. Securities professionals such as J. P. Morgan have been instrumental in shaping firms as large as the United States Steel Corporation.[6] The securities industry has also shaped markets. It helped to develop the junk bond market in the 1980s to meet a need, just as it helped to develop preferred stock in the 1830s to meet a need.

Of all the important components of securities markets, purchasers have changed least over the past two hundred years. The roster of investors willing to put out money at low risk with the prospect of steady return has read the same: institutions, governments, and conservative individuals. When investing opportunities have been attractive enough, significant amounts of capital have come from abroad. It came from England in the early 1800s; it comes from Japan today.

Speculators predicting price changes, many willing to take large risks with the hope of even larger gains, have also been important securities purchasers for as long as there has been a market. Their methods of trading may have changed, but their objectives are essentially the same as when their ancestors entered into time bargains.[7] They are looking to make money. Performance in terms of the greatest increase in share price in the least amount of time motivated many of the earliest securities purchasers, just as it does today.[8]

Performance-motivated trading has periodically led to heavy trading volume. The high share turnover at the NYSE in the 1980s is nothing new.[9] Fast trading, accompanied by speculative excesses, has repeatedly overinflated securities prices in market booms accompanied by trading volume five or ten times greater than just a few years earlier. As part of this pattern, securities markets have then tumbled from these heights, often in "panics."[10] For the most part, such declines can be seen as corrections made necessary when price advances in the markets have outstripped material advances in the corporate world. Following each market collapse, securities prices and trading volume have typically receded slightly and then trudged along until the next growth spurt. Prices and volume rarely lose on the downside anything approaching the advances made on the upside. Even after the crash of October 1987, at year-end 1987, the Dow Jones Industrial Average was higher than at year-end 1986. Similar patterns have repeated themselves from the boom and bust of 1792 to the boom (and bust?) of today.

Speculators are remembered for their contributions to market panics, but they have also made lasting contributions to American economic development. Certainly, their most notable accomplishment is the establishment of the New York securities market, which, in turn, helped to make New York City an important financial center. Furthermore, speculation and risk-taking have launched enterprises that otherwise might never have had a chance. From The Manhattan Company, to the Mohawk & Hudson Railroad, to Xerox Coporation, intrepid risk-takers have bought shares in companies with uncertain futures. At each turn, innovators and speculators have found each other in securities markets and nurtured the enterprises that have made great breakthroughs.

Since the days of William Duer, attempts have existed to beat American securities markets. From Commodore Vanderbilt to Dennis Levine, traders have taken advantage of inside information. Modern regulation has eliminated the most blatant forms of such manipulation from the trading market, and traders or issuers may not now be able to pull off the same schemes, but abuses persist.[11] Corners like those engineered by Jacob Little or bear raids like those Daniel Drew was famous for still occur.[12] Today's stock market barons may not seem as notorious as those of 1850s and 1860s legends, but they are playing the same games and breaking the same rules. Simply put, the regulation of today has improved the integrity of the securities markets, but no matter how thorough, it can never completely tame the human spirit of avarice.

For almost 150 years, United States securities markets were virtually unregulated, and now extensive modern laws, regulations, and administrators are involved in smoothing securities trading. A close look at these regulations, however, reveals that their purpose and effect is to strengthen securities markets by improving investor confidence. The essence of securities law is not to regulate markets in a restrictive sense. Market participants can basically buy or sell as many shares as they wish, in whatever manner they wish. Consistent with this attitude, the NYSE and other self-regulatory organizations have retained a traditional independence from excessive government interference, an independence remarkable for institutions of their importance in this day and age.

Like securities laws that have strengthened securities markets, corporate laws have developed to foster corporate growth and to make corporations more flexible business tools.[13] Corporation law has not inhibited corporations from their important productive tasks. Looking at what has been regulated is important, but examining what has not is equally revealing. Corporate law has protected the public without unduly interfering with business decisions made by corporate managements.

Corporate enterprises have always been in some respects quasi-public and in others quasi-private. Early charters conferred monopoly privileges not so different from today's government defense contractors' insulation from competition. Outside of this type of direct support, governments have been disinclined to interfere with corporations except with attempts to improve their efficiency. Despite the hostile rhetoric of politicians and the popular press, business corporations have always gotten most of what they wanted.

Corporate law has created the basic model: a profit-maximizing enterprise where common shareholders apparently elect the directors responsible for overseeing the management of their company's affairs. In practice, however, ownership and control have been separated. Shareholders in early public corporations were generally as uninterested in corporate management and as supine in corporate governance as the shareholders of today. As corporations have grown and matured, managers have amassed more power, but there has been no fundamental evolution from an era where shareholders participated and contolled. Big public corporations today are built on the same foundation, calling for the same internal government, that supported public corporations like The Manhattan Company in 1800.

Throughout corporate history, securities markets have made the separation of ownership and control less troublesome by constraining managers. The available evidence generally supports the investors' welfare hypothesis and rejects the antagonism between management and shareholder interests described by Berle and Means. Firms must compete for investors' funds, and those that perform the best for investors are those that survive.[14] The stock market has held every management to the same standard: it has honored those who know how to make money.[15] Share prices have always been a measure of corporate performance. The modern corporate officer attempting to keep his share price up to thwart a raider is responding to pressures similar to those felt by managers of the Delaware and Hudson Canal Company, who needed solid share prices in order to maintain access to additional financing.[16] Managers who know how to make money have been kept in power by securities markets, while those who do not have been removed. There has also always been a market for corporate control. Occasionally, battles to topple managements were waged in the stock market in the early nineteenth century; their reappearance in the last twenty years is nothing new.

The restraint on managers is only one connection between securities markets and public corporations. For hundreds of years, the corporation has been an ingenious arrangement for collecting the funds of many savers in a common venture under centralized control, and securities markets have been there to perform their magic and mobilize capital. Citibank uses today's securities markets to raise capital by issuing stock, just as the Bank of New York did two hundred years ago. The methods used by issuers in the markets have grown increasingly intricate as equity and debt have been split into instruments tailored to the needs of issuers and purchasers alike, but the underlying role of securities markets remains unchanged.

The corporate system has always had one foot in the world of banking and credit and the other in the world of goods and services. Securities markets have been central to the development of the corporate system just as the corporate system has been central to the development of the American economy. Lamb stated without hesitation in 1883 that "The New York Stock Exchange is really the most important business organization in the United States,"[17] and a similar claim could still be made today. Whatever its shortcomings, the system of public corporations producing goods, alongside securities markets mobilizing and allocating capital, has thus far survived the market test against potential alternatives.

POLICY IMPLICATIONS

THESE CONTINUITIES in exchanges' efficiency, professionals' assistance, customers' avarice, issuers' needs, governments' noninterference, divorce of ownership and control, and the ability of securities markets to constrain managers all make up the basic structural elements of the corporate system, elements which have existed from the time when securities markets first began to quote and trade shares of corporate stock. Today's public corporations are essentially the same as the joint-stock companies formed hundreds of years ago. Consequently, the contradictions and conflicts that existed in the first public corporations still exist today.

These conflicts provoke age-old controversies. Reformers examine the corporation problem, looking for modifications that will correct whatever it is they see as a misdirected use of public corporations' immense power. In considering this complex issue, any attempt to define relevant questions and to seek responsible answers presupposes an understanding of the development of public corporations and securities markets. An appreciation of how we got here is necessary to know where we are and to plan intelligently where we are going.

Misreadings of corporate history distort attempts at corporate reform. Important proposals are based on replicating a past that never was.[18] Many suggestions for restructuring the corporate system flow from the notion that shareholders once controlled publicly owned corporations, but their controlling position has been eroded.[19] Ownership and control, however, have always been separated in public corporations. Current governance structure and practice are not recent abnormalities, but a natural characteristic of public corporations. Attempts to return control to shareholders who never had it are, therefore, misguided.

A more complete understanding reveals that securities markets replace

some of the restraint that is supposedly lost by the separation of ownership and control. Shareholders express their economic interest in the
corporation and confidence in its management by purchasing, retaining,
or selling shares. They are far less inclined to dissent by action taken within
the corporate framework. The price of shares measures investor interest
better than any vote at a shareholder meeting.

Securities markets have always been the primary forum for shareholders to exercise their rights. Their most important right, the right to sell
shares in a fair market, is now well protected, and that protection should
be maintained. Other regulation of securities trading markets that might
significantly interfere with free market functioning, such as trading halts
when securities prices rise or fall a preset amount, should be approached
with considerable caution.

Additional reforms of the corporate system aimed at protecting shareholders by making shareholder democracy function more effectively,
through improved voting power for example, are hardly worth pursuing.[20] Cumulative voting rights, preemptive rights, and the like merely
enhance the power of a vote that shareholders in large public corporations rarely use.

Shareholder votes are important, however, in one situation: a battle
for control. In that circumstance, shareholder votes have meaning and
should continue to have meaning. Managers should not be permitted to
disenfranchise shareholders by manipulating voting in control contests.
The recent rise of dual class recapitalizations of outstanding stock, which
effectively eliminate the voting rights of public shareholders, is a particularly harmful example of managers' disregard for shareholders.[21] Other
takeover defenses that have the effect of entrenching management are
equally disturbing. Poison pills that have no purpose other than slowing
tender offers need not be permitted to become commonplace. Nor does
there appear to be a compelling reason for new legislation to make takeovers more cumbersome for raiders. Such measures are generally inefficient when they allow corporate officers to escape the discipline of the
market for corporate control and to perpetuate themselves in office.

Elsewhere, corporate regulation is appropriate and necessary. The responsibilities that are the essential task of corporations and governments
can be allocated to each: corporations can continue to produce goods and
services; while governments can continue to lay down standards and
boundaries for corporate action, making it illegal, unprofitable, or both,
for corporations to engage in socially undesirable behavior.[22]

Beyond staying within the letter and spirit of governmental boundaries, corporate social responsibility can be more clearly defined. The term social responsibility is bandied about loosely, but it boils down to the hard case of corporate action requiring shareholders to bear a financial loss in order to effect some socially worthwhile goal. Such sacrifices of shareholder welfare are not the tasks of business corporations and corporate managements. Society is best served by business corporations that concentrate on the efficiency goal, leaving other socially desirable goals for specialized agencies more competent to undertake them.[23]

As long as profit maximization is one of society's highest values, public corporations and securities markets appear to be the best methods for achieving it. If one subscribes to the view that economic growth and prosperity of the type brought about through corporations is a social good, then nothing should be allowed to upset the internal governance structures that have, along with unique capabilities for mobilizing resources and adapting to change, so well served the corporate system in its steady expansion. The potential for the enormous contributions made by public corporations and securities markets has been inherent in their structures and relationships from the beginning. Too much ill-advised reform could restrict their ability to continue performing as well in the future.

New York Securities
Market Statistics: 1790–1840

F OLLOWING ARE assorted tables, accompanied by brief descriptions of their significance, sources, and shortcomings. Numerous conclusions throughout the book are based on these numbers, particularly in chapter 4. For the most part, the tables are a raw reporting of numbers; elaborate statistical techniques have not been used. The sources are, to our knowledge, the best available—primarily early newspapers and journals, but also early stock registers and NYS&EB Call Books. Any distortions due to the inaccuracies of early press reports are unavoidable.

SECURITIES QUOTED IN NEW YORK

T ABLE 1 clearly demonstrates the expanding number of securities issues that were quoted in the New York City press from 1792–1840. According to this indicator, the securities trading market grew steadily throughout its first half-century, while the numbers of stocks and bonds and the various categories of each grew at different rates. The trends in securities listings evident from this table presumably reflect the fortunes of the enterprises behind them. The first publicly quoted bonds were issued by the federal government, but, by the end of the period, state and municipal bonds were also commonly traded. Federal bonds were no longer available for trading after the federal government repaid the national debt in the 1830s. Stock listings increased rapidly while the bond list grew only slightly, particularly after 1800. Publicly traded corporate stocks were exclusively those of financial institutions for many years, with more in-

TABLE 1: Issues publicly quoted in New York: 1792–1840

Year	Total Issues	Bonds				Stocks				
		Total	Fed.	St.	Mun.	Total	Bank	Ins.	RR.	Other
1792	5	3	3			2	2			
1793	5	3	3			2	2			
1794	5	3	3			2	2			
1795	5	3	3			2	2			
1796	5	3	3			2	2			
1797	5	3	3			2	2			
1798	6	3	3			3	2	1		
1799	7	4	4			3	2	1		
1800	9	4	4			5	3	2		
1801	10	4	4			6	3	3		
1802	11	4	4			7	3	4		
1803	12	4	4			8	4	4		
1804	12	4	4			8	4	4		
1805	13	4	4			9	5	4		
1806	14	4	4			10	5	5		
1807	14	3	3			11	5	6		
1808	15	3	3			12	5	7		
1809	15	2	2			13	5	8		
1810	18	2	2			16	6	10		
1811	19	3	3			16	6	10		
1812	19	3	3			16	6	10		
1813	22	3	3			19	9	10		
1814	24	5	4		1	19	8	11		
1815	23	6	4		2	17	8	9		
1816	22	6	5		1	16	8	8		
1817	29	8	5	2	1	21	9	12		
1818	31	8	6	1	1	23	9	14		
1819	37	9	6	2	1	28	10	18		
1820	35	7	7			28	10	18		
1821	43	15	9	3	3	28	11	17		
1822	47	15	9	3	3	32	11	21		
1823	52	16	9	4	3	36	12	24		
1824	72	13	8	2	3	59	18	36		5
1825	85	16	9	4	3	69	20	42		7
1826	99	17	9	5	3	82	24	48		10
1827	102	15	6	9		87	20	45		22
1828	80	19	7	9	3	61	19	36		6
1829	81	20	8	9	3	61	18	38		5
1830	75	17	7	8	2	58	19	35	1	3
1831	74	16	6	8	2	58	18	35	1	4

TABLE 1 (Continued):

Year	Total Issues	Bonds				Stocks				
		Total	Fed.	St.	Mun.	Total	Bank	Ins.	RR.	Other
1832	81	15	6	9		66	25	34	7	
1833	84	14	4	10		70	25	34	7	4
1834	86	12	2	10		74	26	36	9	3
1835	91	11		10	1	80	23	33	9	15
1836	96	9		9		87	25	33	12	17
1837	96	9		9		87	26	27	13	21
1838	110	9		8	1	101	30	32	15	24
1839	107	7		6	1	100	30	31	16	23
1840	117	5		4	1	112	59	36	13	4

SOURCES: *New York Daily Gazette*, April 2, 1792; *Columbia Gazette*, September 2, 1793; *American Minerva*, February 1, 1794; *New York Herald*, December 16, 1795, April 3, 1796; *New York Price Current* (a supplement to the *New York Daily Advertiser*), 1797–1815; *New York Courier*, October 8, 1816; *New York Daily Advertiser*, October 4, 1817; *New York Spectator*, June 26, 1818; *New York Daily Advertiser*, May 15, 1819; *New York Evening Post*, October 13, 1820; *New York Daily Advertiser*, May 18, 1821, July 20, 1822, November 28, 1823, November 26, 1824, July 2, 1825, January 7, 1826, May 18, 1827; *New York Journal of Commerce*, November 27, 1828, January 9, 1829, March 13, 1830, January 12, 1831, December 26, 1832, April 5, 1833, January 7, 1834, February 17, 1835, June 14, 1836, January 4, 1837, January 9, 1838, January 8, 1839, June 3, 1840.

NOTE: Table 1 was compiled from representative quotation lists reported in New York each year. Some of the small discrepancies in the table, particularly the sharp decline in issues quoted in 1827–1828, we believe are attributable to changes in the data source rather than sharp cutbacks in the number of issues in the trading market. Different editors presumably had different standards for what securities to include in issues quoted lists, and different securities professionals presumably traded different securities and would therefore give different information to the press. Gaps in the table such as no reported trading of municipal issues in 1827 where three were reported in 1826 and 1828 can be attributed in the same way. The column of "other" stocks at first contained joint stock company shares and shares of "distant" (i.e., outside New York) companies. By 1840, many of the distant banks and trust companies that had been included in the "other" list were incorporated into the list with New York banks.

surance companies than banks. The number of railroad stocks grew dramatically after their introduction in 1830.

Broad changes in the numbers of securities quoted as reflected in table 1 appear to have been largely immune to changes in general economic fortune. We suggest three theories to explain the fact that significant swings in the number of quoted issues do not correspond well with other economic cycles. First, the number of issues publicly quoted is a blunt indicator and cannot reflect subtle changes in the fortunes of the entities represented; stocks can be traded while enterprises are struggling or while they are thriving. Second, the securities market was so small that the number of issues quoted was somewhat detached from the economy's periodic booms and busts; it was on the rise regardless of economic swings (trading volume, by contrast, was greatly affected by economic swings). Third, shares of other corporations were traded sporadically, but not steadily enough for a listing in the public press, and such unquoted trading likely fluctuated more than did the leading issues that were quoted. Evidence can be found of such trading in issues which never made it to the trading lists. According to Gregory, large denomination ($1,000) shares in manufacturing corporations were bought and sold in Boston, but the selling price rarely appeared in the public press.[1] All sales were through private negotiations, and only a small core of the leaders and their friends knew the actual prices. According to Davis, during the boom of 1792, scrips in the Million Bank and the Tammany Bank were traded, but they were not listed among issues quoted in the press.[2]

Another difficulty with table 1 arises because securities that were listed, but rarely traded, cannot be distinguished from those traded steadily. Listings of securities quoted regularly but traded infrequently were just as likely to represent lack of effort by the dealer providing the information to delete securities that did not belong on the list, or an effort to stretch out the list and use it as an advertisement for the securities business generally. Some listings include securities with large differentials between bid and asked prices, or only a bid or asked price. Securities listed without bid and asked quotations or those without a fairly narrow differential between the two are unlikely to be the subject of active trading. A buyer or seller of a listed, but not regularly traded, security faced difficulties in making a bargain on favorable terms. A world of difference separated quiet issues from those actively traded each day; actively traded securities had a narrow spread between bid and asked quotations, and it was simpler to find buyers or sellers willing and able to make a trade in them.

Therefore, the choices available to customers of the market may have been different from those indicated by table 1. Some securities not on the list were available for trading, and of those on the list, some were more available than others. Nevertheless, table 1 is useful for making comparisons over time, on the assumption that the proportions of actively traded and inactively traded securities remained roughly the same over different periods. It seems reasonable to conclude from table 1 that the choices available to securities purchasers steadily increased. By the 1830s, there were considerably more trading alternatives than in the 1790s.

TRADING VOLUME

THE BEST measure of the size of a trading market is activity as measured by sales volume. The larger the volume of trading, the better the customer's ability to buy or sell a security within a reasonable period of time at a price reasonably close to the last price. Before 1818, trading volume figures are simply not available. Our attempts to estimate trading volume before 1818 based on changes in price quotations proved fruitless. Fortunately, after 1817 and the formation of the NYS&EB, information about trading volume is available. Unfortunately, there are large gaps in that information, some due to a lack of NYS&EB records, some due to newspaper collections that are missing various years. The New York City fire of 1835 presumably destroyed many earlier records.

In the years for which we do have information, the growth of trading volume was dramatic. Table 2 demonstrates that average trading on the NYS&EB rose from 175 shares per day in 1818 to over 8,000 shares per day in 1835. Share volume on the Exchange had grown almost 50 times.

The data for table 2 come primarily from call books in the New York Stock Exchange archives and trades reported in the *New York Journal of Commerce*. The call book data are slightly suspect insofar as they appear to represent the efforts of one secretary to monitor stocks, perhaps only the stocks he was most interested in. The *Journal of Commerce* data have their own potential source of inaccuracies in volume figures reported to the press, yet manages to be the more complete record. In two years when both call book data and *Journal of Commerce* data are available, 1839 and 1840, the *Journal of Commerce* regularly reports 10 to 20 percent more transactions than those recorded in the call book. The call book that exists for 1835, which was not used in compiling table 2, appears to underreport more extremely. Daily average trading volume recorded in the 1835 call book is less than half of that reported by the *Journal of Commerce* (see table 3).

Table 2 records average trading volume over a number of days for each year. Our sample number of days is large enough to get a rough picture of the size of the market, but the yearly numbers can only represent broad changes in trading volume. Market swings clearly happen more quickly than a year at a time. In the crash year of 1837, for a particularly striking example, the average number of shares traded per day in January was 7,393; by June, the average had fallen to 1,534.

TABLE 2: NYS&EB trading volume: 1818–1840

	Daily average	Annualized volume[a]	High day	Low day	No. of days
1818	177	53040	765	0	64
1819	103	30670	498	0	78
1820	156	46710	674	0	101
1821	302	90719	1712	0	53
1824	1309	382656	3716	135	103
1825	1108	332400	2395	269	45
1828	166	49702	444	0	43
1829	158	47492	357	0	39
1830	456	136891	1215	20	49
1831	715	214500	1612	59	40
1832	1069	320711	4729	234	52
1833	1533	459913	2629	159	47
1834	2900	870220	4408	655	41
1835	8475	2542330	14286	1425	71
1836	5954	1786334	8716	1583	38
1837	4170	1251112	10468	724	40
1838	2561	768363	5756	289	38
1839	3843	1152940	8987	1536	45
1840	4266	1279857	6044	2294	42

SOURCES: 1818–1825 New York Stock & Exchange Board Call Books, New York Stock Exchange Archives; 1828–1840 New York Journal of Commerce.
[a]Annualized trading volume based on 300 trading days per year.

TABLE 3: Call books and press reports compared, 1835: shares traded: daily average

	Merchants Bank	Mechanics Bank	Ocean Ins.	Globe Ins.	No. of days
Call Book 1835	4.54	47.2	5.1	3.3	39
Journal of Commerce 1835	18.4	57.4	9.71	8.21	24

NOTE: The only conclusion to draw from these discrepancies between call book and *Journal of Commerce* records in later years is that our table 2 likely underreports the actual volume on the NYS&EB for the earlier years when we rely solely on the call books.

As discussed in chapter 4, trading volume was sensitive to the fortunes of the economy as a whole, much more so than was the number of issues quoted, and it was also subject to speculative booms and busts. Table 2 confirms the weak volume due to the depression of 1819, not recovering until at least 1821. With the speculation of the 1820s, volume first rose steadily, then rapidly into the boom of 1824 and 1825, only to drop off again until the early 1830s.

Trading volume before 1830 fluctuated greatly. On some days no shares were traded, on others nearly 4,000 shares changed hands. An early historian of the Exchange noted that 31 shares were traded on March 16, 1830, and he described this day as the dullest in stock market history.[3] He was wrong; there were actually many duller days, and some where no shares changed hands. There were days when trading would be suspended due to the death of a member, such as December 24, 1831 (Edward Lyde) or November 30, 1832 (Ludlow Dashwood),[4] and other days during slow periods, such as March 14 and 17, 1821, when no trades are recorded in the NYS&EB Call Books. On January 8, 1829, the *Journal of Commerce* claimed there were "no sales at brokers board," and on September 19, 1828, only a United States 6 percent bond was traded.

The boom that expanded later in the 1830s was much larger than that of the 1820s, peaking in the wild trading of 1835 when on October 5, 14,286 shares traded hands. Even after the collapse late in the 1830s, market volume was stronger than it had been ten years before.[5]

ISSUES TRADED

A FASCINATING aspect of the growth of trading volume is the small number of issues into which it was concentrated. With the exception of the boom years in the early 1820s, table 4 demonstrates that the number of issues traded on the exchange was a relatively small fraction of the entire trading list; the figures range roughly from 6 percent to 12 percent. Starting in 1830, the proportion grows, first into double digits on a constant basis, then reaching a peak of 36 percent in 1835 before sinking back at the end of the decade. It appears that trading in the early market, regardless of the number of securities listed, was largely concentrated in a few trusted securities. During the speculative booms of both the 1820s and 1830s, trading volume spread into additional securities, only to retreat during slower periods.

Table 5 on market leaders shows another dimension of the concentration of share volume. As it does today, share volume tended to concentrate in a relatively small number of issues. The Bank of the United States played the role of securities market leader until well into the 1830s. After its federal charter expired, the bank was a falling star. The Delaware and Hudson Canal Company, a favorite of the speculators, also accounted for a large portion of exchange trading in the 1830s. Railroads became market leaders soon after they appeared in 1830, accounting for more than a quarter of the volume after only three years of trading. By their fourth

TABLE 4: Average number of stock issues traded per day compared with the number of issues quoted at the NYS&EB 1818-1840

Year	Stock issues quoted (1)	Stock issues traded per day (2)	(2)/(1)	No. of days
1818	23	2.7	11.7%	64
1819	28	1.8	6.4%	79
1820	28	2.7	9.7%	101
1821	28	3.4	12.1%	53
1824	59	11.1	18.8%	103
1825	69	10.8	15.7%	45
1826	82	5.0	6.1%	24
1827	87	3.0	3.4%	13
1828	61	3.8	6.2%	43
1829	61	3.9	6.4%	39
1830	58	8.1	13.3%	49
1831	58	9.7	16.7%	45
1832	66	10.2	15.4%	52
1833	70	12.7	18.1%	47
1834	74	17.7	23.9%	44
1835	80	28.8	36.0%	71
1836	87	21.9	25.1%	38
1837	87	15.5	17.8%	40
1838	101	18.4	18.2%	38
1839	100	21.9	21.9%	45
1840	112	16.9	15.1%	42

SOURCES: 1818-1825 NYS&EB call books, New York Stock Exchange archives; 1826 *New York Daily Advertiser* price quotations with notations for "sales"; 1827 *New York Spectator* price quotations with notations for "sales"; 1828-1840 *New York Journal of Commerce*.

NOTE: The additional days in this sample not included in table 2 or table 5 are due to newspaper microfilms, where the number of issues quoted can be ascertained but trading volume cannot.

year on the NYS&EB—1834—more railroad shares were traded there than were shares in the Second Bank of the United States.

STOCK TRANSFER BOOK RECORDS

T HE SUBSCRIPTION books of public corporations are another reliable source of information about share trading volume during this period. Share transfers were recorded in books kept by issuers, and we have examined books for the Bank of New York (1791), The Manhattan Company (1800), and the Eagle Fire Insurance Company (1806).[6]

It appears that these institutions had little difficulty in raising the funds necessary to begin operations; upon an offering to sell to the public, shares

TABLE 5: Distribution of exchange volume among market leaders: Second Bank of the United States, Delaware and Hudson Canal Company, and railroads

Year	US Bank	D&H	RR	No. of days
1818	14.7%			64
1819	39.3%			78
1820	41.0%			101
1821	52.3%			53
1824	17.6%			103
1825	26.2%	3.6%		45
1828	39.9%	0.2%		43
1829	20.4%	11.2%		39
1830	23.1%	4.6%	0.1%	49
1831	4.1%	2.5%	9.0%	40
1832	21.9%	15.2%	13.5%	52
1833	38.1%	9.1%	27.5%	47
1834	10.1%	14.7%	41.8%	41
1835	1.9%	10.9%	45.4%	71
1836	10.1%	22.3%	34.8%	37
1837	3.9%	25.6%	42.2%	38
1838	5.2%	26.9%	40.3%	38
1839	2.2%	27.1%	38.3%	45
1840	6.4%	18.8%	24.0%	42

SOURCES: 1818–1825 NYS&EB call books, New York Stock Exchange archives; 1828–1840 *New York Journal of Commerce.*

TABLE 6: Stock transfer book records

	Bank of N.Y.		Eagle Fire Ins.		Manhattan Co.	
Year	Shares traded	Turnover	Shares traded	Turnover	Shares traded	Turnover
1791	2513	139.6%				
1792	2210	122.7%				
1793	1236	68.7%				
1794	759	42.2%				
1795	428	23.8%				
1796	386	21.4%				
1797	245	13.6%				
1798	324	18.0%				
1799	124	6.9%				
1800	110	6.1%			18667	45.4%
1801	112	6.2%			24564	59.9%
1802	141	7.8%			21976	53.6%
1803	154	8.6%				
1804	100	5.6%				
1805	101	5.6%				
1806	47	2.6%	1580	31.6%		
1807	97	5.4%	1280	25.6%		
1808	56	3.1%	2896	58.0%		
1809	64	3.6%	1876	37.6%		
1810	55	3.1%	920	18.4%		
1811	163	9.1%	3456	69.2%		
1812	35	1.9%	208	4.0%		
1813	73	4.1%	812	16.0%		
1814	51	2.7%				
1819	278	14.7%				
1834					10614	25.9%
1835					14364	32.1%
1836					13314	32.4%

NOTE: Turnover numbers represent the percentage of outstanding shares which changed hands during one year.
Bank of New York: shares $500, originally authorized capital $900,000 (1,800 shares), increased to $950,000 in 1813 (1,900 shares). (The 1791 turnover numbers are only for seven months of that year.)
Eagle Fire Insurance Company: shares $100, capital $500,000 (5,000 shares). (The Eagle Fire share trading numbers are based on trading for the last quarter of each year.)
Manhattan Company: shares $50, authorized capital $2,050,000 (41,000 shares).

were typically oversubscribed. At first, these shares were traded rapidly, presumably by speculators who paid their downpayments and then waited to see how the company would fare. After an initial gust of trading and transfer, the activity in these investment-quality issues quieted down some. For the Bank of New York, the activity quieted down considerably, although much of the drop-off in trading was also due to the bursting of the 1792 stockmarket bubble.[7] The Manhattan Company records at the beginning and at the end of the period covered by our research also show a significant decline in share transfers recorded. For the Eagle Fire Insurance Company, the drop-off in the number of share transfers recorded in the subscription books following the initial offer is not as dramatic as for the banks, but the low turnover of shares from 1818–1824, before the boom of the 1830s, as reported in table 7, makes it plausible to conclude that Eagle Fire Insurance trading quieted down after an initial spurt.[8]

OFF-BOARD TRADING

STOCK TRANSFER books provide numbers to back up the well-accepted proposition that considerble trading in the early New York

TABLE 7: Financial Institution Share Turnover

	Manhattan Bank	Eagle Ins.	Merchants Bank	Mechanics Bank	Ocean Ins.	Globe Ins.	No. of days
1818	7.5%	9.1%	1.1%	10.7%	8.9%	10.4%	54
1819	2.5%	1.0%		5.3%		6.7%	88
1820	4.9%						
1824	10.5%	2.1%	22.2%	12.3%	71.2%	14.9%	102
1835			18.5%	21.5%	29.1%	12.3%	24
1836	5.8%	24.7%	25.5%	7.5%	4.8%		25
1837	1.1%	10.5%	8.8%	1.2%			32
1838	3.1%	40.1%	8.1%	5.0%			36
1839	1.0%	6.3%	16.9%	12.5%			33

SOURCES: 1818–1824 from NYS&EB call books, New York Stock Exchange archives; 1835–1839 from New York Journal of Commerce.

NOTE: Manhattan Company: shares $50, capital, $2,050,000 (41,000 shares); Eagle Fire Insurance: shares $100, capital, $500,000 (5,000 shares); Merchants Bank: shares $50, capital, $1,250,000 (25,000 shares), in 1835, $1,490,000 (29,800 shares); Mechanics Bank: shares $25, capital $2,000,000 (80,000 shares); Ocean Insurance: shares $35, capital $350,000 (10,000 shares); Globe Insurance: shares $50, capital $1,000,000 (20,000 shares).

securities markets occurred outside of the NYS&EB, a proposition supported in the secondary sources. In an 1836 "memorial" to the New York
Legislature, the NYS&EB asserted that interest in securities was ascertained at the board's formal trading sessions and then satisfied by trading
"in the street." "[O]ne great object of meeting together in the morning
as a board, is to ascertain who desires to buy and sell a particular stock,
which buying and selling, to a great extent, is done publicly in the street,
or at the exchange after the board adjourns."[9]

In the 1790–1792 period, considerable amounts of trading reportedly
took place in coffee houses and on the street, and similar trading is known
to have taken place away from the Exchange in the 1840s and 1850s.[10]
It seems safe to assume that significant amounts of trading took place away
from the Exchange during the intervening period. The numerous brokers
who were excluded from the NYS&EB were forced to trade elsewhere.[11]
Exchange members themselves had strong incentives to trade off the exchange in order to trade as principals and make a dealer's turn, rather
than merely the low uniform commissions they were allowed on agency
trades at the Exchange.[12]

We have compared the trading in Manhattan Company shares reported in the stock register books with trading in Manhattan Company
shares at the NYS&EB for 1836. The stock register recorded 5.6 times
more trades than the Exchange. Similarly, in two months of 1819 when
we can compare Bank of New York stock register books with Exchange
records, we find the stock register recorded 7.2 times as many trades. This
sample is admittedly small, but it does support the existence of trading
outside of the Exchange.

The actual amount of trading outside the Exchange is very difficult to
estimate from numbers of this type. Actual trading in the securities market differed from stock register reports in two respects. First, stock registers recorded transactions, such as gifts or bequests, which did not origi-
nate in the trading markets. Second, time bargains in the securities markets
which were settled without the transfer of shares were not represented in
stock registers. An additional distortion arises because trades away from
the Exchange were likely to be dealer trades, which required two transactions to transfer shares between public customers: first, a sale by a customer to a dealer and, second, a resale by a dealer to another customer.
In many cases, matching pairs of these transactions were listed in the stock
register books.

Our attempt to come up with a multiplier of Exchange volume to represent actual volume followed this method. First, the stock transfer books

record approximately six times as much volume as the Exchange records. We assume that the necessary reduction of this number to account for nonmarket transfers is at least offset by an equal amount to account for time bargains not reflected in the stock register. We then cut the number in half to account for dealer trades. As so adjusted, our multiplier for off-board trading appears to be three times the volume on the Exchange. Perhaps in slow periods the multiplier was only two. In any event, this figure is an extremely crude ballpark measure. Yet it does seem plausible to conclude that volumes of 3,900 shares per day in 1824 and 25,000 shares per day in 1835 were actually traded in New York.

TURNOVER

S TOCK TRANSFER books provide a glimpse at the turnover of a few stocks as reflected in table 6. Tables 7, 8, and 9, compiled from the NYS&EB call books and the *New York Journal of Commerce*, provide a much larger picture.

Table 7 compiles turnover numbers at the NYS&EB for certain seasoned stocks of banks and insurance companies. With the isolated instance of Ocean Insurance's 71.2 percent turnover in 1824, during the period that speculators such as John Michael O'Connor were trading the stock heavily, the turnover rates rarely exceed 25 percent, and frequently fall below 10 percent. We conclude from this sample that these stocks, and probably most stocks of financial institutions, were not churned on the exchange by speculators; rather, they were primarily bought and sold by investors.[13]

Table 8 compiles turnover numbers for the market leaders of this period. These numbers show incredibly high turnovers for shares that were presumably the objects of speculation. A rate of 2094 percent for Delaware and Hudson Canal Company share turnover in 1836 means the outstanding shares were sold on the exchange more than twenty times over in that year.[14] The high turnover of shares in the Bank of the United States in 1833 and 1836 was likely fueled by speculation stemming from its changing political fortunes. Comparing table 8 with table 5 demonstrates that the tremendous turnover of shares in the Bank of the United States and the Delaware and Hudson Canal Company did not translate into a considerable increase in the percentage of exchange trading these stocks accounted for. Their turnover simply kept pace with a market where shares of many corporations were being traded at very rapid rates.

Table 9 reflects the dramatic development that occurred after 1830. The newly issued railroad stocks, traded on the exchange for the first time, turned over with spectacular velocity. The numbers are sobering; it was common for the entire issue of shares outstanding of a stock "in play" to turn over more than 10 times in a year. In 1835, the entire outstanding issue of shares of the Harlem Railroad was traded over 30 times. In one month alone, February 1835, the entire outstanding issue of Harlem

TABLE 8: Market leader turnover

Year	Second Bank of the United States		Delaware & Hudson Canal Co.		No. of days
	Volume	Turnover	Volume	Turnover	
1818	7710	13.7%			64
1819	12360	22.1%			78
1820	18720	33.4%			101
1821	47451	84.7%			53
1824	68010	121.4%			103
1825	87060	155.5%	24138	160.9%	45
1828	19860	35.4%	75	0.4%	43
1829	9437	16.9%	5310	31.2%	39
1830	31560	56.4%	6369	37.4%	49
1831	8850	15.8%	7313	43.0%	40
1832	70350	125.6%	48818	287.2%	52
1833	175717	313.8%	45548	267.9%	47
1834	88200	157.5%	128260	754.5%	41
1835	48480	86.6%	276608	1627.1%	71
1836	182197	325.4%	397824	2093.8%	38
1837	52410	93.6%	117846	620.2%	40
1838	38730	69.2%	282000	1484.2%	38
1839	25920	46.3%	312747	1646.0%	45
1840	81907	146.3%	240386	1265.2%	42

NOTE: Volume is based on 300 trading days per year.
Second Bank of the United States: shares $100; capital $35,000,000 (350,000 shares). 70,000 shares were held by the federal government. Turnover is based on an estimated 20% of the outstanding publicly issued shares (56,000 of 280,000) in the New York market. For some of these years, the number of shares in the New York market was considerably less, and turnover of those shares that were in the city was therefore even higher. (See Catteral, *The Second Bank of the United States*, p. 508.)
Delaware and Hudson Canal Company: shares $100, capital $1,500,000 (15,000 shares); 1825 $1,700,000 (17,000 shares); 1835 $1,900,000 (19,000 shares). For more on the Delaware and Hudson Canal Company see chapter 7.

Railroad stock turned over 2.71 times. Fowler claims that the whole capital stock sometimes changed hands in a single day.[15] According to Medbery, Harlem Railroad, with 15,000 shares, was subject to an audacious corner, in which 64,000 shares were bought by a ring within a period of seven weeks.[16] Similarly, in June 1836, the outstanding shares in the Mohawk and Hudson Railroad turned over 1.89 times.[17] These stocks were clearly passed around like hot potatoes.[18]

BOND TRADING

TABLE 10 quantifies, by value, the percentage of NYS&EB trading accounted for by bonds. This proportion is a useful index of investment versus speculation on the NYS&EB. Over long periods of time, particularly before the late 1830s, bonds appear to have been considered safer investments than stocks; their prices were more stable, and they were more appropriate as investment-grade securities to be held by the cautious.[19]

The percentages of bond versus stock trading over time reinforces the

TABLE 9: Railroad turnover

	Mohawk	Saratoga	B&P	NYP&B	Harlem	Utica	No. of days
1831	117%						24
1832	310%	86%	891%		114%		35
1834	1240%	1000%	891%	140%	195%	63%	21
1835	1460%	983%	111%	147%	3040%	282%	27
1836	2036%		858%	73%	168%	671%	29
1837	1313%		558%	92%	450%	294%	37
1838	616%		66%	380%	687%	41%	18
1839	624%		23%	210%	1490%	18%	33

NOTE: Mohawk & Hudson Railroad of New York: shares $100, capital 1826, $500,000 (5,000 shares), April 1832, $600,000 (6,000 shares), February 1834, $850,000 (8,500 shares); 1839, $1,000,000 (10,000 shares);
Saratoga & Schenectady Railroad of New York: shares $100, capital, $300,000 (3,000 shares);
Boston & Providence Railroad of Massachusetts: shares $100, capital 1831, $1,000,000 (10,000 shares), 1839, $1,782,000 (17,820 shares);
New York, Providence, & Boston Railroad of Connecticut and Rhode Island: shares $100, capital $1,508,000 (15,080 shares);
Harlem Railroad of New York: shares $50, capital 1831, $350,000 (7,000 shares), April 1832, $500,000 (10,000 shares), April 1835, $750,000 (15,000 shares);
Utica & Schenectady Railroad of New York: shares $100, capital $2,000,000 (20,000 shares).

picture of periods of booms leading up to and resulting in crashes. As speculation advanced in each cycle, the percentages of bond trading fell.[20] Bond trading constituted a large portion of exchange trading volume in the earliest years, when there were few publicly traded corporate stocks and many different bonds available. The percentage of bond as opposed to stock trading fell as the speculative boom grew toward its 1825 peak, and by the crash in 1826, bond trading had virtually disappeared from the Exchange. Speculators were buying the riskier stock issues so heavily

TABLE 10: Bond Trading on the NYS&EB Compared with Stock Trading by Value

	Bond Trading Value Daily Avg. (1)	Stocks Traded Daily Avg. (2)	Stock Value Daily Avg. (3)	Value of Total Trading Daily Avg. (1)+(3)	Bond Trading Percent of Value
1818	$6,260	175	$8,750	$15,010	41.7%
1819	5,463	105	5,250	10,713	50.1%
1820	2,609	152	7,600	10,209	25.6%
1824	2,526	1309	65,450	67,976	3.7%
1828	8,994	166	8,300	17,244	52.2%
1829	4,426	158	7,900	12,362	35.8%
1830	3,356	456	22,800	26,156	12.8%
1831	2,688	715	35,370	38,438	6.9%
1832	2,629	1069	53,450	56,079	4.7%
1833	779	1533	76,650	79,279	3.4%
1834	250	2900	145,000	145,250	0.0%
1835	13	8475	423,750	423,763	0.0%
1836	160	5954	297,700	297,860	0.0%
1837	0	4170	208,500	208,500	0.0%
1838	267	2561	128,050	128,317	0.0%
1839	56	3843	142,150	142,206	0.0%
1840	1,576	4266	213,300	214,876	0.1%

SOURCES: NYS&EB call books, New York Stock Exchange archives; *New York Journal of Commerce.*

NOTE: For table 10, we have made the large assumption that the average value of shares traded on the Exchange at this time was $50. Many shares had a value of $100, but few regularly traded shares had greater values and a considerable number had lesser ones, thus $50 seems a reasonable estimate. Column 3 is column 2 × $50. We added the total value of bonds and stocks (column 1 plus column 3) and calculated the percentage of trading that was accounted for by bonds.

that bond trading was overwhelmed. Then, after the crash of 1826, conservatism returned to the NYS&EB, and bonds again became an important percentage of trades, peaking in 1828, when over 50 percent of the trades at the NYS&EB involved bonds. The pattern repeated itself in the early 1830s, as speculation again engulfed securities markets and bond trading became less significant. Once again, bond trading was dwarfed by stock trading at the peak of the speculative boom. After the tremendous crash in the late 1830s, significant bond trading reappeared on the NYS&EB. The swings up and down of bond trading in opposition to securities market booms and busts tend to confirm the hypothesis that speculators, who preferred stocks, boosted volume in the peaks, and investors, who preferred bonds, were more prevalent market customers during the lulls.

It must be noted that there were other large factors at work in the bond market over this period. The federal government, for example, redeemed all of its bonds in the 1830s; hence, there were no federal issues in the market. States, on the other hand issued bonds freely. By 1839 and 1840, states were on the verge of repudiating their bonds. By then, any who felt bonds were a conservative investment were in for a rude awakening.

TIME TRANSACTIONS

T ABLE 11 represents the fruits of our attempt to determine what percentage of trading on the exchange consisted of time bargains as opposed to cash sales. This table is useful in demonstrating that for much of the pre-1840 period, at least 20 percent of transactions on the Exchange were time bargains. We have reason to believe that the percentage was considerably higher. Clearly, the 1828 numbers from the *Journal of Commerce* reporting no time transactions are inaccurate. The reporter or editor simply did not make a distinction between cash sales and time bargains. In comparing the 1835 NYS&EB call book and the *Journal of Commerce*, it appears that the *Journal of Commerce* only reported approximately half of the time transactions as such. If this pattern were true for all *Journal of Commerce* reporting, then all of the percentages after 1828, calculated from *Journal of Commerce* numbers, should be doubled. Additionally, we designated time bargains to be those with settlement dates more than three days in the future. Typical contracts were those for "cash" to be settled on the same day, contracts in the "regular way" to be settled the next day, and contracts "at three days" to be settled in three days.

We had hoped to demonstrate with table 11 that the frequency of time bargains increased in boom years when speculative trading dominated the NYS&EB. However, due to the discrepancies in reporting of time bargains and the inherent difficulty of lumping together time bargains of four days with those of sixty days, we do not feel that any solid conclusions can be drawn from table 11 in comparing the percentage of Exchange trading that took the form of time bargains from year to year.

BROKER-DEALER TRADES

WITHOUT AN exchange, a smoothly functioning securities market requires persons, today described as market makers, who stand ready to buy or sell certain securities on a continuous basis. Such market

TABLE 11: Time bargains as percentage of NYS&EB trading

	Volume Daily Average	Percent of Exchange Volume	No. of Days
1818	31.3	17.7%	64
1819	35.6	34.6%	78
1820	41.4	26.5%	101
1821	21.2	7.0%	53
1824	259.6	19.8%	103
1825	165.2	14.9%	45
1828	0	0.0	43
1829	12.5	7.9%	39
1830	3.4	0.7%	49
1831	14.4	2.0%	40
1832	19.8	3.6%	52
1833	100.0	18.5%	47
1834	675.1	23.3%	41
1835	413.2	4.9%	71
1836	1098.2	15.5%	38
1837	550.0	13.2%	40
1838	570.2	22.3%	38
1839	841.8	19.7%	45
1840	1116.0	25.9%	42

SOURCES: NYS&EB call books; New York Stock Exchange Archives; New York *Journal of Commerce*.

making appears to have been common in early New York securities trading. Table 12 summarizes broker-dealer principal trading, in Manhattan Company shares, in two different periods. The term "broker-dealer" refers to anyone who devoted at least part of his time to the securities business. Most securities professionals in this period also did other things; they handled foreign exchange, bank notes, commercial paper, commodities, insurance, and more.

In 1800, broker-dealers accounted for 37.4 percent of all trading, a significantly large figure, and in 1835 they accounted for an astounding 89.9 percent of all share volume. Clearly, the broker-dealers were a vital link in the securities trading process. Many of the transfers not involving broker-dealers as principals, particularly by the 1830s when broker-dealers were prevalent in New York, were probably either trades in which they acted as agents or nonmarket transfers.

Analysis of professional trading in Manhattan Company shares for the last five months of 1800 reveals that one broker-dealer, Nathan Prime, probably the most important securities professional in New York during the 1790–1840 era, accounted for 61 of the 87 broker-dealer trades, and for 2,465 of the 2,894 broker-dealer shares traded. These proportions suggest that Prime was acting as a market-maker in Manhattan Company shares, standing ready and announcing his readiness to buy and sell those shares.

That he actually functioned as a market-maker is shown by table 13 which analyzes Prime's trading over eight months from July 1800 to March

TABLE 12: Manhattan Company broker-dealer trading

	Transactions			Volume		
	Total	B-D	B-D%	Total	B-D	B-D%
1800	202	79	34.2%	7222	2699	37.4%
1801	217	94	43.3%	7785	3206	41.2%
1834	96	68	70.8%	3262	2374	72.8%
1835	90	67	74.4%	4819	4333	89.9%

SOURCE: Manhattan Company Stockholder receipt books, Chase Manhattan Company archives, last quarter of each year.

NOTE: Broker-dealer trades include trades as principal or dealer. Brokers could act as both, as evidenced by Nathan Prime buying shares after Prime and Ward formed. Agency trades (as "attny") not included.

TABLE 13: Nathan Prime, trades for own account, Manhattan Company shares, July 29, 1800–March 31, 1801

Date	Buy	Sell	Date	Buy	Sell
Subs.	20		11/17	7	
7/29	100		11/18		7
8/1		10	12/3	25	
		40	12/4	130	20
8/2		8			100
8/13		42	12/6		70
8/29	10		12/10		42
9/2	100		12/15	10	10
9/5		2	1/3	26	
		16	1/5		76
9/6		30			24
		8	1/10		100
9/8		45	1/12	100	
9/10	34		1/15	60	10
9/15		2		100	50
9/22		20			35
		100			30
9/24	34				5
9/27		20			2
9/29	100	50			5
10/1	62	50	1/16	100	200
10/2	100	100		20	
10/3	50	100		25	
10/8	135	45	1/17		20
10/9		100	1/22	10	10
10/16	40		1/30	10	10
10/18		20	2/3	7	7
		19	2/12		10
10/20		25			40
10/21		27	2/13		30
		1	2/14		3
10/23		40	2/20		17
		5	2/23		12
		4			3
		5	2/25	61	40
		1			14
		15			5
		10	2/27	100	33
11/3		100			5
		25			5
		8			30

TABLE 13: (Continued)

Date	Buy	Sell	Date	Buy	Sell
11/6		8	3/6		29
11/7	33	10			8
	4	3	3/8	27	9
		2	3/9		27
11/10		22	3/31	11	

1801. Prime began with a long position of 100 shares acquired by sub-scription on July 29, sold off his shares, replenished his inventory a month later, repeated the sales, and so on. He was in the market continuously. Public customers and probably other broker-dealers came to him to exe-cute orders for Manhattan Company shares. Leonard Bleecker, also a broker-dealer, who did the next largest volume, accounted for only 14 trades and 163 shares during the same period.

By 1835, when professional principal trades accounted for almost 90 percent of share volume, many more professionals were active securities traders. By that time, as table 14 shows, no one broker-dealer accounted for more than 10 percent of the total volume. No one broker had to make a market, because the New York Stock & Exchange Board brought buy-ers and sellers together in a central market.

These five professionals accounted for 67.2 percent of broker-dealer trades and 90.2 percent of broker-dealer share volume. Some fourteen others we can identify as broker-dealers accounted for other professional

TABLE 14: Manhattan Company broker-dealer trading, September through December 1835

Broker-Dealer	Trades	Shares
Coit & Cochrane	12	1071
T. Ward	15	871
Prime, Ward, & King	6	1114
J. Little	8	405
S. Allen	4	450
Total	45	3911

trading. A high proportion consisted of trades in which both sides were broker-dealers. Such inter-dealer activity accounted for 53.7 percent of all professional trading in 1835, much more than in the earlier period.

In many of these trades, a broker-dealer purchased shares and immediately resold them. These appear to have been so-called "riskless principal" transactions that allow a professional to earn a dealer's turn instead of only an agency commission.

Analysis of Eagle Fire Insurance share transfer records reveals that professionals also made markets in relatively small issues. As shown in table 15, broker-dealers accounted for as much as 87.2 percent of the trading during the years from 1806–1813.

Examination of Nathan Prime's trades shows that he or his firm, which was organized at the time, was making a market for Eagle Insurance shares, just as in Manhattan Company Shares. Prime's purchases and sales were almost evenly balanced. His long position rarely exceeded 50 shares, and he appears to have even more rarely gone short. The trading of Leonard Bleecker and Lewis & Lawrence, other broker-dealers, shows a similar pattern. Together, these three broker-dealers accounted for 58.4 percent of the 245 transactions that took place in this small issue between July 16, 1806 and December 31, 1808. As in most new issues, trading activity was high during the issue's first years, high enough for professionals to assume the dealer's risk even in this small issue.

This analysis of professional trading in two issues and three time pe-

TABLE 15: Eagle Fire Insurance Company broker-dealer trading

	Transactions			Share Volume		
	Total	B-D	B-D %	Total	B-D	B-D %
1806	14	3	18.8%	395	50	12.7%
1807	20	7	35.0%	320	108	33.6%
1808	43	35	81.4%	724	632	87.2%
1809	22	12	54.3%	469	146	31.1%
1810	21	15	71.4%	230	157	68.0%
1811	25	19	76.0%	864	549	63.6%
1812	5	4	80.0%	52	42	80.7%
1813	11	4	36.4%	203	14	6.8%

SOURCE: Eagle Fire Insurance Company share transfer book, New-York Historical Society; trades during the last quarter of each year.

NOTE: Broker-dealer trades include trades as principal or dealer; agency trades not included.

riods reveals a great deal about securities professionals in the early market. Less thorough examinations of the shareholder account ledgers for Chemical Bank (1824–1837) and the Bank of New York show a similar concentration of shares traded in the names of broker-dealers. These findings demonstrate that broker-dealers have been a central part of securities trading for as long as there have been securities markets. Trends over time revealed in these tables, particularly the growth in broker-dealer transactions, lead us to the reasonable conclusion that securities professionals became more important to the market as it grew in size and complexity. The increased number of professionals involved reflects the growth of the securities industry generally.

YIELDS TO INVESTORS ON BONDS

I NTEREST-BEARING federal bonds paid a fixed percentage of par to investors. Prices of federal bonds strengthened from 1792 to 1817, gradually resulting in a lower yield to investors on their purchase price. When 6 percent federal bonds dipped below par in the late 1790s, they yielded purchasers a return of more than 6 percent on their investment, but by 1802, when they were again selling at par, they once more provided a 6 percent return.[21] Over the next three decades, with the notable exception of the 1812–1815 years, federal bonds sold at prices that returned between 5 percent and 6 percent to maturity.

Table 16 provides a clear picture of the cost to New York and the corresponding yields to investors for the Erie Canal loans. These loans appear to have cost New York less than federal loans cost the United States Government. The first Erie Canal loan carried a coupon rate of 6 percent and sold at par. The remaining loans were almost evenly divided between 5 percent and 6 percent coupon bonds. In each case the successful bidders either paid a premium or purchased the bonds at a discount from the nominal price. When the premium or discount is factored in, the net cost to the state was generally between 5 percent and 6 percent. A number of the last Erie loans actually carried an effective interest rate of slightly more than 4 percent, and one, the 5 percent loan of July 19, 1824, taken by Prime, Ward, and Sands at a premium of 10.62 percent, cost the state only 3.96 percent.

Most of the Erie Canal issues were presumably resold by the original purchaser to individual investors, many of them foreign investors. The intermediary had to make a profit, and thus the yield to the investor was slightly less than the yield would have been to the original purchasers. The 1824 issue taken by Prime, Ward, and Sands at 3.96 percent was probably resold to give investors a return to maturity of 3.85 percent or less.

Many comparable loans for other state canal projects provided investors with slightly higher yields to compensate for what must have been seen as slightly higher risks. In 1825, a $400,000 Ohio loan at 5 percent interest sold at $97.5 per $100 par, to yield 5.128 percent;[22] in 1827, a $900,000 Ohio Canal Loan at 6 percent interest sold at $107.26 per $100 par for a yield of 5.6 percent;[23] and in 1828 a $1,200,000 Ohio Canal Loan at 6 percent interest sold $107.07 per $100 par for a yield of 5.6 percent.[24]

TABLE 16: Yields to investors on New York Canal loans

Date	Maturity	Amount (thous)	Interest	Subscriber	Price	Yield
6/13/17	1837	$200	6%	NY State Bk	Par	6.00%
7/15/18	1837	200	6%	NY State Bk	104.5	5.49%
3/8/19	1837	175	6%	NY State Bk	101.5	5.83%
5/24/19	1837	200	6%	Fmrs & Mchnks Bk	102.63	5.70%
10/27/19	1837	25	6%	Fmrs & Mchnks Bk	Par	6.00%
1/5/20	1837	130	6%	Fmrs & Mchnks Bk	Par	6.00%
1/25/20	1837	300	6%	Fmrs & Mchnks Bk	101	5.88%
8/21/20	1837	151	6%	NY Savings Bk	108	5.05%
8/21/20	1837	112.5	6%	NY Savings Bk	107.5	5.11%
1/15/21	1837	400	5%	Fmrs & Mchnks Bk	106.5	4.27%
6/25/21	1837	600	5%	Fmrs & Mchnks Bk	106.5	4.27%
10/20/21	1837	400	5%	Fmrs & Mchnks Bk	103.55	4.60%
5/22/22	1837	600	6%	Fmrs & Mchnks Bk	101.25	5.84%
9/23/22	1845	250	6%	JJ Astor & Sons	107.25	5.08%
10/14/22	1845	50	5%	Bank of Troy	99	5.09%
10/14/22	1845	75	5%	Farmers Bank	96.5	5.33%
10/14/22	1845	75	5%	Bank of Troy	97.375	5.25%
10/14/22	1845	50	6%	Farmers Bank	108	5.23%
10/14/22	1845	65	6%	H. Hendricks	107.81	5.25%
10/14/22	1845	52	6%	Levi Colt	107.5	5.22%
10/14/22	1845	100	6%	NY State BK	107.25	5.25%
10/14/22	1845	33	6%	NY State Bk	107.125	5.26%

SOURCE: Report of the Comptroller, New York State Assembly Documents, 60th Sess., Doc. No. 4, Exhibit F (January 4, 1837), pp. 53–57.

NOTE: Amounts are in thousands of dollars. Interest is the coupon rate for the bond. Where

New York State loans not linked to canals but merely for financing government operations were considered safe investments. As such, they offered low yields to investors. $100,000 worth of New York State bonds at 5 percent interest sold at $108.375 per $100 par for a yield of 4.613 percent.[25] Similar government financings by the city of Boston and the commonwealth of Pennsylvania also provided low yields.[26]

The panic of 1837, with its wholesale repudiation by many states of their bonded indebtedness, reminded investors that even bonds backed by the credit of a state carried the risk of default and yields on state bond instruments rose accordingly. In 1835, the New York Canal 5 percent bonds were priced at $112 per $100 par to yield investors a return of 4.4 percent to maturity. In 1840, the same bonds were selling at $88, a price that yielded 6 percent to maturity. The drop in price of Ohio 6 percent

TABLE 16: (Continued)

Date	Maturity	Amount (thous)	Interest	Subscriber	Price	Yield
1/2/23	1845	300	5%	Fmrs & Mchnks Bk	99	5.01%
3/15/23	1845	25	6%	Nathan Warren	100.52	4.95%
3/15/23	1845	25	6%	R.P. Hart	101.05	4.90%
3/15/23	1845	25	6%	Beers & Bunnell	102.08	4.80%
3/15/23	1845	30	6%	S. McCoun	100.31	5.97%
3/15/23	1845	25	6%	H. Hendricks	101.5	5.84%
3/15/23	1845	10	6%	H. Hendricks	100.8	5.92%
3/15/23	1845	15	6%	H. Hendricks	100.76	5.92%
3/15/23	1845	145	6%	Fmrs & Mchnks Bk	100.1	5.99%
6/9/23	1845	500	5%	Fmrs & Mchnks Bk	93.5	5.62%
8/12/23	1845	500	5%	Fmrs & Mchnks Bk	95.5	5.43%
1/5/24	1845	200	5%	Fmrs & Mchnks Bk	99.5	5.05%
5/3/24	1845	200	5%	LeRoy, Bayard & C	108.01	4.22%
7/19/24	1845	200	5%	Prime, Wd & Sands	110.62	3.96%
7/19/24	1845	50	5%	John G. Warren & S.	110	4.02%
7/19/24	1845	100	5%	Fmrs & Mchnks Bk	110	4.02%
7/19/24	1845	68.3	5%	Fmrs & Mchnks Bk	109.6	4.06%
11/24/24	1845	450	5%	General Fund	109.6	4.06%
7/15/25	1826	100	6%	Fmrs & Mchnks Bk	Par	6.00%
7/15/25	1826	170	6%	School Fund	Par	6.00%

there is more than one purchaser recognized in the source, the primary purchaser only is listed here. Price is per $100 nominal bond. Yield to maturity is the bond's nominal interest rate, adjusted for the premium over, or discount from, the face amount, amortized from purchase date to maturity.

bonds during the same period was even greater, from $120 per $100 par in 1835, for a yield of 5 percent, to $91 in 1840, for a yield of 6.6 percent.[27]

YIELDS TO INVESTORS ON STOCKS

E ARLY STOCKS were generally less secure investments than bonds; the assurance of repayment from a group of entrepreneurs was never as solid as that from a government. Accordingly, the earliest bank shares carried a somewhat higher return than bonds.

Well-managed banks paid steady dividends. The Manhattan Company paid 9 percent of par most years ($4\frac{1}{2}$ percent on January 1 and July 1) before 1822, when the dividend dropped to 7 percent. The dividend then rose in 1834 to 8 percent, and reached as high as 12 percent in 1840.[28] The price of Manhattan Company stock ranged during most of this period between 110 and 125, resulting in a yield to purchasers between $5\frac{1}{2}$ percent and 6 percent.[29] The Bank of New York generally paid 8 percent of par per year in the 1830s, but occasionally paid as high as 14 percent,[30] while the stock's price ranged from 115 to 130, resulting in a yield to purchasers between 6 percent and $6\frac{1}{2}$ percent. Shares in the First Bank of the United States averaged dividends of $8\frac{1}{2}$ percent of par during the bank's twenty-year life, and sold at around 150 for a yield of 5.6 percent.[31] The Second Bank of the United States generally paid between 5 percent and 7 percent of par from 1823 to 1834, and shares were priced from 110 to 125, resulting in a yield of $4\frac{1}{2}$ percent to $5\frac{1}{2}$ percent.[32] Generally, bank dividends in New York averaged about 7 percent.[33] Similarly, in Boston, bank dividends were occasionally as high as 12 percent, but usually were about 6 percent to 7 percent.[34]

Insurance company shares, apparently considered riskier investments because the soundness of the projects they insured was often suspect, often provided a higher yield than bank shares. An 1826 comparison of the dividends paid by banks and insurance companies found that insurance companies paid, on average, 2 percent more than banks.[35] An 1828 nine-year review of corporate earnings in New York City reported a 6.6 percent average return on insurance stocks and 5.4 percent on bank shares.[36]

Eagle Fire Insurance company shares ranged in price from 107 to 120, and its annual dividend of 9 percent of par indicated an average return of 8 percent.[37] The other insurance company figures available simply report high, sometimes incredibly high, dividends. The Insurance Company of North America paid dividends of 12 percent, 22 percent and 28.75 percent in 1794, 1795, and 1796.[38] In 1817, the Mutual Insurance Company of New York paid 9 percent,[39] the Globe Insurance Company paid 8 percent,[40] and the National Insurance Company paid 16 percent.[41] The Mississippi Marine and Fire Insurance Company of New Orleans declared a semi-annual dividend of 25 percent in 1828.[42] As Medbery describes it: "From five to ten percent semi-annual dividends were repeatedly declared by Insurance Companies. . . . In 1828 the Ocean Insurance Company netted the holders of its stock twenty percent. . . . The American Insurance Company in 1829 declared a fifteen-percent semi-annual dividend."[43] According to Gregory, insurance stocks showed the greatest profits in Nathan Appleton's portfolio.[44]

Because of the installment method of payment for shares, some of these dividends were being paid to investors who had not fully paid their shares. Thus, the return on the amount the investor had actually paid was often higher than the yields computed above.[45]

Comparisons of Securities Markets in New York and other U.S. Cities: 1790–1840

VOLUME COMPARISONS

THE LITTLE information available on trading volume in other cities tends to confirm that New York City securities markets were the most active in the United States from 1790 to 1840. Reliable comparisons of trading for the years 1837–1840 reveal that reported share volume in Philadelphia was only 13.9 percent of the volume in New York, and reported share volume in Boston was only 9.9 percent of that in New York.

Table 17 is drawn from the *New York Journal of Commerce*. It is likely that the *Journal of Commerce* underreported transactions in the other cities, particularly of issues with a primarily local market. However, a Philadelphia paper, *The Financial Register*, also published securities trading volume information in this period, for both New York and Philadelphia. These numbers, included in table 18, support the conclusion that trading volume in Philadelphia was less than 15 percent of volume in New York.

TABLE 17: Volume of Shares Traded: Daily Average

	N.Y.	Phil.	Bost.	Phil. vs. N.Y.	Bost. vs. N.Y.	No. of Days
1837	3153	937	525	29.7%	16.7%	27
1838	2633	361	353	13.6%	13.4%	18
1839	3882	445	241	11.5%	6.2%	15
1840	4238	181	232	4.3%	5.5%	17
Total				13.9%	9.9%	

TABLE 18: Volume of Shares Traded: Daily Average

	N.Y.	Phil.	Phil. vs. N.Y.	No. of Days
1837	1418	248	17.5%	16
1838	2178	221	10.2%	23
Total			13.0%	

Trading volume data for Philadelphia are also available for 1831 from *Hazard's Magazine* (Philadelphia). A comparison of *Hazard's* Philadelphia trading volume figures with New York trading volume numbers reported in the *Journal of Commerce* also shows Philadelphia volume to be less than 10 percent of New York volume.

This data comparing trading volume is generally consistent with the conclusion that New York securities markets by the 1830s had a trading volume 8 to 10 times as large as that of Philadelphia.

One major assumption in the comparisons of this data is the unconfirmed hypothesis that by the late 1830s, stocks were traded in Philadelphia six days a week, as they were in New York. If Philadelphia brokers were merely trading stocks twice weekly, as they were in the 1811 period, then the annual volume figures for Philadelphia should be calculated by multiplying the daily average by 100 trading days rather than 300 trading days. Thus, it is possible that our figures for Philadelphia volume may be inflated by a factor of three, and Philadelphia's volume may have been less than 5 percent of New York's.

Because the nature of the stocks traded in New York and Philadelphia varied, a comparison of the trading volume in one national stock, the United States Bank of Pennsylvania (before 1837, the Second Bank of the United States) provides a useful comparison of the trading volumes in the securities markets in the two cities. This data confirms the picture

TABLE 19: Volume of Shares Traded: Daily Average

	N.Y.	Phil.	Phil. vs. N.Y.	No. of Days
1831	715	67	9.4%	6 weeks

TABLE 20: United States Bank, Shares Traded: Daily Average

	N.Y.	Phil.	Phil. vs. N.Y.	No. of Days
1837	335	185	52.1%	27
1838	131	42	32.1%	18
1839	82	7	8.6%	15
1840	207	154	74.4%	17
Total			52.5%	

of New York as the center for large trading volume. Although the United States Bank was located in Philadelphia, twice as many shares, on average, were traded in New York—according to the *Journal of Commerce*.

As usual in securities matters, the *Journal of Commerce* data is probably the most reliable. Other sources show an even greater disparity between New York and Philadelphia securities markets in United States Bank shares traded. The *Philadelphia Financial Register* report is shown in table 21.

Data from *Hazard's Magazine* compared with New York data from the *Journal of Commerce* supports the conclusion that New York traded more shares in the Bank of the United States.

Taken together, the information on volume in table 17 through table 22 is compelling. Unfortunately, the information covers only a few years in the 1830s. It is unsafe to hypothesize back to the earlier years of the period on the numbers from the later years alone. Volume information for securities markets outside of New York for the years around the turn of the century has not been found.

TABLE 21: United States Bank, Shares Traded: Daily Average

	N.Y.	Phil.	Phil. vs. N.Y.	No. of Days
1837	180	63	34.9%	16
1838	139	12.4	8.9%	23
Total			22.9%	

TABLE 22: United States Bank, Shares Traded: Daily Average

	N.Y	Phil.	Phil. vs. N.Y.	No. of Days
1831	30	4	13.3%	6 weeks
1834	294	24	8.2%	7.5 month summary

COMPARISONS OF ISSUES QUOTED AND ISSUES TRADED

ONE INDICATOR that is available for the earliest years is a comparison of the numbers of stock issues publicly quoted. Table 23 attempts to measure the number of different corporations with shares that were publicly traded. The numbers do not reflect each corporation whose shares were traded every day, but rather the larger number of corporate shares in which trades occurred or quotes were listed throughout the year.

A different indicator is the average number of issues traded per day. Table 24 compares these figures for New York, Philadelphia, and Boston for trading reported in the *Journal of Commerce*.

An analysis of these issues quoted and traded numbers is difficult. For example, although it is clear that New York does have the largest number of issues quotes by the end of the period, there are years when Philadelphia has more issues quoted, as well as years when Boston has nearly as many issues quoted, and the number of issues traded per day in Boston was greater on average from 1837–1840 than the number of issues traded per day in New York. From this data alone, one could hypothesize that either the Philadelphia or the Boston securities markets were for a time larger than the securities markets in New York.

Some additional observations, however, lead us to believe that more shares were traded in New York than in its rival cities and that New York was the home to the most important securities markets in the United States throughout this entire half century. First, both the Boston and Philadelphia securities listings include a great number of securities for turnpikes, bridges, and other issues of local concern; similar small-time issues simply were not listed in New York, although presumably they were traded. Second, dormant issues (shares quoted without transactions or with only a bid or offered price) are included on the trading lists for Philadelphia and Bos-

TABLE 23: Stock Issues Publicly Quoted

	New York	Philadelphia	Boston
1797	2	3	2
1800	5	6	7
1803	8	8	7
1806	10	17	6
1809	13	20	6
1812	16	22	6
1815	17	24	6
1818	23	26	9
1821	28		9
1824	59	25	
1827	87		
1830	58	30	
1833	70		
1836	87		
1839	100	40	25

SOURCES: The New York data, as in appendix A, come from the New York Price Current until 1818, and from the NYS&EB call books and *Journal of Commerce* afterward. The Philadelphia data is compiled from Poulson's *American Daily Advertiser, Aurora, Claypool's, The Daily Chronicle, The New York Price Current* and *The New York Journal of Commerce.* The Boston data is compiled from the *Boston Centinel*, the *Wholesale Boston Price Current*, the *New York Price Current*, and the *New York Journal of Commerce.* The large gaps in the Philadelphia and Boston listings are due to difficulties with the sources of information. A different source of information for the Boston market comes from Martin, *A Century of Finance*. Rather than distinguish issues traded from issues tradable, Martin year by year, builds his lists of stock issues conceivably in the market by adding every new corporation and its outstanding stock. His list grows quickly, and by 1837 reaches 84 possible issues quoted in Boston. This type of information is helpful, but cannot be used in comparison with issues actually traded. A similar number of issues outstanding and tradable, rather than issues traded, can be found in *Hazard's Magazine* (III (April 1829), p. 215), reporting on an "Auditor General's Report on the Finances" which lists the stock owned at that time by Pennsylvania in well over 100 different enterprises. The same magazine has a daily average of only 10.2 issues quoted in its reports of trading.

TABLE 24: Issues Traded: Daily Average

				No. of Days		
	N.Y.	Phil.	Bost.	N.Y.	Phil.	Bost.
1837	19	7.9	25	27	27	5
1838	18.3	6.7	19.5	16	16	2
1839	20.7	7.2	20	15	15	1
1840	18.3	5.2	16	17	17	1
Average	19.1	6.7	22.2			

TABLE 25: Average Shares Traded per Issue Quoted, 1837–1840

N.Y.	Phil.	Bost.	Phil. vs. N.Y.	Bost. vs. N.Y.	No. of Days
220	87.3	18.9	39.6%	8.5%	75

ton more often than on the trading lists for New York. Thus, the Boston and Philadelphia figures are inflated in a manner that the New York numbers are not. In addition, high numbers of issues quoted do not translate well into large market volume. The average number of shares traded per each issue in New York dwarfed those numbers for Philadelphia and Boston. Table 25, compiled from data in the *New York Journal of Commerce*, demonstrates that for each security traded, volume in New York would be three times that in Philadelphia and ten times that in Boston.

When all of these factors are taken into account, it seems reasonable to conclude that New York was the home of the securities markets with the most active trading throughout the 1790–1840 period.

SECURITIES PRICE COMPARISONS

AS EXPLAINED in chapter 4, the New York securities markets emphasized speculation while Philadelphia and Boston markets did not. One clear confirmation of this proposition is the volatility in securities prices. An informal examination of quotes for shares in the Second Bank of the United States between 1795 and 1820 reveals that the prices in Boston and Philadelphia remained more steady than those in New York. After a more comprehensive examination of securities prices undertaken by Arthur Cole, he indicates that in the 1820–1845 period, values in the Boston region were much more stable than those in New York (see Cole and Smith, *Fluctuations in American Business, 1790–1860*, p. 51.).

Broadside of Securities Trading Rules, September 1791

A T A MEETING of the DEALERS in the PUBLIC FUNDS in the CITY of NEW-YORK held at the COFFEE-HOUSE, on the 21st SEPTEMBER, 1791, it was agreed to be governed by the following rules.

I. That they will not attend the Sales of any, but such as shall make oath not to purchase or sell directly or indirectly on their own account, nor employ any but a Sworn Broker, to purchase or sell Stock for them on Commission.

II. They will not attend more than one Public Sale on each day, which shall be held between the hours of Twelve and Two.

III. Every Lot shall be given to the Auctioneer in writing—it shall be fairly and distinctly described, specifying the article to be sold, and the quantity.

IV. The Lots shall be numbered as they are given in, and shall be put up for sale in the order in which they are numbered.

V. Any Lot, or any part of a Lot may be withdrawn, but no addition shall be made to any Lot after the Sale has begun.

VI. The name of the purchaser shall be asked, distinctly proclaimed, and fairly entered in the Sales Book, unless the Lot is bought by the person who put it up, or by a private bid.

VII. No Lot shall be put up without being subject to the usual Commission on Sales.

VIII. All Purchases and Sales at Auction, shall be settled at the office of the Auctioneer, where the parties shall be bound to attend for that purpose.

IX. Articles sold for cash (unless the hour of delivery and payment is particularly specified at the time of sale) shall be delivered, and the payment made before three o'clock on the succeeding day.

X. In all cases of contract for time, the contracts shall be prepared by the Auctioneer, and the parties shall attend at his office in the course of the second day after the Sale, to execute and exchange them.

XI. In all cases where the Stock sold is not transferred or ready to be delivered at the time specified at the Sale, aggreeably to the foregoing rules, it shall be at the option of the purchaser to make void the bargain or to order a Sworn Broker to make immediate purchase of the same stock for cash, and in case of any loss arising from such purchase, a party who failed in the delivery shall be bound to pay the difference, together with the Broker's Commission.

In like manner, when the purchaser is not ready with his payment, it shall be at the option of the seller to make void the bargain or to order the same Stock to be immediately sold by a Sworn Broker, for cash, and the party failing shall be bound to re-transfer the Stock to the person to whom the Broker may have sold it, and to make good the difference, if any there shall be, to the original seller, besides paying the Broker's Commission.

XII. In any case of the failure of any person to comply with his contract, or to make good the difference, aggreeably to the foregoing, it shall be considered the duty of the other party to report the circumstances of the case to the Dealers at large—who will thereupon determine whether the party failing shall be published as a DeFaulter, and if determined in the affirmative, his Name shall be posted up in the Room, after which he shall not be suffered to purchase or sell at any of the Public Sales.

XIII. Not Lots of Land, or anything foreign to the Public Funds, shall be put up for Auction in the Stock-Room, until the Sale of Stock is declared over.

XIV. These Rules shall take place on the 1st of October; they shall be subscribed by the several Dealers and Auctioneers—and the Dealers shall thereby pledge themselves not to do business with any Auctioneer who shall not have subscribed them.

Richard Platt, Chairman

Printed by Childs and Swaine

New York Stock and Exchange Board 1817 Constitution and Selected Early Resolutions

RULES

TO BE adopted and observed by the "New York Stock and Exchange Board," as reported by a committee appointed at a meeting held on February 25, 1817, and passed March 8, 1817.

1. A President and Secretary shall be elected by ballot on the 2d Saturday of March, annually.

2. It shall be the duty of the President to call the Stocks at the hour that may be fixed upon by the board, from time to time, as the season may require—and that in case of the absence of the President or Secretary the members present may choose one in his stead for the calling of Stocks as President Pro-tempore.

3. It shall be the duty of the Secretary to keep the minutes of the Board in a book for the purpose, an account of all fines, and to collect the same, and also a register of all actual sales of Stocks made at the board, the register to be accessible to the members of the board only.

4. Any member interrupting the President while calling the Stocks, by speaking on any other business, shall pay a fine of not less than six nor more than twenty-five cents for each offence, at the discretion of the President.

5. The election of new members shall be by ballot-he or they must be proposed at least three days preceding the election, and three black balls shall exclude.

6. No motion for altering the rules, the time of meeting, or any other business respecting the board, shall be acted upon until at least ten days

after the motion is made, unless authorized by the unanimous consent of the Board. A motion not seconded shall be considered as lost.

7. In all cases two-thirds of the board must be present to form a quorum to do business, except the calling of the stocks.

8. The President shall decide all questions of order, but an appeal may be made to the board, a majority of the members present shall decide the question of order.

9. When any question is before the board, no member shall speak more than twice on the same question (without leave) nor shall any member be suffered to interrupt another while speaking.

10. Any member being duly elected President or Secretary, refusing to act or neglecting his duty as such, shall be fined a sum not less than five nor more than twenty dollars at the discretion of a majority of the board (provided always that he has not served before in either situation).

11. The rates of commission, viz. not less than

On Funded Debt and net amount	$\frac{1}{4}$ per cent.
On Bank and other complete shares	$\frac{1}{4}$ per cent.
On Insurance Stock complete	$\frac{1}{4}$ per cent.
On Insurance Scrip, Bank and all other Scrip	$\frac{1}{4}$ per cent. on the nominal amount
Foreign Bills of Exchange	$\frac{1}{4}$ per cent.
Inland Bills of Exchange	$\frac{1}{4}$ per cent.
Cashing Promissory Notes and Acceptances Payable in New York	$\frac{1}{2}$ per cent. on the nominal amount
Specie	$\frac{1}{4}$ per cent. on the nominal amount
Obtaining Money on Mortgage,	1 per cent. on the nominal amount

12. All fines shall be at the disposal of a majority of a quorum of the Board.

13. On any motion before the board, at the request of three members, the decision shall be held open for three successive days, in order that every member of the Board may have an opportunity of giving his opinion.

14. The fines for non-attendance at the calling of the Stocks shall be $\frac{1}{16}$th of a dollar, unless sick or out of the city, but when two or more members compose one house of trade, then the attendance of one is sufficient at the calling of Stocks—any member may commute by paying ten dollars, in lieu of fines, per annum. The fines for non-attendance and the sum paid for commutation shall be first applied to the payment of rent. In the payment of rent, each member pays a proportion, whether he belongs to a house of two or more or not.

15. Any member refusing to comply with the foregoing rules may have a hearing before the board, and if he shall persist in refusing, two-thirds of the board may declare him no longer a member.

16. No person shall be considered eligible to be balloted for as a member unless they have been in the business for the term of one or more years, either as a broker or an apprentice, immediately preceding the election.

17. All questions of dispute in the purchase or sale of Stocks shall be decided by a majority of the Board, and in default of any contract for the delivery and payment of Stocks, the defaulter shall be held liable, unless he can surrender a principal who shall be considered competent by a majority of the board. The principals of a purchase or sale to be given at the time of the contract, if required.

18. Passed by unanimous vote March 15, 1817, that no fictitious sale or contract shall be made at this board, any member or members making a fictitious sale or contract shall upon conviction thereof be expelled from the board.

19. Additional Article, the more effectually to carry into execution the 2d Article, for the appointment of a President and Secretary pro tem., viz.: Passed July 1, 1817. That in all cases of such appointment, on the refusal of any member to serve, he shall pay a fine not to exceed five nor less than one dollar.

Additional Article, passed by unanimous vote on September 19, 1817, to amend the Sixteenth Article, viz.: That no person shall be considered eligible to be balloted for as a member unless such person shall have served an apprenticeship to one of the members of the board at least two years immediately preceding his election.

PROCEEDINGS OF THE BOARD

Saturday, March 15, 1817

RESOLVED, THAT sales made at this board are to be settled for on the next day succeeding the day of sale, unless expressed to the contrary.

Resolved, That the 50 shares of Manufacturing Bank sold by Jn. G. Warren to Wm. G. Bucknor at 68 per cent., on the 13th Inst., be expunged from the register of the Board, being a fictitious sale.

Saturday, October 11, 1817

Unanimously Adopted

WHEREAS, It is deemed highly improper and injurious to the interest of this board that its members should transact business without a commission for Brokers who are not members of this Institution.

THEREFORE, Resolved, That no member of this Board shall either directly or indirectly make or cause to be made, any purchases or sales whatever at the board, for any person or persons acting as Broker or Brokers (who are not members of this Board) without first receiving a full commission for the same, and for the faithful performance of which we all mutually pledge our honor.

Thursday, October 23, 1817

Resolved, That in all time bargains the rate of interest is understood to be seven per cent., unless qualified at the time of making the bargain.

November 10, 1817

Resolved, That no member of this Board, nor any partner of a member, shall hereafter give the prices of any kind of Stock, Exchange, or Specie, to any printer for publication, and that the Secretary of the Board only be authorized to give the prices for that purpose.

November 29, 1817

Resolved, That the Secretary be authorized to furnish the prices of stock but once a week, to one price current only, at his discretion, and that no other quotation be made for publication.

John Michael O'Connor—Stock Trading, January to August 1824

January 6   O'Connor sold 7 Bank of America shares, the last of a position of 92 shares he had been selling since December 24, 1823.

January 11   O'Connor bought 50 Life and Fire Insurance Company shares.

January 13 and 16   O'Connor bought 100 New York Insurance Company shares. He had previously been given 100 New York Insurance Company shares as collateral on a loan, but he had sold them. Now he had to purchase new shares and return them to his debtor when the loan was repaid to him.

January 19   O'Connor sold 100 Bank of the United States Shares.

January 20   O'Connor bought 142 Ocean Insurance Company shares.

January 30   O'Connor bought 300 Hope Insurance Company shares.

February 26   O'Connor sold 43 Bank of America shares.

February 26   O'Connor borrowed $700 from Ralph Wells, his broker, giving 100 shares in the Hope Insurance Company as collateral.

March 5   O'Connor borrowed an additional $300 from Wells.

March 21   O'Connor purchased 100 Ocean Insurance Company shares.

March 29   O'Connor sold 50 Pacific Insurance Company shares.

April 1   O'Connor purchased 100 Life and Fire Insurance Company shares.

April 2   O'Connor borrowed $130 from Wells.

April 9   O'Connor borrowed from Ch. Lawton $5,000, using his recently purchased 100 Ocean Insurance Company shares as collateral. The money he borrowed was used to pay his broker for purchasing the shares in the first place. His broker charged interest on that money from March 21 to April 9.

April 9   O'Connor borrowed from Dayton $3,850 with the recently purchased Life and Fire Insurance Company shares as collateral. The money he borrowed was used to pay his broker for purchasing the shares. His broker charged interest on that money from April 1 to April 9.

April 9   O'Connor sold 50 Pacific Insurance Company shares.

April 9   O'Connor bought 100 Ocean Insurance Company shares. May 13, O'Connor borrowed $3,850 from the Union Insurance Company with 100 shares Ocean Insurance Company as collateral.

May 14   O'Connor borrowed $5,000 from the Union Insurance Company.

May 15   O'Connor bought 200 United States Bank shares.

May 17   O'Connor borrowed $2,250 from the Franklin Insurance Company with 72 Ocean Insurance Company shares as collateral.

May 17 or 18   O'Connor borrowed $10,000 from the Phoenix Insurance Company with 100 United States Bank shares as collateral.

June 5   O'Connor borrowed $4,774 from the Union Insurance Company with 124 Ocean Insurance Company shares as collateral.

June 7   Using the proceeds of the June 5 loan, O'Connor repaid the money he owed to Wells for purchasing shares on April 9, with interest.

June 16   O'Connor sold 100 United States Bank shares. He made a profit on the shares he had bought on May 15 without ever putting up his own money. His broker advanced the money and bought the shares, and O'Connor simply paid interest on that money for the intervening month. When he sold the shares, he made a greater profit from the share price increase than the interest and brokerage fees had cost him.

June 16   O'Connor repaid the Union Insurance Company for the loan of May 14.

June 26   O'Connor repaid the Phoenix Insurance Company for the loan of May 17 and the 100 United States Bank were returned to him.

July 29   O'Connor repaid the Franklin Insurance Company on the loan of May 17. He paid the interest costs and the 72 Ocean Insurance Company shares were returned to him.

July 29   O'Connor repaid the Union Insurance Company on the loan of May 13. He paid the interest costs and the 100 Ocean Insurance Company shares were returned to him.

July 30   O'Connor repaid the Union Insurance Company on the loan of June 5. He paid interest costs and the 124 Ocean Insurance Company shares were returned to him.

July 30   O'Connor borrowed $3,500 from City Bank with 100 Ocean Insurance Company shares as collateral. Here he was refinancing his loans by paying off the Union Insurance Company and immediately pledging the same shares on a loan with the City Bank at a more favorable rate of interest.

August found John Michael O'Connor out of town. Letters show that he was interested in selling some of his stock in the United States Bank, Ocean Insurance Company, Hope Insurance Company, and Life and Fire Insurance Company as soon as the prices were high enough.

Early Securities Regulation in New York

A N ACT to Prevent the Pernicious Practice of Stock-Jobbing, and for Regulating Sales at Public Auction. 2 Greenleaf 470, 15th Sess. New York Laws (April 10, 1792).

I. Be it enacted by the people of the state of New-York, represented in Senate and assembly, That it shall and may be lawful for the person administering the government of this state for the time being by and with the advice and consent of the council of appointment, to appoint such and so many vendue masters or auctioneers in and for the city of New-York as they shall judge necessary: Provided, That their number shall not, at any one time, exceed twenty-four, any thing in any law to the contrary notwithstanding.

II. And be it further enacted, That it shall not be lawful for any person or persons whomsoever to sell and dispose of any public securities or stock, created under the acts of Congress of the United States, or of any individual state, at public venue or outcry, within the state of New York, from and after the first day of May next, under the penalty of one hundred pounds for each offence, to be recovered by any prosecutor, or by the attorney general in the manner herein after directed.

III. And be it further enacted, That all contracts, written or verbal, public or private, made after the passing of this act, for the sale or transfer, and all wagers concerning the prices, present or future, of any certificate or evidence of debt, due by or from the United States, or any separate state, or any share or shares of the stock of the bank of the United States, or any other bank, or any share or shares of the stock of any company established or to be established, by law of the United States or any separate state, shall be, and all such contracts are hereby declared to be absolutely null, void, and of no effect: And both parties are hereby discharged from the lien and obligation of such contract or wager, unless the party contracting to sell and transfer the same shall, at the time of making such contract, be in the actual possession of the certificate, or other evidence of such debt or debts, share or shares, or be otherwise entiled [sic] in his own right, or duly authorized and impowered, by some persons so entitled to transfer the said certificate, evidence, debt or debts, share or shares, so to be contracted for; and the party or parties who may have paid any premium, differences or sums of money, in pursuance of any contract hereby declared to be null and void, shall and may recover all such sums of money, together with damages and costs, by action on the case at assumpsit, for money had and received to use of the plaintiff, to be brought in any court of record.

IV. And be it further enacted, That no licensed vendue master or vendue masters, auctioneer or auctioneers, or any other person or persons whatsoever, shall on the day and place when they shall respectively hold their public vendues, sell or dispose of at private sale, any goods, wares, or merchandizes liable to duty by the laws of this state, under the like penalty for every such offence, as is mentioned in the thirteenth section of the act, entitled, "An act for the regulation of sales by public auction," passed the twentieth of February, one thousand seven hundred and eighty-four, to be recovered by any person or persons who shall prosecute for the same, the one half thereof, when so recovered, to be paid to the treasurer for the use of the people of this state, and the other half to the use of the person or persons who shall sue for the same.

V. And be it further enacted, That no person hereafter shall expose to sale at public out-cry or vendue, any goods, wares, merchandize, or effects, on which a duty is laid by the act entitled "An act to amend an act entitled an act for the regulation of sales by public auction," as a deputy to any licensed auctioneer or vendue master, or otherwise, under the penalty of one hundred pounds for each offence, to be recovered by any person suing for such forfeiture, by bill, plaint, or information, in any court having cognizance of the same, the one moiety of such penalty to be for the use of the people of this state, and the other moiety to the person who shall sue for the same. Provided always, That any vendue master may employ his co-partner in trade, or one of his clerks to hold such vendue, in case of his sickness or inability to attend, he being accountable for the conduct of such co-partner or clerk.

VI. And be it further enacted, That if no person or persons shall, within seven days after any offence shall be committed against this or any other act, regulating sales at public auction within this state, prosecute for the penalties therein mentioned, it shall be lawful for the attorney-general to prosecute for the same, which penalties, when recovered, shall be paid to the treasurer, to and for the use of the people of this state.

During the next twenty five years, the New York statute was repeatedly revived and restated, sometimes under confusing titles.

In 1801, "An act to Regulate Sales by Public Auction, and to Prevent Stock-Jobbing" (24th Sess. New York Laws (April 2, 1801)) continued the earlier act. Section 1 provides for auction duty; Section 2 provides for twenty four approved auctioneers. Section 10 prohibits auctioneers from selling on their own account. Section 12 continues the prohibition on sales at auction of "any public securities or stock created under the acts of the Congress of the United States or any individual state, under the penalty of two hundred and fifty dollars for each offense, to be recovered by any person who will sue for the same in any court having cognizance thereof, by action of debt or by information, the one moiety thereof when recovered to be for the use of the people of this state, and the other moiety to the person so prosecuting." Section 17 continues the nullification of time contracts. Note that the statute by this time speaks of dollars, not pounds.

In 1804, the legislature passed "An Act to Amend an Act, entitled An Act to regulate sales by public auction, and to prevent stock-jobbing" (27th Sess. New York Laws (April 6, 1804) p. 222), which modified duties on goods sold in their original packages, but did not alter the provisions outlawing stock-jobbing.

In 1806, buried within "An Act Fixing the Place from Whence to Compute the Sheriff's Mileage Fees for the County of Delaware, and for Other Purposes" (29th Sess. New York Laws (March 28, 1806) p. 210), is the provision: "That the act, entitled "An act to amend an act, entitled an act to regulate sales by public auction, and to prevent stock-jobbing," passed April sixth, one thousand eight hundred and four, shall be and hereby is revived, and shall be deemed to have been revived from the first day of March, in this present year." However, there is no indication of when or why the act lapsed or what the effect of that lapse might have been.

In 1808, the act was again revived with "An Act to revive an Act, entitled An Act to amend an Act, entitled An Act to regulate sales by Public Auction, and to prevent Stock-Jobbing" (5 Webster 438, 31st Sess. New York Laws (November 8, 1808)). "That the act entitled 'an act to amend an act, entitled an act to regulate sales by public auction and to prevent stock jobbing,' shall be and hereby is revived, and shall be deemed to have been revived, from the first day of March last, and shall continue and remain in force until the first day of March, which will be in the year 1812, and no longer." The linkage between the securities market restrictions and the regulations of auctions, which were probably the more important sections of the statute, kept this regulation alive. The act lapsed in 1812, perhaps due to neglect on the part of a legislature concerned with a war.

In 1813, the legislature kept the prohibition on stock-jobbing alive with "An act to Regulate Sales by Public Auction, and to Prevent Stock-Jobbing" (36th Sess. New York Laws (April 6, 1813) p. 181). The statute was in the same form as the previous prohibitions, the only change being a renumbering of the sections. It is noteworthy that the next law passed by the legislature on February 25, 1813 was an act to prevent lotteries and to restrain insurance of lottery tickets. That act had little effect, as lotteries raged throughout this period.

In 1816, the act was again revived by "An ACT to amend the act, entitled an act to regulate sales by public auction, and to prevent stock-jobbing" (39th Sess. New York Laws (November 12, 1816) p. 12). Nothing was changed concerning stock jobbing; the only changes concerned goods damaged at sea.

In 1817, the legislature repealed the restrictions on stock-jobbing with an act to repeal an act entitled "an act to amend the act, entitled, an act to regulate sales by public auction and to prevent stock-jobbing" (40th Sess. New York Laws (April 5, 1817) p. 149). "That the act, entitled 'an act to amend the act, entitled an act to regulate sales by public auction, and to prevent stockjobbing' passed the 12th November, 1816, be and the same hereby is repealed." The decision was reversed in only ten days with "An Act to regulate sales by public auction" (40th Sess. New York Laws (April 15, 1817) p. 326). Section 11 provides "That it shall not be lawful for any person whomsoever, to sell at public auction or vendue within this state, any public securities or stock, created under the acts of the Congress of the United States, or any individual state, except such stock belong to the estate of a person deceased, or to a bankrupt or insolvent debtor, and transferred or conveyed to assignees pursuant to any law concerning bankrupts, or insolvents, or transferred or conveyed to assignees by a general assignment for the benefit of all the creditors of such bankrupt or insolvent, under the penalty of two hundred and fifty dollars for each offence, to be recovered by any person who will sue for the same, in any court having cognizance thereof by action of debt or by information, the one moiety thereof, when recovered, to be for the use of the people of this state, and the other moiety to the person so prosecuting." The first cracks in the foundations of this act were evident by this time, as exceptions were made allowing public auctions of stocks in sales for the benefit of deceased, bankrupt, or insolvent stockholders.

The act lingered on, and was codified in 1830: the revised statutes of New York. 1 Rev. Stat. 710 Section 6.

Finally, after a long but not very useful life, the act was repealed in 1858: An Act to Legalize the Sale of Stocks on Time, (81st Sess. New York Laws (April 10, 1858) p. 251).

Notes

Introduction

1. For a thorough review of the 1987 market collapse, see Nicholas F. Brady et al., "Report of the Presidential Task Force on Market Mechanisms," Washington; GPO, January 1988 (Brady Report). Historically, the decline in the market from the peak of August 25, 1987, to the trough of November 19, 1987, of 30.5 percent was smaller than many postwar declines and was dwarfed by the decline of 89 percent from the 1929 peak to the 1932 low. The singularity of the 1987 market break lies in the rapidity of the decline. Brady Report, appendix II, p. 1. Comparing the crash of 1987 with the crash of 1929, the Brady Report concluded, correctly it seems, that there was less chance of the crash of 1987 bringing on a depression than that of 1929 because the economy was considerably more stable in 1987 than in 1929. Appendix VIII, p. 10.

2. Wall Street is far greater than the NYSE alone. The NYSE is still the largest stock market, but volume in the over-the-counter market made by NASDAQ has grown rapidly in recent years. Overseas exchanges, particularly in Tokyo, also trade tremendous volumes of stocks. Far greater trading occurs in nonstock financial instruments; the value of the average daily trading in U.S. Treasury securities, for example, is roughly twenty times a typical day's trading on the NYSE. The volume of options and futures trading is also tremendous.

3. Capital is the lifeblood of a capitalist economy; it must be both accumulated and mobilized. Allocation of capital is among the most important decisions to be made in any economy, playing a critical role in determining future output. The flexibility and speed of response of the capital allocation mechanism affects directly the adaptability of the productive mechanism, and thereby bears on the long-run prospects of the entire economy. See William J. Baumol, *The Stock Market and Economic Efficiency*, pp. 1–2. Cf. Leonard Silk, "The Market: Why Does It Matter?" The primary market in which corporations raise money by selling new issues of stocks is a small part of the mechanism of corporate finance. Nevertheless, in 1986, $100 billion was raised there. Financings many times more than that were influenced.

4. For corporations, the market is a source of funds. It also provides a perfor-

mance rating for management, and, through tender offers, a disciplinary check on poor management performance. For owners and traders of securities, the market enhances liquidity by providing a forum for moving capital from one enterprise to another. It sets fair prices and provides information on how others expect prices to change. For the securities industry, the market is a place to make a living. For the government, the market is something to be policed to protect the investor, yet promoted as an efficient capital allocation mechanism that does not require massive regulation or intrusion. For economists, the market is an allocator of capital to those businesses most in need of it, a creator of wealth, and a means of keeping society's capital liquid. It is also an indicator of economic performance for corporations and society as a whole.

5. By allocating capital to promising enterprises, Wall Street serves as society's link with the future. See Baumol, *The Stock Market and Economic Efficiency*, p. 2. The fundamental significance of financial markets stems from connections between enterprises producing goods and services in the real world and the paper world of credit and finance. Financial markets also have powerful impact on corporate planning. Some of the most important decisions for our society are made by giant corporations when they determine what to do with retained earnings and with funds raised externally. The single most important factor in making such decisions is usually the impact on the corporations's earnings and the secondary impact on the price of its stock.

6. The American corporate system is different from those of other western countries because of the far more prominent role played by its stock market.

7. Truly corporate bodies, as distinct from partnerships, arise when men devise effective means of participating in an enterprise as a "side-issue," apart from other activity to which they devote their principal business time and effort. Outsiders must find the device attractive and need only be promised the opportunity for profit. Shah Livermore, *Early American Land Companies*, p. 2, n.2.

8. The use here of the term "corporate system" does not suggest concurrence with the analysis used by Adolf Berle and Gardiner Means, who used the term in describing the advent of the "modern corporation" and its relationship with the stock market in their classic study, *The Modern Corporation and Private Property* (hereafter "*The Modern Corporation*"). Our analysis supposes that the corporate system existed when the market began to quote and trade the first shares of corporate stock.

9. Joseph S. Davis, *Essays in the Earlier History of American Corporations* (hereafter "*Essays*"), 2:330.

10. John Kenneth Galbraith, for example, went so far as to stress the independence of the mature corporation from capital markets, as though absence of need to go to the market for funds meant that the corporation was therefore free from the constraints of the marketplace. *The New Industrial State*, p. 75. Galbraith's understanding is simply not so. Today every corporation, large or small, is constrained by the marketplace. For a more complete recognition of the influence of financial markets on corporations, see e.g., Baumol, *The Stock Market and Economic Efficiency*; Thorstein Veblen, *The Theory of Business Enterprise*; Berle and Means, *The Modern Corporation*, bk. 4.

11. For example, a description of the early investment market in securities can be found in Margaret Myers, *The New York Money Market*, 1:10–16. Myers' description is skewed insofar as it downplays the central importance of the speculative influence. Myers views were in step with views of securities market functions current at the time

of her work. The gambling variety of speculation was discouraged, and Congress attempted to outlaw "unnecessary, unwise and destructive" speculation in the Securities and Exchange Act of 1934. See House Comm. on Interstate and Foreign Commerce, H.R. Rep. No. 1383, Securities Bill of 1934, 73d Cong. 2d Sess. (1934). See also Lionel Edie, *Economics: Principles and Problems*, pp. 219, 446–8.

12. Edmund C. Stedman, ed., *The New York Stock Exchange*, p. 85.

13. See appendix A.

14. Joseph Angell and Samuel Ames, the authors of the first corporation text, *Treatise on the Law of Private Corporations Aggregate*, stressed the common elements of all corporations. Davis, Berle, and Means, along with E. Merrick Dodd, *American Business Corporations Until 1860*, and James Hurst, *The Legitimacy of the Business Corporation in the Law of the United States*, have distinguished so-called business corporations from other corporations, and Hurst, and Louis Hartz, *Economic Policy and Democratic Thought*, have gone further to distinguish between business corporations that merely received the privileges associated with the corporate entity from those that received other benefits, but none of these commentators has attributed particular significance in the evolution of public business corporations to the fact that their shares were traded.

15. Historians are correct to point out that the majority of business enterprises did evolve from those which were characterized by direct personal control by a small group of owners to those enterprises without owner control. However, we are stressing the importance of the fact that for public corporations, the change happened much earlier than the late 1800s. For a significant number of American enterprises, it had already happened by the late 1700s.

16. All elements of the corporate system are interconnected. Our stress on securities markets may be no more valid than a similar emphasis on the legal environment or the importance of management. What is cause and what is effect is difficult to determine, and the securities market may have only responded to needs of corporations throughout this history. However, given the importance of securities markets today, it seems safe to assume they have been important throughout the history of public corporations. Our contention is that the importance of this segment of the corporate system, especially in its infancy, has not been sufficiently recognized.

17. The first public corporations whose shares were publicly traded are the ancestors of today's institutions and are the most useful antecedants to study for an understanding of today's corporate world. Enterprises financed with extensive state backing, often called quasi-public corporations, are not nearly as similar to today's public corporations as are the early banks and insurance companies or even unincorporated joint stock companies with transferable shares.

1. The Roots of American Securities Markets

1. See V. E. Morgan and W. A. Thomas, *The London Stock Exchange: Its History and Functions*, pp. 1–27.

2. On the first business corporations and joint stock companies generally, see chapter 7. Each adventurer in a joint stock company received a certificate evidencing his capital contribution and stipulating his rights. As time went on, it became important to

make these certificates transferable. People were more likely to risk their capital and pay more for interests in the venture if those interests could easily be resold. For the enterprise, transferability of shares meant that its capital could remain intact even as the identity of its owners changed. Although the common law generally prohibited the transfer of intangible interests, it found a way to sanction transfers of joint stock company shares. See William S. Holdsworth, A History of English Law, 8:202–3.

3. In 1711, the Earl of Oxford proposed to rescue Queen Anne's government from the financial distress occasioned by Britain's ongoing intervention in the war. The government floated a de facto £10 million sterling offering of government securities. See Charles MacKay, Extraordinary Popular Delusions and the Madness of Crowds (hereafter "Extraordinary Popular Delusions"), p. 46 et seq.

4. The climate for speculation in Europe was fostered by the famous Mississippi scheme of John Law in France in the 1720s. See Morgan, The London Stock Exchange, p. 31; Mackay, Extraordinary Popular Delusions, pp. 1–45.

5. MacKay, Extraordinary Popular Delusions, p. 55.

6. MacKay, Extraordinary Popular Delusions, p. 54, quotes this passage from The Political State.

7. That the credit of the government did not entirely collapse was due to the efforts of Sir Robert Walpole, Whig Prime Minister, 1721–1742. For the government response, including the Bubble Act, see chapter 8.

8. Of the handful of business corporations granted charters before the Revolutionary War, there is no evidence of a market in their shares. See Davis, Essays, 1:87–107.

9. Joint stock companies for manufacturing existed in several instances, but were without popular favor. Davis, Essays, 1:91–98, 178. In 1686, Massachusetts authorized the Bank of Credit Lombard. Davis, Essays, 1:95.

10. In 1751, New York City issued bonds to pay for a corporation pier. Stedman, The New York Stock Exchange, p. 30.

11. Davis mentions wealthy Americans, such as Andrew Cragie of New York, who invested in European securities markets after the war, Essays, 1:180. However, there was no sustained market for these securities in the United States.

12. Arthur Nussbaum, A History of the Dollar, pp. 14, 28.

13. James K. Medbery, Men and Mysteries of Wall Street, pp. 286–7. Some currency may have been overprinted from the time that Massachusetts issued bills of credit in 1690 (see Stedman, The New York Stock Exchange, p. 32), but the new states were considerably more reckless than the colonies had been. Eventually many state notes were accepted in payment of taxes and retired. See, generally, E. James Ferguson, The Power of the Purse.

14. Davis, Essays, 1:180–84. Familiar with practice in the London securities market, and probably also with earlier practice in Amsterdam, merchants and others began to trade desireable securities as soon as they appeared. The English experience is detailed in Peter Dickson, The Financial Revolution in England; the Amsterdam market experience in Violet Barbour, Capitalism in Amsterdam in the 17th Century.

15. The value of bonds issued by Congress depended upon whether the federal government would be given the power to tax. See, generally, Ferguson, The Power of the Purse.

16. Newspaper quotes appeared in Boston as early as 1786. See the Massachusetts

Centinel of July 26, quoted in Davis, Essays, 1:197. Regular quotes in Boston began in March 1789 in the Massachusetts Magazine. Quotes began in Philadelphia in October 1789 in the General Advertiser.

17. Davis, Essays, 1:185.

18. Davis, Essays, 1:185.

19. Rumor has it that when the plans of the new Secretary of the Treasury, Alexander Hamilton, to redeem federal debts and to assume the debts of the states were leaked, some unscrupulous speculators searched remote towns and bought up securities that were soon to appreciate in value. See Davis, Essays, 1:191–2.

20. Robert Morris, Journals of the Continental Congress, 22:429–446, esp. 435, 444; quoted in Davis, Essays, 1:180.

21. For a summary of Hamilton's program, see Stuart Bruchey, The Roots of American Economic Growth, 1607–1861, pp. 108–12. For a description of the trading that preceded the refunding issues, see Davis, Essays, 1:178–211.

22. Between October 1789 and December 1791 prices quadrupled. Davis, Essays, 1:195.

23. Myers, The New York Money Market, 1:10–11.

24. On the corporations that could and could not raise money from the public, see chapter 7.

25. The federal government provided $2 million of the Bank of the United State's $10 million in capital and reserved five of twenty-five seats on the board of directors. The public was to contribute the other $8 million in government bonds and specie. See Bray Hammond, Banks and Politics in the United States, pp. 122–26.

26. On the Bank of New York, see histories by Henry W. Domett, A History of the Bank of New York, and Allan Nevins, The Bank of New York.

27. Shares in both banks soon rose to premium prices. Hammond, Banks and Politics in America, pp. 122–23; Domett, A History of the Bank of New York, p. 44.

28. See Davis, Essays, 1:342–45, 519. On the Society, a New Jersey corporation, see, generally, Davis, 1:349–522. See also chapter 7. Shares in the Bank of North America were also quoted and traded in Philadelphia.

29. See Davis, Essays, 1:198. See Myers, The New York Money Market, p. 12, for a table of prices for federal government securities monthly during 1791 and 1792.

30. Davis, Essays, 1:196. Borrowing stock was apparently unknown in the United States until introduced by financiers with experience in British markets.

31. For more on time bargains, see chapter 6.

32. The discovery, colonization, and early development of America was a speculative enterprise, and it is not surprising that the spirit of speculation ran high both before and after the Revolution. Joseph Edward Hedges, Commercial Banking and the Stock Market Before 1863 (hereafter "Commercial Banking"), p. 27. The period after the Revolution in the United States "was in a peculiar sense an age of speculation," Sereno S. Pratt, The Work of Wall Street, p. 248, quoting William Gouge. The achievement of independence was in itself a "gigantic speculation." Davis, Essays, 2:7.

33. Davis, Essays, 1:286. James Sullivan tells how "The apparent success of some speculators increased the number engaged in that kind of traffic, until the great towns and cities were filled with that kind of gentry." "The Path to Riches," 46(4): extra no. 184; 1933 reprint, p. 199.

34. King to Hamilton, August 15, 1791. Harold C. Syrett, ed., *The Papers of Alexander Hamilton*, 9:59–61; Davis, *Essays*, 1:207.

35. Sullivan, "The Path to Riches," p. 172.

36. Scrips were temporary certificates given to subscribers who paid $25 down on subscribing. Further installments on the $400 par value were apparently not called until January 1. See Davis, *Essays*, 1:341. On prices, see Davis, 1:202–3, 341. In Philadelphia, prices of scrips may have reached $325; Davis, 1:203. See also Hammond, *Banks and Politics in America*, p. 123.

37. *New York Daily Advertiser*, August 13, 1791, p. 3; August 15, 1791, p. 2.

38. July 10, 1791. Robert A. Rutland et al., eds., *The Papers of James Madison*, 14:42–43.

39. See *Columbian Centinel*, March 14, 17, 21, 28, 31, and September 4, 11, and 18, 1792.

40. See Davis, *Essays*, 2:81–91 for a discussion of the banks of 1792. The promotion of these banks as joint stock companies was in the main a speculative device, and after they were unable to win state charters, they were doomed to fail.

41. See Davis, *Essays*, 2:70, 81; 1:285, 342–45, 394. The Tammanial Tontine Association, formed to erect Tammany Hall, was a joint-stock company whose subscription of 4000 shares at $16 each was probably filled, but trading in the shares was restricted by its small capital. The project was hurt by the insolvency of one of its prime movers, John Pintard, in the spring of 1792. A corporation which may have been its successor, the New York Tontine Coffee House Company, was chartered with 203 subscribers at $200 each, and the tontine coffee house subsequently built in 1793 became an important center for merchants and securities traders. See Francis L. Eames, *The New York Stock Exchange*, p. 17; Pratt, *The Work of Wall Street*, p. 5; Medbery, *Men and Mysteries of Wall Street*, p. 287. See also chapter 3.

42. Alexander Hamilton, "Report on Manufactures." Reprinted in Harold C. Syrett, ed., *The Papers of Alexander Hamilton*, 10:233, 267. See also pp. 274–83; especially p. 275. To secure the advantages that will flow from an infusion of foreign capital, "little more is now necessary, than to foster industry, and cultivate order and tranquility, at home and abroad." See also Davis, *Essays*, 2:362–67.

43. "Though induced merely with views to speculation in the funds, [foreign Capital] may afterwards be rendered subservient to the Interests of Agriculture, Commerce and Manufactures." "Report on Manufactures," in Syrett (ed.) 10:276. Later economists would describe this process as capital formation.

44. Hamilton's proposal that government bonds be accepted as payment for the shares of the Bank of United States had its model; the English had used such an arrangement in organizing the Bank of England. Of the public shareholders' capital contribution, $6 million consisted of the government's new securities. $2 million of the bank's $10 million of capital stock was to consist of specie, but this part of its capital probably never exceeded $400,000. See Hammond, *Banks and Politics in America*, p. 123. See also James Wettereau, "New Light on the First Bank of the United States," pp. 263, 270.

45. Davis, *Essays*, 1:194.

46. For an excellent essay on Duer, see Davis, *Essays*, 1:111–338. Duer had been Hamilton's assistant at Treasury, but had resigned rather than move to Washington when the government moved from New York.

47. On Duer's use of government contacts for personal business, see Jones, "William Duer and the Business of Government in the Era of the American Revolution," p. 393. Duer's connections went as high as George Washington. See Robert Sobel, *Panic on Wall Street*, pp. 10–11.

48. The land scheme in Ohio resulted in a number of settlers coming from France only to find hostile Indians and a winter for which they had no provisions. Davis, *Essays*, 1:213–53.

49. Davis, *Essays*, 1:279. On Duer's aborted attempts to organize an international banking house, see Davis, 1:151–73.

50. See, e.g., Bank of New York Stock Register, Bank of New York Archives, which lists many trades in Macomb's name in 1791 and early 1792.

51. Davis, *Essays*, 1:284.

52. Watson to Wadsworth, March 14, 1792 in Wadsworth Papers, Connecticut Historical Society. Quoted in Davis, *Essays*, 1:285.

53. Duer was not above manipulating the market. To maintain an artificial market price, he was known to buy and sell at the same time. He also made attempts to corner the market in certain issues. See Davis, *Essays*, 1:281–2; Sobel, *Panic on Wall Street*, pp. 23–24.

54. Davis, *Essays*, 1:286.

55. One reason for the tumble in prices may have been the introduction of a bill in the Assembly on March 3: "An Act for Laying a Duty on Public Securities and Stock Sold at Auction." See *Journal of the Assembly of the State of New York*. (Albany: Childs and Swaine, 1792), p. 99. A later version of that act, entitled "An Act to Prevent the Pernicious Practice of Stock Jobbing and for Regulating Sales at Public Auction," became law on April 10. See chapter 8; appendix F.

56. See notice of meeting of Duer's creditors, *New York Daily Advertiser*, March 19.

57. Davis, *Essays*, 1:290–94.

58. A contemporary notes that the "little people" who had lent to Duer were aghast; their savings had been lost. These were not entrepreneurial risk-takers, they were later described as "the innocent mechanic, the poor widow and the helpless orphan," *Diary, or Loudon's Register*, April 10, 1792. It was feared that "if not timely appeased . . . [they would] rise to extremities." Watson to Wadsworth, March 14, 1792, Wadsworth Papers, Connecticut Historical Society. Cited in Davis, *Essays*, 1:285.

59. Davis, *Essays*, 1:210, 339–45; Myers, *The New York Money Market*, 1:12.

60. The stock market panic may have been premature, but a deeper reaction set in later in the year. Davis, *Essays*, 2:31. In passing, Sobel, *Panic on Wall Street*, p. 5, mentions an earlier panic in 1785.

61. Johnson's correspondence with Andrew Cragie, describing the distress in New York during this period, appears in Davis, *Essays*, 1:298–303.

62. Letter of April 6, 1792, Anspach Collection, New York Historical Society.

63. See Davis, *Essays*, 1:313–15, 340.

64. On April 10, the New York legislature passed "An Act to Prevent the Pernicious Practice of Stock-Jobbing, and for Regulating Sales at Public Auction." 2 Greenleaf 470, 15th Sess. April 10, 1792. See chapter 8.

65. "Report on Manufactures," 10:256.

2. The Buttonwood Agreement

1. Reprinted in Eames, *The New York Stock Exchange*, p. 14. The subscribers were Leonard Bleecker, Hugh Smith, Armstrong and Barnewall, Samuel March, Bernard Hart, Alexander Zuntz, Andrew D. Barclay, Sutton and Hardy, Benjamin Seixas, John Henry, John A. Hardenbrook, Samuel Beebee, Benjamin Winthrop, John Ferrers, Ephraim Hart, Isaac M. Gomez, Gulian McEvers, Augustine H. Lawrence, G. N. Bleecker, John Bush, Peter Anspach, Charles McEvers, Jr., David Reedy, and Robinson and Hartshorne.

2. Myers, *The New York Money Market*, 1:16. As her sources, Myers cites Martha Lamb, *Wall Street in History*, p. 72; H. G. Hemming, *History of the New York Stock Exchange*, p. 11; Edward J. Meeker, *The Work of the Stock Exchange*, pp. 45, 108 (but see p. 63 for discussion of Buttonwood Agreement). The seeds of the Myers account appear to be Hemming and Eames. Eames bases his version on two items from the *Diary, or Loudon's Register*. For a similar account relying on Eames, see Stedman, *The New York Stock Exchange*, p. 35. The Myers account is cited and accepted in Sidney I. Pomerantz, *New York: An American City 1783–1803*, p. 183; R. Sobel, *The Big Board*, pp. 18–21; C. Welles, *The Last Days of the Club*, p. 9.

3. *New York Daily Advertiser*, July 1, 1791, p. 3.

4. *New York Daily Advertiser*, July 5, 1791, p. 4. Davis, *Essays*, 1:197, reports that public securities auctions were in vogue in Boston before the end of 1790 and quotes a Boston advertisement for an auctioneer and broker as early as April 1, 1789. See chapter 5 for a discussion of early securities professionals in New York.

5. It is uncertain whether members of the general public who were not brokers and dealers participated in the auctions as well. In a record of the purchasers at a McEvers and Barclay auction, October 25, 1791, most of the purchasers can be identified as securities professionals (e.g., Bleecker, Livingston, Hart, Reedy, etc.), but there are some purchasers about whom we cannot be sure. See the letter book of Nicholas Low, New-York Historical Society. See also Davis, *Essays*, 1:198, quoting *The American Daily Advertiser*, January 11, 1792: "it is in the power of every person to try the market by sale of cash for stock or stock for cash, as his inclination may desire, without any risque other than the commission on the lot set up for sale." In March 1792, Standish Forde advised Peter Anspach "to attend the coffee house regularly during the sale of stock" in order to monitor the market. Anspach Collection, New-York Historical Society.

6. Davis points out that securities were traded at both the public auctions and in the private markets. Davis, *Essays*, 1:287.

7. Evans Series of Imprints, Collection of the New-York Historical Society. Reprinted in appendix C. We are grateful to Peter Eisenstadt of the New York Stock Exchange for alerting us to the existence of this broadside. "Sales" in the document refers to public auction sales and "public funds" refers to stocks and bonds in the trading market. It should be noted that in the earliest securities markets of England, government obligations were denominated stocks and company obligations were denominated shares. Henry Clews, *Fifty Years in Wall Street*, p. 87.

8. Rule 1: "That they [Dealers in the public funds] will not attend the Sales of any, but such as make oath not to purchase or sell directly or indirectly on their own account, nor employ any but a Sworn Broker, to purchase or sell Stock for them on

Commission." The reference to sales "of any, but such as make oath," is ambiguous. Broadly construed, dealers agreed to attend only those public auction sales at which all participants retained a sworn broker to handle their business for a commission. A narrow construction only required auctioneers to refrain from buying or selling on their own account. Either way, the rule negates the auctioneers' right to engage in private sales without a broker, a prerogative that they had earlier claimed. See the Pintard and Bleecker advertisement, New York Daily Advertiser, July 5, 1791 ($\frac{1}{8}$ of 1 percent commission on public sales; $\frac{1}{2}$ or $\frac{1}{4}$ of 1 percent on private sales). Despite ambiguities, the rule's objective is clear: to protect brokers against loss of commissions at auction sales.

9. Compare the attempt to hold one auction a day by the formation of the Stock Exchange Office on February 2, 1792. See below.

10. The historians include Eames, The New York Stock Exchange, and Stedman, The New York Stock Exchange. Davis makes an oblique reference to an action of the dealers that might be the one covered by the broadside, but he was obviously unaware of the broadside's existence, Essays, 1:211–12. Pomerantz mentions it in passing, New York: An American City 1783–1803, p. 183, n. 62. It may also be significant that only the name of Richard Platt appears on the document. We know that Platt was a broker at that time, but he did not sign the Buttonwood Agreement and does not appear to have been a leader among securities professionals of the period. Platt was one of the creditors of William Duer and signed the notice of his creditors that appeared on March 19, 1792, in the New York Daily Advertiser. An R. Platt, perhaps a relative, joined the New York Stock & Exchange Board on June 13, 1827. NYS&EB Minute Book, New York Stock Exchange archives.

11. The Broadside Agreement itself mentions sworn brokers. John Hardenbrook and Hugh Smith ran advertisements claiming that they had "taken the oath prescribed by the dealers in stock." Smith's began April 3 and Hardenbrook's May 3, 1792, New York Daily Advertiser. Sutton and Hardy were in the business of "sworn stock brokers," advertisement beginning April 30, and Armstrong and Barnewall were also "sworn stock brokers," advertisement beginning May 14. Others, without reference to the oath, also claimed they would only buy and sell on commission. See, e.g., advertisements of Leonard Bleecker, Bernard Hart, and Samuel Beebee.

12. A class of sworn brokers could simply have evolved without the agreement. John Pintard was sworn on November 25, 1790, before this agreement, by Richard Varrick, Mayor of New York, to perform the office of broker in the public funds and to abstain from dealings for his own account for at least six months, Pintard Collection, New-York Historical Society. Pintard was drawing on the practice in London where brokers were sworn before the aldermen. See chapter 8. Pintard then became an auctioneer, which may indicate that sworn broker simply meant auctioneer. Others who advertised as sworn brokers, however, were not auctioneers, and many who were auctioneers did not claim to be brokers or sworn brokers. Pintard soon stopped confining his activities to those of a sworn broker; as a member of Duer's cabal, he traded for his own account in 1792.

13. Sutton and Hardy, Armstrong and Barnewall, and Hugh Smith all continued their advertisements holding themselves out as sworn brokers after the Buttonwood Agreement. See especially the Hugh Smith advertisement, New York Daily Advertiser, February 14, 1793.

14. Although the Broadside rules were purportedly adopted only by the dealers, some rules clearly presupposed agreement of the auctioneers. Rule 8, for example, called for trades to be settled in the auctioneer's office, and Rule 10 called upon the auctioneer to handle the preparation and execution of time contracts. It is possible in the small financial circles of the time that the auctioneers were involved in the drafting of the rules. At least they participated by being invited to comply, on pain of losing customers at auctions.

15. *New York Daily Advertiser.* February 15, 1792, p. 3, col. 1. Note that A. L. Bleecker was the father of L. A. Bleecker. Jerome B. Holgate, *American Geneology.*

16. See, e.g., *New York Daily Advertiser,* August 9, 1791, p. 3.

17. *Columbian Centinel* (Boston), March 28, 1792. See also *Columbian Centinal,* March 14, April 11, 18; *Diary, or Loudon's Register,* April 4, 7, 9, 10, 13, and 19; *Daily Gazette,* April 2.

18. *New York Journal and Patriotic Register* of March 21, 1792. See notice of meeting of creditors of Leonard Bleecker, a prominent securities professional, in *Diary, or Loudon's Register,* April 18, 1792. John Pintard, an associate of Duer's, was another prominent securities dealer who was forced into insolvency. He escaped from creditors by fleeing to New Jersey. See Pintard's letters to his daughter, 1797–1798, Pintard Collection, New-York Historical Society. In the years that followed, Pintard reclaimed his fortunes and became a pillar of the New York community as founder of both the New-York Historical Society and the Savings Bank of New York.

19. *New York Daily Advertiser,* March 30, 1792, p. 1. B. Livingston was in the chair. There was first a "report of the committee appointed by the Merchants and Dealers in Stock on Monday last" which was taken into consideration before the resolutions. The Committee established to provide a proper room included John Delafield, Nicholas Low, William Henderson, Abijah Hammond, Leonard Bleecker, and Benjamin Walker. Of this group only Leonard Bleecker signed the Buttonwood Agreement. See also *Diary, or Loudon's Register,* March 23; Davis, *Essays,* 1:308; Eames, *The New York Stock Exchange,* p. 13.

20. Letter of March 25, 1792, from William Seton to Alexander Hamilton, in Dommett, *History of the Bank of New York,* p. 46. Seton also states that: "the Dealers in stocks are to have a meeting this evening, and, it is reported, will enter into an absolute agreement not to draw out any specie from the banks for three months to come."

21. Davis, *Essays,* 1:308, quoting the *New Jersey Journal* of April 4.

22. There is no evidence of public securities auctions after April 2. The final Stock Exchange notice signed by five of the auctioneers who published the notice of February 15, 1792, appeared in the *Diary, or Loudon's Register,* March 30, 1792. One more notice, signed only by A. L. Bleecker and Son, appeared in the *Daily Gazette* of April 2, 1792.

23. An Act to prevent the pernicious Practice of Stock-Jobbing, and for regulating sales at Public Auction. Passed April 10, 1792. 2 Greenleaf 470, ch. 62. See chapter 8.

24. The Standish Forde-Peter Anspach correspondence confirms the continuance of trading. Anspach Collection, New-York Historical Society. See, e.g., Forde's letter of April 4, 1792. Forde was deeply concerned by the possible impact of the New York failures on traders in Philadelphia. Auctions ended in Philadelphia on or about

April 12. Forde to Anspach, April 12, 1792. See also *Diary,* or *Loudon's Register,* April 21, 1792, p. 2.

25. *The Daily Gazette* of April 10, 1792, listed prices for the three federal bond issues and shares of the Bank of the United States, but not for shares of the Bank of New York. Nor did it publish, as it had in the past, summaries of prices in Philadelphia and Boston.

26. It is interesting to speculate on what might have happened to the New York market if this panic had not taken place. If, as seems plausible, the securities dealers were happy with the public auctions, and if the auctions had not been declared unlawful, would there have been any reason for change or for the dealers to go underground? Maybe not immediately. However, an exchange would likely have evolved eventually. The forces that pushed for organization of an elitist organization of securities dealers, with its self-regulatory and cartel aspects, would probably have asserted themselves when the volume of trading warranted.

27. Comparing the signers of the February 15 advertisement and the Buttonwood Agreement, one finds Andrew D. Barclay, John Ferrers, Gulian McEvers, Charles McEvers, Leonard Bleecker, and G. N. Bleecker (A. L. Bleecker's son).

28. Compare the broadside, reprinted in appendix C, in which the language is tortured.

29. Exactly what was meant by "preference" is unclear. Preference could mean that signers would charge other signers a lower commission, or it could mean that signers would attempt to direct business to other signers.

30. The signers did not, by any means, include all New York brokers. Not all of those listed in the February advertisement signed the Buttonwood Agreement, nor did all of those associated with the Corre's Hotel meeting of April. Almost half of those listed as brokers in Duncan's 1792 New York directory did not sign the Buttonwood Agreement.

31. See the *New York Daily Advertiser,* May 16 through May 22. Advertisements as brokers were run by Hugh Smith, Samuel Beebee, John Henry, Bernard Hart, John Hardenbrook, John Ferrers, A. Zuntz, Emphriam Hart, David Reedy, Leonard Bleecker, Sutton and Hardy, and Armstrong and Barnewall. The Standish Forde-Peter Anspach arbitrage network continued until at least May 21, 1792. Letter of that date, Anspach Collection, New-York Historical Society.

32. Access to such a price-determining mechanism, when denied to nonsigners, would give the signers a valuable economic benefit, as it later did for the members of the New York Stock & Exchange Board. Adoption of trading rules and provisions for arbitrating disputes are other measures that could have implemented the Buttonwood principles and creating a valuable economic package for the compact's signers. An organized group of traders could have also set up a method for informally enforcing time bargains that the courts would not enforce, as the NYS&EB was to do later.

33. See Davis, *Essays,* 1:308, n. 5.

3. The New York Stock and Exchange Board

1. Hart was the "subscriber" in this notice that appeared in the New York Daily Advertiser, May 17, 1792, on the heels of the Buttonwood Agreement which Hart signed.

2. Securities Professionals at this time were making markets in the absence of any regular auction or exchange. See chapter 5 and appendix A, for more discussion of broker-dealer trading.

3. Medbery, Men and Mysteries of Wall Street, p. 287. The New York Tontine Coffee House Company was chartered for the purpose of a Merchants Exchange with 203 subscribers at $200 each. The building was completed in 1793. Eames, The New York Stock Exchange, p. 17. The building was the center of commercial life in New York until 1827. Pratt, The Work of Wall Street, p. 5; Lamb, Wall Street in History, p. 61. Some of the signers of the Buttonwood Agreement were also subscribers and instrumental supporters of the Tontine Coffee House. See Humphrey B. Neill, The Inside Story of the Stock Exchange, p. 16.

4. Compare The New York Stock Exchange. According to this 1886 history, there was an exchange during the period from 1792 to 1816 that operated under the 1792 principles, and in 1816 this exchange had 28 members. See p. 21. Pratt, The Work of Wall Street, p. 7, agrees. Eames, The New York Stock Exchange, suggests that from 1792 to 1817 the stock brokers of New York dealt together under various agreements in various places. See p. 17.

5. See chapter 2.

6. Philadelphia seems to have had an organized stock trading market in the 1790s and again in the 1820s. See Davis, Essays, 1:287. Myers, The New York Money Market, mentions a belief in a Philadelphia exchange in 1800, but offers no evidence. See p. 17. An advertisement in Poulson's American Daily Advertiser, November 4, 1800, p. 3, gives some indication of a Philadelphia organization: "As there are no such coins in the United States as Pounds, Shillings and Pence, The Brokers of Philadelphia in future intend to buy and sell all kinds of public stock, at so much percent, in Dollars and Cents." Even if the Philadelphia organization had an earlier start, there is no reason to believe it functioned more actively than the group of New York brokers. See appendix B.

7. William Lawton went to Philadelphia in 1816 to obtain a copy of their bylaws for a model, according to Medbery, Men and Mysteries of Wall Street, p. 288. The NYS&EB Memorial, Documents of the Assembly of the State of New York. 59th Sess, no. 291, March 23, 1836, p. 2, agrees that a stock board was established in Philadelphia before New York. "Prior to 1832 the Philadelphia Stock Exchange had no permanent home and the members held their meetings in all sorts of places, especially at the coffee houses." Joseph Jackson, The Encyclopedia of Philadelphia, 4:1115–16. J. T. Scharf and Thompson Westcott, The History of Philadelphia, 1669–1884, pp. 634–35, adds that the Philadelphia exchange searched for a location from 1821 to 1832. That they did not need a location before, and then it took them eleven years to get one, demonstrates their relative insignificance.

8. New York Stock & Exchange Board Minute Book, New York Stock Exchange Archives (also reproduced in Stedman, The New York Stock Exchange, pp. 63–66).

The committee to draw up articles of association included Nathan Prime, Wm. H. Robinson and A. H. Lawrence.

9. Note that Eames, *The New York Stock Exchange*, p. 72, reports A. Stockholm as the first NYS&EB president in 1817, and Stedman, *The New York Stock Exchange*, p. 467, follows him. There is no indication as to why Nathan Prime is not listed as the first president, although one of the most unusual rules in the constitutions relates to a fine to be levied on officers who refuse to serve. Compare Medbery, *Men and Mysteries of Wall Street*, p. 289, suggesting that Prime did his business elsewhere until 1820. Perhaps Prime was merely president of the committee, not of the board after it was organized.

10. See appendix D.

11. Medbery, *Men and Mysteries of Wall Street*, p. 289. The NYS&EB constitution was revised in 1820 by W. H. Robinson, F. A. Tracy, R. H. Nevins, Lebeus Loomis, and Nathan Prime. The 1820 Constitution and bylaws are reproduced in Eames, *The New York Stock Exchange*, pp. 19–26.

12. See NYS&EB Minute Books, NYSE Archives. For later examples, see, e.g., NYSE Archives documents pleading in the dispute between Jacob Little and R. L. Cutting, January 12, 1846, and documents reporting settlement of the dispute between Jacob Little and the firm of Kitchan and Olcott September 14, 1849. See, also, *New York Journal of Commerce*, February 14, 1835, regarding arbitration in the Morris Canal Corner. The strong preference for arbitration of disputes rather than resort to law also contributed to the success of the NYS&EB according to Clews, *Fifty Years in Wall Street*, pp. 561–76.

13. This situation was an archetypal private lawmaking arrangement. See John R. Dos Passos, *A Treatise on the Law of Stock-Brokers and Stock Exchanges*, pp. 34–40, for a general exposition on the power of unincorporated stock exchanges to make and enforce rules. Under the Securities and Exchange Act of 1934, the New York Stock Exchange, as a "Self-Regulatory Organization" retains large discretion to regulate itself.

14. Securities professionals had the same profit-oriented goals of other businessmen. Walton Hamilton, *The Politics of Industry*, pp. 33–34, remarked how the restless pursuit of gain made businessmen the "radicals" who brought forth a new order, "unplanned, unsaluted and unsung." Early securities professionals were, in this sense, radicals.

15. The NYS&EB constitution provided sanctions for violations of the commission rule, but there is little evidence as to how effectively the price-fixing was enforced, particularly in times of slow volume. The records of G. N. Bleecker, however, demonstrate that he charged a commission even in sales of shares for his mother. Bleecker Collection, New-York Historical Society. In 1820, commission rate-fixing was standard practice on the European bourses and the London Stock Exchange. Fixed rates were not abolished on the NYSE until 1975, despite the Sherman Antitrust Act (1890) and the Securities and Exchange Act (1934).

16. There were countervailing pressures to add more members in order to increase the number of trading partners and to cut down on the viability of rival exchanges.

17. Actions of the association, like those of other private clubs, were final. The association determined both the limit on the number of memberships, or "seats," and

the qualifications of members. Seats were not salable at first. For a summary of the prices of seats once they were, see Stedman, *The New York Stock Exchange*, p. 473.

18. The most tangible link between the Buttonwood Agreement of 1792 and the NYS&EB of 1817 consists of the four men—Leonard Bleecker, Bernard Hart, A. H. Lawrence, and Samuel Beebee—who subscribed to both the 1792 agreement and the Exchange's formal constitution. Compare Stedman, *The New York Stock Exchange*, p. 69. For almost 150 years, the unfolding of the relationship between the two groups of securities dealers defined the structure of the securities industry. There is a direct link between the division of the market that finds its roots in the Buttonwood principles of 1792 and Congress' 1975 call to unite the market in a National Market System. See Werner, "Adventure in Social Control of Finance: The National Market System for Securities," p. 1233.

19. Despite the exchange's anticompetitive restrictions, nonmember professionals survived due to the trust of clients or family members, the quality of their financial advice, and probably a discount on their commission charges.

20. At least some off-board brokers in the 1820s charged the same commissions as the NYS&EB brokers. Both Ralph Wells and Clarkson and Company, as brokers for John Michael O'Connor, charged $\frac{1}{4}$ of 1 percent commissions. See chapter 6. The commission cutting may have only been done at this time by fly-by-nights or bucket shops. Later, in the 1860s, both the "Open Board" and the "Old Board" lowered their commissions. See chapter 10.

21. "Resolved that no purchases or sales of stocks shall be made by any member of this Board directly or indirectly in the Street. Any member contravening this order shall be subject to suspension at the pleasure of the Board." NYS&EB Minutes, September 22, 1836, New York Stock Exchange Archives. An attempt was made in 1840 to repeal this ruling, and a compromise was finally reached by changing suspension to a fine of $5 for street trading. By this time, the challenge from the New Board was practically over. See Neill, *The Inside Story of the Stock Exchange*, pp. 48–49.

22. On the New Board, see Eames, *The New York Stock Exchange*, pp. 34–35; Stedman, *The New York Stock Exchange*, pp. 103–4; William Armstrong, *Stocks and Stock Jobbing in Wall Street*, pp. 8–9. A copy of an 1847 constitution and bylaws for the "New Stock Exchange" exists at the New York Stock Exchange Archives. This New Board was also sometimes called the Bourse, after exchanges in Europe. It was formally dissolved in 1848. On other later rival boards, see chapter 10.

23. A market that does the most business in an item, whether a security or not, is likely to be the best market for that item; it tends to produce the narrowest differential between bid and asked quotations and the best executions. Trading then gravitates to that market in a self-fulfilling cycle: size attracts the orders that improve the market and further enhances its attractiveness. Such growth appears to have happened in the first years of the NYS&EB.

24. A stock exchange is a market, controlled by rules, where securities consisting chiefly of the stocks, bonds, and other securities of corporations are bought and sold. Manifestly, a security privileged to be bought and sold on such an exchange obtains a wider market and a more defined current value than one which is not. It may be said therefore, that the true function of such an exchange is 1) to furnish the widest possible market for securities, and 2) to register with greater definiteness their current value. Report of the Committee Appointed Pursuant to House Resolutions 429 and

504 (Pujo Committee) to Investigate the Concentration and Control of Money and Credit, before a subcommittee of the Committee on Banking and Currency, February 28, 1913, 62d Cong. 2d. Sess., p. 33.

25. See Resolutions November 10 and 29, 1817, NYS&EB Minutes, New York Stock Exchange Archives, reprinted in appendix D. The information was published in a *Price Current*, a weekly publication listing prices of hundreds of commodities. Prior to 1817, the *New York Price Current* had included securities prices that were presumably furnished by one or more brokers.

26. Volume information released after 1828 appears in the *New York Journal of Commerce*, in addition to the monthly quotation lists.

27. See appendix A regarding off-board trading; NYS&EB Memorial, Documents of the Assembly of the State of New York, 59th Sess, no. 291, March 23, 1836, p. 5.

28. Today, the New York Stock Exchange's trading list includes issues of most of the nation's largest corporations, but the American Stock Exchange and NASDAQ, the over-the-counter market, trade thousands of other issues. Today, the Exchange trades only securities that meet its listing standards; in the early days, it traded any security that its members wanted to trade.

29. For more on the mechanism of time bargains, see chapter 6.

30. See appendix D. See also the 1820 constitution. Article 11 provides that: "All questions of dispute in the purchases or sales at the Board shall be decided by a majority of the members present. In default of any contract made at the Board for the following day, the defaulter shall be held liable unless he can surrender a principal who shall be considered a responsible person. In all time bargains the parties to surrender principals before one o'clock P.M. of the day of contract, and where either party gives up principal, the other to be allowed until five o'clock P.M. of the same day for consideration. When the principal on either side is not satisfactory, the bargain be void; if no explanation takes place before the time specified, the parties are to be considered bound." Any time transaction executed by a broker was subject to the approval of each principal in the transaction.

31. See Memorial and Remonstrance of the Board of Stock & Exchange Brokers of the City of New York, Documents of the Assembly of the State of New York, 59th Sess. no. 291, March 23, 1836, p. 6. Time bargains were either unenforceable as wagering contracts or were unenforceable under one of the statutes that attempted to outlaw stock jobbing. See chapter 8.

32. Inside their own room, the brokers of the Exchange operated outside the laws of New York. The Exchange had a daily roll call with bids for particular shares, a procedure which resembled auctions, even while auctions for stocks were illegal. See Memorial, Documents of the Assembly of the State of New York, 59th Sess. no. 291, March 23, 1836, p. 3. See also chapter 8. Compare John Michael O'Connor who did not bring his time bargain business to the Exchange. See chapter 6.

33. See Medbery, *Men and Mysteries of Wall Street*, pp. 29–34, for a particularly vivid description of trading prices pushed and pulled by bulls and bears.

34. Medbery, *Men and Mysteries of Wall Street*, p. 14.

35. NYS&EB Minute Book, New York Stock Exchange Archives.

36. *Niles Weekly Register*, February 14, 1835, 47:2. The issue was decided by arbitration under the Exchange's auspices. *New York Journal of Commerce*, February 14, 1835. Later corners were not invalidated on the NYS&EB. Whatever conservative

forces worked against the successful corners in 1835 were no longer felt on the exchange later in the century.

37. See Niles, May 22, 1830, 38:229; July 13, 1833, 44(1138):315. On corners generally, see chapter 6.

38. New York Journal of Commerce, February 14, 1835.

39. Details of this speculation are set out in the chapters 4 and 6.

40. See Documents of the Assembly of the State of New York. 59th Sess, no. 291, March 23, 1836. The bill was entitled An Act to Regulate the Sale of Stocks and Bills of Exchange. See also A Report Of the Select Committee on Stock-Jobbing, Documents of the Assembly of the State of New York, 57th Sess., no. 339, March 28, 1834, recommending legislation.

41. "The city of New-York has for many years past been the great centre of the monied transactions of the Union, and the only market where stocks, to any large amount, could be sold, at any one time, for their intrinsic value, and where money naturally flows to seek employment, or find proper objects of investment; and the great facilities for buying and selling stocks, through the agency of the broker's board, is one reason why the transactions in stock, for foreign and domestic account, are much more extensive in this city than at Philadelphia, or in any other city of the Union." Memorial, Documents of the Assembly of the State of New York, 59th Sess, no. 291, March 23, 1836, p. 2.

42. Memorial, p. 5. The brokers directly make the connection between the stock market and other forms of gambling. They say nothing about the useful aspects of capital allocation that a securities market performs. "Men do not use mathematically exact methods in investing funds. Rather do they tend to accept hunches, personal impressions, alleged tips, and all other wildly speculative leads. Is this not a reflection of man's deep conviction that, after all, life itself is one great gamble?" Timothy Pitkin, The Consumer: His Nature and His Changing Habits, p. 193. Compare Stedman, The New York Stock Exchange, p. 13.

43. Time bargains were said by the memorialists to be enforceable at law in Philadelphia. Memorial, p. 6. Pennsylvania considered a law outlawing time bargains at the same time that New York passed its law, but it was not passed. See chapter 8.

44. On December 14, 1818, The National Advocate printed parts of a letter signed "Seven per cent."

45. On December 18, 1818, in the New York Commercial Advertiser, Messrs. Lewis and Hall responded.

46. William W. Fowler, Ten Years in Wall Street, p. 52.

4. An Overview of New York Securities Markets: 1792–1840

1. The American Minerva published summary prices from January 8, 1794 to October 24, 1794. The prices were then published by The Herald, A Gazette for the Country, in 1795 and 1796. It was not until 1797 that securities prices appeared regularly each week in The New York Price Current, a supplement to the New York Daily Advertiser.

2. Shipping was encouraged by opportunities that resulted from war between Britain and France. Profitable foreign trade kept the United States economy strong, although there were recessions in 1794 and 1798. See Arthur H. Cole and Walter B.

Smith, *Fluctuations in American Business, 1790–1860* (hereafter "*Fluctuations*"), p. 13; Davis, *Essays,* 2:97.

3. See Davis, *Essays,* 2:294. For a summary of securities traded in the earliest years, see Hedges, *Commercial Banking,* pp. 29–33. Hedges discusses government debt and shares in banks and insurance companies.

4. Fritz Redlich, *The Molding of American Banking,* 2:316.

5. *Niles Weekly Register,* April 24, 1813, 4:131.

6. Trading in New York Insurance Company shares began in 1798. See table 1 in appendix A. For more on issuers, see chapter 7.

7. Cole and Smith, *Fluctuations,* p. 17. *Poulson's American Daily Advertiser* contains numerous announcements of bankruptcies and sheriff's sales in this period.

8. See Douglas North, *The Economic Growth of the United States 1790–1860,* p. 56.

9. On the commercial crisis resulting from the war and the closing of the ports, see Pratt, *The Work of Wall Street,* p. 248. New England in general did not support the war, and New England banks would not purchase government bonds to help finance it. They hoarded specie, and banks in the South and West were forced to suspended specie payments during the war. See Cole and Smith, *Fluctuations,* pp. 28–29. Loosely run banks arose elsewhere, and these caused trouble after the war, as did increased competition undermining the new manufacturers after imports resumed. See Murray Rothbard, *The Panic of 1819.*

10. Medbery, *Men and Mysteries of Wall Street,* p. 287. See also Myers, *A Financial History of the United States,* pp. 75–78.

11. On the New York issues, see the *New York Evening Post,* July 7, 1812, p. 3, announcing subscriptions to a $600,000 loan at 6 percent.

12. The New York Legislature incorporated the Phoenix Bank (capital $500,000), Franklin Bank ($500,000), City Bank ($1,500,000) and Bank of America ($2,000,000). See the *New York Journal of Commerce,* November 24, 1828, p. 3.

13. "The recent incorporation of three Banking Companies in this city seems to have, in some degree, depressed the market price of bank stock." *New York Commercial Advertiser,* July 1, 1812. See also *New York Evening Post,* July 8, 1812. The opening of subscription books for the shares of the Bank of America was announced on June 10, 1812, and shares were still available July 22, 1812. See *New York Evening Post* for the intervening period. The Bank of America was conceived as a private sector replacement for the Bank of the United States; it became a cause célèbre when Governor Tompkins prorogued the New York legislature about the charter in 1812. See Hammond, *Banks and Politics in America,* pp. 162–64; *Niles,* February 8, 1812, 1:410–12. Another indicator of the sluggish market was the number of shares listed with nominal quotes. See, e.g., *New York Price Current,* September 5, 12, 19, and 26, and October 3, 1812.

14. See Walter Barret, *The Old Merchants of New York,* 1:398; Medbery, *Men and Mysteries of Wall Street,* p. 287; Meeker, *The Work of the Stock Exchange,* p. 30. See also *New York Price Current* of this period.

15. See Cole and Smith, *Fluctuations,* pp. 7, 23. Many corporate shares had no prices quoted during 1813 and 1814. See, e.g., *New York Price Current,* September 4, 11, 18, and 25, and October 2, 1813; September 3, 10, and 17, and October 18 and 21, 1814.

16. 1815 was clearly a depression year. Cole and Smith, *Fluctuations,* pp. 30–31.

According to Charles Kindleberger, *Manias, Panics and Crashes*, p. 42, 1816 was a crisis year, of the kind that come at the end of a war.

17. *New York Courier*, June 12, 1816, p. 2.

18. Compare Cole and Smith, *Fluctuations*, p. 22: Securities trading during this period was "unimportant."

19. See, e.g., *New York Price Current* September 6, 13, 20, and 27, 1817. Part of the cause of this new strength in the bond market was due to the ability to purchase shares in the Bank of the United States with federal bonds. Federal bonds were commanding a similar premium in 1820. See, e.g., *New York Evening Post*, September 13, 26, 20 and 23, 1820.

20. The amount of outstanding bonds of the United States increased from $45 million in 1812 to $123 million in 1817. New York State and New York City also issued bonds. Eames, *The New York Stock Exchange*, p. 18. See also Adam Seybert, *Statistical Annals*, p. 753.

21. Hammond, *Banks and Politics in America*, pp. 244–45. Many of these shares found their way overseas, and less than 20 percent came into New York. Ralph Catteral, *The Second Bank of the United States*, p. 508.

22. See Joseph Martin, *A Century of Finance*, p. 14. On the speculation in the Bank stock, see chapter 9.

23. See Nathan Miller, *The Enterprise of a Free People*. See also Myers, *The New York Money Market*, p. 24.

24. According to James S. Gibbons, *The Banks of New York*, p. 68, the public debt in 1818 was the highest until 1862, and it is no accident that the formation of the NYS&EB coincided with the peak in the debt. See also Martin, *A Century of Finance*, pp. 15–16. Rothbard, *The Panic of 1819*, p. 20, attributes the boom that led to the NYS&EB formation to easy money policies of the new bank, which did not require redemption of notes in specie.

25. See chapter 7 for more on the Delaware and Hudson. New York Gas and Light was originally listed as a joint stock company in the *New York Journal of Commerce*. See September 13, 1828; June 21, 1831.

26. See, e.g., *New York Journal of Commerce*, September 13, 1828.

27. There are indications that New England with its more prudently managed banks was largely spared. See Rothbard, *The Panic of 1819*. See, also, Pratt, *The Work of Wall Street*, p. 248; North, *The Economic Growth of the United States, 1790–1860*, pp. 182–85; Cole and Smith, *Fluctuations*, p. 30; Clews, *Fifty Years in Wall Street*. Note that as late as June 12, 1824, *Niles*, 26:241, tells of how the Bank of the United States and other monied institutions find it difficult to invest their dollars.

28. Between 1819 and 1824, the spirit of speculation was felt only during a brief expansion during the summer of 1821. However, by late 1824, speculation was active again. William Gouge, *The Curse of Paper Money and Banking*, p. 135. Medbery suggests that the American fever of 1825 was calmness itself compared to the fiery pulsebeat of speculation with which all of England was throbbing. *Men and Mysteries of Wall Street*, pp. 291–92. See appendix A.

29. *Men and Mysteries of Wall Street*, p. 290. *Niles*, May 7, 1825, 28(10):147, describes the opening at Southwark: "Persons appear to have been employed for the express purpose of fighting their way to the books, and bloody noses and black eyes were 'in order.' Many persons were knocked down, and one, at least, is said actually

to have died in consequence of the squeezing and scrambling and fighting that he met with." William Gouge, *A Short History of Paper Money and Banking in the United States*, explains the pressure in Philadelphia: "In New York, the speculator's practice is to subscribe to a much greater amount than the nominal capital, and then clamor for a pro rata division. . . . In Pennsylvania, where subscriptions are not received beyond the amount of nominal capital, draymen and other ablebodied persons are hired by the speculators to get the script for them. They struggle at the windows with so much violence as to give personal injury." See p. 26.

30. *Niles*, Aug. 12, 1826, 30:411. "1826—Considerable excitement in New York in the summer in consequence of the sudden collapse of sundry incorporated bubbles." Martin, *A Century of Finance*, p. 20. The commercial panic of 1826 was brought on by the failure of numerous joint stock companies, "some under the control of fraudulent stock jobbers, and others of visionary enthusiasts." Mary L. Booth, *History of the City of New York*, 2:725. See, also, Frederick Jackson (attributed), *A Week in Wall Street by One Who Knows*.

31. *New York American*, November 25, 1827. See also *New York Journal of Commerce*, March 29, 1828 for an advertisement clamoring for investors without revealing the nature of the project.

32. *Niles*, December 3, 1825, 29:210. See, also, *Niles*, July 3, 1824, 26:281: "The awful and severe castigation that we justly received for our folly or madness some years ago, appears to be forgotten. I did not expect that the lesson would have failed of effect so soon."

33. Gouge, *The Curse of Paper Money and Banking*, p. 136.

34. Pratt, *The Work of Wall Street*, p. 248. Kindleberger discusses this panic as one that fits the pattern of a panic some seven to ten years after every war. *Manias, Panics and Crashes*, p. 211. Pratt feels the panic was due to extensive troubles in England caused by overspeculation in South American enterprises combined with poor harvests, *The Work of Wall Street*, p. 248. Niles also blames the "madness" in England where the abundance of money had led to the "wildest and most visionary projects that had ever had their day." *Niles*, May 7, 1825, 28(10):147; September 10, 1825, 28(10):23.

35. See appendix A. There was a slight decline in the number of publicly quoted issues as well, but that decline may be attributable to a change in the source of data. Note that there were small monetary upheavals in 1829 and 1831. See Pratt, *The Work of Wall Street*, p. 248; Gouge, *The Curse of Paper Money and Banking*, p. 136.

36. See Cole and Smith, *Fluctuations*, p. 51. See also later discussion herein, as to the suitability of the New York market to the trading of railroad stocks.

37. On the contractionary effects of the problems and policies of the Second United States Bank during this period, see McGrane, *The Panic of 1837*, pp. 4–5; Clews, *Fifty Years in Wall Street*, p. 503; Redlich, *The Molding of American Banking*, 2:335 ("engineered depression of 1834"); Cole and Smith, *Fluctuations*, p. 51 ("recession of significance").

36. According to McGrane, *The Panic of 1837*, pp. 3–4, when the Second Bank of the United States abandoned a tight monetary policy in September, an upswing in October resulted. According to Peter Temin, *The Jacksonian Economy*, pp. 22–23, the boom of the early 1830s was due to 1) an increase in silver exported from England, and 2) a decrease in silver wanted in China. Specie flowed in from abroad,

and later that specie fueled inflation. Inflation was the dominant economic fact of 1830s. Temin, p. 68. Interest rates were also high, peaking at 30 percent in 1836. Cole and Smith, *Fluctuations*, pp. 76–77. On securities prices, see Cole and Smith, p. 47. On volume, see appendix A.

39. See Pratt, *The Work of Wall Street*, p. 10.

40. See *The New York Journal of Commerce*, any issue in the mid-1830s.

41. Cole and Smith, *Fluctuations*, p. 51. From August 1833 to January and February 1834, prices were down. Prices shot up at the end of 1834 through the beginning of 1835. Medbery, *Men and Mysteries of Wall Street*, pp. 91, 293–94.

42. See Medbery, *Men and Mysteries of Wall Street*, pp. 13, 295–97. See also chapter 8.

43. Land sales in the 1820s were about $2 million per year. In 1834, they jumped to $5 million, just as the stock market was heating up as well. In 1835, land sales reached $15 million and in 1836, $25 million. After the stock market crash, the real estate market crashed too, and, in 1837, land sales were down to $7 million. See Temin, *The Jacksonian Economy*. The value of land in New York rose from $250 million in 1830 to $403 million in 1835. McGrane, *The Panic of 1837*, p. 45.

44. See George Soule, *Economic Forces in American History*, p. 55. Land speculation was also partially the result of enormous increases in land values because of urbanization and a rapid increase in population. Guy Callender, "The Early Transportation and Banking Enterprises of the State in Relation to the Growth of Corporations," p. 130.

45. For an early example of land speculation, the Scotio land scheme with which William Duer was heavily involved, see Davis, *Essays*, 1:125–50, 213–53. On land speculation generally, see Shah Livermore, *Early American Land Companies*; A. M. Sakolski, *The Great American Land Bubble*. Probably the most famous early American land speculation involved the Yazoo companies. By act of January 7, 1795, the Georgia legislature directed the sale of an enormous area of land comprising most of what are now the states of Alabama and Mississippi. The passage of the bill was secured by open and wholesale bribery. A political turmoil ensued, and a new legislature revoked the sale. See *Fletcher v. Peck*, 6 Cranch (10 U.S.) 87 (1810); Livermore, pp. 146–56.

46. "It is known that those who cannot, with the prospect of advantage, invest their cash in commercial speculations, generally chuse to resort to the finds." *Columbian Centinel*, September 22, 1802, p. 2. Compare: "Speculation was accustomed to concern itself mainly with commodities and land, and only in a minor degree with stocks and government issues." Cole and Smith, *Fluctuations in American Business, 1790–1860*, p. 7.

47. Quoted in Callender, "The Early Transportation and Banking Enterprises of the State in Relation to the Growth of Corporations," pp. 130–31.

48. Michael Chevalier, *Society Manners and Politics in the United States*, p. 305. "Everything" included not only stocks but also commodities and land.

49. According to Medbery, at the time of the fire, "there were several heavy speculative movements under way, and it was deemed indispensable to save the records. One brave fellow went in among the blazing rafters, seized the big iron box, where they were kept, and bore it safely out. The Board voted a generous reward at its very next meeting." *Men and Mysteries of Wall Street*, p. 295. The fire occurred on December 16. For different accounts, see Hedges, *Commercial Banking*, p. 39;

Meeker, *The Work of the Stock Exchange*, p. 65; Eames, *The New York Stock Exchange*, p. 29.

50. A sharp but irregular downward trend in securities prices after 1836 that did not recover until 1842–43 is reported by Cole and Smith, *Fluctuations*, pp. 47–51. See also appendix A.

51. The conventional explanation for this contraction places much of the blame on Andrew Jackson's land policies. The 1836 Specie Circular designed to curb land sales has been blamed for drawing specie from East Coast Banks, and then the distribution of the federal surplus to the states beginning in 1837 drew even more specie from banks. Temin disagrees and blames a crisis in international trade. *The Jacksonian Economy*, pp. 121, 144. He believes the boom and crises were caused by events beyond the control of Andrew Jackson, pp. 11, 17.

52. The bellwether Bank of Pennsylvania, formerly the Second Bank of the United States, suspended specie payments in 1837, resumed again in 1838, only to suspend again in 1839. After Biddle got involved in cotton speculation, the bank failed in 1841.

53. Pratt, *The Work of Wall Street*, pp. 248–49; McGrane, *The Panic of 1837*, p. 1. McGrane saw the panic as tragic, as it resulted in a contraction lasting from 1837–44.

54. See Temin, *The Jacksonian Economy*, p. 148. Temin feels that the depression was not as serious as others have claimed. He claims that deflation is responsible for making many economic indicators appear worse than the underlying economic conditions, pp. 22–23. "The Deflation of 1837 was mild and short-lived; it does not seem to have caused major distress in the economy," p. 120.

55. See Medbery, *Men and Mysteries of Wall Street*, p. 299. Medbery suggests that the stock market had only an incidental connection with the crash of 1837. See appendix A.

56. British willingness to invest in America had not been diminished by the crisis, and the return of easy credit to that country brought a demand for American securities. Temin, *The Jacksonian Economy*, p. 149.

57. In 1841: Florida, Mississippi, Arkansas, and Indiana; in 1842: Illinois, Maryland, Michigan, Pennsylvania, and Louisiana. B. U. Ratchford, *American State Debts*, pp. 98, 101.

58. See Ratchford, *American State Debts*, pp. 153–54.

59. Investment fell dramatically; railroad construction fell by two-thirds from its peak in 1838 to its trough in 1843. Canal construction fell by nine-tenths from its peak in 1839 to its trough in 1844. Ratchford, *American State Debts*, p. 162, quoting Gouge, *A Short History of Paper Money and Banking in the United States*.

60. Thirty had suspended specie payments in the worst of the crisis, occuring in the fall of 1839. Medbery, *Men and Mysteries of Wall Street*, p. 304. Compare the account given in *The New York Stock Exchange*, p. 23. "The panic of 1837 was a commercial panic pure and simple, and the New York Stock Exchange had so little connection with it that its members suffered but slightly."

61. Compare Fowler, who in 1870 writes that "It is only within the past 35 years that Wall Street has got to have a special significance as the centre, not only of money, but of speculation." *Ten Years in Wall Street*, p. 23.

62. "Philadelphia, nevertheless, was fairly important; in Boston there were deal-

ings enough to insure quotable market prices at least in active periods; and outlying cities, like New London and Charleston, were affected to a lesser extent." Davis, *Essays,* 1:200, citing *New York Daily Advertiser,* August 19 and 20, 1791; *Columbian Centinel,* January 18, 1792 ["signed, A Citizen"]; *New York Journal and Patriotic Register,* September 10, 1792. See, also, Davis, 1:286.

63. Arbitrage between markets eliminated, or at least narrowed, differences in yield to investors and cost to issuers for issues that were traded nationally or internationally: primarily federal bonds and shares in the Bank of the United States. For examples of arbitrage, see Anspach Collection, New-York Historical Society. Standish Forde's correspondence furnished Anspach with the prices in Philadelphia while transmitting instructions for handling an account in New York. See, also, letters of Nicholas Low, another New York broker who received information about the Philadelphia market at this time. New-York Historical Society. Davis, *Essays,* 1:200, also discusses arbitrage in the early market. Note that Pomerantz, *New York: An American City,* 1783–1803, p. 164, suggests that increasing arbitrage due to speculation resulted in a demand for better mailing facilities, which a 1792 law sought to provide.

64. See letter from Edward Fox to Andrew Cragie quoted in Davis, *Essays,* 1:200, complaining of market stagnation in Philadelphia: "No man will sell here because he knows more money is to be had in Your City." See also the Forde-Anspach correspondence, New-York Historical Society, which makes the primacy of New York clear, e.g., March 22, 1792: Philadelphia stock prices "will in a great degree depend on the New York market." And see letters from Wm. Wilson, Alexandria merchant, to Andres Clow and Company, January 7 and 27, 1792, recognizing that events in New York run the Philadelphia bond market. Clow Collection, Harvard University Baker Library. Note also that Leonard Bleecker, a New York broker, advertised in the *Gazette of the United States* (Philadelphia) in 1792. See, e.g., the July 4, 1792 issue. Compare Fowler, *Ten Years in Wall Street,* p. 23.

65. In the quiet years before the war of 1812, there is evidence of a small securities market in Philadelphia, dealing largely with local issues such as bridges and turnpikes. By 1811, there was enough trading to sustain public auctions twice weekly. See *New York Price Current* for 1811, listing three bonds, four banks, ten insurance companies, a water loan, a city loan, a masonic loan, two bridges, and five turnpikes. See also appendix B for statistics comparing trading in various cities. On the size of the market, note also an attempt, published in *Niles,* January 24, 1829, 35:350, to estimate the entire capital of monied institutions whose shares were traded in the market. New York is listed as having approximately $35 million, Philadelphia approximately $15 million, and Boston $20 million.

66. *Financial Register,* July 11, 1838.

67. Hammond, *Banks and Politics in America,* p. 149.

68. See Alfred D. Chandler, "Patterns of American Railroad Finance 1830–1850," p. 248. Philadelphia merchants were said to have surplus funds. The Second Bank of the United States (converted in 1836 to the Bank of Pennsylvania) had European connections and the new railroads sold their bonds, often denominated sterling bonds, in the Philadelphia market. See, e.g., the Camden and Amboy Railroad of New Jersey.

69. Entrepreneurs like John Murray Forbes were flush with capital from the China trade or Massachusetts textile mills. During the 1840s, Boston superseded Philadel-

phia as the railroad's chief source of initial investment funds. The Michigan Central is an example of a railroad that went to Boston for capital.

70. Many affluent New Yorkers were heavily involved in New York's glorious new canal system—as owners of bonds, shippers, or owners of land enriched by completion of the canals.

71. New Yorkers purchased railroad stocks for investment in the 1830s and 1840s, as in Boston and Philadelphia. Other projects also found money in New York. See, e.g., Niles, April 16, 1825, 26:103 (Ohio Canal, $400,000); January 13, 1827, p. 31:310 (Ohio Canal, $600,000); December 1, 1827, 33:211 (Ohio Canal, $900,000); October 18, 1828, 35:115 (Ohio Canal, $1,200,000); October 23, 1830, 39:140 (Ohio Canal, $600,000). In 1825, *Niles* declared that New York "is destined to become the monied capital of the whole Union. If internal improvements are projected, or even heavy institutions begun, application must be made to New York." April 16, 26:103. According to Hedges, other than for railroads, New York was recognized as the country's capital market after the Erie Canal bonds were successfully floated. *Commercial Banking*, p. 69. See also Redlich, *The Molding of American Banking*, 2:333–34.

72. Chandler, "Patterns of American Railroad Finance, 1830–1850," pp. 262–63.

73. By 1826, the *New York Evening Post* had a section of their quote list entitled "nationals." Boston securities were strikingly insulated from forces which were active in other parts of the country, and which were producing wide swings in the leading phases of speculation—railroad stocks and public land sales. Cole and Smith, *Fluctuations in American Business, 1790–1860*, p. 47. Other stock markets in commercial cities that were the centerpieces of their regions, such as New Orleans, retained local flavors as well.

74. Hedges, *Commercial Banking*, p. 88. Call loans became the accepted means of financing stock speculation since funds lent on the security of stocks could be called at any time. Call loans grew with the emerging practice of margin trading.

75. Hedges, *Commercial Banking*, p. 139. The liquidity of call loans was illusory. When the market crashed in 1837, the prices of stocks dropped so rapidly that many loans were not fully collateralized after all, p. 105.

76. Hedges, *Commercial Banking*, pp. 77, 89.

77. Formerly Boston, Philadelphia, and Baltimore held large balances from country banks, but by 1859 New York had nearly all of them. Hedges, *Commercial Banking*, p. 58, citing *Bankers Magazine* of August 1859, 14:132–33. See also Hedges, pp. 58–71. Note that New York City banks encouraged "country" banks to keep deposits with them, or they would refuse to accept their notes. See *Niles*, November 19, 1825, 29:180.

78. In turn, foreign balances were held in New York. Hedges, *Commercial Banking*, pp. 71, 138–39. London money definitely preferred Gallatin and New York to Biddle and Philadelphia. The Rothschilds in particular backed the wrong horse, i.e., Biddle, and thereafter stayed out of American finance. Hammond, *Banks and Politics in America*, pp. 516–17. The debacle of 1837 also dimmed the Rothschilds' enthusiasm for investing in the United States.

79. In 1815, "New York in particular became both the center of the import trade and the financial center of the cotton trade." North, *The Economic Growth of the*

United States 1790–1860, p. 63, citing Myers, The New York Money Market, pp. 49, 70. After the Erie Canal and the beginning of railroads more and more western products began to be traded through New England rather than the South. North, pp. 103–05. Payment for goods received from abroad to be shipped to other parts of the country required banks elsewhere to leave funds on deposit in New York. See also Robert Albion, The Rise of New York Port.

80. See Myers, The New York Money Market, pp. 8–9. The failure of Philadelphia banks to break the New York banks in the famous Chestnut Street raid of 1839 indicated that Philadelphia was no longer the nation's financial center. See Hammond, Banks and Politics in America, pp. 329, 514–16; Hammond, "The Chestnut Street Raid on Wall Street," p. 605.

81. North, The Economic Growth of the United States 1790–1860, p. 49.

5. Securities Professionals: The Market's Nucleus

1. See Davis, Essays, 1:199–212; 278–315; Redlich, The Molding of American Banking, 2:304–5.

2. Massachussets Centinel, July 14, 1784, quoted in Davis, Essays, 1:199.

3. Notices to purchase securities, without mentioning the names of the brokers, appear in the New York Daily Advertiser, October 27 and November 6, 1786. Archibald Blair is the only stockbroker listed in the 1786 New York directory. See also Harrison Bayles, Old Taverns of New York, p. 361; Birl E. Schultz, The Securities Market and How It Works, p. 1. By 1790, stockbroker advertisements were common. See, e.g., New York Daily Advertiser, August 27, 1790, with advertisements for George Sutton and John Grahm.

4. The term stockjobbing referred to dealing in general, but often had some sinister overtone; it generally implied some sharp practice or rigging of the market. Morgan, The London Stock Exchange, p. 21. The distinction between brokers and jobbers has always been much more defined on the London Stock Exchange than in New York. Morgan, pp. 146–47. In New York, the distinction between dealers and jobbers may have been that jobbers operated exclusively on their own accounts, where dealers operated both for themselves and others. See Henry Hamon, New York Stock Exchange Manual, p. 107.

5. See Dos Passos, A Treatise on the Law of Stock-Brokers and Stock-Exchanges (hereafter "A Treatise"), pp. 1, 249, 269.

6. See chapter 8. Pennsylvania, in the city charter granted to Philadelphia in March 1789, provided for the licensing of brokers in accordance with regulations established by the city councils. Davis, Essays, 1:200. On the uncertainty surrounding the term "sworn brokers" see chapter 5. Regardless of the precise meaning of the term "sworn broker," there does not appear to have been any conflict between sworn brokers and unsworn brokers.

7. New York Laws, 7th Sess. 1 Greenleaf 64, February 20, 1784. See memorials by L. Bleecker, January 10, 1784, and A. L. Bleecker, January 21, 1784, petitioning the legislature for appointments as auctioneers. Bleecker Collection, New-York Historical Society. When sales of stock at auction were outlawed in 1792, the legislature limited New York to twenty four auctioneers, and required they be sworn before the

mayor. 2 Greenleaf 470, 15th Session, April 10, 1792, Sec. 2. The fact that the number of auctioneers allowed under the statute was twenty four, the same as the number who signed the Buttonwood Agreement of 1792, could be a coincidence, or could reflect some astute lobbying on their part.

8. See Sutton and Hardy's advertisement in the *Daily Advertiser* beginning April 30, 1792, that they will continue as sworn stock brokers and also as auctioneers. See also Emphriam Hart's advertisement in the *Daily Advertiser*, January 15, 1793, explaining that although he had been appointed an auctioneer, he could not find a convenient vendue store, but he would continue to sell stock on commission. See also the *New York Courier* of April 8, 1817, listing of auctioneers in the City of New York (thirty five of them), including James Bleecker (NYS&EB signer), Simon Nathan (NYS&EB signer), and Benjamin Seixas (Buttonwood signer). Brokers would also often act as dealers.

9. See NYS&EB 1817 constitution, article 11, reprinted in appendix D. Brokers were involved with mortgages, foreign exchange, and commercial paper, for which the NYS&EB fixed commission rates.

10. Temple Prime, *Some Account of the Family of Prime of Rowley Mass.*, p. 12.

11. See Barret, *Old Merchants of New York*, 1:11; Wettereau Papers no. 31, Columbia University Butler Library; Phillip G. Hubert, *Merchants National Bank of the City of New York*, p. 49.

12. Acting as agent for a principal, the broker looks for the other side of a transaction that can involve any property or service: a parcel of land, interest in a ship, insurance, a security. He receives a commission for his services only when he puts together a transaction between his principal and the other party. On Prime's aggressiveness, see letter from Matthew Livingston Davis, May 8, 1830, in Nathan Prime Collection, New-York Historical Society; Barret, *Old Merchants of New York*, pp. 11–12.

13. An article in *Niles* on bank notes and exchange provides explanations for the depreciation in value of bank paper, pinning much of the blame on note shavers. "Nor will this public grievance be redressed until our banking institutions are purged of speculators and shavers," October 11, 1817, 13:97.

14. Barret, *Old Merchants of New York*, p. 11; A. Greef, *The Commercial Paper House in the United States*, pp. 7–8.

15. The sources of information about Nathan Prime's career, unfortunately, are far from complete or satisfactory. Prime and his firms left little in the way of original papers or books of account. At times it becomes necessary to fill in some of the gaps in his development by reference to the activities of Prime's contemporaries. Compare advertisement of Isaac M. Gomez, who told the public that he "buys and sells all kinds of public securities, on commission or otherwise, negotiates promissory notes of hand, and bills of exchange, transacts all kinds of business in the brokerage line," *New York Daily Advertiser*, July 2, 1791.

16. Cornelia Sands Prime was born in New York November 8, 1773, the daughter of Comfort Sands, a New York merchant. Nathan and Cornelia may have lived with her father for a year or two, and it is likely that access to his capital boosted Prime's business. See Temple Prime, *Some Account of the Family of Prime of Rowley Mass.*, p. 12.

17. The line between brokerage and dealer business was often thin. The transfer

book for the Eagle Fire Insurance Company, New-York Historical Society, includes trades that were obviously of the kind later to be known as "riskless principal" transactions. Prime would purchase twenty two shares for his own account and then sell twenty two shares the same or following day. The odd number of shares points to the likelihood that Prime was serving as agent for two customers but was taking his compensation in the form of a dealer's turn rather than a broker's commission.

18. N. Gras, *The Massachussets First National Bank of Boston, 1784–1934*, p. 86 discusses trading by a Boston broker-dealer in the shares of the Massachusetts bank that amounted to market-making, but not until 1821–1853. Compare Neill, *The Inside Story of the Stock Exchange*, p. 19.

19. The securities listed were: 8 percent federal bonds; 6 percent federal bonds; Navy 6 percent; 3 percent federal bonds; Bank of the United States shares, Bank of New York shares, Bank of Manhattan shares; New York Insurance Company shares; Columbia Insurance Company shares and United Insurance Company shares. Prime's advertisement also lists exchange on London, Amsterdam, and Hamburg. *New York Commercial Advertiser*, January 2, 9, 16, 1802, p. 3.

20. In 1806, for example, Prime made a market in the relatively small issue of the Eagle Fire Insurance Company when those shares were traded briskly during the first few months after they were issued, as were most new issues. See appendix A.

21. *New York Evening Post*, 1805, reproduced in Neill, *The Inside Story of the Stock Exchange*, p. 32.

22. David Parish, the son of a Hamburg banker who had come to New York, was an extraordinarily interesting man. See P. and R. Walters, "The American Career of David Parish," *Journal of Economic History*, vol. 4, 1944. Parish had come to the United States as a representative of Baring Brothers of London and Hope and Company of Amsterdam. Some of his transactions with Prime were large. On November 21, 1806, for example, Parish forwarded a bill to Prime for $28,042 in Spanish dollars and credited Prime with $6,025 worth of federal bonds. Letter books of David Parish, New-York Historical Society. See especially letters during 1806, 1811, and 1812.

23. See N. Prime's signature as "atty" acknowledging receipt of dividends paid to shareholders of the Union Bank of New York who were apparently his clients. Union Bank Dividend Book, 1806–1814, New-York Historical Society. Redlich describes Prime, Ward, and King as the first American private banking firm because it was the first to take deposits and make loans by discounting paper. *The Molding of American Banking*, 2:67.

24. Ralph W. Hidy, *The House of Baring in American Trade and Finance*, pp. 109–10.

25. Before selling to the syndicate, Gallatin had tried, unsuccessfully, to promote sale of the bonds by offering a $\frac{1}{4}$ of 1 percent commission to anyone arranging to combine individual subscriptions into a single subscription. After the Treasury's success with the 1813 issue, loan contracting became a standard method of distributing securities. The history of loan contracting is detailed in Redlich, *The Molding of American Banking*, 2:304–55.

26. Donald R. Adams, Jr., "The Beginning of Investment Banking in the United States," pp. 99, 109–10; letter of April 3, 1813, to Prime & Ward, Letter books of David Parish, New-York Historical Society. Prime's refusal was an early instance in which an investment banker allowed politics to interfere with business judgment.

27. The Ohio government came to Prime and asked him to form a committee to look into the state's finances as a prelude to borrowing money. On the recommendation of the committee, the loan was made after Ohio inserted a favorable tax provision in the law that authorized the borrowing. See Walter Barret, *Old Merchants of New York*, pp. 391–92; Myers, *The New York Money Market*, 1:24–25, n. 40.

28. In 1818, Prime combined forces with LeRoy Bayard & Co. of New York in bidding for an Erie Canal loan, but lost to the winning bidder, the New York State Bank. *New York Daily Advertiser*, July 18, 1818, p. 2. In 1821, Prime, Ward & Sands did manage to buy $85,000 of an Erie issue, which they proceeded to sell. Miller, *The Enterprise of a Free People*, p. 96. In 1821, an alliance of Prime, Ward, & Sands, Thomas and John Biddle of Philadelphia, and Charles King was established to purchase a $4,000,000 treasury floatation. The alliance's contingent bid of .01 percent above any other offer lost out to the Bank of the United States' ambiguous bid of 1 percent over the average of other offers. Neither argument nor veiled threats swayed the Secretary of the Treasury; rather, they did little more than to demonstrate that the alliance was not above sharp practices. Redlich, *The Molding of American Banking* 2:328.

29. Annual Report of the Comptroller, New York State Assembly Documents, 60th Sess., Doc. no. 4, January 4, 1837, pp. 53–57. See, also, appendix A. Bidding for this loan was highly competitive, and the premium of 10.62 percent paid by Prime, Ward & Sands was the highest on any Erie Canal loan.

30. See e.g. *Niles*, October 18, 1828 35:115 (Ohio Canal 6 percent, $1,200,000); October 23, 1830, 39:140 (Ohio Canal $600,000). See also Redlich, *The Molding of American Banking* 2:333–34, for a discussion of loans sold in New York to Prime, Ward & King in the 1820s and 1830s. Prime, Ward & King only occasionally purchased and resold issues of corporate shares. Compare Girard, who acted as an underwriter in the purchase of shares in the Second Bank of the United States. Adams, "The Beginnings of Investment Banking in the United States," p. 115.

31. The association with the Barings grew out of correspondence begun by Prime in 1810. By 1830, the business between Prime and the Barings had developed into a joint account allowing Prime, Ward & King £50,000 of credit. See Hidy, *The House of Baring in American Trade and Finance*, pp. 49, 109–10, 132, 151, 177.

32. Prime, Ward & King was one of the few firms able to trade foreign currency. Redlich, *The Molding of American Banking*, 2:67. At other times, Alexander Brown and Sons of Baltimore were the leading American dealers in foreign exchange. See Walter B. Smith, *Economic Aspects of the Second Bank of the United States*, p. 46.

33. "Nathaniel Prime, having taken Samuel Ward, Jun. into partnership, the business as Stock and Exchange Brokers, will be transacted in future under the firm of Prime & Ward, 42 Wall St." *New York Commercial Advertiser*, May 5, 1808. Joseph Sands, Cornelia's brother, joined the firm in 1816. A letter from Nathan Prime to J. G. King, June 20, 1823 suggests that Sands had a 5/24ths interest in the firm. Nathan's son Edward joined as a partner in 1820 and received a 3/24ths share. Letter from Nathan to Edward, May 5, 1820. Prime Collection, New York-Historical Society. James Gore King joined the firm in 1825, and the firm was for a time Prime, Ward, Sands, & King, until Sands retired in 1826. See Redlich, *The Molding of American Banking*, 2:67, Martha Lamb and Mrs. Burton Harrison, *History of the City of New York*, 1876.

34. LeRoy Bayard & Co., which took the Erie Canal Loan of May 3, 1824, was such a firm, as was the Baltimore firm of Alexander Brown & Sons, which bought a Maryland bond issue ($2 million) with Cohen & Co., and distributed the bonds with $300,000 of Merchants Bank Stock. See Frank Kent, *The Story of Alexander Brown and Sons*. According to Chandler, "Patterns of Railroad Finance, 1830–1850," this route was followed by firms that later got into the business of loan contracting for railroad securities.

35. J. Joseph was such a representative. See Redlich, *The Molding of American Banking*, 2:335.

36. The best known lottery contractor was S. & M. Allen & Co. Since they took bank notes in payment, they soon engaged in note shaving. See *New York Evening Post*, September 22, 1818, p. 1; "S&M Allen have offices in Philadelphia, Baltimore, Washington D.C., Charleston, etc. and can therefore discount bank notes and drafts at a low rate." When the lottery business dropped off, Allen applied their experience in evaluating the market and merchandising to the securities business. They bid for bond issues, distributing them through branch offices. Allen became one of the roots of E. W. Clark, an important Philadelphia loan contractor and later training ground for Jay Cooke, whose services in helping to finance the Civil War are sometimes considered as marking the beginning of investment banking. See other lottery agents who were also note shavers: G. R. Waite, *New York Evening Post*, February 4, 1812; Van Brunt & Neville, *New York Morning Post*, January 13, 1812.

37. Some institutions, like the Savings Bank of New York, competed with the loan contractors for bond issues, which they apparently held as interest-paying investments. The Savings Bank's charter restricted its investments to state and federal bonds, and it was a large purchaser of Erie Canal bonds. The bank held on to its loans for twelve years or more. Nathan Miller, *The Enterprise of a Free People*, p. 88, n.25.

38. Neill, *The Inside Story of the Stock Exchange*, p. 32; Myers, *The New York Money Market*, p. 67.

39. Medbery, *Men and Mysteries of Wall Street*, p. 289.

40. Henry Wysham Lanier, *A Century of Banking in New York 1822–1922*, p. 127. See *New York Daily Advertiser*, November 11, 1817, which lists the directors of the Globe Insurance Company, including J. J. Astor, Henry Coster, A. H. Lawrence, and Nathan Prime. Prime's candidacy as director in the United States Bank was rejected because of his competition as an exchange dealer. Redlich, *The Molding of American Banking*, 1:117.

41. Redlich, *The Molding of American Banking*, 1:53.

42. Redlich, *The Molding of American Banking*, 1:124; 2:338.

43. We know that its predecessor, Prime, Ward, and Sands, earned $34,000 for its partners in 1823. Prime advised King that a $\frac{7}{24}$ interest in the firm "will give you more than 10,000 dollars per annum." Postscript of July 1 to letter of June 30, 1823, from Prime to King. Prime Collection, New-York Historical Society. It seems reasonable to assume that Prime, Ward & King, which transacted a far larger volume of business than Prime, Ward & Sands, was even more profitable.

44. Barret, *The Old Merchants of New York*, p. 12.

45. See Barret, *The Old Merchants of New York*, pp. 67, 218, 444; Myers, *A Financial History of the United States*, p. 78.

46. William L. Stone, *History of New York City*, p. 418.

47. Advances from his estate to his children amounted to some $345,000 when the will was proved. Indenture of Nathaniel Prime's last will and testament, Prime Collection, New-York Historical Society; Lamb, *History of the City of New York,* 3:710.

48. "Mr. Prime retired from the great banking firm, and his place was filled by his son, Edward Prime. All seemed fair in the future for old Mr. Prime. Vast wealth, excellent sons, daughters all well married, he had nothing else to do but live and enjoy himself. Did he do so? No. The strange fancy seized upon his mind that he was becoming poor—that his destiny was to die in the almshouse. Under this singular monomania, and hallucination of mind, he cut his throat with a razor and died in an instant." Barret, *The Old Merchants of New York,* p. 12.

49. Redlich grudgingly gives some credit for resumption to Prime, Ward & King, *The Molding of American Banking,* 2:67–68, 82–83. See also Myers, *The New York Money Market,* pp. 67–68. According to Medberry, *Men and Mysteries of Wall Street,* pp. 299–301, Samuel Ward worked so hard to get specie payments resumed in 1838 that he fell sick and died soon after.

50. See Redlich, *The Molding of American Banking,* 1:202.

51. The conservative tone he set lasted at least until the 1880s when his firm, now run by his son, would only purchase stocks for cash; they did no margin business, even as margin trading thrived in the 1880s. *The New York Stock Exchange,* p. 61. Charles Christmas, a Prime, Ward & King clerk, and Rufus King founded the firm of Christmas, Livingston, Prime, and Coster and later were instrumental in the rise of the house of Belmont. Redlich, *The Molding of American Banking,* 2:350–53.

52. See text of *Green v. Prime & Ward* in Prime Collection, New-York Historical Society. The plaintiff accused the firm of falsely failing as a ruse to avoid creditors.

53. Chandler, "Patterns of Railroad Finance 1830–1850," p. 254.

54. See Redlich, *The Molding of American Banking,* 2:60–61, 317–18; Armstrong, *Stocks and Stock Jobbing in Wall Street,* p. 32; Robert I. Warshow, *The Story of Wall Street,* p. 63; Matthew W. Smith, *20 Years Among the Bulls and Bears at Wall Street,* p. 246. On Jacob Barker, see the interesting note of a trial of stock-jobbers, including Barker, in *Niles,* October 28, 1826. 31:129. See also *The Speeches of Mr. Jacob Barker and His Counsel on the Trials for Conspiracy,* p. 40: "I am not a broker."

55. Jacob Little was elected into the NYS&EB August 10, 1825. NYS&EB Minutes, New York Stock Exchange Archives.

56. Little functioned as both a broker and dealer. On March 13, 1843, Little was clearly acting as a dealer when he sold to Stephen Allen $2000 of state 6 percent at $102\frac{1}{2}$ ($2050 + $5 commission). Little was acting as a broker on June 24, 1843, when he bought for Stephen Allen $8000 of New York fives at $98\frac{1}{2}$ (7880 + 2 days int. $2.13 + $20 commission = $7902.13). See receipts in Little Collection, Museum of the City of New York.

57. See Hidy, *The House of Baring in American Trade and Finance,* p. 364.

58. See Stedman, *The New York Stock Exchange,* pp. 100–102; Warshow, *The Story of Wall Street,* p. 64; Armstrong, *Stocks and Stock Jobbing in Wall Street,* p. 33.

59. Warshow, *The Story of Wall Street,* p. 63; Smith, *20 Years Among the Bulls and the Bears at Wall Street* (hereafter *20 Years*), p. 247; Medbery, *Men and Mysteries of Wall Street,* p. 100.

60. Smith, *20 Years,* p. 250. Little made a fortune in the panic of 1837. Warshow, *The Story of Wall Street,* p. 63. Some attribute to Little the invention of the

short sale. As we have seen, the short sale or its equivalent with borrowed stocks was evident from the first days of the securities markets.

61. See Stedman, *The New York Stock Exchange*, p. 103. John Ward and Daniel Drew were also important players in the Morris Canal manipulation. See also discussion in chapter 6.

62. Armstrong, *Stocks and Stock Jobbing in Wall Street*, p. 33.

63. See Henry Clews, *Fifty Years in Wall Street*, ch. 59, p. 11; Medbery, *Men and Mysteries of Wall Street*, p. 100; Warshow, *The Story of Wall Street*, pp. 67–68.

64. See Fowler, *Ten Years in Wall Street*, p. 10.

65. Armstrong, *Stocks and Stock Jobbing in Wall Street*, pp. 22, 27, 32–33.

66. Smith, *20 Years*, p. 248; Fowler, *Ten Years in Wall Street*, p. 92. See documents pleading in the dispute between Jacob Little and R. L. Cutting, January 12, 1846, and documents reporting settlement of the dispute between Jacob Little and the late firm of Kitchan and Olcott, September 14, 1849. New York Stock Exchange Archives.

67. Little failed on December 5, 1856. Warshow, *The Story of Wall Street*, p. 79.

68. F. Jackson, *A Week in Wall Street by One Who Knows*. Compare James Sullivan's relatively muted criticism of stock brokers in 1792, "The Path to Riches," p. 182. The criticism was directed more at making customers aware that they should seek out honest advisers than at proposing any regulation of brokers and dealers. See also, *A Report of the Select Committee on Stock-Jobbing*, Documents of the Assembly of the State of New York, 57th Sess., March 28, 1834, no. 339. The report condemns brokers for doing their business in secret and speculating. Brokers, the report claims, "mislead and deceive their employers to a fearful and dangerous degree." The committee proposed a regulatory bill. Later, a bill was proposed to outlaw the board of brokers, but it did not pass. See discussion in chapter 3.

69. James Bleecker, a founding member of the NYSE&B, appears to have been such an adviser. See letters to him from John Rathbone in the Bleecker Collection, New York Historical Society. Armstrong describes Bleecker as "an ancient and very respectable Knickerbocker, who has long been Treasurer to the old Board of Brokers." *Stocks and Stock Jobbing in Wall Street*, p. 38.

6. The Supply of Capital: Purchasers of Securities

1. See Letter from John Rathbone to James W. Bleecker, March 18, 1825, Bleecker Collection, New-York Historical Society. Rathbone boasts that his Phoenix Insurance stock certificates are in his trunk and he has the key.

2. Clews defines speculation as "a method for adjusting differences of opinion as to future values." *Fifty Years in Wall Street*, p. 96. Securities speculators monitor financial markets, corporations, and the overall economic scene, looking for the changes that will affect securities prices. The wheat speculator does not worry much that the wheat he buys and sells may change. The securities speculator has to be on the lookout for the same external economic changes that the wheat speculator looks for, as well as for changes in the security itself, caused by changes in the fortunes of the issuer.

3. See chapter 9.

4. Included in this class are the federal government, state governments, banks pressured by legislatures, and, to a limited extent, individuals. See chapter 7.

5. See chapter 9.

6.. An investor-speculator classification suggests a precision that rarely exists or remains steady for long. Customers' goals are frequently unclear and are constantly evolving, especially in reaction to the changing pressures of mass emotion from the highs of optimism to the lows of pessimism. These blunt categories are, however, commonly used to analyze early securities markets, just as they were used in the 1790s.

7. The dominance of investors as opposed to speculators in the earliest financial markets does not refute the proposition that there were "speculative investors" willing to purchase securities if the risk-reward relationship was attractive. See chapter 7, discusson of Callender's thesis.

8. Compare stockholders listed in Domett, A History of the Bank of New York, pp. 136–39, and Bank of New York Stock Register, Bank of New York Archives.

9. See appendix A.

10. Banks were large purchasers of federal loans. See Adams, "The Beginning of Investment Banking in the United States," p. 112. Banks bid on and took many of the Erie Canal loans. See, e.g., the list of bidders for the Erie Canal loan on July 18, 1818, New York Daily Advertiser, p. 2. The New York Savings Bank's charter restricted its investments to state and federal bonds. Miller, The Enterprise of a Free People, p. 88, fn. 25. See also appendix A.

11. The New York Savings Bank held on to its loans for twelve years or more. Miller, The Enterprise of a Free People, p. 88, fn. 25. Miller, in appendix III, tells how some chartered banks bid for the Erie bonds—not because they wanted them for their portfolios, but because they could pay for the bonds with their own bank notes, which the State then put into circulation to pay contractors and laborers.

12. See Donald R. Adams, Jr., "Portfolio Management and Profitability in Early Nineteenth Century Banking," pp. 61, 66.

13. See Miller, The Enterprise of a Free People, p. 89; Redlich, The Molding of American Banking, 2:327.

14. See Redlich, The Molding of American Banking, 1:49. Although it started well and its shares were tremendously oversubscribed, the Morris Canal & Banking Company soon failed and its shares became a speculative fancy, while its directors became deeply involved in speculation. See chapters 8 and 9. In its last years, the Second Bank of the United States was also a large purchaser of shares in American corporations. Biddle also used the bank to funnel securities into the London market. See Chandler, "Patterns of American Railroad Finance, 1830–1850," p. 253.

15. See Phoenix Insurance Company advertisement in The New York Courier, May 12, 1815. It held 1000 Manhattan Company shares and $110,000 face amount of United States 6 percent bonds. The Phoenix Insurance Company had obtained a charter that included a provision that "one-half of the capital stock to be in shares of the Insurance Company of North America." Marquis James, Biography of a Business, 1792–1942, p. 69. The Insurance Company of North American itself purchased turnpike shares, bank shares, United States bonds, and even lottery tickets. James, Biography, pp. 53, 54, 85, 115. This institutional investor lost money in the crash of 1837, p. 123. Insurance companies were important institutional purchasers of federal bonds. Adams, "The Beginnings of Investment Banking in the United States," p. 112.

Insurance companies were also pioneers in the business of making loans with stock as collateral.

16. See chapter 7.

17. Some states invested in banks to increase state revenues, others to provide for a circulating currency. Callender, "The Early Transportation and Banking Enterprises of the States in Relation to the Growth of Corporations" (hereafter "Early Transportation and Banking Enterprises"), pp. 159–61.

18. New York state-owned Bank of the United States, 152 shares; Bank of New York, 100 shares; 6 percent federal bonds $611,388; 3 percent federal bonds $722,075; deferred debt $385,604. *The Herald*, January 26, 1796.

19. New York owned $747,000 worth of stock in New York banks in 1820. See *New York Daily Advertiser*, February 1, 1820, p. 2. See also Report of the Comptroller, New York State Assembly Documents, 53d Sess., Doc. No. 277 (March 1, 1830).

20. Annual Report of the Comptroller, New York State Assembly Documents, 60 Sess., Doc. No. 4, Exhibit G, January 4, 1837, pp. 57–58, listed in table entitled "Dividend of the Bank Fund Revenue."

21. See J. Cadman, *The Corporation in New Jersey: Business and Politics 1791–1875*, p. 427.

22. See list of stocks owned by the Commonwealth of Pennsylvania, *Hazard's Magazine* (January 2, 1830), 5(1):6–8. Pennsylvania owned stock in 3 banks amounting to over $2,000,000; 61 turnpike companies amounting to nearly $2,000,000; 15 bridges amounting to $410,000 and 3 canals amounting to $200,000. Pennsylvania had similar holdings in 1833. *Hazard's Magazine* (May 4, 1833) 11:327. See also the *New York American*, April 7, 1819.

23. Massachusetts in 1796 owned $1,500,000 federal debt. In 1812, it owned $1,000,000 in bank stock and $700,000 in United States bonds. Revenues from bank stocks were said to defray the costs of Governor Strong's military campaigns. Martin, *A Century of Finance*, p. 18. Maryland in 1824 held $500,000 of federal bonds. *Niles*, January 10, 1824, 25:294. Virginia was said to hold one-third of the stock belonging to its banks in 1829, and was seen as a "partner in the banks." George Clinton, *Essays on Banking*, pp. 42–44. Connecticut owned $424,000 in bank shares and United States bonds in 1824. *Niles*, July 27, 1824, 26:336. In 1824, fourteen different states owned federal bonds. *Niles*, January 24, 1824, 25:336.

24. There is evidence of American stock sales to English investors as early as 1792. A letter from James Brown of Richmond to Leighton Wood, Jr. September 21, 1792, in the Clow Collection, Harvard University Baker Library tells of sale of stock and shipping of certificates to England. See also Davis, *Essays*, 1:151–73, on Duer's attempts to form an international financial organization.

25. See Callender, "The Early Transportation and Banking Enterprises of the States in Relation to the Growth of Corporations," p. 137.

26. See *Columbian Centinel*, April 29, 1797, p. 2; *Columbian Centinel*, September 22, 1802, p. 2. Niles claimed that United States stocks provided higher returns than any other government stocks in the world. *Niles*, July 15, 1815, 8:352.

27. Foreigners owned $23.9 million of United States bonds, as against $66.7 million owned by domestic owners. *Niles*, January 22, 1825, 27:336.

28. See Miller, *The Enterprise of a Free People*, pp. 99–111. The English knew about canals because of their experience with the great canal boom of the eighteenth

century. English capital was available for investment abroad. By 1829, Englishmen owned more Erie Canal bonds than did Americans. Other English investments in canals were profitable and created a predisposition to invest in American canals and banks. See also Callender "The Early Transportation and Banking Enterprises of the States," p. 143.

29. Bruchey, *The Roots of American Economic Growth*, p. 132. The payment of the national debt also encouraged an increase in stock prices because of the money released into the economy. *Niles*, October 8, 1831, 41:98.

30. Callender estimates English investment in the United States to have been over $200 million by 1840. He breaks down this investment as follows: $150 million in state securities, $28 million in United States Bank stock, $9 million in Farmer's Loan & Trust Co., Camden & Amboy Railroad and Commercial Bank of Vicksburg, plus some $19 million in stocks of other corporations, chiefly banks. "The Early Transportation and Banking Enterprises of the States," p. 144. Other Europeans made the total foreign investment in the United States even larger. See *Niles*, September 13, 1834, 47(2):21. Despite the obvious appetite of European investors for American bonds, they did not invest heavily in corporate stocks, leaving those risks to the Americans. Callender, The Early Transportation and Banking Enterprises of the States," p. 153. See also Morgan, *The London Stock Exchange*, pp. 79–88.

31. An example of how extensive these networks could get was the web spun by the Rothschilds, who did business with Prime, Ward, and King; Aaron H. Palmer; Christmas, Livingston, Prime & Coster; I. B. Beers; and J. Joseph—all in New York before 1840. They also had correspondents in Philadelphia and Baltimore. The Rothschilds owned securities in the following issuers: Bank of America, Bank of the United States, The Manhattan Company, Leather Manufacturing Bank, Morris Canal & Banking Company, and Farmers Loan and Trust. They also purchased large quantities of state bonds.

32. See *Niles*, October 3, 1829, 37:83; January 2, 1830, 37:297; January 12, 1830, 37:342; and January 23, 1830, 37:360. The loan was secured to help pay for subscriptions by these cities to the Chesapeake & Ohio Canal. Whether through European investment bankers or through directly opening subscription books, private placement was the most important method for sales of American securities to Europeans; surprisingly few United States stocks or bonds were directly listed on the European exchanges. Callender explains that stocks and bonds of foreign corporations played little part in the London market unless they were endorsed by foreign governments, at least until the middle of the century. "Early Transportation and Banking Enterprises," p. 152. Compare prices of United States securities in London listed in the American press. *Niles*, December 9, 1826, 31:230; November 21, 1830, 37:198.

33. See charter of the First Bank of the United States, section 7, part 1.; Bank of New York Charter, article 5; Charter of the Second Bank of the United States, section 11, part 1.

34. An Act to Recharter the Bank of North America, Ch. 53 Penn., 49th Sess., March 21, 1825, p. 85, article 11. Pennsylvania also passed a statute in 1824 prohibiting all transfers of stock to noncitizens, but this law was easily evaded and was repealed in 1836. See Charles K. Hobson, *The Export of Capital*, p. 110.

35. Callender, "The Early Transportation and Banking Enterprises of the States," p. 139.

36. Foreigners were alleged to own seven million dollars worth of stock in the Second Bank of the United States in 1832. President Jackson's veto message, July 10, 1832, reprinted in Ronald E. Shaw, ed., *Andrew Jackson 1767–1845*, pp. 45–46. Compare comments of Senator Clay, July 12, 1832, reprinted in *Abridgement of the Debates of Congress*, vol. 9, p. 534. Catteral claims that of 4,145 stockholders in 1831, only 466 were foreigners. By 1832, foreigners owned over $8,400,000 worth of stock in the Second Bank of the United States, nearly one third of the outstanding shares. Catteral, *The Second Bank of the United States*, pp. 168, 508.

37. Domett, *The History of the Bank of New York*, p. 137.

38. Manhattan Company Stockholders Cash Receipt Book, Chase Manhattan Archives. Of the 400 initial shareholders of the Merchant's Bank, only 2 had more than 400 shares, and many had only a few. Hubert, *The Merchant's National Bank*, pp. 202–6.

There were 900 shareholders of the Mechanics Bank of New York in 1833, including J. J. Astor with 1,204; J. C. Coster with 1,600; and The Planters and Merchants Bank with 1,700. Many other shareholders had small stakes, some as small as one or two shares. Similar examples can be found in Report of Secretary of the Treasury, 23 Cong. 1st Sess., Senate Doc. no. 73, February 6, 1834, pp. 38–57.

39. It was reported in 1831 that of the 4,145 domestic shareholders of the Second Bank of the United States, 1,449 owned ten shares or less, 900 were females, 329 were executors and trustees, and 126 were corporations and charitable societies. *Niles*, September 10, 1831, 41:31. On women investors, see *New York Courier*, April 13, 1816; Fowler, *Ten Years in Wall Street*, pp. 449–60.

40. See Miller, *The Enterprise of a Free People*, p. 83, n. 14.

41. Most of the large subscribers to New York loans and Erie Canal loans were business and professional men in New York City. Miller, *The Enterprise of a Free People*, p. 83. See Redlich, *The Molding of American Banking*, 2:304 on the prominence of merchants as early customers of the securities markets. Both the Clow and Anspach correspondence support the notion that merchants were early customers of the markets. Clow Collection, Harvard University Baker Library; Anspach Collection, New-York Historical Society.

42. See *New York Spectator*, February 1, 1812; *Niles*, February 8, 1812, 1:410–12.

43. Francis Gregory, *Nathan Appleton: Merchant and Entrepreneur, 1779–1861*, p. 270. Lance E. Davis classifies shareholders of textile firms in 1834. The largest group were merchants and mercantile firms, excluding textile firms, the second were professional persons, the third were textile merchants, the fourth were financial institutions, and the fifth were financiers. Foreign persons (from outside of Massachusetts) had no stock in 1829 and only $6000 in 1834. "Stock Ownership in the Early New England Textile Industry," 204; table 3, p. 220.

44. Hedges, *Commercial Banking*, p. 45; Medbery, *Men and Mysteries of Wall Street*, p. 6; Don Adams, "The Beginning of Investment Banking in America," pp. 112–13; Miller, *The Enterprise of a Free People*, pp. 86–90.

45. Thirty-eight shareholders owned 100 shares or more. The Bank of America also had considerable shareholdings outside of New York City. Some other less secure banks were held largely by New York City residents. See *Report of the Comptroller*,

Legislative Documents of Senate and Assembly of the State of New York, 53d Sess. 1830, Assembly Document no. 277, March 1, 1830.

46. *Niles*, September 10, 1831, 41:31; Catteral, *The Second Bank of the United States*, p. 508.

47. Miller, *The Enterprise of a Free People*, pp. 56–57, 91. Compare letter from Philip Hone to DeWitt Clinton, October 9, 1826, De Witt Clinton Collection, Columbia University Butler Library, "All rich men are timid."

48. The wealthy brokers, i.e., "smart money," did not subscribe to the first Erie Canal loans but came on the bandwagon after the success of the enterprise was established. "These wealthy individuals clearly preferred the stock of the new Bank of the United States. . . . In any case, their names were conspicuously absent from the lists of subscribers to the canal loans, just as they were conspicuously present on the list of subscribers to the Second Bank of the United States." Miller refers to eight wealthy men who subscribed to the Bank of the United States but do not appear on registers for canal loans until 1820–1821 (including Nathan Prime). "Important brokers, who either ignored or make only slight investments in canal stock during this period, such as William G. Bucknor, John G. Warren, LeRoy, Bayard & Company, were actively engaged in the purchase and sale of bank stock." Miller, *The Enterprise of a Free People*, pp. 87–88.

49. Until the end of 1820, "the subscription lists for canal loans contained few names of Americans of great wealth." Miller, *The Enterprise of a Free People*, p. 91. LeRoy, Bayard & Company "followed the pattern of wealthy investors by makings its first purchase of canal stock for $50,000 in 1821, precisely at the time when men of wealth were becoming interested in canal loans." LeRoy, Bayard & Company's investment "proved to be of a purely speculative nature, since it was sold within two years." Miller, *The Enterprise of a Free People*, p. 92, fn. 33. Compare *The New York Daily Advertiser*, July 18, 1818, listing LeRoy, Bayard & Company as one of the unsuccessful bidders for an 1818 loan of $250,000. Along with Prime, Ward & Sands, they were at the bottom of the list with a bid of 101.5. New York State won with a bid of 104.5.

50. Miller, *The Enterprise of a Free People*, pp. 95–96, citing purchases by William Bucknor and Leroy, Bayard & Company, "in order to dispose of the certificates quickly and at a profit." Prime, Ward & Sands also made their first sizable purchase in 1821. Prime, Ward & Sands distributed their holding by successive sales between 1822, when they held $98,000 worth of the bonds, and 1824, when only slightly more than $10,000 of the bonds remained. In 1824, Prime, Ward & Sands purchased $200,000 more.

51. Letter of March 12, 1829, Bleecker Collection, New-York Historical Society.

52. Letter of January 20, 1816, Bleecker Collection, New-York Historical Society.

53. Letter of July 28, 1829, Bleecker Collection, New-York Historical Society.

54. On January 20, 1816, Rathbone recommends the bearer of the letter, a Mr. Fullerton, who has "I understand" $4000 in specie, principally gold "if he should require the assistance of a broker." Bleecker Collection, New-York Historical Society.

55. July 8, 1829, Bleecker Collection, New-York Historical Society.

56. M. Clarkson letter of February 22, 1804, to C. Livingston, Clarkson Collection, New-York Historical Society. See also James Cheetham, an early pamphleteer who complained that the Merchant's Bank issue diminished trading activity and low-

ered the prices of shares in existing banks. Politicus, "Impartial Inquiry into Certain Parts of the Conduct of Governor Lewis," pp. 16–17.

57. See New York Courier, June 12, 1816, p. 2, describing the "danger for widows, orphans and literary institutions, . . ." if they purchase shares in the Bank of the United States. "Bank stock was once the best property in the United States. It is not perhaps extravagant to say it is now among the worst."

58. See appendix A.

59. See Davis, Essays, 2:46.

60. By 1817, the 6 percent war loans were sold at 109¼. See New York Price Current, September 6, 13, 20, and 27, 1817. They were still commanding a similar premium in 1820. See New York Evening Post, September 13, 26, 20, and 23, 1820.

61. Bernard Hart Collection, New-York Historical Society. Bernard Hart later became Secretary of the NYS&EB, a post he held from 1831–1854.

62. The loans were: 1) 68 shares pledged to A. Levine for a loan of $6,179; 2) 50 shares pledged to S. Corwin for a loan of $4,324; and 3) 24 shares pledged to Samuel Beebee for a loan of $2,050.

63. 76 shares Fireman's Insurance Company and 5 shares United Insurance Company.

64. Our reconstruction of O'Connor's trading relies heavily on records in the O'Connor Collection, New-York Historical Society. Many of the specific letters we refer to are contained in the O'Connor Collection, University of Michigan William L. Clements Library.

65. See Powell, List of Officers of the Army of the United States, 1799–1900. O'Connor apparently earned some renown for translating Baron Gay De Vernon's Treatise on the Science of War and Fortifications.

66. O'Connor purchased federal and New York State bonds during his last years in the army. He purchased $4,000 of United States 6 percent in August 1817, from Prime, Ward & Sands. These war debt issues had been the vehicles of speculation, but by 1817 had stabilized somewhat. By the end of his commission, O'Connor was investing in New York State bonds. On April 21, 1818, O'Connor purchased from Samuel Beebee $8,000 of New York State 6 percent. Receipts in O'Connor Collection, New-York Historical Society.

67. See NYS&EB Minute Books, New York Stock Exchange Archives. The New York Directories of this period make it clear that the principal in Clarkson & Co. was the son of Matthew Clarkson, David Clarkson, who later did join the stock exchange. See Longworth's Directory 1825, 1826; Ruth Lawrence, ed., Colonial Families of America, 11:129. David Clarkson signed the 1836 NYS&EB Memorial, and was the NYS&EB president from 1837–1850. Stedman, The New York Stock Exchange, p. 468; Armstrong, Stocks and Stock Jobbing in Wall Street, p. 34. Clarkson & Co. was still operating in the New York market in 1836, according to a share receipt for 50 shares of the United States Bank issued to James W. Bleecker on March 21, 1836. Bleecker Collection, New-York Historical Society.

68. In one transaction, O'Connor apparently loaned money and took in 100 shares in the New York Insurance Company as collateral. He then sold the collateral, taking the risk that the price would fall by the time the loan was repaid and he was forced to repurchase the 100 shares for return to the borrower. Unfortunately for O'Connor, the price rose, and he lost money when he had to repurchase the

shares at a higher price. In his records of this transaction, O'Connor himself calls it a "speculation."

69. By borrowing the purchase price, O'Connor could acquire additional stocks, and if their price rose he would make more money; but, if their price fell, he would lose more money.

70. Letter of March 18, 1825, O'Connor Collection, University of Michigan William L. Clements Library.

71. O'Connor Collection, University of Michigan William L. Clements Library.

72. O'Connor Collection, University of Michigan William L. Clements Library.

73. Hutchinson wrote on August 8, 1822, that "the fall in the price of cotton in England must be followed by considerable failures." On August 11, 1824, Hutchinson wrote that sale of some of O'Connor's stocks will be affected by "the effect produced in England by the last rise here." O'Connor Collection, University of Michigan William L. Clements Library.

74. See appendix F.

75. Financing of this type is very similar to margin trading, which probably began about this time.

76. In late March and early April, O'Connor purchased 100 Ocean Insurance Company shares and 100 Life & Fire Insurance Company shares. He pledged those shares as collateral on a loan to another broker, and used the proceeds of that loan to offset most of the purchse price. He made up the difference and paid off his previous loan to Wells by selling 50 Pacific Insurance Company shares.

77. Ocean Insurance reportedly paid dividends as high as 20 percent in the 1820s. Medbery, *Men and Mysteries of Wall Street*, p. 292. See also appendix A.

78. O'Connor paid off the insurance company loans he had made in June and sold the shares when they were returned to him. He took the proceeds of this sale and paid off another loan.

79. This bank loan actually involved a transfer of the stock certificates to be held as collateral by the lender. See Promissory Note, July 30, 1824, O'Connor Collection, New-York Historical Society. It is not clear that all the other loans, especially those to the brokers, required this degree of care. The certificates were simply held on account for the lender by the broker. Such a system required brokers and their customers to trust each other greatly.

80. Time bargains persisted on the NYS&EB until the Civil War when they gave way once and for all to speculating through margin trading. Hedges, *Commercial Banking*, p. 51.

81. See also letter from John Rathbone to James Bleecker, July 9, 1829, discussing the financing of a purchase of 50 shares of The Manhattan Company. "The Newark Banking and Insurance Co. will give me the money for my check on the Manhattan Bank, if requested—and the Mechanics Bank in New York will give the money for my check on the Newark Banking and Insurance Company." Bleecker Collection, New-York Historical Society.

82. See chapter 4.

83. Hutchinson makes this proposal for Clarkson in letter of June 25, 1822. O'Connor Collection, University of Michigan William L. Clements Library.

84. Evidence on the nature of that activity is much stronger for the years after 1817 than for the years before.

85. Hedges, *Commercial Banking*, p. 48.

86. See Hedges, *Commercial Banking*, p. 50; Hamon, *New York Stock Exchange Manual*, p. 117; Armstrong, *Stocks and Stock Jobbing in Wall Street*, pp. 10–11. *Niles*, June 4, 1814, 6(14):218 presents a reprint of an English article on finance entitled "The Stocks or Public Funds." It tells how "persons who often have no property in the funds" can speculate on price variations by contracting for purchase or sale of the funds at a future day and agreed price. "The business is generally settled without any actual purchase or transfer of stock. . . . This practice, which is really nothing else than a wager concerning the price of the stock, is contrary to law: yet it is carried on to a great extent." The terms bull, bear, and lame duck are defined.

87. Hedges, *Commercial Banking*, p. 50. Time bargains were, however, enforceable at the NYS&EB, according to its rules. See chapter 3.

88. Hedges, *Commercial Banking*, p. 53, citing Myers, *The New York Money Market*, p. 38. See, also, Davis, *Essays*, 1:196.

89. See Hedges, *Commercial Banking*, p. 51; Hamon, *The New York Stock Exchange Manual*, p. 127. Long-term options, however, were subject to considerable abuse. The NYS&EB limited options to 60 days, after an attempt by the Erie Gang to corner Jacob Little on six month's seller's options failed when he sent to England for relief. See chapter 5.

90. Hedges, *Commercial Banking*, p. 52; Medbery, *Men and Mysteries of Wall Street*, pp. 101–8. Aside from their use as a gambling device, puts and calls can also be used to effect a hedge, and early operators used them in that manner. Hedges, *Commercial Banking*, pp. 52–53. An option contract calling for delivery of stock could be hedged against a rise in price by the purchase of a call. If the price of the stock rose, the call could be exercised and the loss checked, while if the price of the stock fell, the cost of the call would be deducted from the profit to leave a net gain.

91. As early as 1820, there were press reports of trading aimed to control prices. See Medbery, *Men and Mysteries of Wall Street*, pp. 289–90. Niles tells how Sun Fire Insurance stock, quoted at 140, "was purchased up to make a run on brokers who were short, after they had liquidated or broke, it fell to 80." August 12, 1826, 30:410. On May 22, 1830, Niles reported on manipulation of stock in the Bank of the United States. He suggests that sharp changes in price were occurring on account of sales where the vendor and purchaser were the same person, 38:229.

92. *Niles*, November 30, 1833, 45(14):209; Armstrong, *Stocks and Stock Jobbing in Wall Street*, p. 14.

93. Securities & Exchange Act of 1934, Section 9. On the modern definition of manipulation under the Exchange Act of 1934, see Norman S. Poser, "Stock Market Manipulation and Corporate Control Transactions," (March 1986), 40:671, et seq. (Manipulation requires deception.)

94. Medbery, *Men and Mysteries of Wall Street*, p. 293. See also *Niles*, July 13, 1833, 44(20):315, reporting on large operations in the stock of the Bank of the United States.

95. Medbery, *Men and Mysteries of Wall Street*, p. 297.

96. *New York American*, June 11, 1825, p. 2.

97. Fowler, *Ten Years in Wall Street*, pp. 336–37. See also Medbery, *Men and Mysteries of Wall Street*, pp. 25–33.

98. See Charles Francis Adams, Jr., "A Chapter of Erie" (1869), reprinted in Adams

and Adams, *Chapters of Erie*, p. 7. Adams compares stock market corners with hoarding goods in commodities markets.

99. Those effecting corners were often not so successful. A failed corner attempt left the operator with large blocks of stocks purchased in a rising market that would have to be sold in a falling market. The results could be tremendous losses. Thus, those attempting corners were taking magnificent risks. Even those who effected successful corners were still saddled with large blocks of stock that could be difficult to unload at favorable prices. See also chapter 10.

100. Fowler, *Ten Years in Wall Street*, p. 32. See also Sakolski, *The Great American Land Bubble*, pp. 232, 253.

101. See Medbery, *Men and Mysteries of Wall Street*, p. 13; Stedman, *The New York Stock Exchange*, p. 102; *New York Journal of Commerce*, February 14, 1835.

102. *Niles*, January 17, 1835, 47(20):331.

103. Armstrong, *Stocks and Stock-Jobbing in Wall Street*, p. 13.

104. See New York State Assembly Document, 60th Sess. no. 328 (1837), pp. 15–17; Myers, *The New York Money Market*, pp. 129–30.

105. A securities holder may use that information in deciding to sell his securities, when he then has a more direct need for the trading market.

106. Most speculators, in any market, are in effect middlemen, who will ultimately sell to one who will use the item. This situation is altered in securities markets when the original purchaser is a speculator paying a small downpayment for common stock. If he reneges on his purchase, the corporate issuer does not receive its capital.

107. Alexis de Tocqueville, *Democracy in America*, vol. 2, part 2, ch. 13.

108. Davis, in describing the purchasers of shares in the Society for Useful Manufactures, states: "A speculative spirit was strong in the whole group, particularly among the New Yorkers." *Essays*, 1:394.

109. Speculators funded the innovation that is an important root of economic development. See Louis Hacker, *The Course of American Economic Growth and Development*, p. 176. Hacker refers also to Schumpeter's theory that innovation is the root source of economic development. See Joseph Schumpeter, *Capitalism, Socialism and Democracy*.

110. Other speculators, the gamblers who buy and sell on hunches or tips, do not help the economy in the same way, but by creating greater trading volume, smoother price fluctuations, more vibrant stock markets, and the like, they make their own contributions to efficient capital allocation.

111. Liquidity, the ability to promptly convert an investment into cash, is crucial to the speculator and investor alike.

112. Intrinsic value would be the present value of the future income stream the securities will produce. On distortion of prices in the trading market compared with earnings, witness the Delaware & Hudson Canal example, chapter 8.

113. Hamon, *The New York Stock Exchange Manual*, pp. 108–9. See also Stedman, *The New York Stock Exchange*, p. 13: "On the whole the outcome of the warfare of the 'bulls' and the 'bears' is a severely scientific test of values by which the safety of the great body of investors is finally promoted."

114. "Continuous" implies that a series of consecutive separate transactions, even though involving price changes, will involve minimum price variations or deviations. "Liquidity" implies that a willing seller can readily (or, perhaps, immediately) find a

buyer, or vice versa, at a mutually agreeable price. "Depth" is a different kind of concept. It refers to the quantity of buying and selling interest and the potential activity on each side of the market.

115. See chapter 4.

116. Michael Chevalier, *Society Manners and Politics in the United States*, p. 309.

117. For a time after the crash of 1837, the stock market was slack, making it difficult for enterprises utilizing the stock market, particularly railroads, to raise the necessary capital. Henry Varnum Poor, concerned by the effect the panics of 1837 and 1839 had on early schemes to build railroads, began an evangelical campaign to popularize railroad investment. Poor believed that state aid should only supplement private capital supplied by individuals living along the railroad route who would benefit from it. They were ones to build and operate a railroad, he believed. Poor favored state endorsement of railroad bonds over state purchase of railroad stock as medium of state support. Alfred D. Chandler, *Henry Varnum Poor*, pp. 64–67.

118. Stedman, *The New York Stock Exchange*, p. 407.

119. This downplaying of the importance of speculation is one reason why early securities markets have been ignored by historians.

120. Studies of the early market that downplayed speculation continue to exert influence. A prime example is Myers, *The New York Money Market*, a pioneering source of valuable information about the early market, frequently cited in later works. In keeping with views of securities markets functions current in 1931, Professor Myers expressly focused on the "investment market." Her description of the early market is therefore skewed insofar as she downplays the central importance of the speculative influence. See Myers, p. 10.

121. Modern financial theory has introduced sophisticated concepts concerning risk-reward relationships, portfolio diversification, and the like, concepts that highlight the shortfalls of gross stereotypes such as investment and speculation.

122. A similar tradition has developed in commodities markets. The "hedger" has been considered legitimate, while the "speculator" has not. This distinction is fading from commodities trading, as well as from stock trading.

123. Government-regulated investment companies, for example, openly solicit the public's savings for the avowed purpose of using them to trade for maximum gains in the shortest possible time. We point out this accepted fact, not to question the propriety of the practice, but solely to underscore the change in perception of investment and speculation.

7. The Demand for Capital: Issuers of Securities

1. The corporation had a legal personality of its own, distinct from the legal personalities of its members. It possessed its own seal, made its own contracts, was responsible for its own debts, and enjoyed perpetual existence.

2. Joint stock companies were similar to large partnerships, created by agreement of the parties, not by the Crown. Funds were pooled in a single "stock" or capital, with complicated agreements setting out the participant's rights. The contracts creating these companies attempted to give them corporate attributes, but they could not wholly insulate contributors from liability for the debts of the enterprise. Some

joint-stock companies were formed as early as the 1550s with goals that varied from early mines to establishing trade links with the Russian empire. See Morgan, *The London Stock Exchange*, pp. 11–27. Similar companies of merchant adventurers, often the merchants of a town banded together in a continuation of earlier guilds, also developed at about this time, and they were often given charters. See, e.g., Elanora Carus-Wilson, *The Records of the Merchant Adventurers of New Castle upon Tyne.*

3. The great majority of American colonists came for neither the glory of God nor the British Empire, but rather to benefit themselves. The pursuit of wealth was a native characteristic of the Americans from their first days. It should be noted that the initial costs of colonization and the hazards of early development proved far greater than estimated, and in no reported instance did American colonization companies pay dividends to their English investors. Within a generation, colonization companies had lost favor as business investments. See Thomas C. Cochran, *Business in American Life: A History*, p. 10.

4. Davis, *Essays*, 2:7–8, 309. Historians often point to the number of corporations in aggregate, without distinguishing between those corporations that were publicly owned and those that were not. The first business corporations were begun immediately; the Bank of North America was chartered by Congress in 1781. See Hammond, *Banks and Politics in America*, pp. 41–50; Davis, *Essays*, 2:10.

5. The English experience was strongly influenced by the Bubble Act of 1720, 6 Geo, 1, C. 18, (1720), even though the law did not expressly regulate issuance of corporate charters. See Armand Budington Dubois, *The English Business Company After the Bubble Act.*

6. Although independent, the trading market and the new issue market responded to the same investor desires. If an issue of new shares was attractive to subscribers, it would be desired by purchasers in the secondary market for the same reason. Thus the corporations whose shares were traded in the secondary market were the same corporations that could raise capital from the public. The corporations whose shares were not traded were either the unprofitable corporations which could not raise capital in the public market, or the close corporations which did not try.

7. See *Briscoe v. The Bank of the Commonwealth of Kentucky*, 11 Pet. (36 U.S.) 257 (1837). States cannot coin money, but can charter banks that can issue currency.

8. See *New York Commercial Advertiser*, July 1, 1812, vol. 15, no. 6223, where the New York Manufacturing Society (also called "the Wire Bank") advertised that it expected to make "the usual banking profits at least, and Gentlemen acquainted with banks do not deny, that a small bank well conducted, is of all others most profitable to shareholders." See, also the discussion of yields to investors in appendix A. Not all banks, however, were profitable. See a pamphlet by Publicola, "Vindication of the Currency of the State of New York and Review of the Report Presented by the Committee on that Subject to the House of Assembly;" *New York Courier*, May 6, 1818, p. 2.

9. Capitalists often preferred to invest their funds in banks instead of lending them on mortgage as they had done in the past." Redlich, *The Molding of American Banking*, 1:9. On share prices, see Cole and Smith, *Fluctuations*, p. 23.

10. See Davis, *Essays*, 2:59–60, for a discussion of how the earliest banks had been experiments. Once their success was assured, many new banks followed, and they found eager investors. The success of the Bank of North America was copied by

numerous banks who often went so far as to use its charter and by-laws as models. See Hammond, *Banks and Politics in America*, pp. 65–66. See also Domett, *A History of the Bank of New York*, p. 4; N. Wainwright, *The Philadelphia National Bank 1803–1953*, p. 6. Compare J. Van Fenstermaker, *The Development of American Commercial Banking: 1782–1837*, p. 3: "The financial success of the Lancaster turnpike in 1794 led to the formation of many private corporations to construct turnpikes and bridges."

11. See Redlich, *The Molding of American Banking*, 1:96–100, 128–131.

12. The crucial roles played by the Banks of the United States in the development of national banking and monetary policy have been clearly acknowledged; while the importance of their role as early corporations, whose shares were publicly traded, has been consistently ignored.

13. See appendix A. As with banks, the management and accounting were straightforward, even simple, yet not all insurance companies succeeded. For a discussion of the dissolution of the Phoenix Insurance Company, see *New York Daily Advertiser*, July 11, 1817, p. 3.

14. See, e.g., list of directors of the New York Insurance Company, including Archibald Gracie, David M. Clarkson, and Samual Ward, *New York Commercial Advertiser*, December 29, 1797; list of directors of the National Insurance Company, including Jacob Barker and Philip Hone, *New York Courier*, December 17, 1816; list of directors of Globe Insurance Company, including John Jacob Astor, Henry Coster, and Nathan Prime, *New York Daily Advertiser*, November 11, 1817, p. 3.

15. *Niles*, August 9, 1828, 34:392.

16. Domett, *A History of the Bank of New York*, p. 108. Insurance stocks, likewise, rarely assumed a speculative character. See Martin, *A Century of Finance*, p. 114.

17. See appendix A. It is estimated that, in 1840, the capital of all nonfinancial institutions amounted to only $300 million. National Bureau of Economic Research, *Securities and Exchange Commission Institutional Investor Study*, 1971, supplementary vol. 1, table 2-2, p. 33. Today, untraded corporations are also far more numerous than traded corporations. For as long as there have been securities markets, corporations have been distinguishable between the relatively few whose shares are traded and the many whose shares are not.

18. See, e.g., Albert Gallatin's April 4, 1808, "Report of the Secretary of the Treasury on the Subject of Roads and Canals" as concluding "that the resources of private enterprise were inadequate to finance the transportation needs of the country." *American State Papers*, (Washington: Gales and Seaton, 1861), class 10, misc. 1, p. 741; Miller, *The Enterprise of a Free People*, p. 31. See also statement by Henry Clay in the Congressional debates on internal improvements: "in a new country the conditions of society may be ripe for public works long before there is, in the hand of individuals, the necessary accumulation of capital to effect them." *Annals of Congress*, 1817–1818, p. 1377; Callender, "Early Transporation and Banking Enterprises," pp. 111, 157.

19. See Callender, "Early Transporation and Banking Enterprises," p. 151; Davis, *Essays*, 2:297–8.

20. According to Callender, the difficulty was rooted in the "means of securing control over the existing supply of capital." The existing capital was owned by small savers, who looked for security rather than handsome returns. "A few speculators freely

played the stock market," but most people viewed securities as risky investments. "Early Transportation and Banking Enterprises," p. 151.

21. Davis, *Essays*, 2:297–98.

22. Issuers could obtain money only if they offered investors the prospect of participating in a venture that would be viable, earn a profit, and pay dividends. The most rash speculators did not care if the enterprise would succeed; indeed, they often sought fancy stocks whose shares could fluctuate excessively in value, precisely because the enterprise the shares represented was not likely to ever succeed. See chapter 6.

23. Bruchey, *The Roots of American Economic Growth*, p. 129; See, generally, Davis, *Essays*, vol. 2.

24. The earliest canals were unable to raise funds in the public market. As the West was opened, the possibility of profit to investors appeared less remote. See Callender, "Early Transporation and Banking Enterprises," pp. 132–133. In addition, the time generally needed for completion of such projects meant that there was likely to be a long interval between the stockholder's contribution of capital and a return from that capital.

25. The Potomac Company, in which George Washington was an active participant, is an example of this kind of company. See Davis, *Essays*, 2:120–136. In the case of *Essex Turnpike Corp. v. Collins*, 8 Mass. 292, 296 (1811), counsel argued: "It is well known that in this country enterprises of this description have not been productive of profit to those who have engaged in them; nor is this generally a primary object of consideration with the subscribers. They are well aware that the community is benefitted by them, and they agree to take a share of the burden." See also E. Merrick Dodd, *American Business Corporations Until 1860*, p. 79 n. 27, p. 115 n. 5; George Taylor, *The Transportation Revolution 1815–1860*, pp. 32–55.

26. Turnpike shareholders had displayed their public spirit. Edward Chase Kirkland, *Men, Cities, and Transportation*, Cambridge; 1:46. Some manufactures "had been inspired in part by local pride and public-spirited motives." Victor Clark, *History of Manufactures in the United States, 1607–1860*, 1:461. During the years of embargo, some state governments felt that chartering manufacturing associations was a matter of patriotism. Bruchey, *The Roots of American Economic Growth*, p. 130.

27. By investing in turnpike shares, stockholders may have initially thought they could make money, but generaly they did not earn any significant return on their investment. "If they could find any compensation, stockholders were driven either to calculating the indirect benefits which might have accrued to them as landowners whose acres had been multiplied or stimulated; or they could brood over the more intangible satisfactions flowing from their display of public spirit. It was an easy step to believe such had been the motives for their investment in the first place." Kirkland, *Men, Cities, and Transportation*, 1:44–46. See, also, Stephen Salsbury, *The State, the Investor and the Railroad*, pp. 41–42.

28. See Davis, *Essays*, 2:291–330. Some toll bridges and turnpikes were successful, but their small and local issues of shares were not traded in New York, although they were occasionally traded in Philadelphia and Boston. Hedges, *Commercial Banking*, pp. 33, 36–37. Small untraded corporations were more like the close corporations discussed *infra*. The extremely profitable Charles River Bridge returned over $7,000 by 1826 to an original subscriber who paid £100. *Niles*, February 18, 1826, 28:402.

No wonder the proprieters fought to protect their monopoly! *Charles River Bridge v. Warren Bridge*, 11 Pet. (36 U.S.) 514 (1830). Most turnpikes and bridges were unprofitable and required considerable state aid. See *Niles*, January 29, 1825, 27:352; Callender, "Early Transportation and Banking Enterprises," p. 150.

29. See, e.g., Myers, *The New York Money Market*, p. 25, for a description of the financing of the Chesapeake & Ohio Canal with an original capital of $3.6 million. One million dollars each was subscribed by the national government and the city of Washington, $500,000 by the State of Maryland, $250,000 each by the cities of Georgetown and Alexandria and only $600,000—one-sixth—by individuals. See, also, *Niles*, January 28, 1827, 32:274–75; October 20, 1827, 33:114; May 31, 1828, 34:277; June 7, 1828, 34:233; June 14, 1828, 34:263–64; October 18, 1828, 35:119. The canal was never completed.

30. "On account of local needs, few canal or navigation companies had difficulty in obtaining their first subscriptions, but most of them experienced trouble in collecting assessments and in obtaining additional subscriptions because canals did not make money." Frederick A. Cleveland and Fred Wilbur Powell, *Railroad Promotion and Capitalization in the United States*, pp. 42–43. Most successful financial institutions did not have this problem; shareholders were eager to fulfill their obligations in order to retain their shares.

31. Much of the early corporate litigation consisted of suits of this nature, with the issuer frequently coming out the loser. The earliest reported suit for nonpayment of a call appears to have been *Union Turnpike Road v. Jenkins*, 1 Caines 381 (N.Y. 1803), rev'd, 1 Caines 86 (N.Y. 1804), where the court found, on the basis of a charter provision, that the sole remedy was forfeiture of the shares belonging to a shareholder who would not pay corporate subscriptions. See E. Merrick Dodd, "American Business Association Law A Hundred Years Ago and Today," 3:280; Dodd, *American Business Corporations Until 1860*, pp. 74–84, 174; Myers, *A Financial History of the United States*, p. 105. See, also, the earliest textbook on American corporation law, Angell and Ames, *Treatise on the Law of Private Corporations Aggregate*.

32. Senior securities (debt and preferred stock) are senior to equities such as common stock because they have a prior, although limited, claim upon earnings. They are attractive to investors who do not wish to take all the risks associated with common stock in unseasoned enterprises. Debentures existed in the Amsterdam financial markets in the late 1600s. See Barbour, *Capitalism in Amsterdam in the 17th Century*, p. 80. Senior securities made their first regular appearance in America in the early 1830s, and then only as emergency financing to bail out ventures running short of capital. The inland transportation companies owned land and other property that could have served as collateral for mortgage bonds, but such issues were rare and were not traded in the securities market. See Cecil Draper, "A Historical Introduction to the Corporate Mortgage," pp. 71, 75–79.

33. See *An Act to Incorporate the Lehigh Coal and Navigation Company*, February 13, 1822, Pennsylvania Laws, vol. 8, p. 86, art. 5; and see notice of declaration of dividend on two types of preferred shares in *Aurora*, January 8, 1824. Compare G. Heberton Evans, Jr., "The Early History of Preferred Stock in the United States," p. 43. The Schuylkill Navigation Company appears to have taken a long term loan in 1823. *Niles*, November 25, 1823, 29:208. The Franklin Manufacturing Company of New York City offered to sell $150,000 bonds at 6 percent in the *New York Daily*

Advertiser, November 12, 1825, p. 1. The federal government received a preferred stock for its investment in the Louisville and Portland Canal, *Niles*, May 13, 1826, 30:189.

34. There were a few isolated examples of brokers facilitating sales of common stock in the prerailroad period. Stephen Girard, for example, contracted for some United States Bank stock which he resold. See Adams, "The Beginnings of Investment Banking in the United States," p. 115. The Delaware and Hudson Canal Company also sold a small secondary issue of $1,000 shares on April 20, 1835, through brokers. A *Century of Progress, 1823–1923*, p. 100.

35. The early Massachusetts textile manufacturing corporations are sometimes pointed to as publicly held corporations. See, e.g., Berle and Means, *The Modern Corporation and Private Property*, pp. 12–13. During the years before 1840, however, these companies were owned by a few shareholders and, despite their corporate charters, resembled partnerships rather than public corporations. Until 1830, their charters did not even grant stockholders immunity from liability for enterprise obligation. See Dodd, *American Business Corporations Until 1860*, pp. 228–30. Their shares were often held by the proprietors and were not regularly traded.

36. In an attempt to explain why manufacturing shareholders in early Massachusetts were subject to full liability while bank and insurance shareholders were not, Dodd suggests that "shareholders in manufacturing corporations were conceived of as having more the status of co-adventurers and less that of mere passive investors than bank and insurance company shareholders." *American Business Corporations Until 1860*, p. 230.

37. See Victor Clark, *History of Manufactures in the United States, 1607–1860*, 1:462. (lack of capital had slowed manufactures); G. Porter and H. Livesay, *Merchants and Manufacturers*, p. 63. Prior to the second war with England, the states frequently granted subsidies to encourage manufacturing, and New York passed a general incorporation statute in 1811 to encourage manufacturing. The war gave impetus to investment in manufactures. See *Niles*, January 16, 1813, 3:328. Books of account were primitive, and although merchants were familiar with the rudiments of double-entry bookkeeping, they often did not distinguish between themselves and the enterprise. Profit and loss statements or balance sheets were unreliable, which further inhibited the potential investor.

38. High stock prices and the demand for securities are two of the reasons why the society was floated as a public corporation. See, generally, John R. Nelson, "Alexander Hamilton and American Manufacturing: A Reexamination," p. 971. Nelson believes Hamilton envisioned the S.U.M. with a threefold purpose: to support the price levels of the speculative market by stabilizing the demand for government bonds, to provide a productive outlet in manufacturing for surplus merchant capital that so many Americans were placing in the securities markets for lack of other opportunities, and to curb the outflow of American securities abroad by requiring their use in subscriptions to the S.U.M. stock. Although the corporation was chartered in New Jersey, the shares were marketed largely in New York City. See Davis, *Essays*, 1:349–522.

39. The S.U.M. was financially injured by the panic in three ways. First, it lost large sums through directors who were bankrupted. Second, many subscribers were speculators hard hit or made more cautious by the disaster, and thus unable or un-

willing to risk more for the society. Third, the prestige of the society, whereby it had
been able to secure subscribers among less speculative men, was so injured that new
contributors were not to be found. Davis, *Essays*, 1:474.

40. Manufacturing corporations were often small in scope and did not require the
amounts of capital other public corporations did. "The stock of manufacturing companies was usually owned by the men directly interested in the enterprise and was
rarely bought and sold." Callender, "Early Transportation and Banking Enterprises,"
p. 150. According to Frances Gregory, *Nathan Appleton*, pp. 270–72, large denomination ($1000) shares, in manufacturing corporations were bought and sold in Bos-
ton, but the selling price rarely appeared in the public press. All sales were through
private negotiations, and only a small core of the leaders and their friends knew the
actual prices.

41. *Niles*, September 15, 1821, n. s. 9 (3):38. "Projects offering clear prospect of
early financial return were almost universally left by common consent to private enterprise." Goodrich, *Government Promotion of American Canals and Railroads 1800–
1890*, p. 279. Legislators sometimes tried to attract investment in otherwise unprofitable enterprises by attaching banking privileges. See chapter 8.

42. Government financing of canals occurred whenever there was little prospect
of return on investment, hence, no prospect of raising the funds from private investors. See Goodrich, *Government Promotion*, pp. 268, 288. For example, the
$1,789,067.20 that Pennsylvania had invested in turnpikes in 1824 yielded the state
only $1,187.50. It was impossible to get private investors excited about that. *Niles*,
January 29, 1825, 27:352. States also had the potential for additional returns, such
as lower transportation costs, that individual investors did not appreciate. See Callender,
"Early Transportation and Banking Enterprises," pp. 155–59. According to Taylor,
The Transportation Revolution 1815–1860, pp. 52–53, once states realized that canals
would not be profitable to them, they stopped investing in them.

43. In many transactions, bonds could be used as the equivalent of money. See
Redlich, *The Molding of American Banking*, 2:304–305.

44. New York State entered the securities market in 1815 when it sold $1.3 mil-
lion of "public and transferable" bonds bearing interest of 7 percent. The flotation
was successful, but only because two banks committed themselves to purchase slightly
more than half the bonds. See Miller, *Enterprise of a Free People*, pp. 81–83. The
city of New York sold at least one issue of its own bonds. It was authorized to sell
"stock" not to exceed $900,000 by the legislature in 1812, in An Act to Regulate
the Finances of the City of New York, 35th Sess. *New York Laws*, (June 8, 1812) p.
172. The city advertised a $600,000 loan bearing interest at 6 percent, and it was
apparently sold. *New York Evening Post*, July 7, 1812, p. 3. See also Miller, *Enterprise*, p. 91 n. 31. State bonds were at first considered on par with federal bonds, but
after their widespread repudiation in the 1840s, they were maligned and avoided for
years. For yields, see appendix A.

45. See Davis, *Essays*, 2:158–66; Miller, *Enterprise*, pp. 20–32.

46. See Miller, *Enterprise*, pp. 77–86. But see Callender's assertion that the state
was confident of its ability to float the loans at 6 percent. "The Early Transportation
and Banking Enterprises of the States," p. 139.

47. The cost of capital to the state was generally low, especially when compared
with the cost of capital to the federal government in the War of 1812. See appendix A.

48. "When the canal commissioners of New York opened their books for subscriptions . . . investment in federal loans and private corporations was a well-established feature of American business." Miller, *Enterprise*, p. 79.

49. The issuance of these state bonds was intertwined with the securities markets. "All these bonds found their way first or last the New York Stock Exchange." Medbery, *Men and Mysteries of Wall Street*, p. 292.

50. Wood and charcoal, with bituminous coal imported from England, then served as the basic fuels. On the Delaware and Hudson Canal Company, see *A Century of Progress, 1823–1923*, and J. Shaugnessey, *Delaware and Hudson*.

51. A charter amendment in 1824 increased the original authorization of $500,000 to $1,500,000. A later 1824 amendment also granted the new company the power to use part of its capital for banking, a profitable business that would presumably provide earnings to help finance construction of the canal. The company actually conducted a small banking operation in its first days, but banking was never a significant part of its activities. The grant of a banking charter, which in those days was dispensed rather infrequently, indicates the high regard for the venture, as well as some adroit lobbying by the Wurts brothers. In 1825, the capital stock was increased to $1,700,000, and, in 1835, increased to $1,900,000.

52. *Commercial Advertiser*, December 10, 1824, quoted in *A Century of Progress, 1823–1923*, p. 19.

53. See *New York Daily Advertiser*, January 7, 1825; *New York American*, January 4–10, 1825.

54. Companies mining anthracite in two other Pennsylvania fields, the Lehigh and Schuylkill, were also seeking entry into the New York market. Either or both of these rivals apparently mounted a vigorous last-minute "dirty trick" press campaign to discredit the Delaware and Hudson and to convince the public that the venture was poorly conceived and bound to end as a bubble. See the long letter in the New York American addressed "To the Citizens of New York" and signed by "A New Yorker" on January 5, 1825, the eve of the Delaware and Hudson subscription opening, which attacked the Delaware and Hudson's estimated costs, engineering, and product quality. It concluded by requesting citizens "to permit the gentlemen who have raised the Lackawaxen steam to endure the explosion." See also *The New York American*, January 6, for another letter, inquiring as to the possibility of success, and a response by the Delaware and Hudson.

55. *A Century of Progress, 1823–1923*, p. 21. Shaugnessey, *Delaware and Hudson*, p. 3 says the issue was fully subscribed in New York City within 2 hours. See also *Niles*, January 22, 1825, 27:336. *A Century of Progress*, p. 18, reproduces the offer to purchase shares at $100 par, with $5 paid. Subscription books were opened not only in New York, but also at Kingston and Goshen.

56. It is interesting to speculate on the Delaware & Hudson's financing alternative had New York been less generous in its support. The company presumably could have issued its own bonds, secured by a mortgage on its properties, as was done later by the railroads. The corporate bonds of course would not have enjoyed the same high credit as the state's bonds, and if the flotation had been successful, the money would undoubtedly have cost the Delaware & Hudson more than the 5 percent and $4\frac{1}{2}$ percent charged by the state.

57. The Delaware and Hudson was not the first nonfinancial corporation with

shares publicly traded in New York. The stock of the New York Gas Light Company was traded on the NYS&EB in 1823. However, Delaware and Hudson shares were the first nonfinancial shares to be market leaders on the Exchange. The Delaware and Hudson example raises doubts concerning the proposition that only a public agency could build a substantial inland transportation facility. Lest the text be taken as a refutation of Callender's position on this point, it must be pointed out that the Delaware and Hudson was primarily engaged in the anthracite coal mining and merchandising business and the canal was its means of bringing the product to market.

58. There was no necessary correlation between a corporation's ability to obtain capital by selling stock to the public and its ability to function effectively. Some companies raised capital on rising markets and then failed when the markets fell.

59. Without an established trading market, the investor wishing to sell his shares would have to search for a purchaser and would never know if the price he obtained was the proper market price. The lack of a secondary market in issues of inland transportation corporations and close corporations diminished their ability to sell issues to the public; investors avoided these issues that were not liquid.

60. For a more detailed discussion, see chapter 9.

61. If stocks are valued in terms of the prospective earnings of the company, the market can serve as an effective disciplinary device. Managements whose operations are inefficient or unprofitable are punished when the market denies funds or provides them on less favorable terms. Baumol, The Stock Market and Economic Efficiency, p. 7.

62. Minutes of the Board of Directors of The Manhattan Company, April 11, 1799 through March 14, 1808 (May 7, 1799), Chase Manhattan Company Archives. Directors reserved most of the stock for themselves in the New Jersey Lombard and Protection Bank, "as is the case with all incorporated monied institutions." New York Spectator, December 23, 1825, pp. 2–3. See also chapter 9.

63. New York Stock and Exchange Board Call Books, New York Stock Exchange Archives.

64. New York Journal of Commerce, September 13, 1828; A Century of Progress, 1823–1923, p. 37.

65. The road was finally powered by gravity and stationary engines, after locomotives purchased from George Stephenson in England proved to be too heavy for the roadbed.

66. A Century of Progress, p. 68. The price of Delaware and Hudson shares actually dropped to $69 on January 25, 1831. New York Journal of Commerce. The Schuylkill Navigation Company shares were not traded on a sufficiently regular basis for market reporting in New York.

67. A Century of Progress, p. 68.

68. Some $300,000 was borrowed at an interest cost of 6 percent. A Century of Progress, p. 74. See, also, the Delaware and Hudson Canal Company Annual Report for 1832.

69. A Century of Progress, p. 80.

70. A Century of Progress, p. 96. Compare prices in the New York Journal of Commerce, January 17, 1832 ($63^{1}/$_{4}$); December 6, 1832 ($134^{3}/$_{4}$); January 10, 1834 ($80).

71. See Armstrong, Stocks and Stock Jobbing in Wall Street, pp. 9–10; Henry Varnum Poor was especially disturbed by the broker's eagerness to speculate in the securities

of new roads. "The favorite footballs in the stock market are those whose value is problematical." *American Railroad Journal*, November 22, 1851, 24:744. See also *American Railroad Journal*, July 1, 1842, 15:41–43; Alfred D. Chandler, *Henry Varnum Poor*, p. 86. Many stocks, including the Morris Canal & Banking Co., became dogs because the managers and directors were more concerned with trading and manipulating the stocks than with managing the company.

72. *American Railroad Journal*, February 1, 1851, 24:73.

73. See Baumol, *The Stock Market and Economic Efficiency*. Baumol's effort shows how the prices are set in the short run at random, yet in the long run prices follow earnings. To serve as an effective resource allocator, it would appear that the market should value a stock partially on the basis of the capitalized value of the company's expected future earnings, as determined by the investment opportunities available to it, p. 6. Though the workings of the market are undoubtedly imperfect, it nevertheless performs a credible job, p. 83. Cf. Paul P. Harbrecht, Jr., "The Modern Corporation Revisited," pp. 1410, 1415. Prices of shares are determined by a number of factors, only one of which is earnings.

74. See Harbrecht, "The Modern Corporation Revisited," p. 1419. Harbrecht claims that for some companies the market value of shares could drop indefinitely without destroying the company.

75. $1,000 par value shares were sold at par to H. Nott & Co., as part of an agreement that he would use the coal in his steamboat business; $1,000 shares were issued on April 20, 1835, for the uneven amount of $109,511.71. *A Century of Progress, 1823–1923*, p. 100.

76. Time bargains had less of an impact on issuers than cash sales, because time bargains did not change the ownership of shares, but they did affect the cash market by influencing the cash market's price.

77. *A Century of Progress*, p. 95.

78. See *New York Journal of Commerce*, June 18, 1839; June 3, 1840. Dividends were 11 percent in 1840. *A Century of Progress*, p. 107.

79. The Delaware and Hudson paid dividends of 8 percent or better during the 1840s. Taylor, *The Transportation Revolution 1815–1860*, p. 39. See Hamon, *Banks and Politics in America*, pp. 328–30 on the later success of the Delaware & Hudson.

8. Government and the Corporate System

1. See Mackay, *Extraordinary Popular Delusions*, pp. 90–97; Burton G. Malkiel, *A Random Walk Down Wall Street*, pp. 32–35.

2. Malkiel, *A Random Walk Down Wall Street*, p. 33.

3. MacKay, *Extraordinary Popular Delusions*, p. 94.

4. An unfortunate tale is told of the ruin brought on the sailor who mistook a bulb for an onion and ate it. See also, the tale of the botanist who inadvertently dissected a valuable bulb. MacKay, *Extraordinary Popular Delusions*, pp. 90–95.

5. Once the selling began in earnest, the dealers got out of the market and the rich no longer bought tulips for their gardens, but only to sell quickly if a profit could be made. Thereafter, bulbs fell to their true value as a commodity. See Mackay, *Extraordinary Popular Delusions*, pp. 95–97. This sequence of events conforms with the

adage that the smart money is leaving by the back door when the small players are coming in.

6. MacKay, *Extraordinary Popular Delusions*, p. 96.

7. MacKay, *Extraordinary Popular Delusions*, p. 96. Debts contracted in gambling have been unenforceable in many countries over countless years.

8. See chapter 1.

9. An Act to Restrain the Extravagant and Unwarrantable Practice of Raising Money by Voluntary Subscriptions for Carrying on Projects Dangerous to the Trade and Subjects of this Kingdom, 6 George I, c. 18 (1720). The Act forbade the issuance of stock certificates without authority by act of Parliament or by Charter from the Crown. See DuBois, *The English Business Company After the Bubble Act* (hereafter "*The English Business Company*"), p. 3.

10. The Lords' order came on July 12, 1720. See MacKay, *Extraordinary Popular Delusions*, pp. 57–64.

11. See DuBois, *The English Business Company*, pp. 12–14.

12. Partnerships with nominal, but not actual, limits on the transferability of their shares flourished. These entities grew with a growing economy, but could not fill the place of corporations. Without a charter or special act, partnerships could not limit shareholder liability.

13. DuBois, *The English Business Company*, p. 39.

14. DuBois, *The English Business Company*, p. 40.

15. The act was repealed in 1825, 6 George IV, c. 91; DuBois, *The English Business Company*, p. 39.

16. John R. Dos Passos, *A Treatise on the Law of Stock-Brokers and Stock-Exchanges* (hereafter "*A Treatise*"), p. 383.

17. 13 Ed. I. Stat. Civ. London, 1285; Dos Passos, *A Treatise*, p. 2. By 1697, a bill was passed restricting the number of sworn brokers to 100. 8 & 9 Wm. III c. 32, 1697, continued by 11 and 12 Wm. III ch. 13; Dos Passos, *A Treatise*, p. 4; Morgan, *The London Stock Exchange*, pp. 22–26.

18. 7 Geo. II c. 8, 1734, extended to perpetuity in 10 Geo. II c. 8, 1737.

19. See Morgan, *The London Stock Exchange*, p. 62. Sir John Barnard's Act did not apply in cases where the sale was bona fide and the stock was actually transferred. The Act only applied to public stocks and not to railways, joint stock companies, or foreign funds. Thus, shares of corporations could still be manipulated. See Dos Passos, *A Treatise*, pp. 385–92.

20. Morgan, *The London Stock Exchange*, p. 63.

21. See Morgan, *The London Stock Exchange*, p. 40.

22. Dos Passos, *A Treatise*, p. 392.

23. 23 and 24 Vict., c. 28, 1860. Leeman's Act of 1867 remained on the books to prevent speculation in bank shares, but Leeman's Act was disregarded by the London brokers, too. Morgan, *The London Stock Exchange*, pp. 147–48.

24. Opinion of the Attorney General and the Solicitor General, D. Ryder and J. Strange, December 28, 1740. Colonial Office Papers 88/2, quoted in DuBois, *The English Business Company*, p. 25.

25. 14 George II, c. 37.

26. See Ronald E. Seavoy, "Laws to Encourage Manufacturing," p. 86. Davis concludes that the Bubble Act had little effect in the Colonies. Davis, *Essays*, 1:25–

27. However, he notes that after Independence, the rise of joint stock companies, such as the Ohio Company, was fostered by the fact that the Bubble Act no longer affected them and they could be organized with impunity. Davis, *Essays*, 1:178; 2:5.

27. The legal status of the Act in the Colonies is uncertain. There is no evidence of Sir John Barnard's Act being directly applied or extended to America, nor any evidence of its being considered an adopted part of the law by any new states after the Revolution. That New York felt compelled in 1791 to enact a law similar to Sir John Barnard's Act is some evidence that the legislature felt that it had not been received as part of the common law of New York.

28. Davis mentions some securities speculation in American cities before the 1790s, but there are no indications that such trading was widespread. See *Essays*, 1:179–212.

29. 2 Greenleaf 470, 15th Sess. (April 10, 1792). See appendix E. The bill was first introduced on March 3 as "An Act for Laying a Duty on Public Securities and Stock Sold at Auction." *Journal of the Assembly of the State of New York*, p. 99. See also *New York Journal and Patriotic Register*, March 28, 1792. On March 23, after the crash in New York, the bill was changed to "An Act for the Regulation of Sales by Public Auction in the City and County of New York." *Journal of Assembly*, p. 136. On March 29, the bill's title was changed again to "An Act Ascertaining the Number of Auctioneers in the City and County of New York, for Securing the Duties, and Prohibiting the Sale of Public Stock at Auction," *Journal of Assembly*, p. 142. The title was changed to its final version in the Senate on April 5, *Journal of the Senate of the State of New York*, p. 77.

30. The securities enumerated in Article II (ban on auctions) are fewer than listed in Article III (ban on futures contracts). Although both lists appear to be comprehensive, it could be argued that the ban on auctions was not meant to apply to certain certificates, such as Bank of the United States shares, not specifically mentioned in Article II, but listed in Article III. At this time, the fact that a fine should be paid in pounds is not so remarkable. Denominations in dollars and cents did not become common until the value of the currency of the United States stabilized. Stock prices were often quoted in pounds and shillings. See quotations reproduced in Davis, *Essays*, 1:339–45. See also chapter 4, the resolution of Philadelphia Brokers.

31. Whether it was the statute that kept public auctions from rising again at a later date is difficult to determine. Compare an advertisement for Wm. F. Pell & Co. reporting an auction sale of $100,000 New York State 5 percent bonds. *New York Journal of Commerce*, January 1, 1828.

32. See Davis, *Essays*, 1:309. See also cases construing the act narrowly, reviewed in Dos Passos, *A Treatise*, pp. 394–97. For example, the burden of proof that the intended seller did not possess the stocks was placed on the party attempting to avoid the contract. *Dykers v. Townsend*, 24 N.Y. 57 (1861). See also *Frost v. Clarkson*, 7 Cowen 26 (N.Y. 1827). Time bargains were also carried out without any risk when the securities were actually in the possession of the seller.

33. The bill considered in Pennsylvania in April was quite similar to the statute passed in New York. See "House of Representatives of Pennsylvania, Tuesday March 27," *Daily Gazette*, April 2, 1792, p. 2, col. 4. The act was read and ordered to lie on the table. An earlier bill had been presented to the Pennsylvania legislature in January. Davis, *Essays*, 1:198.

34. Memorial, Documents of the Assembly of the State of New York, 59th Sess, no. 291, March 23, 1836, p. 6.

35. An Act to Legalize the Sale of Stocks on Time, 81st Sess. New York Laws (April 10, 1858) p. 251. A similar act in Masssachusetts was not repealed, and when a Massachusetts court considered a transaction in New York carried out by a Massachusetts citizen they found the contract against public policy and void. Leonard v. Hart, New York Herald, October 2, 1877, p. 3. By the time the prohibition on time bargains was removed in New York in 1858, speculators were shifting to margin trading.

36. Report of the Select Committee on Stock-Jobbing, Documents of the Assembly of the State of New York, 57th Sess. no. 339, March 28, 1834.

37. See Documents of the Assembly of the State of New York, 59th Sess, no. 291 (Albany March 23, 1836). On the Exchange's spirited defense in light of this bill, see chapter 3.

38. The first state regulations of securities issues and market, known as blue-sky law, were not enacted until 1911.

39. See E. Merrick Dodd, "Lectures on the Growth of the Corporate Structure in the United States with Special Reference to Governmental Regulations," p. 27.

40. See Bank of Utica v. Smalley, 2 Cowen 770 (N.Y. 1824); United States v. Vaughn, 3 Binney 394 (Penn. 1811). Compare Marlborough Mfg. Co. v. Smith, 2 Conn. 579 (1818) (unregistered transferee not liable for assessments); Dodd, "American Business Association Law A Hundred Years Ago and Today," p. 220.

41. Sargent v. Franklin Ins. Co., 8 Pick 90 (Mass. 1829); Shipley v. Mechanic's Bank, 10 Johns. 484, 485 (N.Y. 1813).

42. Dos Passos, A Treatise, p. 405. The NYS&EB Memorialists in 1836 agreed that the legislature is discredited by the laws on "gaming, betting, usury and other penal and restraining acts, (that are) violated every day and almost every hour in the year." Memorial, Documents of the Assembly of the State of New York. 59th Sess., no. 291, March 23, 1836, p. 7.

43. In the development of the mixed economy, active government participation was crucial. See Seavoy, "Laws to Encourage Manufacturing: New York Policy and the 1811 General Incorporation Statute," p. 85. "Down to the Civil War, except in the case of the banking industry, the powers of the government were used to encourage and assist private enterprise, not to restrict it." Callender, "Early Transportation and Banking Enterprises," p. 159. "Nineteenth century judges as well as legislators tended to shape all branches of our commercial law, including that of business corporations, to fit the real or supposed requirements of business expansion." Dodd, "American Business Association Law A Hundred Years Ago and Today," pp. 283–84.

44. As Hamilton put it, economic enterprise "may be beneficially stimulated by prudent aids and encouragements on the part of government," quoted in Bruchey, The Roots of American Economic Growth, p. 112. The First Bank of the United States, for example, had capital with very little specie; it issued money on the basis of the government's own bonds, which were taken as the payment for the bank's shares.

45. Morton Keller, The Life Insurance Enterprise, pp. 5–6. See also North, Growth of the American Economy 1790–1860, p. 50.

46. Trading ventures and land speculations, the largest enterprises of their times, were notable endeavors which eschewed the corporate form.

47. See Robert A. Lively, "The American System: A Review Article," p. 81.

48. See Cadman, *The Corporation in New Jersey: Business and Politics*, pp. 10–11, 61–63; 436–37; Hurst, *The Legitimacy of the Business Corporation in the Law of the United States 1780–1890*, pp. 29, 135. Compare Davis, *Essays*, 2:19–20.

49. Callender, "Early Transportation and Banking Enterprises," p. 148, paraphrasing from Alexis de Tocqueville, *Democracy in America*, p. 513. States promoted banks for the public services they provided, but bank proprietors were primarily seeking profit. See Redlich, *The Molding of American Banking*, 1:8. See also Hammond, "Free Banks and Corporations," p. 185.

50. Compare Livermore, *Early American Land Companies*, p. 258 et seq., for examples of what he interprets as legislative attempts to restrict corporations.

51. See Domett, *A History of the Bank of New York*. The Merchants National Bank also began without a charter in 1803. Its attempts to obtain a charter were hotly contested, but it did obtain one in 1805. See Hubert, *The Merchants National Bank of the City of New York*. The Manhattan Company was begun with the primary goal of bringing water to New York, but buried in its charter were banking privileges. Soon, the water works were abandoned in favor of its large banking operation.

52. An Act to Restrain Unincorporated Banking Associations, 27th Sess. New York Laws (April 11, 1804) p. 251; Hammond traces the roots of such laws to the Bubble Act, *Banks and Politics in America*, pp. 159, 186, 577–78. The 1804 law was strengthened by An Act to Prevent the Passing and Receiving of Bank Notes Less than One Dollar and to Restrain Unincorporated Banking Associations, 36th Sess., New York Laws (April 6, 1815) p. 230, and again with An Act Relative to Banks and for Other Purposes, 41st Sess. New York Laws (April 21, 1818) p. 242. Other states passed similar laws. See also Hammond, "Free Banks and Corporations," p. 184; Livermore, *Early American Land Companies*, p. 252.

53. See Hammond, "Free Banks and Corporations: The New York Free Banking Act of 1838" pp. 186–88.

54. On other similar combinations see Cadman, *The Corporation in New Jersey*, pp. 68–69, 158. On the New York Manufacturing Company, a manufacturing company combined with a bank, see *New York Commercial Advertiser*, July 1, 1812, vol. 15, no. 6223. The Manhattan Company and the Delaware & Hudson Canal Company are two examples of successful corporations begun as joint-purpose enterprises. Both examples also illustrate that an operation with two purposes was often better served by choosing and concentrating on one.

55. *Niles*, November 5, 1825, 29:158–59. Banking and trust powers were included in the charter "to induce capitalists and others to subscribe." Cadman, *The Corporation in New Jersey*, pp. 51, 68, citing New Jersey laws 49 Sess. I sit. (1824), p. 158.

56. *Niles*, May 7, 1825, 28(10):147. See also chapter 4.

57. William J. Lane, *From Indian Trail to Iron Horse, Travel and Transportation in New Jersey 1620–1860*, pp. 228, 236–40. See *Niles*, February 28, 1829, 36:3; George Taylor, *The Transportation Revolution, 1815–1860*, pp. 39–41; Myers, *A Financial History of the United States*, p. 113. By 1848, Armstrong, an early commentator on the New York market, listed Morris Canal common with the "fancy" stocks, those of only speculative interest, as a "miserable abortion." *Stocks and Stock-Jobbing in Wall Street*, p. 29.

58. Legislators knew that banks were necessary, but were afraid of allowing any and all comers to form them. They granted charters sparingly, a policy encourged by existing banks that lobbied heavily against new rivals. In New York, for example, The Manhattan Company joined with the Bank of New York, to oppose issuance of a charter to the Merchant's Bank. For a detailed account, see Hammond, *Banks and Politics in America*, pp. 158–60. Immediately after the passage of a bill extending the charter of the Farmer's Bank of Virginia, the stock of that bank rose from $58 to $103. See George Clinton, *Essays on Banking*, p. 42.

59. Joseph Blandi, *Maryland Business Corporations 1783–1852*, p. 72.

60. Cadman, *The Corporation in New Jersey*, pp. 390–98; Myers, *A Financial History of the United States*, p. 112. When the New Jersey Protection & Lombard Bank was incorporated with a capital of $200,000, the state received a $25,000 bonus, and the bank president also received a $30,000 bonus for obtaining the charter. *New York Spectator*, December 23, 1825, pp. 2–3. See also Hammond, *Banks and Politics in America*, p. 188.

61. See Charter, Section 20. See also Anna J. Schwartz, "The Beginning of Competitive Banking in Philadelphia 1782–1809," p. 417.

62. Gouge, *A Short History of Paper Money and Banking in the United States*, p. 27. See also *Niles*, May 9, 1812, 2:168, reporting on the conviction of John Martin for attempting to bribe a legislator to influence a vote on the Bank of America charter.

63. See Hammond, "Free Banks and Corporations" pp. 188–89. See also a speech raging against banks, by Governor Tompkins earlier that year and reported in *New York Morning Post*, February 6, 1812; *Niles*, February 8, 1812, 1:410–12.

64. The restriction was ineffective and was removed from the constitution in 1845. See Hammond, "Free Banks and Corporations," pp. 188–89.

65. See Jabez Hammond, *The History of Political Parties in New York*, 2:178–79; Hammond, "Free Banks and Corporations," p. 190. See also *Niles*, September 25, 1824, 27:57; November 20, 1824, vol. 27, reporting on indictments for bribery in the case. See *Niles*, October 15, 1825, 29:98–99, complaining about bribery to acquire bank charters; Callender, "Early Transportation and Banking Enterprises," pp. 159–61. See also *Niles*, January 7, 1826, 29:294–95; March 11, 1826, 29:21, regarding Jasper Ward who was accused of accepting bribes to promote a charter. Ward was censured by the legislature and therefore resigned.

66. See Hammond, "Free Banks and Corporations" p. 184; "An Act to Authorize the Business of Banking," 61st Sess. New York Laws (April 18, 1838) p. 245, amended 63rd Sess. New York Laws (May 14, 1840) p. 306.

67. The rapid proliferation of banks founded on insufficient capital was a driving force in a crisis which came to a head late in the 1830s. By the time some modicum of restraint had returned to banking, scores of banks had failed and the public's confidence in them had been sorely tried. See Peter Temin, *The Jacksonian Economy*, p. 158.

68. Act Relative to Incorporations for Manufacturing Purposes 34th Sess. New York Laws (March 22, 1811) p. 111. See Kessler "A Statistical Study of the New York General Incorporation Act of 1811," p. 877; Seavoy, "Laws to Encourage Manufacturing: New York Policy and the 1811 General Incorporation Statute." The statute was applied to corporations formed for manufacturing, textiles, glass, metals, and paints.

69. See Seavoy, "Laws to Encourage Manufacturing, p. 89.

70. Before 1800, charters were often issued as submitted by applicants, with only minor modifications. Davis, *Essays*, 2:316. For some enterprises, banks and insurance companies in particular, charters were requested in a nearly standard format. For other charters, numerous provisions became standard boilerplate.

71. In some states, as in Massachusetts, legislatures enacted laws applicable to whole classes of corporations, and then embodied those laws by reference in special charters, which often consisted of no more than a paragraph. Dodd summarizes charter procedures in different states in *American Business Corporations Until 1860*, pp. 196–201; 268–71. See, also, Dodd, "American Business Association Law a Hundred Years Ago and Today," pp. 254, 263.

72. See Kessler, "A Statistical Study of the New York General Incorporation Act of 1811," p. 877; Hartz, *Economic Policy and Democratic Thought*, p. 41; Cadman, *The Corporation in New Jersey*, pp. 431–38; Hurst, *Legitimacy of the Business Corporation*, pp. 132–33.

73. Compare charter policy in Pennsylvania, where anti-charter rhetoric was most strident (see Hartz, *Economic Policy and Democratic Thought*, pp. 69, 254–67), with Massachusetts, where such sentiment was more muted (see Dodd, *American Business Corporations Until 1860*, pp. 268–71.). In Massachusetts, manufacturing corporations were granted charters freely, but only by special act that between 1808 and 1830 did not relieve shareholders of liability for enterprise debts, while New York sanctioned general incorporation of manufacturing activities in 1811 with "double liability" for shareholders. See Dodd, *American Business Corporations*, 373 et seq.; Shah Livermore, "Unlimited Liability in Early American Corporations," p. 674.

74. See, generally, Dodd, *American Business Corporations*; Davis, *Essays*; J. Blandi, *Maryland Business Corporations 1783–1852*; and Cadman, *The Corporation in New Jersey*.

75. Davis, *Essays*, 2:309. According to Bruchey, the proliferation of charters for business enterprises was "startling." *The Roots of American Economic Growth, 1607–1861*, p. 72.

76. See E. Merrick Dodd, "Statutory Developments in Business Corporation Law, 1886–1936," pp. 27, 28. Compare, generally, Hurst, *Legitimacy of the Business Corporation in the United States*, pp. 18, 44–47; Thomas C. Cochran, "The Business Revolution," pp. 1449, 1459.

77. Dodd, *American Business Corporations Until 1860*, pp. 269, 271.

78. James Kent, *Commentaries on American Law*, pp. 239–40. J. Angel and S. Ames, authors of the first American text on corporation law (*Treatise on the Law of Private Corporations Aggregate*), speculate on the surprise that American corporate growth must cause Europeans. They quote from a jurist in Pennsylvania, a leading anti-charter state, to the effect that his state "was an extensive manufacturer of home-made corporations," p. 35. Angell and Ames assert that this comment "will apply, at the present period more especially, as our readers well know, to every state in the Union," p. 36. President Jackson's feud with the Second Bank of the United States, which spurred a general attack against banks and other chartered corporations by the Locofoco wing of the Democratic Party, had little effect in staunching the flow of charters. Cadman, *The Corporation in New Jersey: Business and Politics*, pp. 75–84.

79. The variations on such epithets are almost endless. See Hurst, *The Legitimacy*

of the Business Corporation, pp. 30–44. See also Davis, Essays, 2:70–72, 304–7; Hammond, Banks and Politics in America, pp. 35, 56; Hartz, Economic Policy and Democratic Thought, pp. 78–79.

80. Ligget v. Lee, 288 U.S. 517, 548–9 (1933), footnotes omitted. Mortmain is "an inalienable possession or tenure of lands; the influence of the past regarded as restricting or controlling the present." On Brandeis' theory, see, also, Werner, "Corporation Law in Search of Its Future," pp. 1611, 1615 et seq.

81. Hammond, Banks and Politics in America, pp. 53–64; Hartz, Economic Policy and Democratic Thought, p. 79.

82. There seems to have been some little fear of possible dangers from them at first, and this was increased toward banking corporations by the political struggles over the United States Bank. But the opposition to corporations as such never became strong or general." Guy Callender, ed., Selections from the Economic History of the United States 1765–1860. Anti-charter sentiment "caused a certain circumspection in granting charters" but "[a]ctions . . . proverbially speak louder than words. . . . The unprecedented growth of corporations emphatically attests to the weakness of the opposition." Davis, Essays, 2:303–39. Compare, generally, J. Hurst, Legitimacy of the Business Corporation in the United States, 1780–1970, pp. 8, 14.

83. Limited shareholder liability was included in many early special charters, and general incorporation laws advanced limited liability as a standard corporate attribute.

84. Under the statute, dissolution was required for any shareholder liability, although at common law, dissolution had not been required. In Slee v. Bloom, 5 Johns Ch. 366 (N.Y. 1821), an unpaid creditor of the Dutchess Cotton Manufactory, which had ceased to do business but had not formally dissolved, brought suit against the shareholders. Chancellor Kent ruled for the shareholders, but was reversed on the grounds that formal dissolution was not necessary for shareholders to be liable. 19 Johns 456 (N.Y. Ct. Err. 1822). Thus, this provision in the general incorporation law expanded the number of situations in which shareholders might be found liable to some extent for corporate debts.

85. In Briggs v. Penniman, 8 Cowen 387 (N.Y. Ct. Err. 1826), affirming 1 Hopkins Ch. 300 (1824), a New York court created the rule that shareholders were subject to "double liability;" when the corporation dissolved without paying its debts, shareholders were liable for: 1) their nominal share amount, and 2) another equal amount. Common law had made shareholders liable to the corporation for the price of their shares; therefore, the statute served to make them liable a second time. See Stanley E. Howard, "Stockholder's Liability Under the New York Act of March 22, 1811," p. 499; Dodd, American Business Corporations Until 1860, pp. 88–89.

86. There were two exceptions. Shareholders would be liable in equity where creditors sought to reach unpaid subscriptions or unpaid assessments as corporate assets, and where creditors sought to recover liquidating dividends which had been paid without reserving sufficient property with which to pay debts. See Dodd, "American Business Association Law A Hundred Years Ago and Today," p. 93. The latter proposition comes from the famous 1824 case of Wood v. Dummer, 30 Fed. Cas. 435 (No 17, 944), 3 Mason 308 (C.C. Maine 1824) (J. Story).

87. The New York legislature had not chosen corporations to be the only form of enterprise with this advantage. An Act Relative to Partnerships, 45th Sess. New York

Laws (April 17, 1822) p. 259, allowed an opportunity to secure the limitation of liability in a limited partnership.

88. Justice Brandeis viewed general incorporation statutes as high point in state control over corporations. He suggested that these statutes served the public interest by curbing the growth of corporations, and by ending the scandals that accompanied the granting of special charters. *Liggett v. Lee,* 288 U.S. 517, 549 (1933). There is scant basis for believing, however, that general laws acted as severe restrictions or that they inhibited corporate growth. See Werner , "Corporation Law in Search of Its Future," pp. 1621–22.

89. Berle and Means, *The Modern Corporation,* pp. 121–22. See Werner, "Corporation Law," p. 1617 et seq.

90. Berle and Means, *The Modern Corporation,* p. 122.

91. Berle later pointed to the abandonment of ultra vires as a factor contributing to decline of state control over corporations. Adolf Berle and William Warren, *Business Organization: Corporations,* pp. 45–48.

92. Berle and Means, *The Modern Corporation,* p. 123.

93. Berle and Means, *The Modern Corporation,* p. 123.

94. Berle and Means, *The Modern Corporation,* pp. 126–28. For a discussion of the relevance of this erosion to the rights of shareholders, see chapter 9.

95. The Berle view of the revolutionary effect of the general incorporation law is challenged in Charles Haar, "Legislative Regulation of New York Industrial Corporations, 1800–1850," p. 191. Some government actions, general incorporation laws for example, did nevertheless have incidental effects which protected corporate investors by limiting the uses to which management could lawfully put shareholders' money. See Dodd, "American Business Association Law A Hundred Years Ago and Today," p. 277.

96. See Justice Marshall's opinion in *The Bank of the United States v. Deveaux,* 5 Cranch (9 U.S.) 61 (1809) where corporations were considered no more or less than the people they consisted of. Later, the Supreme Court, under the leadership of Justice Taney, modified this strict stand. See *Bank of Augusta v. Earle,* 13 Pet. (38 U.S.) 519 (1839); *Louisville Railroad Company v. Letson,* 2 How. (43 U.S.) 497 (1844) (corporations recognized as artificial persons that can sue and be sued). Cf. *Paul v. Virginia,* 8 Wall (75 U.S.) 168 (1868) (corporation is not a "citizen" within the Privileges and Immunities Clause).

97. The typical early charter designated a single activity in a grant that normally conveyed all privileges and franchises incident to a corporation. There is no evidence, however, that promoters attempted to combine activities, except where the power to engage in banking was sought to finance another activity. See Davis, *Essays,* 2:289 n. 87; Callender, "Early Transportation and Banking Enterprises," p. 160. Early enterprises were usually content to confine themselves to the single activity for which they had been chartered.

98. Neither Berle nor other commentators on this subject have shown that the doctrine effectively protected shareholders by restricting the scope of corporate enterprise. See Dodd, *American Business Corporations Until 1860,* pp. 104–8, 188–90. Early shareholders frequently invoked the doctrine of ultra vires, but only as a defense to corporate action to collect unpaid share subscriptions. The shareholder typically

contended that the corporation's construction of a toll road from A to C violated its charter, which called for a road from A to B (where the defendant resided), and therefore relieved him of liability on his subscription. Such effects to channel corporate action were different from a shareholder's efforts to restrict a water company, for example, from entering the gaslight business.

99. Generally, "little or nothing was paid at the outset, it being expected that all or most of the money needed would be obtained by future calls." Dodd, *American Business Corporations* p. 74 (footnote omitted). Until late in the nineteenth century, New York required no more than 10 percent of a newly organized corporation's stock to be paid in cash. See, e.g., *New York Commercial Advertiser*, July 1, 1812, vol. 15, no. 6223, *New York Evening Post* March 3, 1813 (Bank of America); *New York Evening Post*, January 12, 1813 (New York Insurance Company); *New York Courier*, February 14, 1816, p. 3 (National Insurance Company); *New York Daily Advertiser*, May 4, 1819, p. 2 (Mechanics Fire Insurance Company). Compare New York Gen. Stats., 1890, ch. 567, section 3, with New York Gen. Stats. 1895, ch. 671, section 1.

100. Dividends earned by the company could then be applied against these loans until they were paid off. See Hedges, *Commercial Banking*, pp. 49–50; Dodd, *American Business Corporations*, pp. 204, 241, 270; *Niles*, August 21, 1830, 38:445. This sleight-of-hand was practiced even in distribution of stock in the Banks of the United States. See James Wettereau, "New Light on the First Bank of the United States," pp. 263, 281; James Wettereau, *Statistical Records of the First Bank of the United States*. See, also, letter from Secretary of the Treasury Dallas to commissioners for receiving subscriptions, April 1816, reprinted in *Niles*, May 25, 1816, 10:207–8.

101. *Niles*, December 3, 1825, 29:210, tells of "monied institutions without any money at all, the whole being puff and paper." Of the $39.5 million authorized capital of the fifty-nine chartered state banks in existence in 1804, no more than $10 million was estimated to have been actually paid in. See "Gold, Silver, Bank Notes," *Bankers Magazine*, (1856) vol. 10 p. 618. With conservatively managed banks this practice was not a source of trouble, but with poorly managed banks, this practice led many to failure.

102. New Jersey appears to have authorized senior securities before Masschusetts. See Cadman, *The Corporation in New Jersey: Business and Politics*, pp. 416–17; Dodd, *American Business Corporations Until 1860*, pp. 269, 322. On the first senior securities issued, see chapter 7.

103. See Samuel Williston, "History of the Law of Business Corporations Before 1800," pp. 105, 149, 155. Keeping the shareholder's name in a transfer book was "one of the earliest well recognized rights of a shareholder." New York's revised statutes of 1829 codified the right to inspect stock transfer books. 1 N.Y. rev. stat. (1829) pt. 1, c. 18, title 4, 601.

104. See John Michael O'Connor, who in 1825 was leading a campaign to sue the directors of the Hope Insurance Company so that he could inspect the books of account, chapter 9. Later, when books were available, they were as likely as not to be inaccurate. For biting comments on the inaccuracy of financial statements, see Jackson, *A Week in Wall Street by One Who Knows*; Gouge, *A Short History of Paper Money and Commercial Banking in the United States*, p. 19.

105. Some shareholders in the earliest banks had powers to call special, as well

as annual, meetings, and powers to enact or amend bylaws. On the erosion of these safeguards, see David Ratner, "The Government of Business Corporations," p. 1.

106. Corporate officers did have some minimum fiduciary duties to shareholders; they were restricted from the most blatant forms of theft and oppression. See *Attorney General v. Utica Insurance* Co., 2 Johns Chancery 371 (N.Y. 1817); *Ogden v. Kip*, 6 Johns Chancery 160 (N.Y. 1822). In both of these cases, Chancellor Kent suggested, although he did not hold, that principles of fiduciary law were applicable to directors and officers of business corporations.

107. See chapter 9.

9. The Separation of Ownership and Control

1. The neat division between shareholders, directors, and managers often breaks down in practice, particularly as the same individuals can play multiple roles. It is quite common for top management to also be members of the board of directors. Many managers and directors are also shareholders. Because the gamut of shareholders runs from members of management themselves all the way to hostile raiders, the separation of ownership and control is not a sharp cleavage but rather a sliding scale of further widening interests. See Baumol, *The Stock Market and Economic Efficiency*, pp. 84–86.

2. The ability to propose and perhaps pass resolutions also gives shareholders influence in corporate affairs.

3. "The Battle for Corporate Control," *Business Week*, May 18, 1987, 106.

4. This discussion is adapted from Berle and Means, *The Modern Corporation*, pp. 66–84.

5. Minority shares can become a crucial balance of power if the majority is not a monolith but a coalition that can be split.

6. Concern with the minority's loss of control is not great because it is assumed that majority shareholders will act in the best interests of all shareholders. This assumption, however, is often not true, and the law now provides for majority shareholders to be subject to special fiduciary obligations to the corporation and to minority shareholders.

7. Berle and Means also discuss control through legal devices, which discussion we will dispense with here. *The Modern Corporation*, pp. 69–75.

8. A challenge can be very expensive, particularly in relation to a large corporation, because proxy solicitation costs are born by the challenger and only reimbursed if the challenger is successful.

9. In a proxy battle, ordinary shareholders are courted and, if they own a significant block of stock, they can tilt the balance toward one combatant or another.

10. A shareholder rates companies by quality of management, not by credentials of directors or nature of control as share-based or managerial.

11. See Adolf Berle, "The Impact of the Corporation on Classical Economic Theory," pp. 25, 30, 40.

12. See Berle and Means, *The Modern Corporation*, pp. 250–51. Large shareholders may have so many shares that they are not able to find a good market for selling

them. These shareholders may have no recourse but to try and improve their investment by improving the management of the enterprise.

13. Berle and Means, *The Modern Corporation*. We discuss this work mostly as it relates to Berle and his theories. See also W. Werner, "Management, Stock Market and Corporate Reform: Berle and Means Reconsidered" pp. 389, 395 et seq.

14. Berle and Means, *The Modern Corporation*, p. 125 n. 14.

15. Berle and Means, *The Modern Corporation*, pp. 125–26. See chapter 8.

16. In the early days, Berle writes, public corporations were the rare exception. A few utility and textile manufacturing corporations were "quasi-public in character, their stock being held by what was, for the time, a large number of stockholders." Berle and Means, *The Modern Corporation*, p. 11.

17. Berle and Means, *The Modern Corporation*, p. 131. See also Werner, "Corporation Law in Search of Its Future." pp. 1611, 1620.

18. We are told that whereas originally the vote for any fundamental change had to be unanimous, the shareholder later lost the right to block "striking change" in the nature of the business. Berle and Means, *The Modern Corporation*, pp. 129–30.

19. Berle and Means, *The Modern Corporation*, pp. 129.

20. The right to vote by proxy, Berle asserts, was "a century ago denied to the shareholder save where by special provision it was inserted," presumably in the charter. Berle and Means, *The Modern Corporation*, pp. 129.

21. Berle and Means hastened to point out that the erosion of shareholder control was probably as attributable to "his inability to manage as to the obvious willingness of the 'control' to take over the task." Berle and Means, *The Modern Corporation*, p. 131.

22. Berle and Means believed that economic power was being concentrated in a small number of large corporations whose ownership was increasingly dispersed over a large number of shareholders. That dispersion, coupled with gradual elimination of majority and large minority shareholdings, had enabled managers owning few shares, or none, to control the corporation; the resulting separation of ownership and control was dissolving the atom of property. See Berle and Means, *The Modern Corporation*, preface to 1932 edition, pp. xxxix, 3. For earlier expositions of the separation of ownership and control, see W. W. Cook, *The Corporation Problem*, ch. 1, 2, and 6; William Z. Ripley, *Main Street and Wall Street*, ch. 4; Thorstein Veblen, *Absentee Ownership and Business Enterprise*, ch. 5.

23. See chapter 8.

24. See Werner "Corporation Law in Search of Its Future," pp. 1614, 1627–29. Hurst's writings of the 1970s also reject the erosion doctrine.

25. Early cases support the principle, thereafter enacted into statute, that a dissenting shareholder could not block fundamental change, but was entitled to the fair value of his shares. Dodd, who examines these cases in depth, divides them into several classes. Some involved charters in which the legislature had not reserved power to amend or repeal, others contained such "reserve" clauses. Most were corporate actions to collect payment of share subscriptions, a few more shareholder actions to block corporate changes. Dodd points out that different courts gave different answers, concluding that by 1857, investment in a railroad could be diminished or enlarged as legislature and corporate management deemed wise. *American Business Corporations Until 1860*, pp. 133–50. For Berle's analysis of the later law on change in the relative

positions of common shareholders, see Berle and Means, *The Modern Corporation*, pp. 186–95.

26. The sources cited by Berle refer to municipal and other nonbusiness corpo-rations. Whatever authority may have once existed for such a shareholder power of "amotion" in nonstock, nonprofit, membership corporations, there appears to have been none—and Berle cites none—in business corporations. Angell and Ames found no precedent either for, or against, the right of a business corporation to remove of-ficers. J. Angell and S. Ames, *Treatise on the Law of Private Corporations Aggregate* (hereafter "*Treatise*"), p. 247.

27. See Angell and Ames, *Treatise*, p. 68; Blandi, *Maryland Business Corpora-tions, 1783–1852*, p. 64; Dodd, *American Business Corporations Until 1860*, pp. 68–70; DuBois, *The English Business Company*, pp. 288, 304, 324 n. 84.

28. It is no surprise to find advertisements, in 1792, for sale of "approved blank proxies to vote for directors of the Bank of United States" and approved blank powers for transferring the bank's shares. *New York Daily Advertiser*, August 2, 1792. See, also the model blank proxy form in letter from Secretary of the Treasury Dallas to commissioners for receiving subscriptions to the Second Bank of the United States, April 1816, reprinted in *Niles*, May 25, 1816, 10:207–8. The right to vote by proxy was described as a weakening of the shareholder's control over the enterprise, Berle and Means, *The Modern Corporation*, pp. 128–29, but the right existed from the beginning.

29. See, e.g., reference in *McKin v. Odom*, 3 Bland 407, 416–17 (Md. Ch. 1828). Other cases involving early proxy practice include *State ex rel. Kilbourn v. Tudor*, 5 Day 329 (Conn. 1812); *Livingston v. Lynch*, 4 Johns. Ch. 573 (N.Y. 1820); *Ex Parte Holmes*, 5 Cowen 426 (N.Y. Sup. Ct. 1826).

30. The inherence thesis is experiential, not normative; it expresses no opinion concerning the values served by the behavior it describes.

31. See Gras, *The Massachusetts First National Bank of Boston 1784–1934*. At a similar meeting October 18, 1845, there were only 44 votes. On each occasion, six directors were elected. The inactivity of the stockholders was reflected in the routine election of the directors and ultimately, perhaps, in the low dividends earned and paid. Gras, pp. 35–36, 87. See also Redlich, *The Molding of American Banking*, 1:17.

32. The rationale for proxy voting was said to be that it would be "singular if shareholders of a business corporation could not be represented at shareholder's meet-ings by an attorney of their own choice." Angell and Ames, *Treatise*, p. 277. On proxy voting generally, see Dodd, *American Business Corporations Until 1860*, pp. 69–70. In the event of a proxy contest for corporate control, the only time votes might have some effect, the market provided an easy exit for shareholders who chose to avoid discord.

33. The top twenty shareholders controlled less than one-third of the shares. Hu-bert, *Merchants National Bank*, pp. 202–6.

34. *Niles*, July 25, 1829, 36:349.

35. Many similar examples can be found in *Report of Secretary of the Treasury*, 23 Cong. 1st Sess., Senate Doc. No. 73 (February 6, 1834) pp. 38–57.

36. *Niles*, September 10, 1831, 41:31. Compare Davis, *Essays*, 2:301–4.

37. See chapter 6, discussion of shareholder dispersal.

38. Securities professionals affected ownership and control by making shares more financial assets and less potential instruments of control. First, the broker's interest was likely to be quick share turnover, regardless of its effect on corporate control. Second, some brokers, also operators, were interested in driving down the price of a company's shares to make a profit, without regard to the effect of the price decline on the company. Third, loan contractors, the fledgling investment bankers, found that their experience in the securities markets was useful to issuers coming to the market for funds. Fourth, the ordinary customer's need to rely on the securities professional for advice was bound to affect corporate control. In the event of an offer to purchase customer's shares, or of a proxy contest, the customer was likely to turn to the professional for guidance.

39. Early public corporations appear to have paid out most of their earnings as dividends, rather than reinvesting them in the enterprise. See Dodd, *American Business Corporations Until 1860*, p. 212. See also Donald Kehl, "The Origin and Early Development of Early Dividend Law," p. 36. This practice of antebellum New England textile companies was sharply criticized by E. Bigelow, *Remarks on the Depressed Condition of Manufacturers in Massachusetts.*

40. Banks have been singled out for attention here because, before 1835, they were the nation's largest, best known, and most controversial corporations, with the largest number of shareholders and the most active trading markets. Banks enjoyed this primacy from the end of the Revolution until well into the 1830s, and then appear to have been second to the railroads as issuers of publicly held securities until the Civil War. For growth to 1818, see J. Van Fenstermaker, "The Statistics of American Commercial Banking, 1782–1818," p. 400.

41. Redlich, *The Molding of American Banking*, 1:17–20. Compare, generally, Gras, *The Massachusetts First National Bank of Boston*, pp. 26–27.

42. See Gibbons, *The Banks of New York, Their Dealers, The Clearing House and the Panic of 1857*, pp. 23–69; Redlich, *The Molding of American Banking*, 1:60.

43. Redlich, *The Molding of American Banking*, 1:55–64. Beginnings of the evolution are seen in the role played by William Seton, the first cashier of the Bank of New York, in the growth of that bank. See Domett, *The History of the Bank of New York*, p. 16. For a detailed description of the later relationship between president and board of a city bank, see James Gibbons, *The Banks of New York*. The New Jersey Protection and Lombard Bank of was run, in effect, by the president "on no competent authority," but rather by default because the finance committee did not meet. *The New York Spectator*, December 16, 1825.

44. See Thomas P. Govan, *Nicholas Biddle: Nationalist and Public Banker 1786–1844*, pp. 78–87, 377.

45. For a description of Biddle's administrative style, see Redlich, *The Molding of American Banking*, 1:113–124. Redlich sees an evolution in Biddle toward autocracy, but generally sees Biddle as a manager with considerable power, who also accepted and utilized the inputs of directors and subordinates.

46. For the change in the nature of administration between the First and Second Banks of the United States, see James Wettereau, "New Light on the First Bank of the United States," pp. 263, 276.

47. Many shares in the Bank of the United States were apparently owned by foreigners, who, under the bank's charter, were legally disenfranchised. After the scan-

dal of the Jones administration, shareholders tried to limit the power of management, but failed.

48. The absence of involvement in management by outside directors, who typically have not participated in important enterprise decisions or even seriously questioned the actions of those to whom they owe their board seats, is not surprising. See James A. Ward, "Power and Accountability in the Pennsylvania Railroad 1846–1878," pp. 48–59; Chandler, *Henry Varnum Poor*, pp. 160–61; Alfred D. Chandler, *Strategy and Structure: Chapters in the History of American Industrial Enterprise*, p. 313. Banks also had a tripartite internal government structure, and share market that dispersed shareholdings and divided ownership and control.

49. Although this discussion of the move toward centralization sounds like "erosion," the distinctions are clear. First, if this change in management style is what is meant by some who point to erosion, it happened much earlier than is commonly accepted. Second, and more importantly, this erosion was a division of power among managers and directors; shareholders were already outside of the controlling group. Original shareholders in manufacturing corporations were holdouts against the trend of broad delegation to management; they maintained significant control over management until a later period. See Gregory, *Nathan Appleton: Merchant and Entrepreneur*; L. Davis, "Stock Ownership in the Early New England Textile Industry."

50. The Wurts family started the company and made the original important decisions. They petitioned the legislatures on the company's behalf. No Wurts was president until 1831, apparently because the family wanted a prominent public figure as president, to insure the investors' confidence. After Governor De Witt Clinton refused the post of first president, the Wurts enlisted Philip Hone, soon to be mayor of New York. After Hone, John Bolton served as president until 1831. John Wurts succeeded him when Bolton was forced to resign because of differences with the Wurts Brothers. See Shaugnessey, *Delaware and Hudson*, p. 6; *A Century of Progress: 1823–1923*, p. 23; and chapter 7.

51. In the early 1800s, there was a popular suspicion that a few rich individuals controlled the Massachusetts First National Bank of Boston and managed it for their own benefit. Gras, *The Massachusetts First National Bank of Boston*, p. 70. The president of the New Jersey Protection and Lombard Bank received a $30,000 bonus for procuring the charter from legislature. *New York Spectator*, December 23, 1825, pp. 2–3.

52. The first Directors of The Manhattan Company signed for 12,000 of that company's 40,000 shares. Minutes of the Board of Directors of The Manhattan Company, April 11, 1799 to March 14, 1808 (May 7, 1799) p. 17, Chase Manhattan Company Archives. Directors reserved most of the stock for themselves in the New Jersey Lombard and Protection Bank, "as is the case with all incorporated monied institutions." *New York Spectator*, December 23, 1825, pp. 2–3. See also *Ex Parte Willocks*, 7 Cowen 402 (N.Y. Sup. Ct. 1827) (director's attempted vote of hypothecated stock invalid).

53. See editorial in *New York American*, June 11, 1825, p. 2, for a vivid description of manipulation in the stock market by company managers.

54. *Niles*, December 21, 1822, 23:241. North Carolina Bank directors acted in violation of their charter. *Niles*, January 18, 1823, 23:309.

55. *Niles*, March 22, 1823, 24:35.

56. *Niles*, February 20, 1830, 37:427–28, November 26, 1831, 41:237.

57. *Niles*, March 20, 1830, 38:69.

58. *New York Daily Advertiser*, October 26, 1819, p. 2. See, also, Hedges, *Commercial Banking*, p. 20.

59. William Gouge discusses the Eagle Bank at New Haven and the self-dealing and fraud by the president ruining what was a sound institution. Gouge, *The Curse of Paper Money and Banking*, pp. 119–120.

60. See *Niles*, February 28, 1829, 36:3; George Taylor, *The Transportation Revolution, 1815–1860*, pp. 39–41; Myers, *A Financial History of the United States*, p. 113; Lane, *From Indian Trail to Iron Horse, Travel and Transportation in New Jersey 1620–1860*, pp. 228, 236–40. See also chapter 8.

61. Hammond, *Banks and Politics in America*, pp. 172–76; Gouge, *The Curse of Paper Money and Banking* (hereafter "*The Curse of Paper Money*"), pp. 6–11.

62. *Niles*, December 3, 1825, 29:210. Gouge discusses banks in the various regions and periods. He mentions a number of New England banks with little or no capital. *The Curse of Paper Money*, pp. 114–17. See also chapter 8, on the practice of stock not being fully paid in.

63. Gouge, *The Curse of Paper Money*, pp. 117–18, discussing the Sutton Bank in 1828.

64. See generally, Gouge, *The Curse of Paper Money*. Some of these banks were the so-called wildcat banks, allowed to grow under the promotion of the Jacksonians who wanted all to have the ability to receive corporate privileges. Wildcat banks were located in out of the way places, where only wildcats lived, which made it difficult for their notes to be presented for redemption in specie. Gouge, for example, discusses the bank of Vincennes, Indiana, which issued its notes with a legend in "very small letters" that the notes could only be redeemed "nine months after date," p. 91.

65. May 26, 1819.

66. *New York Daily Advertiser*, October 26, 1819, p. 2.

67. *New York Daily Advertiser*, June 4, 1819, reprint from the *Baltimore Federal Republican*, June 1, 1819, letter from a stockholder.

68. *New York Daily Advertiser*, January 14, 1818, p. 2, reprint of article from the *Courier of London*. See also *New York Daily Advertiser*, Dec 21, 1818, p. 2.

69. *Niles*, September 6, 1817, 13:31.

70. *New York Daily Advertiser*, January 14, 1818. The stock was concentrated largely in Baltimore, with four times as much stock as New York. Even Charleston held more stock than New York. *New York Daily Advertiser*, December 22, 1818, p. 2.

71. See *New York Daily Advertiser*, December 14, 1818, p. 2.

72. *New York Daily Advertiser*, December 14, 1818, p. 2.

73. Report of the Committee to Inspect the Books and Examine into the Proceedings of the Bank of the United States, and to report whether the Provisions of its Charter have been violated or not. House Report No. 92, 15th Cong. 2d Sess. January 16, 1819, reprinted in M. St. Claire Clarke and D. A. Hall, *Legislative and Documentary History of the Bank of the United States*, pp. 714–32. See, also, "Mr. Spencer, House of Representatives," *New York Daily Advertiser*, January 20, 1819, p. 1–2.

74. William Drayton, chairman of general committee of the United States Bank, report on the bank, *New York Daily Advertiser*, November 8, 1819, p. 2.

75. Congress did reiterate the provisions of the charter that related to voting rights.

76. See *New York Daily Advertiser*, January 25, 1819, p. 2, for a discussion of this alternative, along with the recognition that determined speculators cannot be stopped.

77. This letter was written in 1824 or 1825. The existing copy is handwritten, but was suitable for publication in a newspaper or pamphlet. O'Connor Collection, New-York Historical Society.

78. Even financial reports that were available were of little use to shareholders, because their accuracy was suspect. See Jackson, *A Week in Wall Street by One Who Knows*, for biting statements on the inaccuracy of financial statements. Compelling banks to give an annual statement does not compel them to give a faithful statement. They who know the secrets of bank management say "little reliance is to be placed on these accounts." Gouge, *A Short History of Paper Money and Banking in the United States*, p. 19.

79. O'Connor contemplated an early shareholder's derivative action.

80. *New York Courier*, November 23, 1815, p. 2.

81. L. Davis, "Stock Ownership in the Early New England Textile Industry," p. 210.

82. Gregory, *Nathan Appleton: Merchant and Entrepreneur*, p. 296. Appleton was not a typical shareholder: "his dominant characteristic was active participation in the management of the ventures he supported."

83. See Gibbons, *The Banks of New York, Their Dealers, The Clearing House, and the Panic of 1857*.

84. Bank of New York Charter, Article V; see, also, First Bank of the United States Charter, Section 7, 1; Second Bank of the United States Charter Section 11, 1. Similar provisions existed in some insurance companies; see Dodd, *American Business Corporations Until 1860*, p. 231; and some manufacturing companies, see Gregory, *Nathan Appleton: Merchant and Entrepreneur*, p. 253. Regressive voting schemes were most common for banks.

85. For the most part, restrictions creating regressive voting in early corporations were ineffective, as large shareholders who were interested parcelled shares to straw men. Later, regressive voting restrictions were eliminated.

86. Gras, *The Massachusetts First National Bank of Boston*, p. 35.

87. See, e.g., *Kilbourn v. Tudor*, 5 Day 329 (Conn. 1812); *Livingston v. Lynch*, 4 Johns. Ch. 573 (N.Y. 1820); *Ex Parte Holmes*, 5 Cowen 426 (N.Y. Sup. Ct. 1826). One hotly contested election for directors of the Manhattan Company was split along political party lines, *American Citizen and General Advertiser*, November 30, December 1, 1801. See, also, a description of the Bank of Darien contested election, *Niles* February 4, 1826 30:369.

88. *New York American*, June 11, 1825, p. 2.

89. *New York Enquirer*, July 6, 1826, p. 2; Gouge, *A Short History of Paper Money and Commercial Banking in the United States*, p. 26.

90. See, e.g., *Robinson v. Smith*, 3 Paige Chancery 222 (N.Y. 1832). A "raider" acquired the shares that carried control and changed the board of directors. The purchases were financed by loans with the shares as collateral, but with the owner retaining the right to vote.

91. Harold van B. Cleveland and Thomas F. Huertas, *Citibank, 1812–1970*, p. 11.

92. The new directors bought fifteen thousand shares (a majority of the outstand-

ing stock) from Lawton on September 9, 1825, at a 7 percent premium. Greenmail involves threatening some action against the directors' interest, which they will pay to prevent. Directors pay by purchasing, at a premium, the shares that are the basis of the greenmailer's power. See "Greenmail: Targetted Stock Repurchases and the Management Entrenchment Hypothesis," p. 1045.

93. City Bank, Board of Directors, Minutes June 25, 1825, and September 24, 1827; cited in Cleveland and Huertas, *Citibank, 1812–1970*.

94. Compare Louis Lowenstein, "Pruning Deadwood in Hostile Takeovers: A Proposal for Legislation," pp. 249, 257. ("Tender Offers developed only recently in the United States.")

95. Berle and Means, *The Modern Corporation*, p. 114. The problem had become a serious public concern because, for the first time, many of these shareholders were members of an "investing public" who had purchased common stocks as property interests that purported to assure participation in corporate earnings and assets, p. 6.

96. Berle and Means, "Property and the Stock Market," *The Modern Corporation*, bk. 3, p. 255.

97. W. Werner, "Management Stock Market and Corporate Reform: Berle and Means Reconsidered," p. 398.

10. The Railroad Age: 1840–1890

1. In the 1860s, a Jerome, Riggs & Co. weekly circular noted: "Although only about thirty years have elapsed since [the railroad] came into use, it now includes all the operations of society. It has created by far the greater proportion of the value of the property of the country. Without it there could be neither domestic nor foreign commerce to any considerable extent. It brings together the producer and consumer, who could be united by no other tie. Every day increases its usefulness and power. Society cannot now put forth a single great effort in which the railroad is not the chief agent and actor." Quoted in Hamon, *The New York Stock Exchange Manual*, p. 217. Compare Robert Fogel, *Railroads in American Economic Growth*.

2. See Louis Grodinsky, *Transcontinental Railway Strategy 1869–1893*, p. 424. See, also, Hamon, *The New York Stock Exchange Manual*, p. 218.

3. *The New York Stock Exchange*, p. 17.

4. Following examples from Britain, steam coaches running on rails were in the news by the 1820s. Some railroad enterprises were begun in the United States without charters. A railroad was actually chartered in New Jersey in 1817, but not enough funds were raised to get the project rolling. See Cleveland and Powell, *Railroad Promotion and Capitalization in the United States*, p. 59. A successful railroad was chartered in Massachusetts in 1825, and constructed by 1827. See Henry Varnum Poor, *History of the Railroads and Canals of the United States* (hereafter "History"), 1:85. In New York, the first chartered railroad was the Mohawk and Hudson, chartered in 1826, and completed in 1831. Poor, *History*, 1:218.

5. According to Pratt, the Mohawk and Husdon Railroad was the first railroad whose shares were traded at the NYS&EB in 1830. Pratt, *The Work of Wall Street*, p. 9. We have found no earlier trading of railroad shares reported in the *Journal of Commerce*.

6. *Niles*, January 7, 1832, 41:337.

7. For an example of railroad shares bought for investment, see discussions in Niles of purchases in the Baltimore and Ohio Railroad: "The greater part of the stock subscribed, is held by persons who have no purpose of speculation," September 29, 1827, 33:75; December 22, 1827, 33:266; April 7, 1827, 32:100.

8. See chapter 7. Cole and Smith report that railroad stocks and land became the major vehicles of speculation, *Fluctuations*, pp. 46–48.

9. Hedges, *Commercial Banking*, pp. 53–55.

10. See Henry Adams, "The New York Gold Conspiracy 1870," reprinted in C. F. Adams and H. Adams, *Chapters of Erie*, p. 101. Adams refers to pounds at at time when greenback currency had sunk to only 37 cents to a metallic dollar. Margin trading, simple in principle, rested on two important innovations. One was daily settlement: payment by buyer against certificates delivered by seller, no mean accomplishment in an age of high bookkeepers' desks. The other was bank loans to brokers, also on a daily basis, that permitted brokers to carry their customers' margin accounts. By the 1850s, call loans were the accepted means of financing stock transactions. Hedges, *Commercial Banking*, pp. 55, 89, 103. See also chapter 4. The loan market became a regular part of Wall Street trading. Stedman, *The New York Stock Exchange*, pp. 445–46.

11. For examples of speculation this extreme, see Medbery, *Men and Mysteries of Wall Street*, p. 205.

12. When an investor borrows money to buy stock, he is leveraged. If the price of the stock increases, he gains proportionately more on the amount of his own money he risked. On the leverage of railroad share purchasers, see William Z. Ripley, *Railroads: Finance and Organization*, pp. 105–11; Cleveland and Powell, *Railroad Promotion and Capitalization in the United States*, p. 143.

13. Margin trading fueled increasingly rampant speculation. Many stocks became fancies, vehicles of speculation, whose prices rose and fell sharply with little relation to the inherent value of a share in the enterprise. See Armstrong, *Stocks and Stock Jobbing in Wall Street*, for descriptions of fancy stocks and a list of fancy stocks that had developed by that time. See also chapter 4.

14. See Cole and Smith, *Fluctuations*, pp. 87–138, for an overview of the period from 1843–1860. There was a sharp rise in stock prices in 1843–4 and those prices were maintained through the mid-1850s, pp. 108–9.

15. There was a drop in September 1853, followed by a renewed burst of speculation in 1855. *The New York Stock Exchange*, p. 24.

16. See Stedman, *The New York Stock Exchange*, p. 118.

17. See Stedman, *The New York Stock Exchange*, p. 124. Cole and Smith report that prices of stocks declined from 1852 to the trough in the panic of 1857. The speculative boom before the panic of 1857 was not very excited. Prices recovered late in 1857. Cole and Smith, *Fluctuations*, pp. 109–110.

18. After Lincoln was elected, the South made it plain that secession was inevitable. The spread of economic timidity in New York showed itself through a tightening of the money market and the rapidly falling prices of securities. With ominous speed, the contraction of the money market paralyzed commerce. Foreign exchanges reflected the condition of the public mind. Ships half-laden with grain and flour lay in dock, unable to put to sea because shippers could find no one to take their bills.

For a similar reason, agents of British houses were unable to purchase supplies. Importers, failing to dispose of their paper, had no funds with which to purchase exchange. Cotton could not be stored because of the condition of the money market. Banks were extravagantly cautious and independent; they refused to take any but the least risky paper. In the South, there were bankruptcies; in the North, a general shutting down of business. Stedman, *The New York Stock Exchange*, p. 127.

19. According to Stedman, the gigantic stock speculation which has played so prominent a part on the stage of America's financial affairs arose at the time of the Civil War. Stedman, *The New York Stock Exchange*, pp. 100, 119.

20. Henry Adams, "The New York Gold Conspiracy," p. 101.

21. Trading in this annex, also called "Goodwin's Room," began about the time of the outbreak of the war. "The members of the Old Board (NYS&EB) looked down, from an immeasurable height, upon the motley crowd in the Annex." Fowler, *Ten Years in Wall Street*, pp. 55–56. See also Eames, *The New York Stock Exchange*, p. 42.

22. The New York Mining Exchange existed for six months of 1857 and was restarted in 1859. Stedman, *The New York Stock Exchange*, pp. 124–25. "Some legitimate business in Lake Superior copper shares served the purpose of attracting the public to the market . . . where skilled manipulators combined to sell various ornamental pieces of paper to innocent investors." Hamon, *The New York Stock Exchange Manual*, p. 8; Medbery, *Men and Mysteries of Wall Street*, pp. 274–85. Some unregulated trading was also conducted in a basement nicknamed the Coal Hole, because of coal company shares traded there.

23. On February 1, 1865, a Petroleum Board, corner of Broadway and Rector Street was opened for the petroleum concern; another petroleum association was formed at 16 Broad Street. Hamon, *The New York Stock Exchange Manual*, p. 8. The petroleum and mining boards merged in January 1866. Stedman, *The New York Stock Exchange*, p. 159.

24. After the issuance of paper money, gold began selling at a premium. Gold was listed in the NYS&EB for a time, but soon was banned from trading on the floor, the brokers finding it disloyal to the Union to trade in gold while the war progressed. Stedman, *The New York Stock Exchange*, pp. 148–49; Eames, *The New York Stock Exchange*, p. 45. On October 14, 1864, a Gold Exchange was formed. Stedman, *The New York Stock Exchange*, p. 153; Hamon, *The New York Stock Exchange Manual*, p. 8. See also Eames, *The New York Stock Exchange*, pp. 109–120; Medbery, *Men and Mysteries of Wall Street*, pp. 231–73. The Gold Exchange flourished until May 1877. Specie payments were resumed by the United States in 1879.

25. The organization that evolved into the Open Board was first called the Public Stock Exchange and its records date from December 1863. See Hamon, *The New York Stock Exchange Manual*, p. 8; Eames, *The New York Stock Exchange*, p. 50; Stedman, *The New York Stock Exchange*, p. 155. The Constitution of the Open Board is dated March 16, 1864, New York Stock Exchange Archives.

26. This board got off to a slow start until finally, in March 1864, it was removed from the Fifth Avenue Hotel to the Republican Headquarters. See Stedman, *The New York Stock Exchange*, p. 164. "Mammon is worshipped from daylight in New York till midnight." Hamon, *The New York Stock Exchange Manual*, p. 8. Evening trading, as well, existed during the 1790s boom.

27. After only a year or so, the Evening Exchange collapsed in fraud and failure when it was discovered that numerous forgeries had been peddled there. Trading on the Mining Board dropped off, as the blatant deception and fraud led the majority of its members to quit the organization by 1867. See Stedman, *The New York Stock Exchange*, p. 160; Medbery, *Men and Mysteries of Wall Street*, p. 285.

28. In August 1865, the evening exchanges were stigmatized. Eames, *The New York Stock Exchange*, pp. 120–22; Stedman, *The New York Stock Exchange*, pp. 164–65. Although the Open Board and the NYS&EB were in direct competition, they managed to act together on such matters as clearing the industry of fraud-ridden exchanges. Discrimination by one exchange against another, by prohibiting members to trade with members of a rival exchange, was outlawed in New York by "An Act to Amend the Penal Law in Relation to Discrimination by Exchanges or the Members Thereof," New York Laws, ch. 477, p. 998 (May 9, 1913).

29. Although the popular name "New York Stock Exchange" was in use by the 1850s, the title of the organization was not officially changed from the New York Stock & Exchange Board to the New York Stock Exchange until January 29, 1863. See Eames, *The New York Stock Exchange*, p. 43; Stedman, *The New York Stock Exchange*, p. 147. The NYS&EB or NYSE was also called the Old Board and the Regular Board.

30. Fowler, *Ten Years in Wall Street*, p. 55. According to Fowler, the Open Board had lower commissions, which forced the NYSE to cut rates to be competitive. However, it appears that the NYS&EB lowered commissions on trades among members from $\frac{1}{4}$ of 1 percent to $\frac{1}{8}$ of 1 percent on November 7, 1861, well before the Open Board was formed. Report of the Committee on Commissions, New York Stock Exchange Archives; Eames, *The New York Stock Exchange*, p. 42. There may, however, be a grain of truth in Fowler's comment. In the 1865 NYSE Consititution, it was made clear that the $\frac{1}{8}$ of 1 percent commission applied to trades among members, and that $\frac{1}{4}$ of 1 percent commissions would still be charged by members to nonmembers, including Open Board brokers. Thus the NYS&EB may have clarified their commission structure between 1861 and 1865, in response to a challenge by the Open Board, to the detriment of the business of the Open Board brokers.

31. Stedman, *The New York Stock Exchange*, p. 162.

32. Stedman, *The New York Stock Exchange*, p. 119.

33. Vanderbilt had demonstrated the usefulness of the securities markets and the corporation as instruments for consolidating different enterprises when he combined eleven different railroads into the New York Central system in 1852. Gould, Huntington, and Villard advanced the technique into an art by developing the strategy and tactics required to obtain control of roads necessary to their plans. On control by a voting trust see also Fredrick Lewis Allen, *The Great Pierpont Morgan*, pp. 66–79.

34. For a detailed and scathing description of this battle, see C. F. Adams, "A Chapter of Erie 1869," in *Chapters of Erie*. On Drew, see Bouck White, *The Book of Daniel Drew*.

35. H. Adams, "The New York Gold Conspiracy," in *Chapters of Erie*. p. 104. On Erie corners, see also Clews, *Fifty Years in Wall Street*, pp. 137–46; Fowler, *Ten Years in Wall Street*, pp. 494–511. On Fisk, see W. A. Swanberg, *Jim Fisk, The Career of an Improbable Rascal*.

36. See Charles F. Adams, "An Erie Raid," in *Chapters of Erie*, pp. 137–193.

37. Members of the council were deeply involved in the speculation of Harlem. They attempted to rig the prices by granting and then rescinding privileges to lay rails on Broadway. Vanderbilt foiled their scheme by cornering the stock and foisting great losses upon them.

38. State legislators attempted to make money on stock price fluctuations they influenced with their grants and rescissions of privileges. Vanderbilt outmaneuvered them by cornering Harlem stock and forcing them to pay him large sums in settlement. See Fowler, *Ten Years in Wall Street*, pp. 198–211; 343–58; Stedman, *The New York Stock Exchange*, pp. 174–81. See, generally, on operators, Medbery, *Men and Mysteries of Wall Street*, pp. 153–91.

39. This exchange was the child of a federal policy that rather than tax the population to pay for the Civil War, had issued legal tender known as greenbacks. The value of greenbacks was rooted in the financial stability and credibility of the United States government, and that value fluctuated with the fortunes of the war. Greenbacks were also depreciated because of their oversupply for the normal needs of trade. When the value of greenbacks fell, all prices, including the price of gold, increased. Fluctuating gold prices fostered gold future trading, which served important financial and commercial interests. Gold futures trading was necessary to aid importers and foreign exchange bankers; all who had obligations to meet in gold, at some definite future time, could secure themselves in the interim against market fluctuations. Merchants and manufacturers, by selling gold for future delivery, could guard against fluctuations in currency values that would lessen the prices obtainable for their wares.

40. At that time, the country was estimated to have only $4 million in gold in priviate hands, with the government holding $15–$20 million. Adams, "The New York Gold Conspiracy," in *Chapters of Erie*. p. 113. There were others involved in the gold conspiracy, but Gould and Fisk emerged as the key players.

41. See Adams, "The New York Gold Conspiracy" in *Chapters of Erie*; Clews, *Fifty Years in Wall Street*, pp. 181–200; Fowler, *Ten Years in Wall Street*, pp. 512–31.

42. There were hints that Gould had quietly sold out most of his position before the crash, leaving Fisk in the breach. Fisk tried to pin his deals on another he claimed to be acting as agent for.

43. New York and federal statutes of 1863 had managed, with taxes and a prohibition on loans with gold or gold certificates as collateral, to briefly slacken the market. See Hamon, *The New York Stock Exchange Manual*, pp. 209–14. On March 3, 1863, Congress imposed a tax on all sales of gold, Statutes at Large, vol. 12, p. 719, sec. 4. These laws themselves were of little influence in stopping a rise. They served, however, to turn the current of speculation from operation for a rise to operation for a fall. In turn, gold became cheaper, which favored those who sent it out of the country. Ultimately, a greater scarcity of gold resulted, which put upward pressure on the price. Obviously, the laws did not smooth the markets as intended. The act of March 3, 1863, was virtually repealed by the act of June 30, 1864 (Statutes at Large 13:223), and the act of March 3, 1865 (Statutes at Large 13:478).

44. An Act to Prohibit Certain Sales of Gold and Foreign Exchange, June 17, 1864 (Statutes at Large 13:132). This act also criminalized the sale of foreign exchange more than ten days in the future.

45. Legislation on this subject causes worse evils than gold gambling. As long as gold is a commodity that economic forces dictate must be dealt in, all restrictions imposed by law on the mode of buying or selling it may affect the fair trader injuriously, while offering little obstacle to the rogues. None but the honest law-abiding dealers would comply with the legal formalities; the real gamblers would evade them. Hamon, *The New York Stock Exchange Manual*, p. 213.

46. July 2, 1864 (Statutes at Large: 13:344).

47. The NYS&EB itself had formed a separate government section or government board in 1867. The Government Board was merged into the NYSE first, then the Open Board. Eames, *The New York Stock Exchange*, p. 52.

48. Calls in stock were discontinued 1882; calls in bonds were discontinued 1902.

49. Legend has it that a disabled broker used to regularly trade one security on one part of the Exchange floor, and the specialist system evolved from this happenstance. Like many myths about early securities markets, this story does not appear to have any foundation in fact.

50. Fowler, *Ten Years in Wall Street*, p. 58.

51. Although securities professionals had specialized prior to this period, specialization became more pronounced as markets grew. In 1835, John H. Thompson of no. 12 Wall Street New York, "Pledges himself to his customers and friends that in his stock negotiations he will do nothing on his own account—his time and ability in all cases shall be devoted for the benefit of those who favor him with their orders." Reprinted in Eames, *The New York Stock Exchange*, p. 30. Medbery commented, in 1878, that the great majority of brokers made it their pride that they performed a purely commission business, but all of them were actually engaged in their own speculation. See, generally, Medbery, *Men and Mysteries of Wall Street*, pp. 7–8, 109–38.

52. See Stedman, *The New York Stock Exchange*, p. 162. In 1835, with volume of approximately 140,000 shares traded with an average value of $50, the entire NYS&EB trading amounted to $7 million in stocks, and perhaps half again as much in bonds.

53. In 1878, Medbery wrote: "The full number of these broker offices is between four and five hundred. Some of the smaller firms have lodgement several flights up, and the region between Williams and New Streets is literally honeycombed with them. They differ in amount of capital, credit, capacity; but otherwise are nearly of a kin." *Men and Mysteries of Wall Street*, pp. 116–17.

54. The distinction between the two markets is fundamental: the trading market merely changes the identity of the security holder; the new issue market allows corporations to obtain capital. However, the line between the two is blurred; it is difficult to determine where initial distribution ends and trading begins, and distributions by large shareholders may not benefit the corporate issuer but are nevertheless often classified as part of the distribution market. In addition, the new issue market depends on the trading market; corporations can sell securities only if the purchasers know they can be resold. Prices in the trading market also profoundly affect success in the distribution market.

55. See Chandler, "Patterns of American Railroad Fianance 1830–1850." These middlemen were at first primarily loan contractors. Chandler traces change in the most important city for raising railroad investment capital from Philadelphia at first,

then Boston through the 1840s, and finally New York. Regardless of when New York became the most important financial center for drumming up investment capital, it was from the start the most important center for both speculative capital and the secondary trading market.

56. Investment banking's roots can be traced back to the financing for the War of 1812. See Adams, "The Beginning of Investment Banking in the United States"; chapter 5; Redlich, The Molding of American Banking, 2:67.

57. Alfred Chandler, "The Role of Business in the United States," p. 28.

58. Investment bankers' foreign connections were crucial; capital from overseas financed many early railroads. Foreign capital was particularly interested in business loan issues, railroad bonds especially. After the repudiation of state issues, foreigners were not interested in state debt. In the generation before the Civil War, investment banking in the United States was conducted largely by private bankers, chiefly the agents of foreign banking houses. See Vincent Carosso, Investment Banking in America, p. 10; Chandler, Henry Varnum Poor, pp. 94–97; Hidy, The House of Baring in American Trade and Finance, pp. 407–18.

59. See History of Investment Banking in New England, p. 26; Redlich, The Molding of American Banking, 2:357.

60. Jay Cooke's syndication began when he marketed over $2 billion of Civil War bonds. A syndicate is a group of houses who together will promote the securities and stand ready to buy them if they are not sold. Investment bankers spread their risks while helping the issuers receive prompt payment for securities. Syndication by investment bankers has been oftimes seen as a development of the late 1800s, but really has roots in Parish, Girard, and Astor jointly taking 1812 war bonds the government had been unable to sell. See Adams, "The Beginning of Investment Banking in the United States"; Carosso, Investment Banking in America, p. 52. Similar practices were carried out in Morgan's time when powerful firms often cooperated with each other by taking responsibillity for a portion of a large issue being handled by one of them.

61. Drexel, Morgan; August Belmont; Winslow, Lanier; Kuhn, Loeb; and others merchandised railroad securities in quantity. See Chandler, Henry Varnum Poor, pp. 89–97. Some of these investment bankers were operating in the 1840s and 1850s. See, e.g., Redlich, The Molding of American Banking, 2:353–55, regarding Winslow, Lanier.

62. Morgan was the prime mover in selling some $30 million of New York Central shares in London for William Vanderbilt, distributing $40 million of Northern Pacific bonds in New York, successfully mediating a dispute between the New York Central and Pennsylvania railroads, and reorganizing the Chesapeake and Ohio, Southern, Erie, and other railroads. The reorganizations invariably involved distribution of new securities to replace existing issues and to scale down the road's fixed charges.

63. See Cochran, Business in American Life: A History, pp. 155–56.

64. See Chandler, Henry Varnum Poor, pp. 106–7. When a railroad failed, investment bankers were likely to take an important role in reorganizing it. Investment bankers often became directors of roads whose securities they sold, in order to be able to watch over corporate affairs more closely.

65. Government assistance continued well into the railroad age. Where a legislature refused to purchase common shares of a railroad as too risky, it purchased preferred or guaranteed railroad bonds or issued state bonds for railroads to raise capital.

Promoters sold preferred shares, often to a governmental entity, when the capital contributed by common shareholders had been depleted before completion of the road.

66. A high point of shareholder's democracy was reached for some of the so-called Dowager Railroads of the greater Boston area, such as the Boston and Maine, before 1850. At first, these railroads were entirely financed by common stock; stockholders attended meetings and elected the directors and officers, who selected and guided the paid managers. Shareholders even elected committees to check upon their directors. Shares were traded in the market, but share marketability does not seem to have diluted the relationship between ownership and residual control. Directors also took their duties seriously; they met weekly, made management decisions, selected and monitored top administration. See Werner, "Corporation Law in Search of its Future," p. 1637. On British shareholders exercising control at this time, see R. Lambert, *The Railway King*, pp. 112–24, 244.

67. See Alfred Chandler, *The Visible Hand*, pp. 89–94; George Burgess and Miles Kennedy, *Centennial History of the Pennsylvania Railroad Company 1846–1946*; William Wilson, *History of the Pennsylvania Railroad Company*.

68. Sometimes money was borrowed on the collateral of the shares themselves. See Cleveland and Powell, *Railroad Promotion and Capitalization in the United States*, pp. 198–201.

69. On early dividends of from 6.5 percent to 16.75 percent see *Merchants Magazine and Commercial Review* (1840) 2:355, 357; (July 1843) 8:188.

70. See *Niles*, March 19, 1831, 40:50—railroad in Patterson New Jersey; March 26, 1831, 40:64—Norristown Railroad and Philadelphia and Westchester railroad; June 18, 1831, 40:283—New York and Harlem Railroad; August 6, 1831, 40:405—Utica and Troy railroad.

71. Some of the earliest railroads were financed with bonds that could be sold to distant investors who preferred bonds, with their appearance of secure principal and guaranteed income. Chandler, "Patterns of American Railroad Finance 1830—1850" p. 248.

72. See W. Ripley, *Railroads: Finance and Organization*, pp. 59–61, 105–16. See also chapter 7. Some early preferred stock had the same voting privileges as common. See G. H. Evans, "The Early History of Preferred Stock in the United States," p. 43.

73. The bonds of the time were long-term debt instruments secured by a mortgage on part or all of the road's physical property. After the legality of bonds was assured by statutory authorization, mortgage bonds became a major source of railroad financing, and they were particularly attractive to foreign investors. Chandler, "Patterns of American Railroad Finance 1830–1850," p. 248.

74. Packages of common stock, preferred stock, and bonds were sold together. See, e.g., packages of securities were available in Rio Grande ($1650 for package of one $1000 9 percent bond and $1000 par common stock). Grodinsky, *Transcontinental Railway Strategy 1869–1893*, p. 63.

75. Leverage concerns a debt to equity ratio; when corporate debt is high compared to equity, a firm is considered highly leveraged. See Poor, *History of the Railroads and Canals of the United States of America*. Poor's state-by-state analysis demonstrates the dominance of share capital over funded debt in the earliest years, and demonstrates the steady increase in the percent of capital represented by debt.

76. When the capital base of an enterprise is increased by borrowing, the number

of shareholders remains the same while the size of the enterprise grows. Thus each common shareholder is taking a larger risk; he or she will receive a greater dividend or increase in stock price if the enterprise succeeds. If the enterprise fails, the bondholders and preferred shareholders will be paid first, and the common shareholder can lose his or her entire investment.

77. The existence of senior securities effected, as Veblen described it, a "thoroughgoing separation between management and the ownership of industrial equipment." See Veblen, *The Theory of Business Enterprise*, pp. 72–74. One reason for financing railroads by sale of preferred shares was to disenfranchise investors. Ripley, *Railroads: Finance and Organization*, p. 100.

78. See Werner, "Corporation Law in Search of its Future," pp. 1637–38.

79. Compare the Vanderbilts, who managed to hold on to majority control of the New York Central until 1883.

80. Charles F. Adams, "Railroad Inflation," p. 130. Adams commented that this feat occurred at a time (apparently about 1852) when considerable amounts of railroad "stock was considered worthless and almost given away." See also Chandler, *Henry Varnum Poor*, pp. 99–100. Huntington raised $4 million to be used as "front money" for common shares of the Union Pacific Railroad and the Credit Mobilier, a separate corporation created to construct the road, and this slim equity base supported a total of $63.5 million of bonds. The bond sales paid for the road and the promoters were able to withdraw their own capital. Charles Crocker followed the same pattern in building the Central Pacific. See, generally, Charles Edgar Ames, *Pioneering the Union Pacific*; Grodinsky, *Transcontinental Railroad Strategy*.

81. The managerially controlled Pennsylvania Railroad developed an organizational structure very different from that of roads dominated by financial leaders. Chandler, *The Visible Hand*, pp. 175–85. This management control conformed to the law's governance standards, which were the same for the Pennsylvania Railroad in 1885 as they had been for the Bank of North America in 1785. The evolution to management control is detailed in Ward, "Power and Accountability in the Pennsylvania Railroad, 1846–1878" p. 37. The swift transfer of control is notable because Pennsylvania, the domiciliary state, was supposed to have pursued a firmer anti-charter policy before the Civil War than other industrial states. See Hartz, *Economic Policy and Democratic Thought*, pp. 290–97.

82. See Adams, "The New York Gold Conspiracy," p. 109.

83. See, generally, Chandler, *The Visible Hand*.

84. White, *The Book of Daniel Drew*, p. 59.

85. George W. Edwards, *The Evolution of Finance Capitalism*, p. 156.

86. On watered stock, see Adams, "Railroad Inflation," pp. 141–64.

87. With preemptive rights, shareholders of a corporation have the right to buy a share of any new issue proportional to the presently outstanding shares they already own. Thus, a shareholder's proportional stake in a corporation cannot be diluted without his first being given a chance to refuse to purchase a proportional number of shares in the new issue.

88. Among the doctrines developed at this time was the ultra vires doctrine, which prevented a corporation from incurring a debt for an enterprise outside of the scope of its charter, and the doctrine that directors acted as trustees for creditors.

89. NYS&EB Minutes October 5, 1847, New York Stock Exchange Archives.

90. NYS&EB Minutes January 25, 1853, New York Stock Exchange Archives.

91. NYS&EB Minutes, February 8, 1861, New York Stock Exchange Archives. See also Clews, *Fifty Years in Wall Street,* lauding this practice.

92. See B. Schultz, *The Securities Market and How It Works.* p. 11.

93. Act of June 3, 1864. Along with positive encouragement, corporations benefited from noninterference in regulation and taxation. See Hacker, *The Course of American Economic Growth and Development,* pp. 172–73. Hacker stresses the risk-taking mores of the time, which approved private and unequal accumulation in the harsh judgment of the marketplace. Not all federal moves were permissive, however. Federal action taken on "the railroad problem," in essence the corporation problem, resulted in the Interstate Commerce Commission, formed in 1887 to regulate railroads, particularly to enforce reasonable and just rates. See Gabriel Kolko, *Railroads and Regulation.* After the Interstate Commerce Commission was formed in 1887, legislative attention turned to mergers and consolidations.

94. See C. Peter MacGrath, *Yazoo: Law and Politics in the New Republic,* pp. 101–06. In the Charles River Bridge Case (1837), for example, a new supreme court cleared the way for newer "private" corporations to act without the fear that older "public" corporations with ambiguously worded charters would successfully claim that their monopoly or other charter rights were invaded. 11 Pet. (36 U.S.) 420 (1837).

95. Initially, corporations were denied access to federal courts on the grounds that they were not "persons." See *The Bank of the United States v. Deveaux,* 5 Cranch (9 U.S.) 61 (1809). By the time of *Bank of Augusta v. Earle,* 13 Pet (38 U.S.) 519 (1839), corporations were allowed into federal court, and a few years later in *Louisville Railroad Company v. Letson,* 2 How. (43 U.S.) 497 (1844), they were allowed into court outright and granted the legal fiction of personhood. The original position had been outmoded by the reality that corporations were important to the national economy and needed access to the federal courts in order to seek review of assaults on them by state legislatures.

96. This tradition of sympathy with corporations continued for years on the Supreme Court. Later in the century, corporations were protected under the rubric of substantive due process—see, e.g., The Minnesota Freight Rate Case (*Chicago, Milwaukee and St. Paul Railway Co. v. Minnesota,* 134 U.S. 418 (1890))—and the doctrine of liberty of contract—see, e.g., *Allegeyer v. Louisiana,* 165 U.S. 578 (1897) and *Lochner v. New York,* 198 U.S. 45 (1905).

97. Jay Cooke failed on speculation in Northern Pacific. See Eames, *The New York Stock Exchange,* p. 60; Stedman, *The New York Stock Exchange,* p. 266.

98. The NYSE was closed from September 20 to September 30, 1873. Eames, *The New York Stock Exchange,* p. 60; Stedman, *The New York Stock Exchange,* p. 271.

99. See Grodinsky, *Transcontinental Railway Strategy, 1869–1893,* pp. 122–144.

100. See Richard N. Owen and Charles O. Hardy, *Interest Rates and Stock Speculation,* pp. 147–48. The average annual volume was calculated as 51 million shares during the peirod 1875–1879 and 104 million five years later. See H. Parker Williams and Jules I. Bogen, *Investment Banking* (New York: Harper, 1936), p. 228, quoted in Robert Sobel, *The Big Board,* p. 116. See, also, annual volume reported in Eames, *The New York Stock Exchange;* Stedman, *The New York Stock Exchange.* A great boom in business occurred in the early 1880s, and the whirl of speculation was tremendous; everybody was buying and selling stocks and bonds of all descriptions.

Volume for a single day rose to an early peak of 700,000 shares on November 28, 1879. The *Commercial and Financial Chronicle*, November 29, 1879, vol. 29, supplement, p. 3; December 18, 1886, 43:739; Edwards, *The Evolution of Finance Capitalism*, p. 167.

101. See Alexander D. Noyes, *Forty Years of American Finance*, pp. 101–2.

102. Edwards, *The Evolution of Finance Capitalism*, p. 167.

103. Congress, for example, passed antitrust legislation in 1890, after spending considerable time and energy on the subject. While the history of antitrust legislation is beyond the scope of this work, it is evident that antitrust questions and corporation questions were closely related. Popular fear of economic power was a driving force behind the legislation. See generally, William Letwin, *Law and Economic Policy in America*; Hans Thorelli, *The Federal Anti-Trust Policy*. At first, the act was laxly enforced, narrowly interpreted, and effective only against loose combines. See Ellis W. Hawley, *The New Deal and the Problem of Monopoly*.

104. There was a panic in 1893, triggered somewhat by the Sherman Silver Purchase Act, which was quickly repealed in August 1893. In the panic of 1893, railroads and industrials both were hard hit. One-fourth of the railroads in the country were in bankruptcy courts, including the Union Pacific, Northern Pacific, Santa Fe, and Reading. George Leffler, *The Stock Market*, p. 103. NYSE governors seriously considered closing the exchange on July 25, 1893, as they had in November 1873. Noyes, *Forty Years of American Finance*, p. 194.

105. Railroadmen by and large could not delist their securities, stop margin trading in them, or prevent pool operations that affected the price of their shares. The nature of the market, an important factor affecting the corporation and its control, was a given that railroad operators had to accept.

11. Conclusions

1. Securities markets facilitated government aid to railroads by allowing unconvinced legislators to take on reduced risks through the mechanisms of preferred stock or simply through guarantees on mortgage bonds. Markets facilitated the corporate combinations that built large railroad conglomerates due to the ease with which stock could be purchased when compared with the difficulties in amassing real assets. See, for example, the description of the consolidation of the New York Central Railroad from ten pre-existing railroads by exchange of stock. Irene D. Neu, *Erastus Corning, Merchant and Financier*, pp. 161–63.

2. See Navin and Sears, "The Rise of a Market for Industrial Securities 1877–1902," p. 105.

3. See Walter Werner, "The SEC as a Market Regulator," p. 757.

4. White knights are called in to outbid raiders. Crown jewels, attractive assets of target companies, are sold to competing bidders. Targets acquire businesses that create antitrust obstacles for raiders. Shares held by unwanted shareholders are repurchased at prices above market value that amount to greenmail. Corporations have become leveraged as a takeover defense; using up their capacity to borrow money, they make themselves less attractive. See L. Lowenstein, "Management Buy-Outs,"

p. 730; L. Lowenstein, "No More Cozy Management Buy-Outs," p. 147; Michael Bradley and Michael Rosenzweig, "Defensive Stock Repurchases," p. 1377. Defensive tactics have become further complicated with poison pills. See Susan S. Dawson, Robert J. Pense, and David S. Stone, "Poison Pill Defensive Measures," p. 423.

5. Brokers' chief interests have been quick share turnover, regardless of the effect on corporate control. Rapid turnover can affect a company, however, in different ways; it can make it easier for incumbent managers to remain in power or for outsiders to displace the incumbents. In addition, some brokers, following the example of Jacob Little, have manipulated the price of a company's shares to make a profit in operations for their own account, without regard to the effect on the company.

6. See Allen, *The Great Pierpont Morgan,* pp. 138–48, for a discussion of the creation of the United States Steel Corporation of New Jersey. See also John Moody, *The Truth about the Trusts;* Robert H. Weibe, *The Search for Order 1877–1920;* Ralph Nelson, *Merger Movements in American Industry 1895–1956.*

7. See Kenneth Garbade, *Securities Markets,* p. 199.

8. In the 1960s, common stocks that promised "performance" became the core of the securities markets. Among the better known popular works on this phenomenon are Adam Smith, *The Money Game.* and J. Brooks, *The Go-Go Years.* See also Walter Werner, testimony before the Subcommittee on Fiscal Policy of the Joint Economic Committee.

9. Although turnover was high in the 1980s, it was less than one-third the turnover in 1910. See *New York Stock Exchange Fact Book 1987,* p. 77; Brady et al., "Report of the Presidential Task Force on Market Mechanisms," appendix II, p. 15.

10. One synopsis of these panics claims that the panic of 1837 was a land panic; that of 1857, a banking panic; that of 1873, a railroad panic; and that of 1893, a currency and industrial panic. "The fundamental cause of all these misfortunes was the excessive passion for speculation, which inflated credit to the bursting point." Stedman, *The New York Stock Exchange,* p. 261.

11. In the 1970s, OPM, National Student Marketing, Investors Overseas Service, and other companies with high share values but little to no real value were every bit as fraudulent as notorious issues of earlier days. One conclusion to draw is that the SEC has not stamped fraudulent issuers out. See Frank Easterbrook and Daniel Fisher, "Mandatory Disclosure and the Protection of Investors," pp. 669, 670.

12. There are still bear raids and bull pools, although not as blatant as in the nineteenth century. See, e.g., *Wall Street Journal,* September 2, 1986, p. 8.

13. See Hurst, *Legitimacy of the Business Corporation,* p. 157.

14. See Frank Easterbrook, "Managers' Discretion and Investors' Welfare: Theories and Evidence," pp. 540, 570. The conventional theory of management behavior as antagonistic to shareholders appears flawed at its core by its failure to recognize how significantly managers are influenced by financial markets. The influence is basic and explains much that otherwise appears inexplicable: why, despite the separation of ownership and control, managers behave as though they owned their corporations, often at their own expense.

15. The stock market holds every company, however lofty or lowly its products or purpose, to the same qualifying standard: it honors the enterprise that knows how to make a buck. Executives learn that the market takes their measure. Its constantly

fluctuating prices pronounce them effective managers, irresistible salesmen, inspirers of others, daring innovators, maybe geniuses—or sluggards, milquetoasts, wrong-guessers, incompetent turkeys whose inaction has left their companies ripe for take-overs by sharp-eyed, sharp-penciled raiders. Leonard Silk, "The Market: Why Does It Matter?," pp. A1, D17.

16. Despite all of the possible defensive measures a corporate management can take, the best defense is to keep the share price up and the shareholders happy. See John Coffee, "The Strain in the Corporate Web," p. 1.

17. Martha Lamb, *Wall Street in History*, p. 89.

18. For examples of how the historical concept lingers and how it effects propos-als for reform, see Werner, "Corporation Law in Search of its Future," pp. 1612–1613.

19. Professor Galbraith finds it a "commonplace" that shareholders have yielded their power to managers. John Galbraith, *The New Industrial State*, p. 52. Ralph Nader rests far-ranging proposals for corporate reform on the "collapse" of state law and "ev-isceration" of shareholder power. Ralph Nader et al., *Taming the Giant Corporation*, pp. 33, 46. Bayless Manning tells how the whole body of corporation law "slowly perforated and rotted away" and became today's "great empty corporate statutes—towering skyscrapers of rusted girders . . . containing nothing but wind." B. Manning, "The Shareholder's Appraisal Remedy," pp. 223, 245 n. 37. Each describes, or sug-gests, a process of erosion: once effective shareholder control or state regulation, or both, withered and died, and was no more.

20. This generalization does not embrace efforts to keep managers honest and to provide shareholders with disclosures that will also have this effect. William L. Cary's proposal to set minimum federal standards was obviously a worthy endeavor; federal standards could serves the emminently important goal of keeping the corporate sys-tem operating within high moral code. See Cary, "Minimum Federal Standards," pp. 319, 321–22.

21. See "Dual Class Recapitalization and Shareholder Voting Rights," p. 106. In July 1988, the SEC voted to prevent public corporations from issuing new classes of stock that would diminish the voting power or the existing shareholders. See 12 C.F.R. section 240.19c-4 (1989).

22. Werner, "Management, Stock Market, and Corporate Reform: Berle and Means Reconsidered," p. 416.

23. Werner, "Corporation Law in Search of Its Future," p. 1665.

Appendix A. New York Securities Market Statistics: 1790–1840

1. Gregory, *Nathan Appleton: Merchant and Entrepreneur, 1779–1861*, pp. 270–72.

2. See Davis, *Essays*, 2:81–82.

3. Stedman, *The New York Stock Exchange*, p. 85. See Introduction.

4. New York Stock & Exchange Board Minute Books, New York Stock Exchange Archives.

5. For more on volume in later years, see Eames, *The New York Stock Exchange*, p. 95 (1875–1893); Stedman, *The New York Stock Exchange*, pp. 473–74 (1879–1903); Richard Owens and Charles Hardy, *Interest Rates and Stock Speculation*, monthly

reports for 1881–1913; *New York Stock Exchange Fact Book 1987* see listings for 1900–1987.

6. Bank of New York Archives, Chase Manhattan Company Archives, and New-York Historical Society respectively. Segments of such books also exist for the Merchant's National Bank and the Chemical Bank. We have used what we can from those books, but there does not appear to be enough information to include them in table 6.

7. A considerable amount of the 1791 and 1792 trading was in the name of Alexander Macomb, Duer's associate.

8. See Louis N. Geldert, *Centennial History of Eagle Fire Insurance Company 1806–1906.* Eagle's shares were initially oversubscribed, and the company paid consistent dividends from its first year. Prices of its shares ranged from 107 to 120, thus its annual dividend of 9 percent of par indicated an average return of 8 percent. Eagle was a slow stock on the NYS&EB. From what we know of other fire insurance companies of the period, Eagle seems to be typical of those that were conservatively managed and financially successful.

9. Memorial, Documents of the Assembly of the State of New York. 59th Sess, No. 291, March 23, 1836, p. 5. The "New Board" also had volume equal to the "Old Board" in 1836. Eames, *The New York Stock Exchange,* p. 34; Armstrong, *Stocks and Stock-Jobbing in Wall Street,* pp. 8–9.

10. See Davis, *Essays,* 1:287; Armstrong, *Stocks and Stock-Jobbing,* pp. 8–9, 18.

11. Ralph Wells and Clarkson & Co., brokers for John Michael O'Connor in the 1820s, were not members of the NYS&EB. See chapter 6.

12. Exchange members were not then restricted from doing business with non-members on a principal basis, i.e., without a commission. This restriction became part of the Exchange's Rule 390, adopted after World War II. That Exchange members traded in the street is also supported by the Resolution of September 22, 1836 that members shall not trade in the Street on pain of expulsion, later reduced to a fine of $5.

13. Steady prices for shares in financial institutions confirm their investment-grade quality. Cole and Smith conclude that the value of bank shares was relatively constant from 1785–1820. *Fluctuations,* pp. xxv–xxvi; 23.

14. For more on the Delaware & Hudson Canal Company, see chapter 7. See also Pratt, *The Work of Wall Street,* p. 45, listing 9 stocks in 1901 whose outstanding shares were turned over more than 10 times, and two (the St. Paul Railroad and the Union Pacific Railroad) whose shares were turned over 20 times.

15. Fowler, *Ten Years in Wall Street,* p. 204.

16. Medbery, *Men and Mysteries of Wall Street,* p. 91–92. Medbery states that the capital consisted of 7,000 shares, which was true in 1831. By 1835, however, the capital consisted of 15,000 shares. See New York Statutes of April 6, 1832, and April 18, 1835.

17. Pratt reports similar turnover in 1901 for nine stocks that were sold nearly fifteen times over. *The Work of Wall Street,* p. 45.

18. Many of these transactions were time bargains where the stocks never changed hands, but only the difference in the contract price and the market price at the time of settlement changed hands. For the effect of such rampant speculation on issuers, see chapter 7.

19. Cole and Smith, *Fluctuations*, pp. 7, 23, note that the early bonds were less speculative than corporate stocks. Bonds tended to be looked on as investments, stocks as speculations.

20. It is safe to assume that these assets can be considered substitutes for each other. "It is known that those who cannot with the prospect of advantage invest their cash in commercial speculations, generally chuse to resort to the funds [government obligations], in preference to private obligation, or even landed estate." *Columbian Centinel*, September 22, 1802, p. 2.

21. See, e.g., *Columbian Centinel*, September 2, 1802.

22. See *Niles*, April 16, 1825, 26:103.

23. See *Niles*, December 1, 1827, 31:211.

24. See *Niles*, October 18, 1828, 35:115.

25. See *New York Journal of Commerce*, January 1, 1828.

26. *Niles*, June 19, 1824, 26:252, reports a Pennsylvania state loan of $220,000 at 5 percent sold at $103.8 for a yield to investors of 4.816 percent. The same issue reports a Boston loan of $55,000 at 4 percent sold at $94.42 for a yield of 4.236 percent.

27. See *New York Journal of Commerce* price listings.

28. See "Stock Record," Manhattan Company Records, Chase Manhattan Company Archives.

29. Stock prices were quoted in percent of par, not dollars. Thus a quote of 110 for the $50 par Manhattan Company shares meant a cash price of $55. Similarly, a quote of 110 for the $400 par First Bank of the United States shares signified a cash price of $440. Note that par of shares in the Second Bank of the United States was $100.

30. See dividend record kept by G. N. Bleecker, Bleecker Collection. New-York Historical Society.

31. See James Wetereau, "New Light on the First Bank of the United States," p. 284; Martin, *A Century of Finance*, p. 13.

32. See Catteral, *The Second Bank of the United States*, p. 504.

33. See *Niles*, January 29, 1825, 27:339.

34. See *Niles*, April 16, 1814, 6:119; April 10, 1824, 26:86; March 4, 1826, 30:2. Because dividends on bank shares in Boston were similar to those in New York, presumably yields were similar as well.

35. *New York Daily Advertiser*, January 2, 1826.

36. *New York Journal of Commerce*, January 24, 1828.

37. See Louis Geldert, *Centenial History of the Eagle Fire Insurance Company 1806–1906*.

38. Marquis James, *Biography of a Business: Insurance Company of North America*, pp. 52–53.

39. See *New York Daily Advertiser*, May 9, 1817.

40. See *New York Daily Advertiser*, May 14, 1817.

41. See *New York Daily Advertiser*, July 8, 1817.

42. See *Niles*, August 9, 1828, 34:392.

43. Medbery, *Men and Mysteries of Wall Street*, p. 292. See also *The New York Stock Exchange*, p. 21.

44. Gregory, *Nathan Appleton: Merchant and Entrepreneur*, p. 283.

45. See *Niles*, October 30, 1824, 27:144.

Selected Bibliography

Manuscripts

Anspach Collection. New-York Historical Society.
Bank of New York Stock Register. Bank of New York Archives.
Bleecker Collection. New-York Historical Society.
Charter of the Bank of New York.
Charter of the First Bank of the United States.
Charter of the Second Bank of the United States.
Clarkson Collection. New-York Historical Society.
Clow Collection. Harvard University Baker Library.
Committee on Commission Report. New York Stock Exchange Archives.
Delaware and Hudson Canal Company. Annual Report [1832].
De Witt Clinton Collection. Columbia University Butler Library.
Eagle Fire Insurance Company Stock Register. New York-Historical Society.
Little Collection. Museum of the City of New York.
Longworth's Directory. 1825, 1826.
Low, Nicholas. Letter Book. New-York Historical Society.
Manhattan Company Stockholders Cash Receipt Book. Chase Manhattan Company
    Archives.
Minutes of the Board of Directors of the Manhattan Company. April 11, 1799–1808.
    Chase Manhattan Company Archives.
New York Stock and Exchange Board. Minute Books. New York Stock Exchange
    Archives.
New York Stock and Exchange Board Call Books. New York Stock Exchange Archives.
New York Stock and Exchange Board Constitution [1820]. New York Stock Ex-
    change Archives.
O'Connor Collection. New-York Historical Society.
O'Connor Collection. University of Michigan William L. Clements Library.
Open Board of Brokers. Constitution [1864]. New York Stock Exchange Archives.
Parish, David. Letter Books. New-York Historical Society
Pintard Collection. New-York Historical Society.
Prime Collection. New-York Historical Society.

"Stock Record" Manhattan Company Records. Chase Manhattan Archives.
Union Bank Dividend Book [1806–1814]. New-York Historical Society.
Wettereau Papers. Columbia Unviersity Butler Library.

Legal Authorities

Abridgement of the Debates of Congress. New York: D. Appleton, 1832.
Allegeyer v. Louisiana. 165 U.S. 578 (1897).
An Act for Laying a Duty on Public Securities and Stock Sold at Auction. 2 Greenleaf 470. April 10, 1792.
An Act Relative to Banks and for Other Purposes. 41st Sess. New York Laws. April 21, 1818.
An Act Relative to Incorporations for Manufacturing Purposes. 34th Sess. New York Laws. March 22, 1811.
An Act Relative to Partnerships. 45th Sess. New York Laws. April 17, 1822.
An Act To Authorize the Business of Banking. 61st Sess. New York Laws. April 18, 1838. Amended 63rd Sess. New York Laws. May 14, 1840.
An Act To Incorporate the Lehigh Coal and Navigation Company. Pennsylvania Laws, vol. VIII, p. 86, Art. V. February 13, 1822.
An Act To Legalize the Sale of Stocks on Time, 81st Sess. New York Laws. April 10, 1858.
An Act To Prevent the Passing and Receiving of Bank Notes Less than One Dollar and To Restrain Unincorporated Banking Associations. 36th Sess. New York Laws. April 6, 1813.
An Act To Prevent the Pernicious Practice of Stock-Jobbing, and for Regulating Sales at Public Auction. 2 Greenleaf 470. April 10, 1792.
An Act To Recharter the Bank of North America, Ch. LIII 49th Sess. Pennyslvania Laws. March 21, 1825.
An Act To Regulate the Finances of the City of New York. 35th Sess. New York Laws. June 8, 1812.
An Act To Restrain the Extravagant and Unwarrantable Practice of Raising Money by Voluntary Subscriptions for Carrying on Projects Dangerous to the Trade and Subjects of this Kingdom. 6 George I, c. 18 (1720).
An Act To Restrain Unincorporated Banking Associations. 27th Sess. New York Laws. April 11, 1804.
Annals of Congress. 1817–1818.
A Report of the Select Committee on Stock-Jobbing. Documents of the Assembly of the State of New York. 57th Sess. No. 339. March 28, 1834.
Attorney General v. Utica Insurance Co. 2 Johns Chancery 371 (N.Y. 1817).
Bank of Augusta v. Earle. 13 Pet. (38 U.S.) 519 (1839).
Bank of Utica v. Smalley. 2 Cowen 770 (N.Y. 1824).
Briggs v. Penniman. 8 Cowen 387 (N.Y. Ct. Err., 1826).
Briscoe v. The Bank of the Commonwealth of Kentucky. 11 Pet. (36 U.S.) 257 (1837).
Charles River Bridge v. Warren Bridge. 11 Pet. (36 U.S.) 514 (1830).
Chicago, Milwaukee and St. Paul Railway Co. v. Minnesota. 134 U.S. 418 (1890).

Documents of the Assembly of the State of New York. 59th Sess., No. 291. March 23, 1836.

Dykers v. Townsend. 24 N.Y. 57 (1861).

Essex Turnpike Corp. v. Collins. 8 Mass. 292 (1811).

Ex Parte Holmes. 5 Cowen 426 (N.Y. Sup. Ct. 1826).

Ex Parte Willocks. 7 Cowen 402 (N.Y. Sup. Ct. 1827).

Fletcher v. Peck. 6 Cranch (10 U.S.) 87 (1810).

Frost v. Clarkson. 7 Cowen 26 (N.Y. 1827).

House Committee on Interstate and Foreign Commerce. H.R. Rep. No. 1383. Securities Bill of 1934. 73d Cong. 2d Sess. (1934).

Journal of the Assembly of the State of New York. Albany: Childs and Swaine, 1792. New-York Historical Society.

Kilbourn v. Tudor. 5 Day 329 (Conn. 1812).

Ligget v. Lee. 288 U.S. 517 (1933).

Livingston v. Lynch. 4 Johns. Ch. 573 (N.Y. 1820).

Lochner v. New York. 198 U.S. 45 (1905).

Louisville Railroad Company v. Letson. 2 How. (43 U.S.) 497 (1844).

Marlborough Mfg. Co. v. Smith. 2 Conn. 579 (1818).

McKin v. Odom. 3 Bland 407 (Md. Ch. 1828).

Memorial and Remonstrance of the Board of Stock & Exchange Brokers of the City of New York. Documents of the Assembly of the State of New York. 59th Sess. No. 291. March 23, 1836.

Ogden v. Kip. 6 Johns Chancery 160 (N.Y. 1822).

Paul v. Virginia. 8 Wall (75 U.S.) 168 (1868).

Report of the Committee Appointed Pursuant to House Resolutions 429 and 504 (Pujo Committee) to Investigate the Concentration and Control of Money and Credit, before a subcommittee of the Committee on Banking and Currency. February 28, 1913. 62d Cong. 2d. Sess.

Report of the Comptroller. Legislative Documents of the Senate and Assembly of the State of New York. 53d Sess. 1830. Assembly Doc. No. 277. March 1, 1830.

Report of the Comptroller. Legislative Documents of the Senate and Assembly of the State of New York. 60th Sess. 1837. Assembly Doc. No. 4. January 4, 1837.

Report of Secretary of the Treasury. 23 Cong. 1st Sess. Senate Doc. No. 73. February 6, 1834.

Report of the Select Committee on Stock-Jobbing. Documents of the Assembly of the State of New York. 57th Sess. 1834. No. 339. March 28, 1834.

Robinson v. Smith. 3 Paige Chancery 222 (N.Y. 1832).

Sargent v. Franklin Ins. Co. 8 Pick 90 (Mass. 1829).

Shipley v. Mechanic's Bank. 10 Johns. 484 (N.Y. 1813).

Slee v. Bloom. 5 Johns Ch. 366 (N.Y. 1821), 19 Johns 456 (N.Y. Ct. Err. 1822).

The Bank of the United States v. Deveaux. 5 Cranch (9 U.S.) 61 (1809).

Union Turnpike Road v. Jenkins. 1 Caines 381 (N.Y. 1803), rev'd, 1 Caines 86 (N.Y. 1804).

United States v. Vaughn. 3 Binney 394 (Penn. 1811).

Werner, Walter. Testimony before the Subcommittee on Fiscal Policy of the Joint Economic Committee. 91st Cong. 2d Sess. (April 28, 1970).

Wood v. Drummer, 30 Fed. Cas. 435 (no 17, 944), 3 Mason 308 (C. C. Maine 1824).

Books and Articles

A Century of Progress, 1823–1923, the History of the Delaware and Hudson Canal Company. Albany: J. B. Lyon, 1925.

Adams, Charles Francis and Henry Adams. Chapters of Erie. Ithaca: Cornell University Press, 1956.

Adams, Charles Francis. "Railroad Inflation." North American Review (1869), vol. 108.

Adams, Donald R., Jr. "The Beginning of Investment Banking in the United States." Pennsylvania Magazine (1977), vol. 101.

——. "Portfolio Management and Profitability in Early Nineteenth Century Banking." Business History Review (1978), vol. 52.

Albion, Robert. The Rise of New York Port. New York: Scribners, 1939.

Allen, Frederick Lewis. The Great Pierpont Morgan. New York: Harper and Row, 1948.

Ames, Charles Edgar. Pioneering the Union Pacific. New York: Appleton-Century Crofts, 1969.

Angell, Joseph and Samuel Ames. Treatise on the Law of Private Corporations Aggregate. Boston: Little and Brown, 1832.

Armstrong, William. Stocks and Stock-Jobbing in Wall Street. New York: New York Publishing, 1848.

Barbour, Violet. Capitalism in Amsterdam in the 17th Century. Baltimore: Johns Hopkins Press, 1950. Reprinted Ann Arbor: University of Michigan Press, 1963.

Barret, Walter. The Old Merchants of New York. New York: Carleton, 1864.

Baumol, William J. The Stock Market and Economic Efficiency. New York: Fordham University Press, 1965.

Bayles, Harrison. Old Taverns of New York. New York: Frank Allen Genealogical Company, 1915.

Berle, Adolf and William Warren. Business Organization: Corporations. Brooklyn: Foundation Press, 1948.

Berle, Adolf. "The Impact of the Corporation on Classical Economic Theory." Quarterly Journal of Economics (1965), vol. 79.

Berle, Adolf and Gardiner Means. The Modern Corporation and Private Property. 2d ed. New York: Harcourt, Brace & World, 1968.

Bigelow, E. Remarks on the Depressed Condition of Manufacturers in Massachusetts. Boston: Little, Brown, 1858.

Blandi, Joseph. Maryland Business Corporations: 1783–1852. Baltimore: Johns Hopkins Press, 1934.

Booth, Mary L. History of the City of New York. New York: E. P. Dutton, 1880.

Bradley, Michael and Michael Rozenzweig. "Defensive Stock Repurchases." Harvard Law Review (May 1986), vol. 99.

Brady, Nicholas F. et al. "Report of the Presidential Task Force on Market Mechanisms." Washington: Government Printing Office, January 1988.

Brooks, J. The Go-Go Years. New York: Weybright and Talley, 1973.

Bruchey, Stuart. The Roots of American Economic Growth: 1607–1861. New York: Harper and Row, 1965.

Burgess, George and Miles Kennedy. Centennial History of the Pennsylvania Railroad Company: 1846–1946. Philadelphia: The Pennsylvania Railroad, 1949.

Buxbaum, Richard M. "The Relation of the Large Corporation's Structure to the Role of Shareholders and Directors: Some American Historical Perspectives." In Norman Horn, ed., *Law and the Formation of Big Business Enterprise in the 19th and 20th Centuries.* Gottingen: Vanderbrook and Ruprecht, 1979.

Cadman, J. *The Corporation in New Jersey: Business and Politics, 1791–1875.* Cambridge: Harvard University Press, 1949.

Callender, Guy S., ed., *Selections from the Economic History of the United States: 1765–1860.* Boston: Grim, 1909.

Callender, Guy S. "The Early Transportation and Banking Enterprises of the State in Relation to the Growth of Corporations." *Quarterly Journal of Economics* (1902)., vol. 17.

Carosso, Vincent. *Investment Banking in America.* Cambridge: Harvard University Press, 1970.

——. *The Morgans.* Cambridge: Harvard University Press, 1987.

Carus-Wilson, Elanora. *The Records of the Merchant Adventurers of New Castle upon Tyne.* Durham: Surtees Society Publication (1899), vol. 93.

Cary, William L. "Minimum Federal Standards." In D. Schwartz, ed., *Commentaries on Corporate Structure and Governance.* Philadelphia: American Law Institute, 1979.

Catteral, Ralph. *The Second Bank of the United States.* Chicago: University of Chicago Press, 1903.

Chandler, Alfred D. *Henry Varnum Poor.* Cambridge: Harvard University Press, 1956.

——. "Patterns of American Railroad Finance 1830–1850." *Business History Review* (1954), vol. 28.

——. *Strategy and Structure: Chapters in the History of American Industrial Enterprise.* Cambridge: MIT Press, 1962.

——. *The Visible Hand: The Managerial Revolution in American Business.* Cambridge: Harvard University Press, 1977.

Chevalier, Michael. *Society Manners and Politics in the United States.* Boston: Weeks, Jordan, 1839. Reprinted New York: A. M. Kelley, 1966.

Clark, Victor. *History of Manufactures in the United States, 1607–1860.* Washington: Carnegie Institution, 1916.

Clarke, M. St. Claire and D. A. Hall. *Legislative and Documentary History of the Bank of the United States.* Washington: 1832. Reprinted New York: Kelley, 1967.

Cleveland, Frederick A. and Fred Wilbur Powell. *Railroad Promotion and Capitalization in the United States.* London: Longmans Green, 1909. Reprinted New York: Johnson Reprint, 1966.

Cleveland, Harold van B. and Thomas F. Huertas. *Citibank, 1812–1970.* Cambridge: Harvard University Press, 1985.

Clews, Henry. *Fifty Years in Wall Street.* New York: Irving Publishing, 1908.

Clinton, George. *Essays on Banking.* Richmond: Collins, 1829.

Cochran, Thomas C. *Business in American Life: A History.* New York: McGraw-Hill, 1972.

——. *The Basic History of American Business.* Princeton: D. van Nostrand, 1959.

——. "The Business Revolution." *American Historical Review* (1974), vol. 79.

Coffee, John. "The Strain in the Corporate Web." *Michigan Law Review* (October 1986), vol. 85.

Cole, Arthur H., and Walter B. Smith. *Fluctuations in American Business, 1790–1860.* Cambridge: Harvard University Press, 1935.

Cook, W. W. *The Corporation Problem.* 1891.

Davis, Joseph S. *Essays in the Earlier History of American Corporations.* 2 vols. Cambridge: Harvard University Press, 1917.

Davis, Lance E. "Stock Ownership in the Early New England Textile Industry." *Business History Review* (1958), vol. 32.

Dawson, Susan S., Robert J. Pense, and David S. Stone. "Poison Pill Defensive Measures." *The Business Lawyer* (February 1987), vol. 42.

de Tocqueville, Alexis. *Democracy in America.* 1848. Reprinted Garden City: Doubleday, 1966.

Dickson, Peter. *The Financial Revolution in England.* New York: Macmillan, 1967.

Dodd, E. Merrick. "American Business Association Law a Hundred Years Ago and Today." Reprinted in *Law, A Century of Progress, 1835–1935.* New York: New York Univeristy Press. 1937.

——. *American Business Corporations Until 1860.* Cambridge: Harvard University Press, 1954.

——. "Lectures on the Growth of the Corporate Structure in the United States with Special Reference to Governmental Regulations." Cleveland: Cleveland Bar Association, 1937.

——. "Statutory Developments in Business Corporation Law, 1886–1936." *Harvard Law Review* (1936), vol. 50.

Domett, Henry W. *A History of the Bank of New York.* New York: G. P. Putnam, 1884. Reprinted New York: Greenwood Press, 1969.

Dos Passos, John R. *A Treatise on the Law of Stock-Brokers and Stock Exchanges.* New York: Harper, 1882. Reprinted New York: Greenwood Press, 1968.

Draper, Cecil. "A Historical Introduction to the Corporate Mortgage." *Rocky Mountain Law Review* (1930), vol. 2.

"Dual Class Recapitalization and Shareholder Voting Rights." *Columbia Law Review* (1987), vol. 87.

Dubois, Armand Budington. *The English Business Company After the Bubble Act.* New York: The Commonwealth Fund, 1938.

Eames, Francis L. *The New York Stock Exchange.* New York: Thomas G. Hall, 1894. Reprinted New York: Greenwood Press, 1968.

Easterbrook, Frank. "Managers' Discretion and Investors' Welfare: Theories and Evidence." *Delaware Journal of Corporate Law* (1984), vol. 9.

Easterbrook, Frank and Daniel Fisher. "Mandatory Disclosure and the Protection of Investors." *Virginia Law Review* (May 1984), vol. 70.

Edie, Lionel. *Economics: Principles and Problems.* New York: Thomas Y. Crowell, 1926.

Edwards, George W. *The Evolution of Finance Capitalism.* London: Longmans, Green, 1938.

Evans, G. Heberton Jr. "The Early History of Preferred Stock in the United States." *American Economic Review* (1929), vol. 19.

Fenstermaker, J. Van. *The Development of American Commercial Banking: 1782–1837.* Kent: Bureau of Economics and Business Research, 1965.

——. "The Statistics of American Commercial Banking, 1782–1818." *Journal of Economic History* (1965), vol. 25.

Ferguson, E. James. *The Power of the Purse*. Chapel Hill: University of North Carolina Press, 1961.

Fogel, Robert. *Railroads in American Economic Growth: Essays in Economic History*. Baltimore: Johns Hopkins University Press, 1964.

Fowler, William W. *Ten Years in Wall Street*. Hartford: Worthington, Dustin, 1871.

Friedman, Lawrence M. *A History of American Law*. New York: Simon & Schuster, 1973.

Galbraith, John Kenneth. *The New Industrial State*. 3d ed. New York: Mentor, 1978.

Gallatin, Albert. "Report of the Secretary of the Treasury on the Subject of Roads and Canals." Reprinted in *American State Papers*. Washington: Gales & Seaton, 1861.

Garbade, Kenneth. *Securities Markets*. New York: McGraw-Hill, 1982.

Geldert, Louis N. *Centennial History of Eagle Fire Insurance Company 1806–1906*. New York: Eagle Insurance, 1906.

Gibbons, James S. *The Banks of New York, Their Dealers, The Clearing House, and the Panic of 1857*. New York: D. Appleton, 1858.

Goodrich, Carter. *Government Promotion of American Canals and Railraods 1800–1890*. New York: Columbia University Press, 1960.

Gouge, William. *The Curse of Paper Money and Banking*. London: Mills, Jowett, and Mills, 1833. Reprinted New York: Greenwood Press, 1968.

——. *A Short History of Paper Money and Banking in the United States*. 2d ed. New York: B. & S. Collins, 1835.

Govan, Thomas P. *Nicholas Biddle: Nationalist and Public Banker, 1786–1844*. Chicago: University of Chicago Press, 1959.

Gras, N. *The Massachusetts First National Bank of Boston, 1784–1934*. Cambridge: Harvard University Press, 1938.

Greef, A. *The Commercial Paper House in the United States*. Cambridge: Harvard University Press, 1938.

Gregory, Francis. *Nathan Appleton: Merchant and Entrepreneur, 1779–1861*. Charlottesville: University of Virginia Press, 1975.

Grodinsky, Louis. *Transcontinental Railway Strategy, 1869–1893*. Philadelphia: University of Pennsylvania Press, 1962.

Haar, Charles. "Legislative Regulation of New York Industrial Corporations, 1800–1850." *New York History Magazine* (1941), vol. 22.

Hacker, Louis. *The Course of American Economic Growth and Development*. New York: Wiley, 1970.

Hamilton, Walton. *The Politics of Industry*. New York: Knopf, 1957.

Hammond, Bray. *Banks and Politics in the United States*. Princeton: Princeton University Press, 1957.

——. "Free Banks and Corporations: The New York Free Banking Act of 1838." *Journal of Political Economy* (1936), vol. 44.

——. "The Chestnut Street Raid on Wall Street." *Quarterly Journal of Economics* (1946), vol. 61.

Hammond, Jabez. *The History of Political Parties in New York*. Albany: Van Benthuysen, 1843.

Hamon, Henry. *New York Stock Exchange Manual*. New York: John F. Trow, 1865. Reprinted New York: Greenwood Press, 1970.

Harbrecht, Paul P. Jr. "The Modern Corporation Revisited." *Columbia Law Review* (1964), vol. 64.

Hartz, Louis. *Economic Policy and Democratic Thought.* Cambridge: Harvard University Press, 1948.

Hawley, Ellis W. *The New Deal and the Problem of Monopoly.* Princeton: Princeton University Press, 1966.

Hayes, Samuel L. "The Transformation of Investment Banking." *Harvard Business Review* (January–February 1979) vol. 57.

Hedges, Joseph Edward. *Commercial Banking and the Stock Market Before 1863.* Baltimore: Johns Hopkins University Press, 1938.

Hemming, H. G., *History of the New York Stock Exchange.* New York: H. Glover, 1905.

Hidy, Ralph W. *The House of Baring in American Trade and Finance.* Cambridge: Harvard University Press, 1949.

History of Investment Banking in New England. Federal Reserve Bank of Boston, 1969.

Hobson, Charles K. *The Export of Capital.* London: Constable, 1914.

Holdsworth, William S. *A History of English Law.* vol. 8. London: Methuen, 1926.

Holgate, Jerome B. *American Genealogy.* New York: private printing, 1848.

Howard, Stanley E. "Stockholder's Liability Under the New York Act of March 22, 1811." *Journal of Political Economy* (1938), vol. 46.

Hubert, Phillip G. *Merchants National Bank of the City of New York.* New York: Merchants National Bank, 1903.

Hurst, James. *The Legitimacy of the Business Corporation in the Law of the United States.* Charlottesville: University of Virginia Press, 1970.

Jackson, Frederick (attributed). *A Week in Wall Street by One Who Knows.* New York: J. F. Trow, 1841.

Jackson, Joseph. *The Encyclopedia of Philadelphia.* Harrisburg: National Historical Association, 1933.

James, Marquis. *Biography of a Business, 1792–1942: The Insurance Company of North America.* New York: Bobbs-Merrill, 1942.

Jones, Robert F. "William Duer and the Business of Government in the Era of the American Revolution." *William and Mary Quarterly* (1975), vol. 32.

Kehl, Donald. "The Origin and Early Development of Early Dividend Law." *Harvard Law Review* (1939), vol. 53.

Keller, Morton. *The Life Insurance Enterprise.* Cambridge: Belknap Press, 1963.

Kent, Frank. *The Story of Alexander Brown and Sons.* Baltimore: Private printing. 1925.

Kent, James. *Commentaries on American Law.* 6th ed. New York: 1848.

Kessler, William C. "A Statistical Study of the New York General Incorporation Act of 1811." *Journal of Political Economy* (1940), vol. 48.

Kindleberger, Charles. *Manias, Panics, and Crashes.* New York: Basic Books, 1978.

Kirkland, Edward Chase. *Men, Cities and Transportation.* Cambridge: Harvard University Press, 1948.

Kolko, Gabriel. *Railroads and Regulation.* New York: Norton, 1970.

Lamb, Martha. *Wall Street in History.* New York: Funk and Wagnalls, 1883.

Lamb, Martha and Mrs. Burton Harrison. *History of the City of New York.* New York: Barnes, 1876.

Lambert, Richard. *The Railway King.* London: Allen and Unwin, 1954.

Lane, W. J. *From Indian Trail to Iron Horse: Travel and Transportation in New Jersey, 1620–1860.* Princeton: Princeton University Press, 1939.

Lanier, Henry Wysham. *A Century of Banking in New York, 1822–1922.* New York: Gilliss Press, 1922.

Lawrence, Ruth, ed. *Colonial Families of America.* New York: National Americana Society, 1928.

Leffler, George. *The Stock Market.* New York: Ronald Press, 1957.

Letwin, William. *Law and Economic Policy in America: The Evolution of the Sherman Anti-Trust Act.* New York: Random House, 1965.

Lively, Robert A. "The American System: A Review Article." *Business History Review* (1955), vol. 29.

Livermore, Shah. *Early American Land Companies: Their Influence on Corporate Development.* New York: The Commonwealth Fund, 1939.

——. "Unlimited Liability in Early American Corporations." *Journal of Political Economy* (1935), vol. 43.

Lowenstein, L. "Management Buy-Outs." *Columbia Law Review.* (1985), vol. 85.

——. "No More Cozy Management Buy-Outs." *Harvard Business Review* (January–February 1986) vol. 64.

——. "Pruning Deadwood in Hostile Takeovers: A Proposal for Legislation." *Columbia Law Review* (1983), vol. 83.

MacGrath, C. Peter. *Yazoo: Law and Politics in the New Republic; The Case of Fletcher v. Peck.* Providence: Brown University Press, 1966.

MacKay, Charles. *Extraordinary Popular Delusions and the Madness of Crowds.* 2d ed. New York: Farrar, Strauss and Giroux. 1852.

Malkiel, Burton G. *A Random Walk Down Wall Street.* New York: Norton, 1973.

Manning, B. "The Shareholder's Appraisal Remedy: An Essay for Frank Coker." *Yale Law Journal* (1962), vol. 72.

Martin, Joseph. *A Century of Finance.* Boston: Joseph Martin, 1898. Reprinted New York: Greenwood Press, 1969.

McGrane, Reginald Charles. *The Panic of 1837.* New York: Russell and Russell, 1965.

Medbery, James K. *Men and Mysteries of Wall Street.* New York: R. Worthington, 1878. Reprinted Ann Arbor: University Microfilms, 1968.

Means, Gardiner. *The Corporate Revolution in America.* New York: Collier Books, 1962.

Meeker, Edward J. *The Work of the Stock Exchange.* New York: Ronald Press, 1930.

Miller, Nathan. *The Enterprise of a Free People.* Ithaca: American Historical Association, 1962.

Moody, John. *The Truth about the Trusts.* New York: Moody, 1904.

Morgan, V. E. and W. A. Thomas. *The London Stock Exchange, Its History and Functions.* New York: St. Martin's Press, 1962.

Myers, Margaret. *The New York Money Market,* vol. 1. New York: Columbia University Press, 1931.

——. *A Financial History of the United States.* New York: Columbia University Press, 1970.

Nader, Ralph, et al. *Taming the Giant Corporation.* New York: Norton, 1976.

National Bureau of Economic Research. *Securities and Exchange Commission Institutional Investor Study.* 1971.

Navin, Thomas R. and Marian V. Sears. "The Rise of a Market for Industrial Securities, 1887–1902." *Business History Review* (June 1955), vol. 29.

Neill, Humphrey B. *The Inside Story of the Stock Exchange.* New York: B. C. Forbes, 1950.

Nelson, John R. "Alexander Hamilton and American Manufacturing: A Reexamination." *Journal of American History* (1979), vol. 65.

Nelson, Ralph. *Merger Movements in American Industry 1895–1956.* Princeton: Princeton University Press, 1959.

New York Stock Exchange Fact Book 1987. New York: New York Stock Exchange, 1987.

Neu, Irene D. *Erastus Corning, Merchant and Financier.* Ithaca: Cornell University Press, 1960.

Nevins, Allan. *The Bank of New York.* New York: private printing, 1934.

North, Douglas. *The Economic Growth of the United States 1790–1860.* New York: Norton, 1966.

Noyes, Alexander D. *Forty Years of American Finance.* New York: G. P. Putnam, 1909.

Nussbaum, Arthur. *A History of the Dollar.* New York: Columbia University Press, 1957.

Owens, Richard N. and Charles O. Hardy. *Interest Rates and Stock Speculation.* New York: Macmillan, 1925.

Pitkin, Timothy. *The Consumer: His Nature and His Changing Habits.* New York: McGraw-Hill, 1932.

Politicus. "Impartial Inquiry into Certain Parts of the Conduct of Governor Lewis." New York: James Cheetham, 1806.

Pomerantz, Sidney I. *New York: An American City 1783–1803.* New York: Columbia University Press, 1938.

Poor, Henry Varnum. *History of the Railroads and Canals of the United States.* New York: Schultz, 1860.

Porter, G. and H. Livesay. *Merchants and Manufacturers.* Baltimore: Johns Hopkins University Press, 1971.

Poser, Norman S. "Stock Market Manipulation and Corporate Control Transaction." *University of Miami Law Review* (1986), vol. 40.

Powell. *List of Officers of the Army of the United States, 1799–1900.* New York. 1900.

Pratt, Sereno S. *The Work of Wall Street.* New York: D. Appleton, 1906.

Prime, Temple. *Some Account of the Family of Prime of Rowley, Mass.* New York: De Vinne Press, 1897.

Publicola. "Vindication of the Currency of the State of New York and Review of the Report Presented by the Committee on that Subject to the House of Assembly." New York: 1818.

Ratchford, B. U. *American State Debts.* Durham, N.C.: Duke University Press, 1941.

Ratner, David. "The Government of Business Corporations." *Cornell Law Review* (1970), vol. 56.

Redlich, Fritz. *The Molding of American Banking.* 2d ed. New York: Johnson Reprint Corporation, 1968.

Ripley, William Z. *Main Street and Wall Street.* Boston: Little, Brown, 1927.

——. *Railroads: Finance and Organization.* New York, Longmans, Green, 1915.

Rothbard, Murray. "The Panic of 1819." Ph.D. dissertation, Columbia University, New York.

Rutland, Robert A., et al., eds. *The Papers of James Madison.* Charlottesville: University of Virginia Press, 1983. vol. 14.

Sakolski, A. M. *The Great American Land Bubble.* New York: Harper, 1932.

Salsbury, Stephen. *The State, the Investor, and the Railroad.* Cambridge: Harvard University Press, 1967.

Scharf, J. T. and Thompson Westcott. *The History of Philadelphia 1669–1884.* Philadelphia: L. H. Everts, 1884.

Schultz, Birl E. *The Securities Market and How It Works.* New York: Harper, 1942.

Schumpter, Joseph. *Capitalism, Socialism and Democracy.* New York: Harper, 1942.

Schwartz, Anna J. "The Beginning of Competitive Banking in Philadelphia 1782–1809." *Journal of Political Economy* (1947), vol. 55.

Seavoy, Ronald E. "Laws to Encourage Manufacturing: New York Policy and the 1811 General Incorporation Statute." *Business History Review* (1972), vol. 46.

Seybert, Adam. *Statistical Annals.* Philadelphia: Thomas Dobson, 1818.

Shaugnessey, J. *Delaware and Hudson.* Berkeley, Calif: Howell-North Books, 1967.

Shaw, Ronald E., ed. *Andrew Jackson 1767–1845.* Dobbs Ferry, N.Y.: Oceana Publications, 1969.

Silk, Leonard. "The Market: Why Does It Matter?" *New York Times,* October 21, 1987, p. A1.

Smiley, Gene. "The Expansion of the New York Securities Market at the Turn of the Century." *Business History Review* (1981), vol. 55.

Smith, Adam. *The Money Game.* New York: Random House, 1967.

Smith, Matthew W. *20 Years Among the Bulls and Bears at Wall Street.* Hartford: J. B. Burr, 1871.

Smith, Walter B. *Economic Aspects of the Second Bank of the United States.* Cambridge: Harvard University Press, 1953.

Sobel, Robert. *History of the New York Stock Exchange 1935–1975.* New York: Weybright and Talley, 1976.

——. *Panic on Wall Street.* New York: Macmillan, 1968.

——. *The Big Board.* New York: The Free Press, 1965.

——. *The Curbstone Brokers.* London: Macmillan, 1970.

Soule, George. *Economic Forces in American History.* New York: William Sloan Associates, 1952.

Stedman, Edmund C., ed. *The New York Stock Exchange.* New York: Stock Exchange Historical, 1905. Reprinted New York: Greenwood Press, 1969.

Stone, William L. *History of New York City.* New York: Virtue and Yorston, 1872.

Sullivan, James, "The Path to Riches." *The Magazine of History* (1792), vol. 46 (no. 4); extra no. 184. Reprinted New York: William Abbatt, 1933.

Swanberg, W. A. *Jim Fisk: The Career of an Improbable Rascal.* New York: Scribners, 1959.

Syrett, Harold C., ed. *The Papers of Alexander Hamilton.* 27 vols. New York: Columbia University Press, 1965–1987.

Taylor, George. The Transportation Revolution 1815–1860. New York: Harper and Row, 1951.

Temin, Peter. The Jacksonian Economy. New York: Norton, 1969.

"The Battle for Corporate Control." Business Week, May 18, 1987.

The New York Stock Exchange. New York: New York and Philadelphia Historical Pub., 1886. Reprinted New York: Arno Press, 1975.

The Speeches of Mr. Jacob Barker and His Counsel on the Trials for Conspiracy. New York: William A. Mercein, 1826.

Thorelli, Hans. The Federal Anti-Trust Policy. Baltimore: Johns Hopkins University Press, 1955.

Veblen, Thorstein. The Theory of Business Enterprise. New York: Scribners, 1904.

Wainwright, N. The Philadelphia National Bank 1803–1953. Philadelphia: Philadelphia National Bank, 1953.

Ward, James A. "Power and Accountability in the Pennyslvania Railroad 1846–1878." Business History Review (1975), vol. 49.

Warshow, Robert I. The Story of Wall Street. New York: Greenberg, 1929.

Weibe, Robert H. The Search for Order 1877–1920. New York: Hill and Wang, 1968.

Welles, C. The Last Days of the Club. New York: Dutton, 1975.

Werner, Walter. "Adventure in Social Control of Finance: The National Market System for Securities." Columbia Law Review (1975), vol. 75.

——. "Corporation Law in Search of its Future." Columbia Law Review (1981), vol. 81.

——. "Management, Stock Market, and Corporate Reform: Berle and Means Reconsidered." Columbia Law Review (1977), vol. 77.

——. "The SEC as a Market Regulator." Virginia Law Review (1984), vol. 70.

Werner, Walter and William Cary. "Outlook for the Securities Markets." Harvard Business Review (1971), vol. 49.

Wettereau, James. "New Light on the First Bank of the United States." Pennsylvania Magazine of History and Biography (1937), vol. 61.

——. Statistical Records of the First Bank of the United States. New York: Garland Publishing. 1985.

White, Bouck. The Book of Daniel Drew. New York: Doubleday, 1910.

Williston, Samuel. "History of the Law of Business Corporations Before 1800." Harvard Law Review (1888), vol. 2.

Wilson, William. History of the Pennsylvania Railroad Company. Philadelphia: H. T. Coates, 1899.

Newspapers and Periodicals

American Citizen and General Advertiser
American Minerva
American Railroad Journal
Bankers Magazine
Claypool's Daily Advertiser
Columbia Gazette (New York)
Columbian Centinel (Boston)

Commercial and Financial Chronicle
Daily Gazette (New York)
Diary, or Loudon's Register (New York)
Financial Register (Philadelphia)
Gazette of the United States (Philadelphia)
General Advertiser (New York)
Hazard's Magazine (Philadelphia)
Herald, a Gazette for the Country (New York)
Massachusetts Magazine (Boston)
Merchant's Magazine and Commercial Review (New York)
National Advocate (New York)
New York American
New York Commercial Advertiser
New York Courier
New York Daily Advertiser
New York Daily Gazette
New York Enquirer
New York Evening Post
New York Herald
New York Journal and Patriotic Register
New York Journal of Commerce
New York Morning Post
New York Price Current
New York Spectator
Niles Weekly Register (Baltimore)
Poulson's American Daily Advertiser (Philadelphia)

Index